Praise for *The Goddess and the Guru*

"Any serious seeker after truth will find in Amritananda's story a wonderful example of just how vivid life can become when you enter into a real relationship with the Divine."—Dr. Robert Svoboda, author of *Aghora: At the Left Hand of God* and a dozen other books

"In *The Goddess and the Guru*, Bowden has brought forth a work that is a joy to read, whose wisdom calls for more than a single reading...So read it again and again: You will find yourself traversing many dimensions with ease and in wonder." —Professor Ambika Talwar, Cypress College, author of *Poems in Color* and *In the Folds of Your Sari*

"Just as an ocean cannot be held in one's palm, a life cannot be fully contained in a book. But what readers of *The Goddess and the Guru* will glean is an experience— even if only for a short while—of what this *particular* ocean truly felt like. And that glimpse can become the prod, the catalyst, by which they might carry their individual *sadhana* forward."—Anantalakshmi Pisipati, eldest daughter of Sri Amritananda Natha Saraswati

"Here we find the life and legacy of a spiritual innovator—and nuclear scientist, no less—whose existence was as Goddess-filled as it was insistently human, a case study in sacred wonder carved by the challenges of everyday life. A page-turning gem of a book."—Corinne Dempsey, author of *The Goddess Lives in Upstate New York*

"The Goddess tradition lives and breathes in Michael Bowden's riveting account of Dr. Prahlada Sastry (Sri Amritananda Natha Saraswati, or Guruji), a pioneering physicist who passionately engaged the provocative goddess of India's Sri Vidya tradition. A must-read for explorers of Tantra, mysticism, and the feminine divine."—Linda Johnsen, author of *The Living Goddess*, *Daughters of the Goddess* and *The Complete Idiot's Guide to Hinduism*

"An important book if you're interested in authentic Tantra, especially Śrīvidyā Śākta Tantra."—Christopher Hareesh Wallis, author of *Tantra Illuminated* and *The Recognition Sutras*

"Guruji was an unusual personality, able to mask what he was to perfection. Nobody would ever begin to suspect what he was. I think he eventually became the human face of the Goddess, so that everyone who met him had an experience of Her. I am happy that his journey and his wisdom have been collected and shared in *The Goddess and the Guru* for the benefit of all. The world has rarely known his like."—Wijayaharan Aiya, founder and head priest of Sri Rajarajeshwari Peetam, Rochester, New York

"Pay close attention: *The Goddess and the Guru* has the potential to realign your world."—Roxanne Kamayani Gupta, Ph.D., author of *The Yogini's Mirror*

"Riveting storytelling and revolutionary teachings...on the miraculous possibilities that open up when we bring our spiritual and worldly lives together."—Sarah Tomlinson, author of *Nine Designs for Inner Peace*

"Not since Yogananda's *Autobiography of a Yogi* have we had such an intimate look into the making of a spiritual master and teacher. More than mere biography, *The Goddess and the Guru* is a reflection of us all...tracing not just how and what we practice, but what leads us to practice."—Maya Devi Georg, founder and editor of *Brahmaloka or Bust*

The Goddess and the Guru

The Goddess and the Guru

A Spiritual Biography of Sri Amritananda Natha Saraswati

ॐ Michael M. Bowden ॐ

The Goddess and the Guru

A Spiritual Biography of Sri Amritananda Natha Saraswati

Text © 2017 by Michael M. Bowden

Photos © by Michael M. Bowden unless otherwise indicated. Other photos © the listed creators.

45th Parallel Press

P.O. Box 9551

PROVIDENCE, RI 02940

Cover design by Darinka Aguirre and Jeff Werner
Front cover photo © 2015 Julianne Reynolds
Back cover photo © 2014 Oleg Zinkovetsky
Interior design and typesetting by Jeff Werner
Copy-editing by Amy Haagsma
Proofreading by Hazel Boydell
Indexing by Sheilagh and Elspeth Simpson

Publisher's Cataloging-In-Publication Data
(Prepared by The Donohue Group, Inc.)

Names: Bowden, Michael M.
Title: The goddess and the guru. [Volume 1], A spiritual biography of
    Sri Amritananda Natha Saraswati / Michael M. Bowden.
Other Titles: Spiritual biography of Sri Amritananda Natha Saraswati
Description: Charlotte, Maine : 45th Parallel Press, [2017] | Includes bibliographical references and index.
Identifiers: ISBN 978-0-9979466-0-4 (paperback) | ISBN 978-0-9979466-4-2 (international paperback) | ISBN 978-
    0-9979466-3-5 (hardcover) | ISBN 978-0-9979466-1-1 (ePub) | ISBN 978-0-9979466-2-8 (Mobipocket)
Subjects: LCSH: Saraswati, Amritananda Natha, Sri. | Gurus--India--Biography. | Physicists--India--Biography. |
    Hindu goddesses. | Spiritual life--Hinduism. | Tantrism. | LCGFT: Biographies.
Classification: LCC BL1175.S37 B69 2017 (print) | LCC BL1175.S37 (ebook) | DDC 294.5092--dc23

Digital print edition v1.0

For Guruji

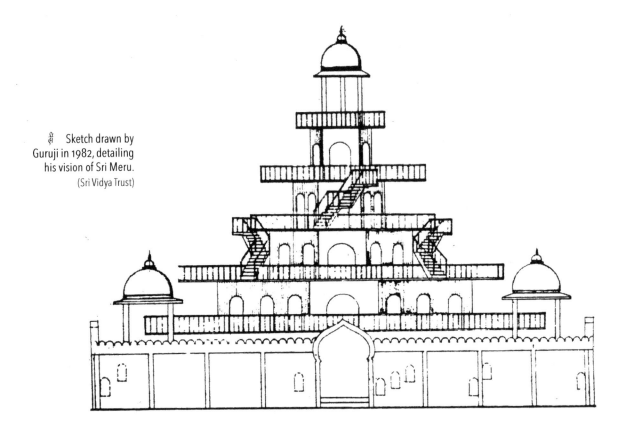

श्री Sketch drawn by
Guruji in 1982, detailing
his vision of Sri Meru.
(Sri Vidya Trust)

Only try to see for yourself.

Don't blindly accept what others say.

~ Sri Amritananda Natha Saraswati

Contents

THE GODDESS AND THE GURU

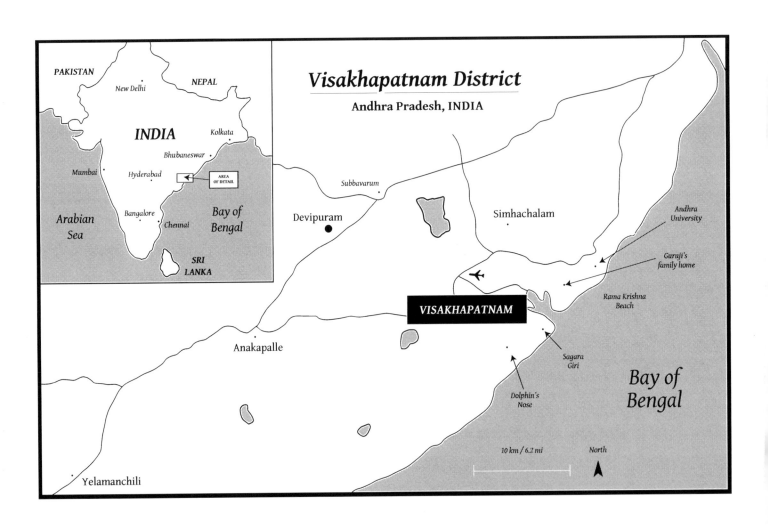

Visakhapatnam District

Andhra Pradesh, INDIA

INDIA

PAKISTAN

New Delhi

NEPAL

Kolkata

Bhubaneswar

Mumbai

Hyderabad

AREA OF DETAIL

Bangalore

Chennai

Bay of Bengal

Arabian Sea

SRI LANKA

Subbavarum

Simhachalam

Devipuram

Andhra University

Guruji's family home

VISAKHAPATNAM

Rama Krishna Beach

Anakapalle

Sagara Giri

Dolphin's Nose

Bay of Bengal

10 km / 6.2 mi

North

Yelamanchili

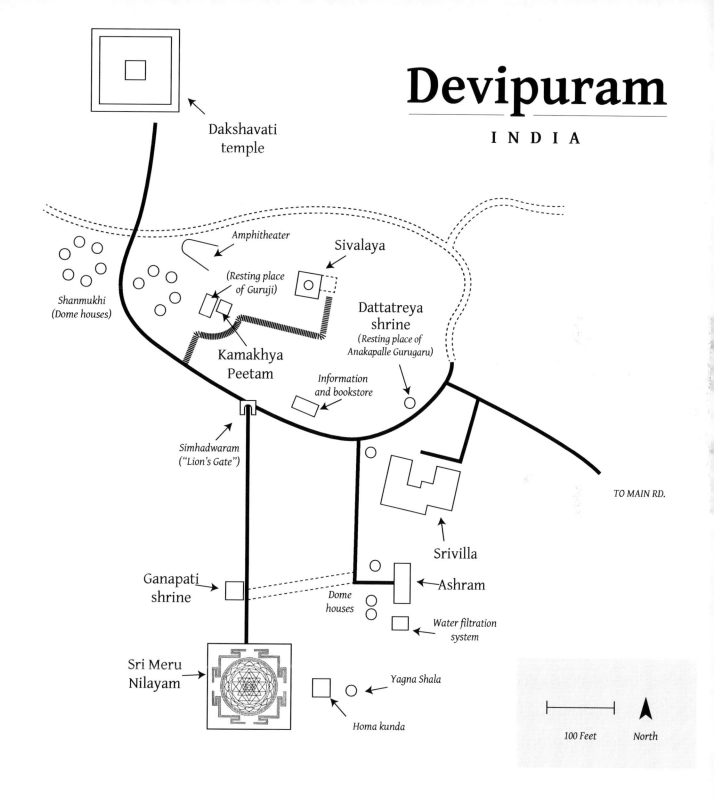

Devipuram

I N D I A

Dakshavati
temple

Amphitheater

Sivalaya

Shanmukhi
(Dome houses)

(Resting place
of Guruji)

Kamakhya
Peetam

Dattatreya
shrine
(Resting place of
Anakapalle Gurugaru)

Information
and bookstore

Simhadwaram
("Lion's Gate")

TO MAIN RD.

Srivilla

Ganapati
shrine

Dome
houses

Ashram

Water filtration
system

Sri Meru
Nilayam

Yagna Shala

Homa kunda

100 Feet   North

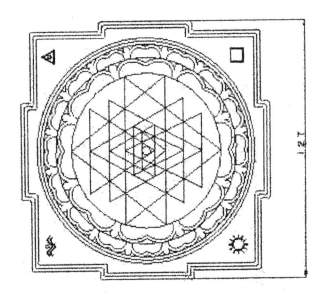

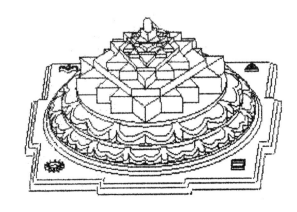

ALL DIMENSIONS ARE IN mm

127

X.X +-0.1
X.XX +-0.01
X.XXX +-0.001
ANG. +-0.5

NAME: MERU_CHAKRA_5INCH   SIZE: A3

श्री The original 2005 CAD
schematic for the Devipu-
ram Merus, as edited and
corrected by Guruji.
(Sri Vidya Trust)

A Note from Guruji

On behalf of the Goddess's devotees,
Thank you for your Herculean effort
in writing and assembling these materials.
May Her work, beyond the Three Worlds of Space, Time and Matter,
continue unimpeded.

Among the Hindu traditions, Sri Vidya is that which explores the connections
between the Mother, the Child and the Father–Mother unity,
via the invariant geometries that define our Universe and beyond.
Attempts to clarify these constructs are much needed by the present generation,
which is so hungry for authentic information on why certain practices help
and others hinder our progress and quality of life.
Your work will help in this process.
I appreciate your time and trust in me.

I don't claim to be a perfect *upasaka*.
I don't have the scientific depth to understand the Creator's ideas.
But like so many others before me, I have tried—and I am trying still.
So please do not put me on a pedestal or give me unwarranted credit.
Just say that I am a learner too.

Love, Guruji

Foreword

By Sri Chaitanyananda[1]

I first met Guruji back in 1979 when I was an architect in Lusaka, Zambia. I was still in my 30s then. I had arrived there from Sri Lanka by way of India in 1970 and was working at the buildings department of the Ministry of Power, Transport & Works. On my own time, I used to perform *pujas*—Hindu rituals—in my home, for the city's South Asian expatriate community. There was a thirst for that kind of thing; there were no Hindu temples in Lusaka in those days.

Guruji, meanwhile, was a visiting professor of nuclear physics at the University of Zambia, where he was known as Dr. N. Prahlada Sastry. He was walking along the corridors there one day when he met a good friend of mine, Dr. Ramaswamy, then dean of the engineering department. They shook hands, exchanged introductions and decided to have a cup of tea in the cafeteria. As they chatted, Guruji casually asked, "So what do the Hindus do around here without any temples?"

Ramaswamy replied, "There's a young Sri Lankan couple that holds *pujas*, so we go there." Well, Guruji must have been a little curious. He said, "Oh? What do they do?" Ramaswamy told him, "Among some other things, they chant the Lalita Sahasranama..."[2] And that was all Guruji needed to hear.

"Really! Can you take me there?" That was it.

It happened to be a Tuesday, the day he first walked into our *puja*. After we finished chanting, Dr. Ramaswamy introduced us. I looked into Guruji's eyes and was dumbstruck; I couldn't take my eyes off them. I kept thinking, "My God, what does this man know that the rest of us don't know?" I knew there was something *completely* unusual about him. There was a depth in his eyes that I had never seen in anyone's eyes before. You keep looking into those eyes, and—almost without your knowledge—you feel peaceful, you want to cry, you want to laugh; you want to do all these things at once. But I finally got hold of myself, thinking, "How embarrassing! He must be wondering, why is this fellow staring at me?"

1 Srilasri Chaitanyananda Natha Saraswati–better known as Haran Aiya or simply "Aiya"–is one of Guruji's early disciples and the founder and head of the Sri Rajarajeswari Peetam Temple in Rush, NY, and was referred to by Guruji as his "spiritual son." This foreword was prepared shortly before Guruji's death; Aiya's use of the present tense has not been altered.

2 The *Lalita Sahasranama* ("One Thousand Names of the Goddess Lalita"), c. 900 CE, is one of the most important devotional hymns/chants in the Hindu Sri Vidya tradition. See "Introduction: The World of Sri Vidya" in *The Goddess and the Guru, Volume II*.

3 A Tantric path that honors the great goddess Tripurasundari and places considerable emphasis on harnessing her powers through ritual. For further explanation, see "Introduction: The World of Sri Vidya" in *The Goddess and the Guru, Volume II.*

Anyway, I soon came to know that Dr. Sastry was a master of Sri Vidya *upasana*,[3] initiated by an accomplished guru in India. As it happened, I had long been seeking initiation into Sri Vidya, but it was a very secretive and basically impenetrable sect in those days, unless by chance you knew an initiate—or happened to be a Brahmin, which I am not.

The very next day I visited the home of a close friend of mine, Mr. Balasubrahmanyam. He was a Tamil Brahmin in his 60s, an absolutely brilliant man. We called him Balu. He was then chief engineer at the Zambia Electricity Transmission Company, the state-owned power corporation. He was a regular at our *pujas* and very knowledgeable about these things.

He too knew Guruji, and so I eagerly asked him, "Balu, should I go to Dr. Sastry and ask whether he will initiate me into Sri Vidya?"

"Why not?" Balu said. "Go ask him!"

I said, "But what if he tells me I'm not a Brahmin, so I can't have it?" I'd had that experience before.

Balu said, "So what's the big deal? If he says no, he will join all the others who have refused it to you before. That's the worst thing that could happen. But imagine if he says yes!"

4 *Sri Chakra Puja* is a central Sri Vidya ritual discussed elsewhere in this book and at length in *The Goddess and the Guru, Volume II.*

That decided it for me. I said, "Okay, we're going."

A few days later we went to his house, knocked on the door, and who should answer but Guruji's eldest daughter, Anantalakshmi. I said, "Is Dr. Sastry at home? Can we see him please?" She called out, "Daddy!" and he emerged from the *puja* room. "Ah! Haran and Balu! Come in!" he said. "I have just finished a *Sri Chakra Puja*.[4] Come into the shrine room." We went in, he offered us the *amritam*;[5] we took it. Then Balu discreetly withdrew into the living room, and left me alone with him.

5 *Amritam* means "nectar" in Sanskrit. Here, Guruji is offering his guests the *prasadam*–food offerings made to the deity and then distributed to worshipers– from his *Sri Chakra Puja.*

Now, Guruji *knew* why I had come. Later on, I found out *he knew.* But I plucked up my courage and asked him, "Aiya,[6] you know Sri Vidya, and you have a guru. Will you take me on as a disciple? Will you teach it to me?"

Not even for a fraction of a second did he hesitate. "Yes," he said, "I will."

"But Aiya," I felt compelled to tell him, "I am not a Brahmin."

6 *Aiya* is a Tamil honorific literally meaning "Father." It is often used in same sense as "Sir."

He looked me squarely in the eyes and said, "Well, what difference should that make? I have the knowledge; you are thirsting for it—why shouldn't I give it to you? It's fine; there are no problems."

That happened in October of 1979. The next spring my contract with the Zambian government ended, and on April 26, 1980, I left for the United States. Shortly thereafter, Guruji completed his professorship and returned to India. So it was only six months that we were together there; that's all. But that brief time completely changed my life, the life of my family and the lives of everyone around me at that time. Everything took on new dimensions, extraordinary depth; in the realm of *puja*, we understood more and more of what we were chanting and why.

Our encounter changed things for many others as well. Because Guruji made that one decision, so long ago—to initiate me into Sri Vidya and give me the mantras—just look around today and see how many it has benefited over the years.[7] With that one little act of compassion toward an unknown person (*ostensibly* unknown, I should say; again, I am *sure* he knew who I was and how this was going to spread)—just look at what he accomplished!

That in itself should tell you he is no ordinary human being.

Here is the bottom line: Guruji cannot see the color of a person's skin. He doesn't care about their nationality or their past or their future or any of that. All he can see is the Mother. He doesn't see a person as Indian or non-Indian, Brahmin or non-Brahmin, male or female, good or bad; nothing like that. There are no compartments in his mind. All of us are the Divine Mother's children; that is how he looks at it. Nowadays, of course, there are many people who *say* things like that—but I've never seen or met anybody else who so genuinely exemplifies and lives that worldview as he does.

What is it that makes Guruji so different? I think he arrived here with the whole package, whereas most of us have to strive to get the package. I think he's been coming back with it for, oh, to the best of my knowledge, 800 years at least. He keeps coming back with the same package. What he did before that, I have no idea. He is an unusual

7 In the years since this incident, Aiya has himself initiated many thousands of disciples into Sri Vidya *upasana*. These are the people he describes as benefiting from Guruji's act in initiating him.

personality, able to mask what he is to perfection. Nobody would even begin to suspect what he is.

Some time ago he told me, "I am not working on a human timeline. My job is to sow the seed. If it germinates within two months, good; if it germinates after 2,000 years, that's also good. My job is simply to sow the seed; let her take care of the rest in her own sweet time."

I think that since Guruji has been at Devipuram, the main temple deity there, Sahasrakshi, has expanded her presence to such an extent that her consciousness and his are one and the same. I believe that his consciousness has blended with that of the Devi herself. He has *become* Sahasrakshi. And what he expresses is exactly what she would express. What he gives out is what she would give. I think he's become the human face of the Devi so that everyone who meets him—sophisticated, worldly people and simple villagers alike; everyone who comes to see him—will have an experience of her. I am happy that his journey and his wisdom have been collected and shared in *The Goddess and the Guru* for the benefit of all.

The world has rarely known his like.

Sri Gurubhyonamah!

Haran Aiya
Chaitanyananda
Sri Rajarajeswari Peetam
Rochester, NY

Introduction

By Michael M. Bowden

PERHAPS MOMENTS OF ENLIGHTENMENT ONLY REALLY COME
WHEN THERE IS DEEP CONFLICT.
~ *Sri Amritananda Natha Saraswati*

Everything seemed so tidy, so symmetrical.

In the autumn of 2014, I was nearing completion of my research and reporting for this biography of Sri Amritananda Natha Saraswati, an Indian nuclear scientist who abandoned a top post at the peak of his professional career to become a spiritual teacher. Now widely known as "Guruji,"[1] Amritananda worked within an esoteric Hindu religious tradition called Sri Vidya *upasana*—literally, the "Path of Auspicious Wisdom."[2] Sri Vidya is an ancient and influential tradition, remarkable, among other things, for worshiping the supreme divine almost exclusively in female form, as the *Mahadevi*, or Great Goddess.[3]

As I was wrapping up my work, Guruji turned 80. By chance, his late September birthday fell in the midst of *Navratri*, the most important yearly festival of the Goddess, which unfolds over nine nights each autumn. This fortuitous convergence was marked by large, enthusiastic crowds at Devipuram—"The Goddess's Abode"—the temple complex that Guruji had spent more than three decades building up from almost nothing in the rural wilds of eastern India. Even for a man not known to rest upon his laurels, it was a time of celebration, of looking back with satisfaction on a lifetime well spent and a job well-done. From my own, more mundane perspective, the event also beautifully bookended his biographical narrative. The timing could not have been more perfect.

Or so it seemed until two weeks later, when everything suddenly changed.

Early on the morning of Sunday, October 12, 2014, a severe cyclonic storm designated "Hudhud"[4] swept in fiercely off the Bay of Bengal, making violent landfall in

1 The name Guruji means "Respected Teacher," *guru* meaning "spiritual teacher" and *-ji* being a Hindi honorific.

2 *Upasana* means a spiritual path. An *upasaka* is a follower of that path. The word "*Sri*," besides meaning "auspicious," is also a name of the Goddess. Thus an alternate rendering of Sri Vidya *upasana* could be "The Path of the Goddess's Wisdom."

3 See "Introduction: The World of Sri Vidya" in *The Goddess and the Guru, Volume II*.

4 An unexpectedly harmless name for such a ferocious storm, *hudhud* in Arabic refers to a delicate, crested songbird also known as the hoopoe.

Guruji's home city of Visakhapatnam on India's east coast. It was the first time in more than a century that an Indian city had suffered a direct cyclonic hit, and destruction was extensive. Tearing relentlessly inland, Hudhud wreaked havoc in smaller towns and villages as well—including Devipuram, located about 25 miles west of the city. Within a matter of hours, it flattened much of what Guruji had spent half a lifetime building up.

"Cyclone Hudhud caused heavy damage to Devipuram," he confirmed two days later, when communications were partially restored. "Wind speeds were above 200 kilometers per hour, the takeoff speed of a Boeing aircraft.[5] If buildings are damaged, they can be repaired or rebuilt. But it also erased all the greenery, which will be hard to replace. All kinds of cashew, teak, *neem* and other trees were uprooted. No vegetation was left untouched."

Indeed, fallen trees and other debris blocked all major and minor roadways approaching Devipuram, and lay strewn haphazardly across the temple complex itself. It would all have to be cleared before structural repairs and replanting could even begin. "To limp back to normal may take about two months," Guruji said, offering about as optimistic an estimate as the circumstances could possibly accommodate.

Octogenarian or not, his moment for celebration and reflection had passed, almost as soon as it began.

It was time to get back to work.

ॐ

Years ago, Guruji was approached by a longtime female disciple who complained that she had been praying and praying to the Goddess, yet her life only seemed to keep getting more difficult. What, she asked him, could she possibly be doing wrong?

"If we knock at the Goddess's door persistently enough, she'll eventually let us inside," Guruji replied. "The problem is that she rarely lets us in the usual way, by simply opening the door. Instead, she reaches out through the keyhole, grabs hold of us tightly, and then pulls us back in through that same keyhole, very slowly."

His reply, of course, was half in jest—a gesture of commiseration and understanding to lighten a heavy moment. But it contained a serious core. Guruji was not implying that this "keyhole" was some sort of punishment or that the Goddess is intrinsically

5 Hudhud made landfall in Visakhapatnam at wind speeds of 206 kilometers per hour (128 miles per hour).

cruel to mere humans—quite the opposite; he continually emphasized that we are all part of her essence, and that her essence is love. What he was getting at is that, sometimes, in order to begin seeing and understanding the world as it really is, we must surrender some of our most ingrained, cherished assumptions and preconceptions about its (and our own) nature. By metaphorically pulling us through the keyhole, the Goddess is really just giving us what we need to further evolve—stripping away layers of ego and attachment, and enabling us to perceive something much deeper and truer.

So it was perhaps unsurprising to find that less than a week after Hudhud dragged Devipuram through its keyhole—with roads still impassable, and electricity and communications yet to be fully restored—Guruji was already focused resolutely on the future. "The cyclone has left us with a clean slate to rewrite our vision of Devipuram," he told a group of volunteers. "This is a special gift given to us by the Mother Goddess, the silver lining in a dark cloud. The question facing us now is: what is the way forward, with both individual and societal happiness as our twin goals?"

The Goddess, in other words, had not destroyed Devipuram at all; on the contrary, she had thrown down a challenge, created an opening, pointed toward a goal—and now his role, and ours, was to interpret and set into motion whatever that intended outcome might be. One of her names in Sri Vidya practice, after all, is *Sarva-Samkshobhini*, "she who agitates all," shaking things up in order to free us from our complacency and open our eyes to new possibilities. By his own assessment of the situation, Guruji was once again—as he had been repeatedly throughout his life—being given an opportunity to put his beliefs into action, to truly practice what he preached.

It was a challenge he never declined.

Keyhole Stories

HE WHO WRITES IN BLOOD AND PROVERBS DOES NOT WANT TO BE READ;
HE MUST BE LEARNED BY HEART.
~ *Friedrich Nietzsche*

During an extended stay at Devipuram in 2012, I mentioned Guruji's keyhole parable to Karthika, a Tamil woman in her early 30s serving as a sort of all-purpose hostess and events coordinator there. Her eyes lit up with recognition. "Well that explains a lot!" she said with a laugh. "I definitely feel as though I've been pulled through a keyhole or two." And she went on to narrate the fairly harrowing tale of how she ended up at Devipuram. When she finished she asked me, "So what about you? What's *your* keyhole story?"

It became a sort of catchphrase. We took to asking new visitors, "What's your keyhole story?" It was a powerful icebreaker. Something about the general vibe at Devipuram seemed to open people's hearts—emotions always floated close to the surface. People wanted to talk and to share. So the keyhole stories flowed, and many of them were truly astonishing.

For example, Montserrat, a young dancer from Mexico, came to Devipuram to decompress after a terrifying few months in which her family desperately negotiated the release of her father, a government official kidnapped by an organized crime group. Then there was Cliff, a sweet, 60-something gentleman from Washington State, diagnosed with an inoperable brain tumor and given less than a year to live. He and his wife had been planning to visit Devipuram together, but their savings were insufficient, and he could no longer wait—so she pitched in her half and bought him an airline ticket to use while he was still physically capable of traveling.

Most stories were far less dramatic, of course. But virtually everyone had experienced some sort of striking epiphany, large or small, that caused them to question conventional definitions of success, fulfillment, happiness and meaning; to see life in a new, fundamentally different way; to start grappling with big, existential questions.

Keyholes will do that.

The theme of my own keyhole story, I suppose, was loss. Within a fairly compressed period of time, my wife Anna and I lost a baby daughter; then my father—a strapping man in the midst of hand-building his dream retirement cottage on a lake in the Maine woods—was diagnosed with late-stage pleural cancer and, in the blink of an eye, he was gone too, the cottage left unfinished. Around the same time, my best friend since childhood, a funny, brilliant bioengineer and classical pianist, lost his mind and committed suicide. Almost simultaneously, a series of unpredictable circumstances largely beyond my control threatened my fledgling legal career as well.

Barely had I weathered those squalls when I suffered a spinal injury requiring immediate surgery. Lying on a curtained-off cot at 3 a.m., in a dim corner of the hospital emergency room, I experienced a strange, probably morphine-induced, moment of disconnection. My awareness drifted up to the ceiling and hovered there for a while, looking impassively down at my unconscious body. I watched as a male African–American nurse with a shaved head stopped in for a routine check, realized I wasn't breathing and called for help. After a brief flurry of activity, I was revived. The surgery was a success; however, rehabilitation was a challenge. I wasn't able to walk normally and unassisted for well over a year. The seemingly logical, upward trajectory of my life—which I had always taken more or less for granted—seemed to be palpably disintegrating before my eyes.

Yet, as anyone who has survived such rough patches—and much worse, of course—can readily attest, there are abundant blessings even in times of deepest personal crisis. However intense one's downward flow, there is always an updraft to be found. I bounced back nicely from my injury, better than the brightest prognoses. I recovered professionally too, though I veered away from active law practice and more toward legal journalism (I had been a New York Times Company reporter before law school and had never really stopped freelancing, so the shift made sense in its own way). My wife and I had two beautiful sons; we moved into a lovely home overlooking Narragansett Bay.

Nonetheless, the long barrage of successive crises had left me with a certain siege mentality; I was plagued by a jittery, defensive anxiety, as though perpetually bracing for the next shoe to drop. The sensation was disagreeable and distracting. Realizing that a fearful mind can produce a vicious feedback loop, perversely attracting more and more of whatever is feared, I wondered how—short of chemical or pharmaceutical masking—I might begin to overcome the cycle.

At some point, I remembered a time when, as a child, I was dragged by a couple of older cousins to a horror movie they wanted to see—something way more intense than I was equipped to handle at that age. Rather than risk losing my credibility by freaking out, I forced myself to look away from the film, concentrating instead on the glowing red exit signs and drapes and architectural details of the theater. This offered me instant, reassuring relief from the disturbing images unfolding onscreen.

Now as an adult, immersed in real-life events that sometimes felt like a horror film, I tried using the same trick on a larger scale, looking for "exit signs" to pull me out of my personal dramas for at least a little while (which is, it turns out, a pretty good working definition of meditation). Even in very rudimentary form, the practice dialed down my anxiety a notch or three. I began to see people and situations with a bit more equanimity. I lost a lot of fear. I mellowed out somewhat. It was nice. The more I tried it, the more I wanted to learn.

I began devouring the spiritual writings of Swami Vivekananda, Swami Yogananda, Sri Ramakrishna and other classic teachers of Eastern philosophy. I especially enjoyed the work of Sir John Woodroffe (1865–1936), a.k.a. "Arthur Avalon," who—while prominently serving as Chief Justice of the Calcutta High Court in British India—spent his private hours explaining, defending and ultimately practicing in the then widely reviled Hindu religious schools of Shaiva and Shakta Tantrism.[6] During those disruptive years of my life, Woodroffe's prolix, fussy Victorian prose—written in an arcane, quasi-legalese voice that struck me as both endearing and mildly hilarious—soothed me like a sedative, while also affording a first partial glimpse into the mysterious world of Sri Vidya Tantra. Reading about these magnificently complex and

6 See "Introduction: The World of Sri Vidya" in *The Goddess and the Guru, Volume II.*

beautiful forms of meditation, I became intensely curious about their actual practice, beyond mere theory.

Information began trickling in soon thereafter, when I met a curmudgeonly but likeable fellow attorney named N. Sankara Menon, who was at that time India's sole representative on the prosecutorial team spearheading the United Nations' International Criminal Tribunal for Rwanda in Arusha, Tanzania. Before long, our shop talk veered into discussions of Indian philosophy. We became friends and he eventually revealed that he had been initiated into Sri Vidya by an elderly female guru at just 16 years of age (when we met, he was in his mid-50s). As a child, he had attended both Muslim and Christian religious schools, as his grandfather wanted him to learn about different paths to God. As a youth, he spent months practicing meditation in a cave infested with snakes and scorpions. In short, he was not your garden-variety prosecutor.

Menon and I kept in touch. We talked about Sri Vidya and about life in general; he was being tossed by severe personal and professional storms of his own during this period. Yet he gamely fielded my increasingly detailed questions and, late one night, gave me a basic Sri Vidya mantra over the phone. He added the caveat that he was unsure of its efficacy in the absence of an in-person, hands-on initiation by an authentic Sri Vidya guru. Unfortunately, he told me, such individuals were exceedingly hard to find—even in India, never mind the United States.

Fakes and wannabes abounded everywhere.

I wasn't particularly concerned. At that point in my life—with a new home to maintain, busy young children to parent, a recently changed job to get acclimated to, and now terminally ill in-laws demanding increasing slabs of my wife's time and attention—the matter was purely academic.

I wasn't in the market for a guru anyway.

I kept reading about Sri Vidya, though, and—as I learned more and began dabbling a little in Sanskrit—I got into the habit of writing about what I learned and posting it online, using the pseudonym "Devi Bhakta" (bestowed upon me by a senior diplomat at the Consulate of India in Edinburgh, but that's another story). At the time, there was precious little information about Sri Vidya on the Internet, so I teamed up with Menon to create a website called Shakti Sadhana, and an associated Yahoo Group of the same name. The third leg of our founding triad was a kind and brave Singaporean woman of exactly my age named Nora, who lived in Malaysia. Born to a Muslim family, she had incurred the wrath of Islamist watchdogs by marrying a Tamil Hindu and converting to Hinduism—a religion she now taught and practiced openly. Branded an apostate, she had been harassed and even received death threats for her beliefs. Nonetheless, as an indefatigable contrarian, she was probably the most outspoken of us all.

And when our unlikely team started uploading Sri Vidya scriptural excerpts, translations and ritual guides to the site, people began joining Shakti Sadhana in droves. The quality of discussion and debate was often quite high. We eventually drew thousands of members, for a time becoming the largest Yahoo Group in the "Hinduism" category—no small achievement for a little-known esoteric practice competing for attention with countless more mainstream and organizationally vast groups during Yahoo's early dot-com boom days.

One day in early 2002, Menon mailed me the link to a website he'd discovered. It was titled simply Guruji: Sri Amritananda Natha Saraswati.

"Now this fellow is the real thing!" he enthused. "If you read—*and understand*—everything he has written here, you'll have a pretty comprehensive understanding of what Sri Vidya and Tantra are really all about." So I started reading—and pretty soon I was hooked. Amritananda's authorial voice struck me as startlingly original: erudite but plainspoken; compassionate and practical; spiritually resonant, yet down-to-earth and even humorous. I liked him. In a way I had not come across before, his work seemed to combine a distinct intellectual rigor with a matter-of-fact mysticism that for me, on an intuitive level, registered as spine-tinglingly genuine.

But who was he? A brief, sketchy biographical paragraph on the site indicated that he was a nuclear scientist, Dr. N. Prahlada Sastry by name, who had somehow become a spiritual guru and built some kind of unusual temple. The whole thing sounded unlikely at best, but the facts were tantalizing if true. For years, spiritual self-help writers have loosely cited cutting-edge physics (how many New Age books have the word "quantum" in their title?) as a means of validating alternative spirituality, with often eye-rolling results. "To the chagrin of many scientists," one critic scoffed, "the language of physics was mixed with psychobabble and Eastern mysticism by laypeople who wouldn't know a supercollider from the Super Shuttle."[7] But how worthwhile it would be to encounter a man who could speak authoritatively to *both* sides of the equation—an accomplished nuclear physicist who was *also* a self-realized spiritual master!

Still, I wondered, why hadn't I come across his name or work before? Was he indeed the "real thing," as Menon suggested? How could I know for sure?

I didn't have to wait long for an answer. In mid-2003, Menon called again to tell me that Dr. Sastry—or "Guruji," as nearly everyone called him—was in the United States as we spoke, and would soon be visiting my area, staying with a disciple, Subbarao Kompella, an engineer then living in a Boston suburb just 30 miles north of my home. Menon telephoned one of the organizers of the U.S. visit to introduce me, and I followed up with a call to Subbarao's wife, Usha, who arranged a time when I could come and meet Guruji for myself.

Our first encounter was pleasant and interesting, if a bit anticlimactic. I probably set a wildly inappropriate tone by arriving straight from the office in a business suit. I was—accordingly, I guess—greeted by Guruji in a brisk, businesslike manner.

He looked exactly as his did in his photographs on the Web: a ruggedly handsome man of 68, his white beard still containing a few dark strands, wearing a white cotton shirt and *dhoti*. He was cordial and attentive, with an extremely soft voice (I continually found myself leaning in closer to follow his conversation) and remarkably deep, focused and intense dark-brown eyes. His presence, however, was comfortable and almost disarmingly "normal," particularly given his formidable reputation and the strange, passionate wisdom of his writing. Yet he also projected an unmistakably holy aura, a very peaceful energy. I found it calming to be around him.

As we talked, Guruji was working on an educational computer animation with the help of a pair of local teenagers who sat busily tapping on their laptops, occasionally consulting with him in whispered tones. A bit starstruck at first, I told Guruji how impressed I was by his work. He thanked me and returned the compliment, stating that he enjoyed the Shakti Sadhana group and was grateful to us for discussing Devipuram

7 From Deepak Chopra's 1990 *Quantum Healing* to Sandra Anne Taylor's 2006 *Quantum Success*, the casual association of physics and spirituality has become something of a cottage industry. "To ordinary readers, [Chopra's work] was a visionary leap; to many scientists, it was a simplistic interpretation of physics made worse by grandiose claims. But never mind the critics. Deepak had *Oprah*."

and disseminating his work there. Politely but single-mindedly, he questioned me about the popularity of the group and sounded me out for ideas on creating an on-line community, sharing knowledge and widening the diversity of people attracted to the community.

We chatted for a couple of hours. During one long silence I abruptly—and, upon reflection, rather incongruously—decided to list off some of my personal and professional misfortunes of the moment. (Wasn't that what one did with a guru?) Guruji stopped typing and looked up from the computer screen. His eyes met mine silently for a few moments. Then he nodded sympathetically, mumbled something like, "Yes, life can be full of difficulties," and returned to his work. I dropped the therapy-session talk.

We touched on some broad ideas about Sri Vidya, but not in any great depth; he was preoccupied with his computer project. After a while I stood and took my leave. It was a perfectly pleasant meeting—but certainly nothing like I expected an intimate audience with a spiritual master might be.

Still, we arranged to meet again a few days later. I had asked if he would be willing to grant me Sri Vidya *diksha*—formal initiation into his spiritual lineage. Guruji readily agreed. I arrived in an entirely different mode this time, having deliberately striven for a more "spiritual" frame of mind: I took the day off from work, dressed comfortably and casually, read some of his writings in the morning, meditated a little and listened to a CD of the Sri Vidya prayer chant *Sri Lalita Sahasranama* on my drive up to see him. Ours would be his final meeting in Boston. Immediately afterward, he was leaving for upstate New York.

The atmosphere at Subbarao's home was also very different this time. There seemed to be no other outside visitors; those present were preparing for the day's journey. Usha again received me with a smile, led me into the living room, sat me on the sofa, handed me a glass of orange juice and returned to packing. I looked around the room, my eyes coming to rest on the household shrine, over which loomed a large photo portrait of Guruji. When I returned my attention to the room again a few moments later, it was empty and dim; everyone had left. Someone had closed the blinds.

Guruji entered, nodded a greeting, and sat in a chair perpendicular to the sofa where I was seated. "So you would like to receive *diksha*, initiation into Sri Vidya?" he said.

"Yes," I replied, my mouth suddenly dry.

He nodded and said, "Let's meditate together for a few minutes before we begin, all right?"

I nodded back.

Guruji assumed a loose meditational posture, straightening his back and neck, and then closed his eyes. I watched him settle into an enormous stillness, and after a moment—overcome with nervousness—I tried to do the same. There was no way. I closed my eyes and tried a simple breath-counting technique. That helped a little, but my concentration remained scattered. I snuck a peek at Guruji. He was deep in meditation, hadn't moved an inch. I closed my eyes again and tried unsuccessfully to focus. I was beating back a creeping sense of failure when, suddenly, it felt as if a trap door had swung open beneath me, and I fell with an intense jerk into darkness.

When the sense of falling stopped a moment later, I looked around, but I was no longer seeing with physical eyes. They say the human mind processes unfamiliar experiences by using familiar ones as analogies, and that is my best explanation for what I saw: a dark, windowless, cinderblock room crammed with file cabinets, their drawers stuffed to overflowing. Additional stacks of files teetered high atop the cabinets, disappearing up into the darkness. I was viewing the scene from above. At its center, Guruji sat in a chair, calmly going through the files with what seemed to be amazing speed. In general, I could not see what he was looking at; the "work" was proceeding far too quickly.

Only twice did he pause long enough for me to look over his shoulder at a specific "file"—once he stopped to examine a black-and-white photo of my recently deceased father, and once he paused on a photograph of my friend who committed suicide a year earlier. Why those images? Did they loom as significant markers in my consciousness? Before I could consider the matter further, I felt myself yanked back up through the darkness. Opening my eyes, I found myself still sitting in Subbarao's dimmed living room; Guruji looking at me patiently.

"Shall we begin?" he said.

He gave me four Sri Vidya mantras that day—Guru, Bala Tripurasundari, Ganapati and Panchadasi—repeating each of them three times, correcting my pronunciation as I repeated them back, and then giving me simple instructions for their use. I asked if there was anything else I needed to know or do. "That is enough for now, I think," he said. As if to ensure that I understood the significance of the exchange, he added, "So I am your guru, and you are my disciple." I bent and touched his feet in the Indian manner of paying respect; he placed his hand on my head.

As if on cue, the room brightened again; people returned, the bustle of packing resumed.

"I can teach you more, if you like," Guruji said, standing as we both prepared to part. "Come and spend a few months with us at Devipuram. You will learn a lot."

It was my turn to mumble—well, I said, I have a wife and young kids, work obligations, home to maintain, mortgage to pay, etc. He listened with no trace of disappointment or disapproval. Then, with a nod and a polite farewell, he turned and allowed himself to be led away to a waiting car. I stood off to one side by my own car for a few minutes, watching as a caravan of several vehicles slowly pulled out of the driveway and disappeared down the road. Then I left too.

A few minutes later, I stopped at a local coffee drive-through—I was in serious need of some gesture of "normalcy," I think—and then continued my drive home. The coffee sat untouched in the car's cup holder. I had no appetite for it. I tried to think about what had just happened and what I was feeling, but found I could not approach any of it analytically.

A pressure was growing in my chest, and I had to pull the car into the breakdown lane. Overcome by an indefinable jumble of emotions, I sobbed explosively, convulsively for several long minutes (a highly unusual reaction for me; I've never been much of a crier). Then the feeling passed as quickly as it had arrived. I wiped my face, collected myself, took a sip of my lukewarm coffee and turned back onto the road again.

I arrived home without further incident.

The Work of Guruji

BE GLAD THAT YOU HAVE SOME LITTLE KNOWLEDGE
OF SOMETHING THAT YOU CANNOT PENETRATE.
IT IS ENOUGH IF ONE TRIES MERELY
TO COMPREHEND A LITTLE OF THIS MYSTERY EVERY DAY.
NEVER LOSE A HOLY CURIOSITY.
~ *Albert Einstein, final interview*, LIFE, 1955

Guruji, one quickly learned, lived very much in the present moment. Once a lecture was delivered, an essay written, a ritual perfected, he did not linger for long in its glow, but immediately moved on to new challenges. At various junctures in our association, however, I did endeavor to help him with a few minor "preservative" tasks: managing a couple of Devipuram publications, editing and arranging some raw transcripts of his addresses into more reader-friendly form. I first floated the idea for this book about five years after we met. The more I learned about Guruji, the more convinced I became that his story was worth telling; the more I read of his work, the more I felt it deserved a wider audience.

His manner of expressing himself struck me as genuine and original. He was an evocative writer and natural teacher with a compassionate, compelling and practical message that, I felt, could genuinely benefit many people on many different spiritual paths. Over time, I came to view him as a quiet but profound game-changer, a true iconoclast, a living exemplar of the ancient archetype of the *jivanmukta*—the enlightened being alive in the world. (In fairness, this is a claim he has never made, to my knowledge. Quite the contrary: "I don't accept any claims of me being a realized soul," he once said. "To me, material and spiritual are all the same. There is only one realized soul. That is God. And *you* are it.")

As I pondered his work, I often found myself wondering (1) "Why on earth isn't he better known?" and (2) "Why hasn't anyone told his story?"

The answer to the first question, I came to believe, was a matter of both personality and cultural context. In terms of personality, Guruji simply didn't seem wired for self-promotion. He possessed a daunting intellect, a lively curiosity and a terrific sense of humor. He was a low-key but engaging speaker who radiated honesty and authenticity. Yet he remained, if not quite self-effacing then genuinely humble, downplaying himself tremendously, always shifting attention and credit to others. And while he related episodes from his life with the flair of a natural storyteller, he also seemed entirely uninterested in reliving his past or conveying any particular, coherent "narrative" about himself.

Regarding culture, Guruji's life and teachings unfolded, for the most part, within a Hindu spiritual context and a distinctly South Indian social milieu. To understand and appreciate his work, at least a rudimentary grasp of that context is helpful, even for people from other parts of India. (This I have attempted to provide, both in the text and footnotes of this volume, and in a section called "The World of Sri Vidya" in *The Goddess and the Guru, Volume II: Selected Works of Sri Amritananda Natha Saraswati*.)

And as to my second question, about why no one had ever comprehensively told his story before? The answer that finally sprang into my mind was this:

"So tell it."

One day, after we'd worked on a number of projects together, Guruji asked me to have a look at an extraordinary unfinished manuscript that he'd begun more than a decade earlier. Entitled *Understanding Sri Chakra Puja*, it was a comprehensive manifesto on Sri Vidya philosophy and ritual. Draft versions of the work had unofficially circulated for years among his disciples, but he felt it still needed substantial work. So Guruji and I set about refining, editing, re-sequencing and updating the text, to which he contributed some fascinating new material (much of which is included in *The Goddess and the Guru, Volume II*).

Again, the idea of a book surfaced in my mind. As our work proceeded, I ventured the opinion that *Understanding Sri Chakra Puja* merited "real" publication, perhaps anthologized together with a selection of his other works. These, I was coming to realize, existed in dozens of far-flung locales and forms—decades-old cassette tapes stacked in moldering storage boxes; random electronic files of unedited, unformatted plain text; one-of-a-kind typescripts and manuscripts hidden away in private collections. I argued that a vastly wider audience could be reached if only some of this material were to be properly edited, organized, published and distributed.

Guruji, however, strongly objected to the idea of commercial publication—primarily on the grounds that he claimed no intellectual ownership of his writings and ideas. He was, he explained, a mere conduit for the Goddess's wisdom: it was her work, not his. He had simply written or said whatever she put into his head—so how could he, in good conscience, presume to copyright that material? "The Goddess doesn't copyright the water we drink or the air we breathe," he told me. "If she did, what would become of us?"

This argument made perfect sense to me as a Sri Vidya *upasaka*, even if my inner lawyer and editor were somewhat crestfallen. At any rate, time and events interceded: over the next few years, major changes in Guruji's life and that of Devipuram took center stage (as recounted in this biography). Meanwhile, 8,000 miles away, my own life began drifting in divergent directions as well. My kids were growing older, my professional obligations more demanding. I had all but abandoned the Shakti Sadhana group and long since fallen short of the technical and ritual knowledge required to complete the remaining edits to *Understanding Sri Chakra Puja*. The entire project quietly shuddered to a halt and several fallow years passed, with the whole idea of ever completing a "Guruji book" growing less and less likely every day.

Then in the summer of 2010 a few old friends, concerned over my disappearance from the Sri Vidya "scene," prevailed upon me to come and spend a few days at a massive *Atirudram Yagna*[8] event being held to commemorate the reconsecration of Sri Rajarajeswari Peetam, a Sri Vidya temple founded some 30 years prior by Wijayaharan Aiya—one of Guruji's earliest and best-known disciples—in Rush, NY, a farming community on the outskirts of Rochester.

When I arrived there, the energy was extraordinary. Smoke from 121 fire pits rose and mingled with the chants of hundreds of devotees gathered under a vast tent during the 11-day festival. The crowds milling outside the tent and around the temple grounds

8 *Atirudram Yagna* is a three-millennia-old Vedic fire ceremony dedicated to Lord Shiva.

15

were huge, enthusiastic and celebratory in unmistakably South Asian fashion—rainbows of brightly colored silk saris, the flash of 22-karat gold jewelry and gems, the scent of cow manure and raw milk, of fresh flowers, deep-frying samosas and simmering spices, of wood fires and incense—all combined with the continual, hypnotic, primordial chanting of the ancient *Atirudram* to intoxicating effect.

The event drew participants from across the United States as well as Australia, Canada, Germany, India, Japan, New Zealand, Singapore, Sri Lanka and a dozen other countries. Television news cameras bobbed through the crowds; a *Washington Post* photographer dashed about, capturing the event for an article and photo essay that would appear a few days later. The seeds that Guruji had begun sowing decades earlier were seemingly reaching rich fruition in this unlikely corner of rural upstate New York.

During a break in the ceremonies, I was fortunate to enjoy some private time with—and inspiring words from—Haran Aiya himself, who was presiding over the event. Upon his advice, I also had a serious "chat" with *Vazhi Ganapati*, a small, black granite statue of Lord Ganesh that resided on a tree-shaded deck behind the temple. Figuring I had nothing to lose, I asked him to either facilitate completion of the book or definitively relieve me of the task. Perhaps it worked, for in the days, weeks and months that followed, doors began to open and pieces of the story—leads, documents, referrals—began to manifest. People began to manifest, too.

Needless to say, Guruji himself was my central source, sharing reams of personal letters, writings, computer files and—most precious of all—countless hours of his time, in person, by phone and by email. As the book began to gel, Guruji's daughters Anantalakshmi Pisipati, Radha Marthi and Rama Kandarpa came to the fore, sharing their memories, insights and encouragement, while also opening the family archives and facilitating connections with some of Guruji's closest and earliest associates who might otherwise have never agreed to speak with me in depth.

Saru Janahan—*danseuse extraordinaire*, patron of the visual arts and the definition of a friend in need—began appearing in my life at unexpected intervals, quietly, good-naturedly (and repeatedly) steering me toward reliable connections and resources as I gradually assembled the elements of Guruji's biography. She could be both forceful (telling me, for example, "*You* have to write this book; *you* are the only one who can do it the way it needs to be done!") and remarkably subtle (it took me an embarrassingly long time, as a journalist, to make the connection that she was Haran Aiya's daughter). New Delhi native Megha Chatterjee, a former *Hindustan Times* columnist I'd known for a number of years, also came to the rescue—transcribing hours of interviews and recorded talks, reading drafts and offering occasionally transformative advice on structure and flow, even allowing me to commandeer her dining room during a particularly fruitful week of writing and interviews.

Professor Alok Baveja of Rutgers Business School lent his critical eye and considerable analytical prowess to the manuscript as well, acting almost as a dissertation advisor as he helped me shape, refine and focus its underlying themes and ideas. For more than a year Mrs. Prasanna Nair, a Mumbai businesswoman, adopted me as something of a pet project, leveraging her considerable force of will to talk me into a sabbatical in India for purposes of gathering still-needed interviews and materials. Prasanna met me when I arrived in Mumbai, booked my internal flights and lodgings, and introduced me to an impressive group of Sri Vidya practitioners, including Sri Gopal Narayan, who welcomed me into his home, coached me through a couple of beautiful Devi *pujas*, offered mind-blowing tutorials on the *Devi Mahatmyam*, the empowerment of mantras and the role of the guru—and treated me to an epic Sunday luncheon at Govinda's in Juhu.

The Guruji book, it seemed, was finally back on track.

By this time Guruji's aversion to copyright had softened a bit, and my narrative plan had grown more sophisticated. *The Goddess and the Guru* would consist of two volumes, not one: the first would be Guruji's biography, researched, reported and written as an original manuscript using multiple interviews and documents; the second would present a selected, edited and curated collection of his most significant, representative writings. These developments in themselves largely eliminated most copyright concerns: Guruji's raw online materials would remain in place for any who sought them out; meanwhile, lost and forgotten gems could be polished and displayed for discovery by a much wider audience.

Publishing such an "authoritative version" had become increasingly important. Because although Guruji's writings had indeed spread far and wide online, they had sometimes done so in unexpected ways. Disembodied phrases cherry-picked from his work popped up as social media quotes and memes, stripped of their original context. Sometimes their content was edited or bowdlerized to reflect the sharer's viewpoint rather than Guruji's own. Occasionally his writings were attributed to other authors; in other cases he was identified as the author of others' works. A reliable printed volume could help resolve some of this confusion.

A book would also help disseminate Guruji's message in a way the Internet alone could not. For despite the early promise of the Web and the advent of the Information Age, reaching an audience online had in some ways become more difficult than ever. For at least a millennium, it had been virtually impossible to access the knowledge of Sri Vidya that Guruji had freely shared. But now the metrics of search engine results were erecting entirely new obstacles: people seeking genuine information on Tantra and Sri Vidya were less and less likely to find Guruji unless they specifically sought him out by name—otherwise, his writings were lost in a blizzard of Tantra-themed pages of broadly varying character and quality.

His tentative efforts to teach Sri Vidya via Facebook likewise evaporated in the ephemeral nature of the medium itself. "Google cares what you know, but not who you are; Facebook cares who you are, but not what you know," Guruji quipped one warm autumn evening on his favorite bench outside Devipuram's Ashram. "When someone comes up with a medium that cares about both, then I might be interested!"

His growing ambivalence about online technology surfaced again one night when a disciple phoned with a question about his *sadhana*. "I am not your guru anymore!" Guruji jokingly replied. Before the confused caller could formulate a response, he added, "Haven't you heard? Human gurus are obsolete! The real guru now is Google. Any question you have, just Google it and you'll get an instant answer!"

Yet it was precisely Guruji's down-to-earth humanity that most profoundly informed his particular brand of "magic."

For all the depths and antiquity of Sri Vidya philosophy, and all the multilayered complexity of its ritual, Guruji's interest in the tradition always remained resolutely human-focused—offering *access* and *empowerment* to the largest possible number of people. Even as he trained professional priests in the most elevated and arcane details of ritual practice, he seemed equally engaged when advising, assisting and encouraging those with only the most tenuous knowledge of Sri Vidya, or whose spiritual interests lay elsewhere entirely. Among his followers were not only masses of Indians, but also thousands of foreigners. His admirers included an inordinate number of professionals and intellectuals—doctors, scientists, engineers, academics, college students, entrepreneurs and artists all seemed quite comfortable in his company—yet urban wage-earners and housewives, local villagers and farmers also turned out in droves.

For his part, Guruji appeared remarkably at ease at whatever level he was approached.

"You could have a very casual conversation with him, or a very engaged one," said Megha, the Toronto-based journalist. "It was basically all about what you wanted; it was very '*you*-centric.' You felt there was somebody who loved you in a way you had not been loved before—no like or dislike; no critiquing, no judgment, no expectation; a very different kind of association."

Others echoed her experience. "Coming from an empirical background, to have someone talk about spirituality with a sense of mathematics and science made it easier to digest," said Rachael Hensley of Kauai, Hawaii, who had visited Devipuram several times. "Guruji has also given me a real gift in being able to tap back into things that science *can't* explain."

Alexey Somov, a Russian commodities trader based in Switzerland, also cited Guruji's scientific approach, noting his "unique ability to formulate a complex philosophy and very subtle spiritual experiences into clear and understandable forms. He is great, but he's easy—easy to speak with, easy to be with, easy to work with."

Krishna Ramesh, a nuclear scientist from Bangalore, added, "Every time I look at him I feel a sense of motherly love; someone who is very compassionate, who is open to hear anything you have to say, and who welcomes you wholeheartedly."

One night in Devipuram, under the stars at the Sri Meru temple, a dozen or so visitors were asking Guruji a series of very involved spiritual questions. He would close his eyes for a long time after each query before answering—sometimes to the point where

I wondered if he'd fallen asleep. But then he would abruptly open his eyes and reply in detail. I too found myself closing my eyes during those long intervals of silence. Sitting beside him, I could strongly "feel" his presence, as one can with most people, but at one point I suddenly felt his absence, as distinctly as if he had gotten up and walked away. Curious, I opened my eyes. He was still physically sitting there, but whatever "presence" one usually feels from another person's proximity was gone; it was as though he was merely a projection in space. Within a few moments the sense of his presence returned as he began to speak, but it was a highly unusual sensation—and one that several others seem to have felt from him.

"It's almost like there's nothing there, and yet there's something really big there at the same time," Megha noted. "It's very strange. But whatever it is, you come away feeling that you have met somebody the likes of whom you're not easily going to meet ever again. He is one of a kind among gurus."

If there was any time that Guruji appeared *least* at ease, it was when his undeniably mystical qualities were overemphasized, or when he was too persistently placed upon a pedestal. As a man of science and a Tantric adept, he was justified in this reticence. After all, attempting to elevate him into any kind of separate category—to emphasize his "specialness"—in a way minimized his achievements, precisely by treating them as miracles far beyond the reach of ordinary human beings. When in fact his underlying message was always, "I am *not* extraordinary. What I am, you are too. You are *all* God. You only have to *realize* it."

So in a way, my goal in this book was to emphasize the man behind the superlatives—especially since so many of the qualities that made Guruji "special" were precisely the ones that made him most human. As David Godman, biographer of Sri Ramana Maharshi, once said of his subject, "I don't feel I need to burnish his image at all, because the uncensored truth of his life speaks for itself."

A lovely example of Guruji's "ordinary specialness" is seen in the keyhole story of Cliff Pollick, whom I encountered at Devipuram in 2012, when he was 61. A spiritual seeker by disposition, Cliff worked with the sick and dying in a Seattle-area nursing home and rehabilitation center. He and his wife Micha were saving money for a multi-national spiritual pilgrimage when Cliff was diagnosed with an inoperable brain tumor and given less than a year to live. Micha gifted him with her half of their savings so that he could make the grand pilgrimage alone before he died. He chose to visit the Great Pyramids in Egypt, the holy Hindu city of Kashi (Varanasi), India—and Guruji at Devipuram.

"I believed my journey to India and Devipuram to be the last major undertaking of a full, happy and blessed life," he told me. "The opportunity to actually spend time with other folks studying Sri Vidya, to take part in so many beautiful rites and rituals, to meet Guruji and thank him in person for his writings and teachings was extremely important to me. His work had been the key to my understanding of and access to the richness of this tradition."

Cliff arrived at Devipuram toting a small, pyramidal Sri Meru he had ordered by mail from Devipuram five years earlier.[9] One day he brought the Meru to Guruji for his blessing. Handing it back afterward, Guruji told him, "This is for your healing."

Cliff's only real disappointment in his visit, he told me the day before he left Devipuram, was that he didn't get a chance to enjoy any one-on-one time with Guruji. So that evening, after completing an interview with Guruji for this book, I hurried back to Cliff's room and told him Guruji was at the temple with just a couple of visitors, and that now might be a good time to find a moment alone with him. Though preoccupied with packing and departure preparations (he was scheduled to leave for the airport at 4 a.m.), Cliff sprang at the opportunity.

"I got there as quickly as possible, and was happy to see that the group was so small," he told me later. "It was wonderful to just sit and converse with Guruji—and then I realized at one point that I was all alone with him."

Aware of Cliff's medical condition, Guruji inquired how he was feeling, and Cliff replied as well as could be expected.

Guruji nodded, then looked intently at Cliff and asked, "What do you need?"

Cliff found himself unable to reply. After a moment Guruji stood and said, "How about a hug?"

9   A Sri Meru is a three-dimensional projection of a Sri Chakra, used in Sri Vidya worship, that figures heavily in Guruji's life and work. See also "Introduction: The World of Sri Vidya" in *The Goddess and the Guru, Volume II.*

"So I stood up and stepped closer to him and he surrounded me with a feeling so peaceful that I felt something crumbling inside myself," Cliff recalled. "I said, 'It's not what I *need*, so much as that I *want* so very much to receive *diksha* from you.'"

"But what do you mean by that?" asked Guruji, who had, after all, shared several major Sri Vidya mantras with the classes Cliff had participated in.

"I was really not quite sure," Cliff recounted later. "So I told Guruji something to the effect that I thought a formal, one-on-one initiation would involve some kind of grand ceremonial gesture—like him placing a foot on my head, or whispering the mantra into my ear, or tying a red string to my wrist and bringing me into the lineage. I really wasn't sure *what* was involved! So finally I said that, although I had limited time left in this life, I wanted his blessing to practice Sri Vidya for the remainder of my time and for him to be my guru."

In the gathering dusk, Guruji looked into Cliff's eyes and whispered, "I have *always* been your guru. That's why you are here. And I will still be your guru when this body"—he touched his own chest—"is ash."

Cliff found himself in tears. He thanked Guruji, palms pressed together in *namaskaram*,[10] and the two parted. "Had nothing else happened on the entire journey, I believe that I could have returned home a happy man," he said.

ॐ
ह्रीं

Back in the United States a few months later, Cliff's physician introduced him to a neurosurgeon of Indian descent at a major New York hospital,[11] who specialized in treating hard-to-reach brain tumors using minimally invasive technologies. The neurosurgeon had reviewed Cliff's case and "offered to do the surgery as an opportunity to demonstrate his breakthrough techniques to the Seattle medical community," Cliff said.

After Cliff shared a "*Reader's Digest* version" of his experience at Devipuram, the specialist "was kind enough to let me keep my Meru in the operating theater during the surgery," Cliff said. "It was sealed in a plastic bag under the operating table I was lying on."

Cliff underwent successful catheter-probe laser brain surgery on May 1, 2013. "My wife told me that as I emerged from anesthesia, she recognized I was mumbling the Panchadasi mantra," he said.[12] In the months that followed, Cliff underwent a long, grueling rehabilitation program to overcome lingering neural deficits caused by his illness. By two years out from his visit to Devipuram, he had almost entirely recovered.

On the topic of keyholes, I remember chatting with Guruji one pleasant evening at Devipuram. "You know," I told him, "back when you first gave me *diksha* 10 years ago, at some level I actually thought, 'Now I'm really on my way—this is the big turning point! Here's where I leave my troubles behind!'"

Guruji smiled gently. "Mistake number one," he said.

"But seriously," I persisted, "does there ever come a point in one's *sadhana* where things *do* begin to get easier?"

He smiled again. "I'll let you know when I find out," he said.

In truth, however, Guruji's own life and actions had already answered the question to perfection: things *never* really get easier—life is what it is, even for a spiritual master in the midst of his ninth decade. If there was ever any doubt on that score, Cyclone Hudhud's visit to Devipuram stood as a stark reminder.

What *does* get better with time and *sadhana* is our ability to process and absorb such disappointments and setbacks, realizing that they are in fact neither, that they're really just interesting (if occasionally harrowing) turns in the road—each offering new opportunities to put our professed beliefs and values to the test, to discover the nature and expression of the divinity that dwells within us all. To experience, at the highest possible level (at least once in a while) just how vast and grand and beautiful this life and this world can be; how powerful and divine *we* are capable of being; and how much good we can do with our power and divinity if only we learn how to properly use, focus and direct it while we're here.

As Guruji's own life vividly illustrates, that's a trick easier said than done. But if we set our mind, body and spirit fully to the task—as we all eventually must—it's a goal that is eminently achievable.

A Spiritual Biography

Q: *You say you've talked with divine beings; are you a prophet?*

A: No, I am not a prophet, trying to change the world. I am too small for that. I am only saying that I happened to talk to the Goddess in meditation. Thousands of people do that, and they are not all prophets. I am just another person like you, who believes in doing good to others.

Q: *What if I don't believe what you say?*

A: It is your doubt, and you have every right to choose the answer you like. But it is also my experience, and I have every right to tell about it. If you believe in me, that I am telling the truth, then you may benefit. If you don't believe what I say, you certainly don't lose anything because she is already with you. So accept, and be happy, or don't accept, and be happy. Either way, I want only your happiness and spiritual growth.

~ Sri Amritananda Natha Saraswati,
Conversation with the author, 2007

Prologue: A Grand Consecration

February 25, 1994

The temple was remarkable, unprecedented—a startlingly bright Technicolor wonder soaring high into the tropical sky amid the deep-green, jungle-covered hills of rural eastern India.

Utterly unique in design, the structure presented a sort of open pyramid—or, more precisely, a three-dimensional, geometrically precise projection of the Sri Chakra, one of Hinduism's holiest symbols. Nine interlocking triangles surrounding and radiating out from a central point, forming a network of 43 smaller triangles, those in turn encircled by lotus petals and gated walls, in a mystical diagram symbolic of the entire cosmos: the very womb of creation.

And a womb it was, for this was a temple dedicated to Hinduism's Great Goddess, here in the form of Lalita Tripurasundari, the supreme deity of Sri Vidya, one of India's oldest, most sophisticated schools of Tantric worship. Dating back a millennium in its present form, Sri Vidya is fed by Vedic streams of philosophy another 2,000 years older than that, as well as indigenous goddess-worship traditions rooted in the deep subsoil of prehistory. The Sri Chakra is Sri Vidya's primary symbol. Practitioners, in fact, insist it isn't a symbol at all, but, by its very nature, a direct manifestation of the Goddess herself.

Possibly even more remarkable than the temple itself, however, was the man who had coaxed it into existence. More than a dozen years earlier, a series of powerful spiritual visions led Dr. N. Prahlada Sastry, then a nuclear physicist at India's premier scientific research institute, to walk away from his prestigious position at the heart of the country's military defense complex. Retreating to a remote and empty wilderness, he discovered the remains of a long-forgotten Mother Goddess shrine, then embarked upon a lifelong journey to revive and expand it—along the way revealing the deepest secrets of a religious tradition that had remained essentially inaccessible for centuries to all but the most privileged few.

In so doing he attracted tens of thousands of followers from across India and around the world. They called him Guruji and his temple complex Devipuram. Huge crowds of devotees—multiple estimates exceed 10,000; some veer closer to 20,000—were present on that warm winter morning for the culmination of a three-day *Maha Kumbha Abhishekam,* or Grand Consecration ritual, which formally breathed life into the temple as a vital center of worship.

When Guruji ascended to the temple's spire at the culmination of the event, spectators gasped in unison as a streak of white light shaped like a *lingam*—an emblem of Hinduism's Supreme God, Lord Shiva—suddenly flashed into view, briefly engulfed the temple, and then vanished into the cloudless blue sky. A *Times of India* photographer covering the event captured the phenomenon in a compelling series of snapshots—and yet another credibility-stretching story was born about the strange powers of this singularly focused scientist-guru and his unlikely temple.

It was a pivotal episode in an amazing life, but only one of many transformative stops on an inner and outer journey that, in many ways, continues to this day—a journey that began a lifetime earlier in a small coastal city just 25 miles to the east.

ॐ A massive statue of Lord Vishnu's Man-Lion avatar, Lord Narasimha, shown here disemboweling King Hiranyakashipu, at Simhachalam Temple near Vizag. (Adityamadhav83/ Wikimedia Commons)

1 The Man-Lion's Son

"Father! Father! Prahlada is born!"

The clock was nearing 10:30 on the warm, autumn Wednesday night of September 26, 1934,[13] but four-year-old Suryalakshmi was still wide awake, keeping vigil on her father's lap when the midwife finally emerged from the birthing room with happy tidings of a newborn son.

"Father, come on! Let's go see Prahlada!"

Even in the excitement of the moment, Nishtala Narasimha Rao paused at his daughter's exclamations. Prahlada? That was the name of a legendary boy-saint, for whom the great god Vishnu manifested as Narasimha, the Man-Lion,[14] to defeat a demonic king.[15]

"While we were sitting and waiting, my father was reading me the story of Prahlada," Suryalakshmi explained. "Just as he got to the line '*He is here, He is there; it is certain, He is everywhere!*' the midwife arrived with news that my brother had been born. When I saw him, they said, I kept repeating the name Prahlada."

Taking their daughter's enthusiastic exclamations as a divine suggestion, Narasimha Rao (who himself shared the Man-Lion's name) and his wife Lakshmi Narasayamma named their first son accordingly.

13 In Hindu astrology, this was *Krishna Chaturthi*, the fourth day of the dark half of the moon in the month of *Bhadrapada*. *Bharani Nakshatra* was ascendant, consisting of three stars in the shape of a downward-facing triangle, or *yoni*, extending from 13°20' to 26°40' in Aries. *Bharani* is governed by the planet *Shukra* (Venus) and presided over by Lord Yama (Death). Those born under its influence are said to be focused, hardworking, creative and poetically inclined.

14 King Hiranyakashipu won a boon from Lord Brahma that he could not be killed by man or animal, inside or outside, in daylight or at night, on earth or in the heavens, by any weapon living or inanimate. So Lord Vishnu descended in the form of Narasimha, having the body of a man and the head and claws of a lion. He killed Hiranyakashipu on the threshold of his temple, at dusk, with his claws, while the demon lay across his thighs.

15 As Hiranyakashipu prepared to kill the devout Prahlada, he mockingly asked, "Where is your God now?" Prahlada replied that God is here, there and everywhere. Striking a post of the temple, Hiranyakashipu said, "Is he in this pillar?" Whereupon Vishnu, in the form of Narasimha, emerged from the pillar and disemboweled the evil king.

So it was that Nishtala Prahlada Sastry,the man who would later become known to thousands as Sri Amritananda Natha Saraswati, or simply "Guruji," was named by his big sister.[16]

ॐ
ह्रीं

The young Smarta Brahmin[17] family resided close to the center of Visakhapatnam, a bustling port city in what was then the Madras Presidency of British India, and now lies in the state of Andhra Pradesh. Picturesquely situated on India's eastern coastal plain, where the dramatic, angular hills of the Eastern Ghats tumble into the vast blue expanse of the Bay of Bengal, the city is sometimes called "The Jewel of the East Coast."

Visakhapatnam—also known as Vizag (from an older transliteration, "Vizagapatnam")—is a small city by Indian standards, but more than two million people call it home. The city's rich street life is on full display along the broad waterfront boulevard of Beach Road, with its vendors, street performers, playgrounds, aquarium, zoo, military memorials—all under the watchful gaze of a monumental white sculpture of Lord Shiva and Goddess Parvati at Tenneti Park. Vizag also hosts the Eastern Command of the Indian Navy, and supports both a massive state-owned shipyard and a vast steel refinery, yet its leafy, intimate neighborhoods still nurture a friendly, small-town feel that recalls the fishing community it was for thousands of years. The area also retains much of its natural beauty, including miles of sandy beaches, craggy cliffs and hilltop parks overlooking the sea.

In Visakhapatnam's immediate environs, one can explore the extraordinary limestone formations of the Borra Caves, or hike the breathtaking forested hills of the Araku Valley, known for its gardens, valleys, waterfalls and streams (and, more recently, for Araku Emerald, a fair-trade organic coffee produced by a local indigenous tribe). The area is bursting with temples and shrines, none more formidable than the stately, thousand-year-old Simhachalam complex, located on a hilltop just north of town— and dedicated, of course, to Lord Narasimha (the Man-Lion association would surface repeatedly throughout Guruji's life).

In an early photograph of the family on an outing to Simhachalam in 1939, Prahlada, age four, is held in one arm by his bare-chested father. His mother holds brother Prasad Rao,[18] two years younger, while sister Suryalakshmi,[19] age eight, stands

16 Guruji's full name was Nishtala Surya Somayajula Prahlada Sastry. Nishtala was his surname (given first in Telugu usage). Surya was added because he was born soon after his parents visited Arasavalli Sri Suryanarayana Swami Temple in nearby Srikakulam. Somayajula is his paternal grandfather's name. Prahlada Sastry was his given name. In his professional life, Guruji generally referred to himself as Dr. N.P. Sastry, and that convention is followed in this book.

17 An elite subcaste within the priestly Brahmin fold, the Smarta community is traditionally associated with esoteric spiritual knowledge and the practice of Vedic fire rituals.

18 Guruji's younger brother, Nishtala Venkata Surya Prasad Rao, was born on August 15, 1936.

19 Guruji's elder sister, Gunturu Suryalakshmi, née Nishtala Venkata Suryalakshmi, was born on November 25, 1930, and is the oldest of the three siblings. Two earlier daughters had died in infancy.

between her parents. Towering behind them is the temple's massive bas-relief sculpture of Varaha, Lord Vishnu's boar avatar.

Like many Hindu temples, Simhachalam is considered a *tirtha*—literally a ford, or crossing point—a place where the borders between the mundane and the transcendent, the human and the divine, are permeable and ever-shifting. It was a touchstone in a world that the child observed with penetrating curiosity and intelligence.

"I first began becoming aware of myself around that time," Guruji said. Even in early childhood, he remembers analyzing the world in "a highly logical manner; I was always able to arrange things in neat compartments in my mind."

"He had tremendous concentration, even then," sister Suryalakshmi agreed. She recalled Prahlada's *Akshara Abhyasa*[20] ceremony, a ritual to Saraswati, Hindu goddess of knowledge, the arts and education, in which children are formally taught their first letters. At the age of five, the boy took the pen and—saying, "Here comes *Aim*! *Aim* is coming!"—proceeded to write the syllable, which is the *bija*, or seed mantra, of the goddess Saraswati. ("This from a child who had no previous knowledge of letters," Suryalakshmi noted.) The presiding priest then guided him in writing *Om Namah Shivaya*—the primary mantra of the god Shiva—as his first full sentence.

His innate intelligence served Prahlada well as he began formally attending school, where he quickly distinguished himself as an outstanding student—despite occasionally significant financial restraints. "My father could not afford to buy us textbooks, so I used to borrow my schoolmates' books and copy them neatly into my notebook," Guruji said. "It was around this time that I discovered I could look at any page, and then close my eyes and see every letter, every paragraph, from beginning to end, exactly as if I were viewing a photograph. So exams were easy for me. Since the questions mainly depended on testing memory, all I had to do was to close my eyes, read the book and then write down the answers. As you might have guessed, I was getting good grades."

His intellectual curiosity extended beyond academic subjects. Even as a young child, Prahlada displayed a prodigious interest in matters spiritual, habitually posing such imponderable questions as: *Why did God create the world? Was it just for fun? Is he here with us, having fun too? Why is there religion? Why do we worship God? What happens if we*

don't? Sometimes an adult, charmed by the boy's innocent curiosity, would attempt to indulge him—but one question invariably led to another until his interlocutor finally gave up in exasperation.

In his leisure time, Prahlada immersed himself in Hinduism's great religious epics, the *Ramayana* and *Mahabharata*. Beginning at about age eight, he undertook to read each of the 18 *Maha Puranas*[21]—massive cultural repositories of religious stories and teachings—in turn, gradually absorbing the elemental storehouses of Hindu lore. These pastimes gave him "immense happiness," and the stories sprang vividly to life in his mind's eye, blending seamlessly with the features of his everyday world.

"So when I was reading the story of Prahlada, I thought it was my own story," he explained. "I began to see divine figures such as Krishna, Ganesh, Hanuman and Saraswati—my favorite goddess—in the patterns of the leaves in the trees. I used to talk with them and play with them." Sister Suryalakshmi remembers him climbing a *parijat* (coral jasmine) tree near their home, holding a stick to his lips and telling her, "Isn't this how Lord Krishna plays the flute? This is what I can see! This is what I hear!" At first, he thought everyone else could perceive the divinities as well, and would sometimes call out to his friends, "Look, Lord Krishna is sitting up in that tree! See?"

His companions would turn, mouths agape, to wherever he was pointing—and, of course, see nothing at all. Laughing at their friend's overactive imagination, they would return to their games, leaving him alone with his visions. "Immersed in such pastimes, and being pretty much an introvert by nature at any rate," he recalled, "I was aptly nicknamed 'the absentminded professor.'"

Young Prahlada could often be found staring off into space, lost in thought, listening intently to sounds that no one else could hear—sometimes a *veena*,[22] sometimes a flute, sometimes ankle bells or temple bells. At that age, he had no idea why he was hearing these sounds or where they came from; he only knew that they made him happy. "As a youngster, I used to get the feeling that if I ever stopped hearing those sounds, I would die," he said. "I don't know why that feeling was there, but it was."

ॐ
ह्रीं

Of course, life was not all dreamy reflection. Prahlada was an ordinary boy in many respects, who enjoyed, for example, playing football (soccer) with his friends after

21 The *Puranas* are a genre comprising scores of ancient Hindu spiritual texts; however, the *Ashta-adasha Mahapurana* ("18 Great Puranas") are generally considered the most significant.

22 An Indian plucked string instrument similar to a lute.

school. "We used to play on the slopes of a steep sand hill—*isaka konda* in Telugu—near King George Hospital in Visakhapatnam," he said. "Our feet would get stuck in the sand; scaling the hill was pretty tough going. We would arrive at the Hanuman Temple—opposite the Prabhat Talkies Theater—utterly exhausted, just in time for *prasadam*[23] and then go home giggling."

But the sporting life was not his forte. "One day while playing football, I broke my right arm in half at a 90-degree bend—after that, I was asked not to play these rough games." It was not so much that Prahlada was fragile; he was built sturdily enough. It was more an issue of his innate gentleness, a quality his younger brother vividly remembers.

"He was called '*Samka*,' the kind and soft-natured; I was '*Dhumka*,' the rough and aggressive!" said Prasad Rao. "One fine day when we were quite young, *Annayya* (big brother) and I had an argument and in a fit of anger I gave him a couple of punches and he started crying." Their father stepped in, demanding that Prasad Rao apologize and promise never to repeat the offense—but "*Dhumka*" refused and was locked in an anteroom without food until he relented.

"Well, it seems I never complied!" Prasad Rao recalled with a laugh. "But after a couple of hours, *Annayya* could no longer bear my plight. He started crying and pleading with Amma to release me. When that didn't work, he too refused to eat until food was given to me. Finally, she had no option but to release me and give us both something to eat!"

Prahlada's sensitivity also had its creative aspects, one of which was a distinct gift for drawing and painting. Studying under a professional artist friend of the family, Mr. P.J. John, he produced excellent likenesses of family members, including his grandparents from photographs, and even one of Mahatma Gandhi; unfortunately, none of these early works have survived into the present. As an adult, however, Guruji would frequently call upon these skills to illustrate his visions, ideas and teachings. (According to one early disciple, "When I commented to Guruji once about his artistic talent, he told me that when he settled down to draw, at times Saraswati would hold his hand and sketch intricate images for him.")

It wasn't long before he began displaying more mystical talents as well.

23 Distribution of blessed food offerings.

"In 1941, when I was about seven, I discovered that I had a very long tongue, the tip of which I could extend halfway up my long nose!" he said. "I could roll my tongue back, up behind the uvula and into the cavity above the palate, for no apparent reason. I found I could touch the septum dividing my right and left nostrils; when I did, I would experience a sharp pleasure, bordering on pain."[24]

He would sometimes press his tongue further into the nasal cavity until he experienced "a sweet liquid falling from somewhere up above; whenever this used to happen, I had the experience of not being hungry for days on end. When my mother would try to force me to eat, I would get very upset and protest that I was full and couldn't eat anymore!"

It was around the age of 11, however, that Guruji had what he calls his first true spiritual experience. He was playing in his home's open courtyard, when suddenly "bright sparks appeared in the sky" and the world began spinning around him, faster and faster, as if everything was being sucked into a vast vortex, with himself at its center.

The sparks resolved into "gray, misty globes of light floating in front of me, then collapsing into my eyes and entering my body. I felt myself growing larger, flying high; I could see the city of Visakhapatnam, the streets and houses and temples, the seashore. They all began collapsing into me. Then entire countries were collapsing into me, then the earth, the sun, the moon, the stars; space itself—the whole cosmic vision. And then I lost consciousness."

His mother called for Prahlada's father, who immediately scooped him up and carried him inside. A doctor was called. "I was nearly in a state of semicoma, half aware," Guruji said. "I would ask my parents and elder sister, 'Who are you? Why are you here? How am I related to you?'" With a fierce fever sometimes reaching as high as 107°F, "I was wrongly diagnosed as having cerebral malaria, and treated with heavy doses of quinine."

But the treatments eventually broke the fever, and after a few days Prahlada began returning to himself. His sister Suryalakshmi, by then 15, sat by his bedside and asked him exactly what had happened. He told her he wasn't sure. "I didn't hear anything, but I saw different worlds," he said. "I wandered in the skies. It was great!" Guruji began excitedly speculating to his sister about the meaning of life and the nature of God, but she stopped him abruptly, warning him not to share such thoughts with his elders and peers—no one would believe or understand him.

"I was all right in a week, but by then I had become nearly deaf," he said, though his hearing slowly returned over time. The most unfortunate outcome of the illness? "I lost the photographic memory that I'd had up until that time. The drugs killed all that. If I had to guess, I'd say my intelligence came down by roughly a factor of a hundred. There were so many things I couldn't remember anymore." In retrospect, Guruji added, "I think it could have been a spiritual experience of *jada samadhi*, wherein bodily consciousness is absent and any sense of 'I and mine' is lost, even when awake."

Nonetheless he continued to excel at school and his intellectual life remained rich. "I was pretty good at math, but I hated chemistry—I could never figure out why the colors in the beakers had to change!" he said, with a laugh. "I also learned a little Sanskrit and passed an entrance test for proficiency in Telugu," his native tongue.

In fact, Prahlada knew more than "a little" Sanskrit, his brother recalled. "I still remember the plight of our Sanskrit teacher, when I insisted that I too wanted to learn," he said. "I could hardly pronounce the *Sabda Manjari*," an introductory primer, "while my brother progressed to the *Kalidasa Kavyas*," a collection of verses by Kalidasa, the Shakespeare of Sanskrit literature.

श्री Rama Krishna Beach in Visakhapatnam, as it looked during Guruji's childhood.

(Public domain)

2 Do As You Will

Though the Nishtala household was never wealthy, the family always had enough to cover its basic needs, and generously showered hospitality on visiting relatives and friends. "To my parents, wealth and poverty were not important concepts," Surya-lakshmi said. "Whatever they had, they shared."

Prahlada's father, Narasimha Rao, was educated up to the tenth standard,[25] but never progressed any further in school "though he made several attempts," Guruji said. He was a large, imposing, even burly man who had been a skilled football player in his younger days—with a strong jaw and intense dark eyes that flashed fierce independence, stubborn self-confidence and perhaps a hint of sly humor. Though scrupulously honest and ethical by all accounts, Narasimha Rao had no particular interest in formal religion or ritual.

"He was deeply religious inside, but rarely exhibited any outward signs of it," Guruji explained. The elder Nishtala was, however, a staunch admirer of Mahatma Gandhi who tried to follow the great man's precepts, leading a frugal life and working hard. "My father was a highly principled man, a true Gandhian who cared deeply for his Motherland, which was at that time still under the yoke of the British Empire," Guruji noted.

25 India's first through 12th "standards" closely correspond to U.S. and Canadian "grades."

Narasimha Rao had, in turn, imbibed much of his outlook from his own father, Nishtala Somayajulu, a highly regarded and "very handsome" Vizag lawyer "who used to drive around the city in a horse and buggy," Guruji said. "He had received orders to be a high court judge, but passed away before he could assume office." Narasimha Rao was one of Somayajulu's six children—who included two daughters and three more sons. "My father's eldest brother Nishtala Bhagawanulu was an auditor. Next came Nannalu, who learned French but never held any job, and then Venkatarao, who was a public prosecutor and lawyer in the city."

Narasimha Rao was the artistic idealist of the clan, earning his living as a professional photographer (younger relatives knew him as Photo-*Tatayya*—"Photo-Grandpa"). He worked out of an old stable behind the house, which he'd converted into a studio called *Roopa Rekha Kanti Grahakam*: roughly, the "Beauty and Glow Picture Studio." On the side, he offered lessons. "Most of the photographers in Visakhapatnam had been apprentices under him at one time or another," Guruji said. "In fact, he was the first to start a photography business in the city. I remember that he was a strong believer in Kodak products as superior to all other brands. Though Agfa and Gevaert were also around at the time, he used to only stock the Kodak items—'All Kodak Supplies' was his motto."

During World War II, Narasimha Rao volunteered his photographic skills to the Allied war effort. As a major naval center, Vizag figured prominently in the defense strategy of British India—to the extent that it had once been the target of a Japanese bombing raid. So Guruji's father teamed up with a friend—no less a personage than the princely Kishor Chandra Deo Bhanj, 23rd Raja of Daspalla—to conduct regular reconnaissance missions in the Raja's helicopter, photographing the Japanese fleet's positions and movements off the coast. He won the trust of local British military officials by supplying his prints along with their destroyed negatives to guarantee that the images remained secret (apparently a practice few Indian photographers followed in those days). The pair's wartime adventures came to an abrupt end when they crashed into a pineapple orchard in the Simhachalam Hills north of the city. Both men were fortunate enough to escape with just a few scratches, but the chopper was a total loss. Narasimha Rao made the best of a bad situation by photographing the wreckage and selling the images to a local newspaper.

Guruji's mother, Lakshmi Narasayamma—though schooled only through the third standard and functionally illiterate (as was fairly common among middle-class women of her era and milieu)—was a walking treasure trove of stories from the Hindu epics and *Puranas*. Like her husband, she possessed a strong and vivacious character, and she was, by inclination, also a committed Gandhian. An only child herself, Lakshmi Narasayamma was proud of and ambitious for her children, and provided most of the structure and routine in their early lives. Under her austere encouragement and guidance, Guruji remembers a childhood that was "quite happy," albeit largely lacking in such "extravagances" as movies and other entertainments.

The family home was nestled on a street in central Vizag known as Kothasalipeta.[26] A single-story structure laid out in typical South Indian style, it consisted of 14 rooms surrounding and opening onto a spacious central courtyard. The house had been brought to the marriage by Lakshmi Narasayamma, whose father—Jayanti Venkanna Pantulu, well-placed as Vizag's Deputy Collector—had built it a generation earlier, in 1900. "My maternal grandfather earned a name as a good arbitrator," Guruji noted of Venkanna Pantulu. "Everyone used to appreciate that he would do justice to both sides."

The structure's amenities included two deep and reliable wells (a true luxury in the drier seasons), a large rooftop terrace and the stable (Jayanti had kept horses) that would eventually become Narasimha Rao's photo studio. Constructed of white-washed masonry, the home was open and airy, with high ceilings, stone floors and a tiled roof—an extremely practical design for the city's hot, humid climate. It was aesthetically pleasing as well, buttressed by networks of pillars and arches, and accented by heavy wooden support beams over the internal windows and doors. Yet it lacked any ornate architectural flourishes: like the man who built it, the house was ultimately straightforward and sensible.

26 An apartment complex named Lakshmi Residency (after Guruji's mother) now stands on the site of Guruji's childhood home, which was demolished in 2001. According to his daughter Radha, "As the years went by, the old house was in need of constant repair, and maintenance costs were escalating. So with a heavy heart it was decided to raze the house and build afresh."

Though they took no direct part in India's freedom struggle against the British Empire, Guruji's parents proudly adopted Gandhi's principle of wearing homespun (*khadi*) clothing. Lakshmi Narasayamma even insisted on wearing heavy *khadi* saris during pregnancies, when their considerable weight became difficult to manage. Her spinning skills reached such levels of refinement that she won several local competitions, once bringing home a silver trophy bowl that the family still preserves.

"My father never purchased mill cloth because it wasn't *swadeshi*—not made in the country," Guruji recalled. "So we became adept at spinning thread with the *taklis*, a metal disk attached to a spindle, and we would make our own clothes from the thread we spun. That situation continued all the way up to my college days. When everyone else was wearing pants, I was still wearing half-pants made from handspun *khadi*. My fellow students used to heckle my poor style of dress—but they were still jealous of my performance at exams!"

Such compromises were simply a part of everyday life in the Nishtala household. When he was around 11 years old, Guruji recalled, he asked his father for pocket change to see a popular film then playing at the local cinema. His father, in typical fashion, turned the request into a moral lesson: "Should I spend that money on some *dal* (lentils) for our family dinner, or would you rather take it and watch a movie for your own enjoyment? Which would you prefer?" Always keenly aware of his family's economic constraints, Prahlada chose the *dal*, though he remembers feeling a little disappointed about it. In general, however, from an early age worldly pleasures never much enticed him. He was content, he said, just to have loving and affectionate parents who took good care of him.

"That was childhood for us," Suryalakshmi said. "We were always together, never apart. The three of us children used to sleep on the same bed, between our mother and father. I played with my brothers, we tried to stay out of mischief, we ate what our mother gave us to eat, and we wore what she gave us to wear—none of those fancy outfits that children wear today!"

Even as a teenager routinely topping his class at Saint Anthony's High School, a Roman Catholic institution in Visakhapatnam, Guruji continued to hear strange sounds emanating from deep within himself. He struggled to understand their meaning and origin—and kept asking difficult and precocious questions: *What is the significance of*

divine visions? Does everyone have them? What is the difference between sleep and death? What is this thing called samadhi?[27]

27 *Samadhi* is a higher level of concentrated meditation described as a non-dualistic state of consciousness in which the subject's consciousness becomes one with the object experienced.

By that time, however, he had come to understand that his parents were neither equipped nor inclined to answer, nor were any of his teachers, elders or peers. Yet the visions and sounds continued to evoke strong emotions. They did not adversely affect his schoolwork, though; he finished first in his 10th-standard class.

Soon afterward, however, Guruji's peaceful childhood existence changed permanently and dramatically when the stalwart Narasimha Rao suffered a paralytic stroke. Gravely ill and unable to leave his bed, his condition deteriorated swiftly and doctors soon confirmed the worst—death was imminent. Suryalakshmi, who helped nurse her father through his final days, recalled that he suffered emotionally as much as physically, tortured by the thought of abandoning his children just as they were reaching the prime of life.

"What weighed most heavily on him was that he'd told his sons if they got good marks in school, he would make sure they got a top education in engineering," she said. "He bitterly regretted that they kept their part of the bargain, while he—because of his illness and financial constraints—was unable to keep his." Heartbroken, he told a friend, "I spent my career photographing other people's children on their graduation days, but I won't be able to photograph my own."

Guruji's distant cousin Sundari Amma—who would, years later, marry his younger brother—recalled her first meeting with Guruji, when she was about 12 and he was a teenager sitting at his father's bedside.

"As we entered the house, I remember seeing Guruji's father—a well-built older man afflicted by paralysis—lying on a bed, and beside him Guruji himself—a young man wearing a traditional *dhoti* with a towel thrown over his shoulder," she said. "When my parents entered, he rose and greeted them with folded palms, introducing himself as his father's eldest son. I was impressed by the attention and affection he showed toward his father, and by his simplicity and deference toward my parents, by how naturally he struck up a conversation and made us feel welcome and comfortable."

Narasimha Rao passed away in July 1952 at the age of 55. "I was hardly 17, barely out of the 10th grade," Guruji recalled. "We were left with no means, and my mother, brother and elder sister and brother-in-law"—then newlyweds just setting up household in the Nishtala family home—"also had to be taken care of." For the time being, the family's scope of options was decidedly narrow. "On the advice of my illiterate mother and the pressures of my family, we took a small loan of ₹3,000[28] at a compound interest of 120 percent per annum, which I had to repay, nearly 50 times over, by selling my father's house." (Guruji clarified, "The house I sold was paternal property. The house we lived in was maternal property.")

To supplement the family income, it was decided to divide Venkanna Pantulu's sprawling homestead into apartments and take in tenants. Suryalakshmi and her family occupied one unit. Their father's elder sister and her husband moved in as caretakers. In years to come the house would be continually modified to suit its new role, and for the next three decades most of it would be occupied by renters.

In an intimate farewell exchange shortly before his death, Narasimha Rao had imparted to his son one final piece of advice—a tiny seed that would grow to become Guruji's guiding philosophy. Guruji had asked his father for a compass, a beacon to carry with him through the years to come.

His father's reply: "Do as you will."

Simple though it was, the phrase effectively distilled Narasimha Rao's own approach to life as well. "Guruji's father was an independent thinker, and he gave a lot of weight to his own beliefs," daughter Radha explained. "He was advising his son to use the same guiding principle that he himself had followed; that is, to believe in yourself most of all, and be answerable only to your own conscience. He placed his full confidence in his eldest son when he left him with those words."

Their impact would ultimately prove to be nothing less than transformative. "They stuck with me all my life," Guruji said. Their influence can be seen in nearly every major decision he made, and over time took on an almost mystical significance. "Strangely enough, my guru at Anakapalle[29]—who also shared my father's name, Narasimha, by the way—would later give me the very same advice."

28 In 2010, the Government of India adopted ₹ as the symbol for rupee; it was incorporated into its currency notes in 2012.

29 Swami Swaprakasananda, discussed in chapter 8.

ॐ
ह्रीं

So it was that the dreamy, spiritually inclined child suddenly found himself thrust abruptly into the responsibilities of adulthood, decisively rerouted toward the workaday existence of a householder—a path he would follow for decades before finally embracing a life of spiritual exploration and service.

Religious visions and absentmindedness fell by the wayside overnight, becoming irrelevant luxuries. Faced with onerous new family responsibilities, Guruji resolved to take his sister's advice at last, and give up his apparently useless preoccupations with God, creation, the meaning of life and other such "big questions." He told himself, "I'll worry about all that when I'm in my 40s perhaps. For now, I can't be bothered." And that is indeed how his life would eventually unfold.

"It was probably my destiny to study the truths of science and the external world before I could turn my mind inward much, much later on in my life," he said. For the time being, education—for both himself and his younger brother—would take top priority. Yet even that was problematic.

While Guruji's academic promise was undeniable—he finished high school at the top of his class and won admission into India's premier engineering school, the prestigious Indian Institute of Technology (IIT) at Kharagpur—the money simply wasn't there.

"I couldn't even muster the funds to buy a railway ticket," he said. No solutions presented themselves in the time available, so finally, "I had to drop the idea of IIT." When his brother reached college age several years later, Guruji ensured that his own frustration was not repeated, sending Prasad Rao to the Directorate of Marine Engineering Training (now the Marine Engineering and Research Institute) in Calcutta.

Guruji settled for his more accessible and more affordable hometown college, Andhra University, in Visakhapatnam, which happened to be opening a brand-new nuclear physics department that autumn. One of his father's close friends, Neelayya Garu, arranged Guruji's admission into the program as well as a scholarship to cover his tuition. "Any friend worthy of the name should be like Neelayya Garu," Suryalakshmi said. "During my father's illness, when hardly anyone ever came to visit us— even his own brothers didn't turn up to see him on his deathbed because they were

45

afraid he might ask them for financial help—even then, Neelayya Garu came and tried to make sure we would be okay."

On the darker side of the moral spectrum, several distant cousins—in the immediate wake of Narasimha Rao's death—appeared with false claims to the family home, in a cynical maneuver that would have deprived the Nishtalas of their sole means of financial support. In an early show of "do as you will" self-reliance, "their attempt was foiled, mainly due to a message Guruji received in a dream, which helped him locate some crucial documents that disproved the false allegations," his daughter Radha said.

It was under these disheartening circumstances that young Guruji reported to his first day as a physics major at Andhra University in the autumn of 1952. His enthusiasm was low—he had only agreed to enter the program, he said, because a relative assured him that "nuclear studies were the 'in' thing to do. I would have preferred to do the engineering degree at IIT, because I had an aptitude for engineering kinds of things—but that was no longer an option."

So Guruji determined to make the best of it—and he made an impression. Classmate Dr. E.V.R. Rao[30] remembered their first encounter: "I was sitting on the university bus when Sastry boarded at the Turner's Choultry stop. What first attracted my attention was his rather disheveled, unshaven appearance and his peculiar voice, which was notably high-pitched and soft. Soon enough, however, I learned he had a reputation as one of the school's brightest students. We became social friends, too; for example, we used to relax outside of class by playing cricket on the Yellamma Thota grounds."[31]

Still, Andhra University seemed a rather lackluster substitute for IIT—and it might well have been but for one fateful circumstance: the school's fledgling Department of Nuclear Physics was being developed under the leadership of one of 20th-century India's more extraordinary and unusual figures, the nuclear-physicist-cum-holy-man known as Professor Swami Jnanananda.

$$\triangledown$$

30 Upon graduating from Andhra University, Dr. E.V.R. Rao (b. 1936) secured a position at the Bhabha Atomic Research Centre, one of TIFR's sister organizations, in Bombay. Rao's and Guruji's social and professional paths crossed frequently, and they remained friends throughout their lives. Their final meeting took place just months before Guruji's death.

31 Yellamma is a local form of the Mother Goddess, whose worship is said to date back to the Nagas, early indigenous inhabitants of the Vizag area. Yellamma Thota was her temple in the city.

3   The Yogi, the Nazis and the Cyclotron

Professor Swami Jnanananda—newly anointed as the founding director of Andhra University's Nuclear Physics program—was never a "guru" to Guruji in the formal, religious sense of the word; they hail from different lineages, and their philosophies and teachings differ significantly in many details. But by any ordinary definition of the word—the guru as an influential teacher, mentor or guide—Jnanananda abundantly fits the bill. He was the first to impress upon a youthful Guruji the complementary, rather than contradictory, nature of science and spirituality, and he did so with a direct, analytical and informed approach that Guruji, even in his youth, instinctively recognized and respected.

"We were not 'friends,' heavens no," Guruji said. "Our relationship was more that of a respectful and affectionate guru and his *shishya*. But our personal talks were few and far between, and mostly confined to creating the nuclear research facility at Andhra University and helping him write a book on vacuum physics."

Yet the interactions they did enjoy were significant in multiple, enduring ways. At a juncture when Guruji had resolutely abandoned spiritual practice for academic and worldly pursuits, Jnanananda served as powerful reminder that those two worlds were not necessarily in conflict. Moreover, a number of unignorable parallels link these two men of India who, at various points in their lives, excelled both as successful practicing nuclear scientists and as advanced spiritual adepts.

Born Bhupathiraju Lakshmi-Narasimha Raju (Narasimha appears again) on December 5, 1896, in the village of Goraganamudi, about 180 miles (300 kilometers) south of Vizag, Swami Jnanananda was a mathematics prodigy who delved deeply into yoga and spirituality in his youth. As a teenager he ran away from home and became a disciple to Swami Purnananda, an orthodox Shaiva guru in Calcutta. His parents located him and brought him home. But in 1917 at age 21, he "ran away" again—this time to avoid marrying and settling into the family agricultural business as his wealthy parents were insisting.

Walking tirelessly and freight-hopping trains, he traveled deep into the northern wilderness, finally settling in under "a big rock" on the banks of the Gandaki River in Nepal, near Lumbini, birthplace of the Buddha. "I had no food," Jnanananda wrote in a 1961 Telugu memoir. "The forest was very thick. I had heard that ancient *rishis* lived on air and ate fruits, roots and fresh leaves. I started doing the same. I began practicing yoga. I spent my time doing *asanas* and meditation."

He made a somewhat unusual yogi, with long hair and a beard, completely naked save for a loincloth (and a pair of prescription eyeglasses)—yet fully fluent in the King's English. He also read voraciously, immersing himself not only in Sanskrit scripture, but in Western philosophical classics such as Plato's *Republic* and Kant's *Critique of Pure Reason*. People would gather to stare at—and stay to seek the blessings of—this unusually urbane and intellectual young spiritual master. Jnanananda would duly oblige, and then slip away under cover of night to seek his beloved solitude again.

During the winter months, when most *sadhus* migrated south, Jnanananda remained in the frozen north, relishing the deep quiet and developing advanced yogic abilities—including, reputedly, the ability to generate intense heat from inside his body. During a long winter spent at the source of the Ganges River, high in the hills of northern Uttarakhand on the border with China, he lived in a cave a few miles outside the pilgrimage center of Gangotri. A local caretaker priest named Bhumananda looked after him. Jnanananda recalled:

Bhumananda used to bring me food every day, walking in the snow for about a mile to reach the Bodhi Cave. One day it snowed very heavily. It was a blizzard. Bhumananda brought food even that day; however, he got so cold that his fingers were frozen and were unable to hold the plates and bowls. I was naked as usual. He put his hands on my back and he told me it was like a stove. He left me that day after he got control of his fingers. It snowed more and more all through December, January and February. From then onwards he would warm his fingers on my back, whenever they would freeze.

On another occasion Jnanananda led a group of prominent, politically connected pilgrims on a ritual circumambulation of Mount Kailash in Tibet, refusing to ride any animal and again wearing only a loincloth despite the cold.[32] Early in the climb, he slipped and fell into a rushing torrent of glacial meltwater, tumbling "800 or 900 feet" in the slushy current before managing to grab a boulder and gradually make his way "to the other side of the stream, with great difficulty." Apparently unfazed by the incident, he merely paused to thank God for saving his life and then "continued walking back onto the route that we were supposed to take, proceeding most cautiously and slowly into the mountains."

Through a full decade of such austerity and physical adventure, Jnanananda's reputation spread steadily across India and even abroad. (Guruji remembers fellow students at Andhra University gossiping about Jnanananda's youthful exploits—so incongruous with the sober, dignified gentleman who taught their classes each day.) Along the way he also composed hundreds of poems, mostly in English, and completed a verse distillation of his philosophy titled *Purna Sutras* ("Complete Aphorisms"). A sample, written beside Aharbal Falls in Kashmir in August 1920:

> *Behold!*
> *Spheres on spheres!*
> *Systems after systems,*
> *Countless worlds and suns,*
> *Moons and stars and all,*
> *Moving in measures, band by band,*

32 Over the centuries, countless Hindus, Buddhists and Jains have undertaken ritual circumambulations of Mount Kailash, the traditional abode of Lord Shiva. Though Kailash towers 21,778 feet (6,638 meters) above sea level, the clockwise circumambulation takes place between 15,000 feet (4,600 meters) and 18,000 feet (5,500 meters). Setting foot on the slopes of the peak itself is considered taboo.

The shining islands of the spatial sea
Stirred with the dreadful waves,
Which roll in restless tides of change,
Slowly, slowly drown
In the darkest abyss of space
Infinite, unfathomed, undiminished,
Leaving behind image-worlds and suns,
Moons and stars and all mere images,
The shadow islands of the infinite sea.

In 1927, at the age of 31, Jnanananda abruptly set aside the renunciate's life and returned to the workaday world, where he found himself widely hailed as "1,008 Sri Jnanananda Swami." This title, Guruji explained, meant "his attainments were such that 1,008 honorific 'Sris' were to be uttered before speaking his *dikshanama*," or initiatory spiritual name.

Reverting to conventional modes of dress and grooming, Jnanananda traveled to Europe to oversee publication of his *Purna Sutras* in German translation, along the way delivering lectures on Hinduism to audiences in Italy, Austria and Germany. Among the attendees at a Dresden event was one Professor Dember, mathematical physicist and acolyte of Dr. Albert Einstein. Dember found Jnanananda's lectures—"centered on unbounded time and space experienced in higher states of consciousness"—to be deeply thought-provoking, and the two began meeting to discuss the connections between their respective fields.

Upon Dember's recommendation—and having completed a summer crash course in university-level German—the young swami enrolled at Dresden's College of Science and Technology as an undergraduate that very autumn, eventually earning degrees in both mathematics and physics. His intense academic workload did not dampen his spiritual passion: he continued to prolifically publish books, pamphlets and articles on Hindu spirituality, and delivered scores of lectures on the topic.

With the rise of Adolf Hitler and the Third Reich, however, Jnanananda became concerned about Germany's darkening socio-political climate—in particular the "distasteful and deplorable" treatment of Jews (including his beloved mentor Professor Dember, who was summarily dismissed from his tenured position at the university and forced to flee the country), and the increasingly "irrational" behavior of "even educated Germans."

As the situation grew increasingly "unbearable," he relocated to Prague, where he earned a master's degree in x-ray spectroscopy at the venerable Charles University in 1936. When the Nazis invaded Czechoslovakia in 1939, Jnanananda boarded a train out of the country—only to be detained at the border for questioning, accused of "sabotage," and sent back to Prague with orders to report to Nazi authorities on a biweekly basis. Displaying a fearless steadiness of mind born from years of yogic austerity, Jnanananda refused to cooperate.

"I challenged them to put me in jail if they could prove their suspicion on any count," he recalled. "I strongly [stated] that I would not report to the police station." Astonishingly, the Nazis thereupon "withdrew their summons." Jnanananda next penned a letter to a top-ranking officer in the German occupying force, arguing, "It would be a shame on your part to detain a guest from India for no reason. I would like to go to England, and it would be fair on your part to let me go." Again, against all apparent odds, the letter worked: Jnanananda was granted safe passage through war-torn Europe to Holland, whence he caught a steamer to London. During the trip he handed the last of his pocket money to a dispossessed Jewish family he met onboard, fleeing Nazi persecution.

Recalling these actions years later Jnanananda said, "Although I did not know what was going on, I was not afraid. I took the developments as they happened, only as a witness. As a seeker of truth and an ardent practitioner of yoga, my mind and heart were always in bliss, and I had no fear. I would speak my mind if the occasion demanded, without weighing ramifications."

Guruji would later display a similar propensity.

Following a short stay in London, Jnanananda accepted a teaching position at the University of Liverpool, where he researched the spectroscopy of beta radiation and was awarded his Ph.D. in 1943. The following year, however, he left England under a cloud of British allegations (cheerfully admitted by him, of course) that he was a sympathizer with the cause of Indian independence. Arriving in New York City on Christmas Day 1944, he proceeded by train to Ann Arbor to accept a position at the University of Michigan, where he engaged in "the nuclear research that was going on at the Cyclotron," the university's early particle accelerator. He also completed a textbook titled *High Vacuua* (which Guruji would assist him in updating a decade later). But when tapped to participate in the development of the United States' first atomic bomb in 1945, Jnanananda declined on moral grounds.

"I followed the events [when the United States] used it as a weapon against Japan during that year," he wrote. "I received a general letter from Professor Einstein soliciting support to express scientists' concerns against the use of atomic energy for destruction, and I sent him my letter of agreement." In a typical display of understatement, he added, "While this was going on, I also became known for my philosophical pursuits as a yogi and gave a lecture on this subject at the university."

When India won its independence in 1947, Jnanananda returned to his homeland, accepting a direct invitation from Prime Minister Jawaharlal Nehru to head the country's new National Physics Laboratory in New Delhi. There he would remain until 1954 when—during a family visit in Andhra Pradesh—he suffered a bad fall down a flight of stairs, sustaining a broken right shoulder and arm, and several breaks to his right leg. Transported to Visakhapatnam for a long period of recovery and rehabilitation at King George Hospital (overlooking the very "sand hill" where Guruji played football as a boy), he was invited by Andhra University to lead development of its new Department of Nuclear Physics. After some consideration, Jnanananda resigned his position in Delhi and accepted the university's offer.

Jnanananda threw himself into his new role with characteristic vigor—calling in favors from political VIPs in New Delhi, soliciting funds and equipment, attracting academic talent to fill the faculty rolls and inviting prominent guest lecturers from abroad (one from the Massachusetts Institute of Technology was so impressed by Jnanananda's program that he convinced MIT to make a significant in-kind gift to Andhra University). He actively encouraged student input as well, "giving them full freedom in developing the new department," which in turn generated "a tremendous enthusiasm to get things rolling." As would happen repeatedly throughout his life, Guruji had found himself in a fresh and exciting hothouse environment, governed by a free-thinking leader with a distinctively "do as you will" philosophy.

Guruji studied at Andhra University from 1952 until 1956. He spent his first three years in the Department of Physics at Mrs. A.V.N. College (the University's arts and sciences affiliate), where he earned his Bachelor of Science (B.Sc.) with honors. In his fourth and final year, he completed his Master of Science (M.Sc.) under Jnanananda in the new Department of Nuclear Physics.

"My master's research thesis was on all the possible ways that scalars could be made," Guruji said, referring to the digital counters used in calculator and computer displays. "My contribution was in the number of ways a binary number could be rendered into a decimal scale through hardware, and in theory through software. I demoed some of the simpler methods by actually making the hardware."

This was a highly unusual approach to a thesis project, noted Dr. Rao, his former classmate. Whereas most master's candidates expanded upon topics studied at the undergraduate level, Guruji took his work in an entirely different direction. "We'd had very little exposure to electronics in the B.Sc. program," Rao said. "Sastry undertook the task based solely upon his research in books and some guidance from Jnanananda. Most of us found this extraordinary. It was my first indication that this Sastry was always up to something new and original. I was quite impressed by his versatility and ability to pick up on new ideas and areas quickly. He had a way of going very deeply into any subject he took up."

Religion and spirituality were at this point, however, decidedly not among those subjects. "I did not find him to be 'spiritual' in any sense back then," Rao said. "He was quite scientific in all of his attitudes."

In awarding Guruji his M.Sc. degree, Jnanananda paid high praise. "Sastry, you have made your thesis like Panini's grammar—simple yet complete," he said.[33] "Nobody can add to it now. The *Maheswara Sutras* gave us semantics and the *sutras* Panini

33 The *Ashtadhyayi* ("Eight Chapters") is a treatise on Sanskrit grammar, written in the sixth or fifth century BCE by the Indian grammarian Panini. It set the linguistic standards for Classical Sanskrit.

34 The *Pratyahara Sutras*, also known as the *Maheshwara Sutras*, are attributed to Lord Shiva himself.

35 A compiler is a computer program that transforms source code written in one programming language into another.

derived from them gave us grammar for Sanskrit language in just about 20-odd *sutras*.[34] No other language has such a complete grammar in so few *sutras*. And now, using the approach in your thesis, people can write a compiler for computers in the Sanskrit language!"[35]

"Only he could have made such a comment," Guruji reflected. "When I replied that I had studied Sanskrit 'til the age of 11 years, he patted my back and said, 'Very good. This will stand you well in your spiritual and scientific journeys for a long time to come. I appreciate your work.'"

Just as Jnanananda had cut an unorthodox figure as a wandering *sadhu* in his youth, the mature Swami made for an atypical academic, donning the saffron robes of a renunciate even while teaching. "People used to fall at his feet and seek his blessings" as he walked across campus to class, recalled G. Siva Prasada Rao, a former student who later became a senior scientist with India's Central Groundwater Board.

It was Jnanananda who first demonstrated to Guruji that science could actually validate religious belief rather than undermine it. "He used to say that his life would have been incomplete without involvement in both of these seemingly opposing aspects of his work," recalled Professor V. Lakshminarayana, an early student who went on to teach at Andhra University himself. "He treated these aspects, the spiritual and the materialistic, as 'two arms with which to embrace the divine.'"

Jnanananda taught his students, "Yogic practices are intended to train a yogi to gain mastery over mind and body. A devoted scientific trainee should do the same thing. In both cases, *sadhana* is needed. In both cases, there should be an urge to search for an understanding of the inner secrets of nature."

Such ideas predictably fascinated the young Guruji, and perhaps Jnanananda recognized a kindred spirit in his student as well—he undoubtedly possessed both the conventional and yogic wherewithal to make such an assessment. He would also have noticed in Guruji a certain selflessness uncommon among accomplished young men in competitive settings.

"Learning, for my father, was never about making the grade or getting a good job," Guruji's daughter Anantalakshmi explained. "For him, it was purely the love of the subject. Guruji would make detailed notes for his B.Sc. and M.Sc. exams, but he never hesitated to share them freely with any classmate who asked. His mother—who understood just how much effort had gone into those notes—was inclined to be less generous. Yet he would persist, saying 'What will I do with the marks?'"

Perceiving these qualities in the young Guruji, Jnanananda would also have appreciated the unlikely synchronicity that brought them together in that particular time and place: the seasoned scientist and enlightened adept who had, quite literally by accident, found himself teaching school in Vizag, and the gentle, gifted student, still freshly wounded by the loss of both his father and his coveted admission to distant IIT. The opportunity for a meeting of the minds could hardly have been more perfect.

Fully aware of Guruji's precarious financial straits, Jnanananda would sometimes lend him textbooks from his personal library. One day while visiting the oceanside hut that Jnanananda called home, the younger man's eyes were drawn to a print on the wall depicting two interwoven serpents with a row of lotuses aligned between them—a mystical chart symbolically depicting the practice of Kundalini Yoga. Noticing his attention, Jnanananda grinned. "Ah, so it seems that you are interested in these things as well!" he said. "Good! Well, the time has not yet come for you to know about them, but don't worry. You will come to know when the time is right."

Perhaps given time, the relationship between Jnanananda and Guruji would have further deepened, but fate had other plans.

"I could have continued on to the Ph.D. program in Andhra University," Guruji said. "But I had lost my father, and I had to support my extended family and take care of my younger brother's costly engineering education. So when I got a good offer of employment in Bombay after earning my M.Sc., I had no choice. I took it."[36]

36 On November 23, 2014, Guruji received the Professor Swami Jnanananda Award, given to outstanding alumni of the nuclear physics department at Andhra University. At the ceremony, he joined other surviving members of the program's first two classes to share memories and mark Jnanananda's December 5th birthday.

🕉 Guruji at left as a senior scientist at the Tata Institute of Fundamental Research in Bombay, mid-1970s.
(Sri Vidya Trust)

4   The Cradle of Cutting-Edge Science

By the time he graduated from Andhra University with his M.Sc. in 1956, Guruji had managed to secure a highly competitive position with the renowned Tata Institute of Fundamental Research (TIFR) in Bombay. It was the beginning of a successful career that would span 25 years until he stepped down in 1981 to pursue his spiritual calling.

It is nearly impossible to overstate the prestige involved in such an offer being extended to a freshly minted graduate from an unproven university program. Guruji was among a select few—the cream of India's scientific talent—handpicked by an organization that has since expanded to employ, directly or indirectly, more than 50,000 scientists through various satellite organizations across India. "I grew up with the Institute, almost from its inception," Guruji said, with more than a trace of lingering affection in his voice.

"It was India's cradle of cutting-edge science," he said. "Out of it came the Atomic Energy Institute, which led in turn to the Electronics Corporation of India Ltd., and onward to the Indian Space Research Organisation, the Thumba Equatorial Rocket Launching Station, and so on. It was the country's scientific nucleus and in those days it was in the process of exploding."

Indeed, TIFR was and remains one of modern India's premier scientific success stories—as was its charismatic founder, Dr. Homi Jehangir Bhabha (1909–1966).

Remembered today mainly as a pioneering nuclear physicist, Bhabha was, during his heyday in the 1950s and '60s, even more widely admired as a handsome and charming *bon vivant* and gifted polymath who juggled prodigious expertise in physics, electronics, astronomy and microbiology while also dabbling successfully in politics, diplomacy and the visual arts. Perhaps unsurprisingly, he was a friend and admirer of Swami Jnanananda as well, and—while Guruji could not say for certain—it is hardly a stretch to imagine the good Swami applying the considerable leverage of his recommendation to bring a prize student from his upstart Andhra University program to Bhabha's attention.

In an article celebrating Bhabha's centenary in 2009, the Indian newsmagazine *Frontline* recounted TIFR's unlikely genesis:

It all began with a letter that Bhabha wrote to his friend, industrialist J.R.D. Tata, in August 1943. [At the time,] Bhabha was a reader[37] at the Indian Institute of Science (IISC), Bangalore. He had come to India from Cambridge on a brief holiday in 1939, but the [outbreak of the] Second World War forced him to [extend his stay]. Bhabha joined the IISC's physics department ... and established a Cosmic Ray Research Unit there. He also began wondering about the development of science in India and in his letter to Tata expressed his ideas about setting up an institute for fundamental research. ...

"The lack of proper conditions and intelligent financial support," Bhabha [wrote] to Tata, "hampers the development of science in India at the pace the talent in the country would warrant." In reply, Tata said: "If you and/or some of your colleagues in the scientific world put up concrete proposals backed by a sound case, I think there is a very good chance that the Sir Dorab Tata Trust will respond."

Encouraged, Bhabha wrote to Sir Dorab Saklatvala, chairman of the trust, in March 1944. "There is at the moment in India no big school of research in the fundamental problems of physics, both theoretical and experimental. There are, however, scattered all over India competent workers who are not doing as good work as they would do if brought together in one place under proper direction. ... [P]rovided proper appreciation and financial support are

37 A "reader," in the British and Indian systems, is an academic rank above senior lecturer that corresponds to professor in the United States.

58

forthcoming, ... I am convinced that within five years we could make Bombay the centre of fundamental physical research in India. ... The scheme that I am now submitting to you is but an embryo from which I hope to build up in the course of time a school of physics comparable with the best anywhere."

Tata backed Bhabha's proposal, and on the trust's approval, the institute was established on June 1, 1945, under a tripartite agreement between the trust, the Government of Bombay and the Government of India. Soon TIFR emerged as a major research centre on the world map, a standing that it continues to enjoy to this day.

In 1948 Bhabha left TIFR to direct independent India's new Atomic Energy Commission. However, the eminent scientist remained deeply involved with the institute and remained an active presence there when Guruji arrived from Vizag in 1956. The younger man was predictably starstruck.

"As a young, aspiring scientist, I was awed by his presence," Guruji said. "Dr. Bhabha was, in many ways, the father of science and mathematics in modern India. He was a charismatic leader, a powerful speaker and always impeccably dressed. He was also an artist, whose paintings were regularly exhibited in famous art galleries—and, I would add, he was the most coveted bachelor in Bombay. None could match him for wit or style."

Bhabha's management policies made a similarly arresting impression; they were decades ahead of their time. Once a week he would hold large seminars, inviting scientific innovators and political luminaries to address his scientists. Bhabha made every effort to enhance their sense of autonomy and creative latitude.

"He provided music and sofas to senior scientists so that they could sleep during office hours at their will," Guruji said. "He gave absolute freedom to every scientist and full control to every administrator." In other words, Guruji had yet again found himself in a resolutely "do as you will" environment. Yet this freedom initially struck him as perplexing—and possibly pointless.

"There we were, supposedly the best scientific brains in the whole of India—and we were essentially vacation artisans in a holiday camp," he joked. "There was nobody to report to, nobody to check on what we were doing. There was a huge library, and the beautiful section containing all the magazines was the most frequently populated. For a long time, we did absolutely nothing! We'd go to the magazine department, sit and read; then go to the canteen and sip tea and chit chat; then come back and read more magazines; then go to lunch; then come back to the labs and sleep; then have another cup of tea; then go back..."

But such empty pastimes soon grew boring, and then boredom gave way to experimentation. "The motivation came from inside, and once it came there was no stopping us," Guruji said. "We were at it from 6 o'clock in the morning until 12 o'clock midnight, and then coming back for more."

His direct supervisor Professor B.V. Thoson was, like Bhabha himself, a staunch advocate of complete intellectual freedom for his scientists. Without it, he believed, they would devolve into mere wage-earners doing their bosses' bidding. He wanted his scientists to break boundaries, not submit to them.

"That was his guiding precept," Guruji said of Dr. Thoson. "I believe he was a true guru in that sense. He wanted his disciples not to remain under his control, but to get beyond him, to transcend him. That, in turn, enabled a continuous growth process. By contrast, if your theory is that the guru must know more than the disciple—then, by extrapolation, when the disciple becomes a guru, *his* disciple has to know less than *him*, and so on down the line, until eventually you arrive at zero!"

ॐ

In addition to his research activities, Guruji became deeply involved in designing and building first integrated chips, and then eight-bit processors. At one point he devised a floating-point desk calculator using early transistor-transistor logic chips.[38]

"Not the large-scale ones, but the small-scale integrated circuits using NAND gates, NOR gates, flip-flops and so on,[39] and so on, trying to learn how to put them together into systems," he explained. "Then I designed a small microprocessor and wrote software to make it work as a desk calculator. All these were my attempts to understand how to put the building blocks of integrated circuits together and make systems that worked."

38 The term "floating point" refers to the fact that a number's decimal point can "float"; that is, it can be placed anywhere relative to the significant digits of the number. This function enables increased range and capacity by trading off redundant degrees of precision.

39 In digital electronics, a negated AND (NAND) gate is a logic gate that produces an output that is false only if all its inputs are true. Like NAND gates, negated OR (NOR) gates are so-called "universal gates" that can be combined to form any other kind of logic gate. A flip-flop or latch is a circuit that has two stable states and can be used to store state information. Flip-flops are a fundamental building block of digital electronics systems used in computers, communications and many other systems.

In the realm of nuclear physics, Guruji's doctoral thesis on the Mössbauer Effect led to a Ph.D. in solid state physics from Bombay University in 1964.[40] "My thesis concerned crystal field interactions with the hyperfine fields of the iron nucleus in crystalline $KFeF_3$ and the gamma rays emitted from the iron nucleus," he said. "I did some studies on how the hyperfine fields relax and change with the electrical fields of the crystal during the phase-transition transformation of the crystalline structure at liquid helium temperatures." Professor K.S. Singhvi served as his external examiner for the degree, which was awarded "more for the novel design of my cryostat than the content of the topic," Guruji said.[41]

He also dabbled in more down-to-earth subjects—for example, earning a master's degree in marketing from Kishinchand Chellaram College of Arts, Commerce and Science (better known as K.C. College), an affiliate of Bombay University, in 1977, where he topped his class and even earned a gold medal. "The classes took place in the evening and most of his fellow students were less than half his age," daughter Anantalakshmi recalled. "But he turned out to be an excellent student—diligent, attentive, creative; a favorite among teachers and fellow students alike."

That goodwill proved to be a blessing one day when Guruji failed to show up for a major exam. While college administrators and classmates frantically tried to reach him at his office, he was at home fast asleep, resting up for the exam he mistakenly thought was still a few hours away. When Guruji finally arrived and realized his error, the professor made a special exception, allowing him to write the exam in a faculty office.

The next year, by coincidence, Guruji's brother Prasad Rao took the same course at the same college. "Due to his hectic work schedule, he missed a number of lectures and fell behind," Anantalakshmi said. "So the professor told him, 'Last year, we had another older gentleman who was an excellent student. I am sure he won't mind sharing his notes with you.' And he referred him to—you guessed it—his own brother, Guruji. A small world, indeed!"

ॐ
ह्री

Despite the many rewards and fascinations of Guruji's work at TIFR, the lumbering socialist economic policies that hamstrung India economically in the 1960s and '70s sometimes made his work onerous and unnecessarily difficult.

40 The Mössbauer Effect—also known as recoilless nuclear resonance fluorescence—is a process in which a nucleus emits or absorbs gamma rays without loss of energy to a nuclear recoil.

41 A cryostat is a device used to maintain super-low cryogenic temperatures in the samples or devices mounted within it.

"India was going through a very difficult foreign-exchange crisis in those days," he recalled. "For a grant of $100, we had to wait six months. And we had to make everything with our own hands—do the drilling, do the lathe work, sharpen the tools, everything. We had to make our own glass dewars with silver plating on the glass for low-temperature research.[42] This made it very tough for us. We really regretted being unable to compete in international markets—but they could do in one month what it took us two years to do."

Perhaps due in part to such frustrations, Guruji's long tenure at TIFR was marked by a distinct restlessness. "Roughly every five years I would change my field," he said. "I would get fed up with whatever I was doing in about that time. Just as I was about to reap the benefits of a certain specialty, I would move out of it: that was the pattern. I could never just be comfortable with any one particular level of understanding."

At some level he already sensed that he had a higher calling in life. But as the 1950s and '60s unfurled, professional and familial obligations exerted a gravity he simply couldn't ignore.

42 Dewars are scientific containers described by Guruji as being "used for transporting very cold liquids from point A to point B across our sprawling lab."

5   An Absentminded Professor?

In 1957, a year after beginning work at TIFR, Guruji traveled home to consummate a long-anticipated milestone in his personal life. Several years earlier, he had become engaged to a beautiful young woman—a distant cousin, in fact—whom he had known and admired for years.[43]

"My grandfather had two sisters," he recalled. "The younger one was Visalakshi, who had a granddaughter called Annapurna." Born at the peak of a lunar eclipse on March 13, 1941, Annapurna Gunturu was predicted by astrologers to have an auspicious future ahead. The fourth among six children (her siblings were an older brother, two elder sisters and two younger sisters), she grew up in a large, extended-family home in Yelamanchili, about 100 miles (175 kilometers) southwest of Vizag; it was a busy trading hub for the sugar cane and rice crops that grew profusely in the surrounding countryside. A cultured and literate family, the Gunturus maintained a household, daughter Radha noted, where "knowledge was revered and nurtured."

Though amiable by nature, with a cheerful and happy-go-lucky personality, young Annapurna had a somewhat delicate disposition—she suffered from asthma and tended to prefer quieter pastimes. A habitual reader and consistently good student, she studied through the 10th standard but never sat for her year-end exam. Annapurna's mother Yashoda kept house; her father, Lakshmana Somayajulu, was a prominent

43   Though comparatively rare today, in the 1950s it was still common for Hindu cousins to marry in the South Indian states of Andhra Pradesh, Karnataka, Kerala and Tamil Nadu.

lawyer with a brisk practice in town. Those who knew her then remember the young Annapurna as an inveterate "Daddy's girl," indulged by and inseparable from her beloved father.

Through her paternal grandparents, Annapurna imbibed a broad spiritual education. Grandfather Gunturu Subbarao was, like her father, a lawyer—but also president of the Theosophical Society of the Madras Presidency,[44] and he often hosted meetings and visiting dignitaries on Society business. His wife Visalakshi was also spiritually inclined and very much involved in theosophy, holding regular public readings and discussions on Hindu scripture and tales from the Epics.

Under her grandmother's tutelage, Annapurna learned to recite these Sanskrit passages beautifully, often memorizing long passages by heart. In his twilight years, old Subbarao—his eyesight failing due to cataracts—would ask her to sit and read to him from Theosophical Society journals. As she did so, he would explain the terminology and arguments to enhance her understanding.

As a distant relative, Guruji had encountered Gunturu Subbarao on several occasions over the years, once engaging in a two-hour discussion on theosophy—"mostly about the 'seven planes of existence' theory, Madam Blavatsky's derogatory views on science, the nature of soul and its travails and so on," Guruji said. As he recalled it, "the discussion was detailed. He appreciated my inquisitiveness and answered my vexing questions patiently. But our conversation did not really affect me spiritually, because even then I could never agree with derisive statements about science."

Annapurna and Guruji had also crossed paths at weddings and other family events, and as they grew older, he began taking more serious note of this pretty out-of-town visitor—nor did Annapurna fail to notice the handsome young Bombay scientist.

"Since Guruji and I are cousins, we would sometimes go to the beach with Prasad Rao and the others," she recalled. "One time, after we had all dried ourselves off and gone back to the house, Guruji's father gave me either the *Ranganatha Ramayanam*[45] or the *Rukmini Kalyanam*,[46] and asked me to read some stanzas from it. I knew many of them by heart because my grandmother had taught them to me. Guruji's father was very impressed by the way I recited, and so was Guruji." As Guruji remembers the incident, Annapurna's recitation was definitely from the *Rukmini Kalyanam*. "I liked her

44 The Theosophical Society was formed in the United States in 1875 by Madame Helena Petrovna Blavatsky and Henry Steel Olcott, aiming "'to vindicate the importance of old Asiatic literature, and to investigate the hidden mysteries of Nature and the physical and spiritual powers latent in man especially.' Blavatsky and Olcott moved to India in 1879, where they attracted more members than they had in the West."

45 The *Ranganatha Ramayanam* is a Telugu-language version of the epic *Ramayana*.

46 The *Rukmini Kalyanam* is a story from the *Bhagavata Purana* in which Rukmini is a princess, and Lord Krishna is a cowherd. Rukmini falls in love with Krishna, and her brother tries unsuccessfully to prevent their marriage.

voice and I liked her face," he said. "I told my parents I didn't want to look at any other marriage proposals when I grew up. I told them I liked this girl."

More than just "liked," in fact. "I fell in love with her!" Guruji admitted. "Love at that age is not normal, so it must have been predetermined in one way or the other. I think it was arranged by the Goddess that I should marry her." Radha added that "Guruji's father was always very affectionate towards my mother, and this may have subconsciously affected Guruji's feelings about her as well."

The attraction was mutual, though Annapurna's version of events reflected the strict Indian social conventions of an earlier time. "Well they did also ask me at home what my opinion about the match was, but in those days the bride had no separate aspirations [from her family's] about how the groom should be," she said. "So I happily gave my consent."

Guruji's manner of proposing was also highly unusual in a time and place when marital alliances were negotiated between families with great formality. "He went personally to Annapurna's home and directly asked her parents for her hand in marriage," his sister-in-law Sundari Amma noted. "This simple approach—no highhandedness on the part of the groom—was very much appreciated by them, too."

The engagement was agreed upon in 1954; the marriage was celebrated three years later upon Guruji's return from his first year at TIFR. The ceremony took place on August 2, 1957, in Yelamanchili. Guruji was 22, Annapurna was 16. "The bride was golden and doll-like, the groom a proficient scientist, the wedding a feast for the eyes," Sundari Amma would recall years later. "It was a happy union, and a means through which much worldly good would be achieved."

At the time, however, the new couple's ambitions were considerably more modest than that. Leaving the familiar environs of Andhra Pradesh for a new life in Bombay (even then a vast metropolis of four million, though still a mere fraction of the megalopolis it has since become) was a daunting challenge for a small-town girl.

"It was a big move for my mother," daughter Rama said. "By then, Guruji was already working at TIFR and familiar with Bombay. Amma, on the other hand, still knew only Telugu—she hadn't yet learned Hindi or English, so she found it difficult at first. But she soon learned both languages by herself and with the help of friendly neighbors."

Annapurna honed her English skills by studying issues of *Reader's Digest*, and eventually developed a taste for English novels, including a particular weakness for the works of British novelist Nevil Shute. "When we were a little older, she would play Scrabble with us, and she surprised us on many occasions with the size of her vocabulary, though we'd sometimes help her out with the spellings," Radha noted, adding, "today, of course, she converses and holds her own with people of all different nationalities."

Guruji too was "always reading something different" in those days, former classmate and TIFR colleague Dr. E.V.R. Rao recalled. "Whatever subject interested him, he would get totally involved in it. Many years later, but when he was still at TIFR, I first learned that he was getting into Tantric books. No one in our circle of friends took that kind of stuff seriously! But typical of Sastry, he got very deeply involved in the subject—possibly that was an early indicator of his new avatar to come!"

Guruji and Annapurna also shared an enthusiastic taste for Carnatic (South Indian classical) music. "My father was always keen to promote classical music, dance and other cultural activities," Radha recalled. "Both Amma and Guruji used to listen to radio programs of vocal and instrumental music. Once, when he was already in his 40s, a friend gave Guruji a violin and he actually taught himself some basics!"

Dr. Rao, too, vividly remembered the music that filled the family's home.

"We all used to meet there on holidays and sing songs together," he said. "We would listen to the recordings of M. Balamuralikrishna[47] and Srirangam Gopalaratnam.[48] Their renderings of the *Yenki Patalu* songs[49] held a great appeal for us and were a source of much common interest and inspiration. Occasionally other friends would join in as well. Sastry and his family were always good hosts."

In the early days of their union, however, Guruji and Annapurna were not extravagant hosts. Their Bombay lodgings were cramped, Spartan and decidedly inelegant. "We initially stayed in small apartments with shared facilities," Amma said. "It was unfamiliar, but we had no real complaints. That's just the way it was. Later we moved

47 M. Balamuralikrishna (1930-2016) is a renowned Indian Carnatic vocalist, multi-instrumentalist, composer and actor.

48 Srirangam Gopalaratnam (1939-1993) was a noted female Telugu classical vocalist.

49 The *Yenki Patalu* songs are Telugu folk songs written by the renowned poet Naduri Subba Rao (1895-1957).

to Ghatkopar, a suburban neighborhood of eastern Mumbai, where we had a bigger place." Eventually, the family would end up at the comparatively posh TIFR Quarters, located in the well-heeled Bombay suburb of Colaba, close to Guruji's office. But that all lay in the future.

Despite the prestige of his position, Guruji's early salary was by his own description "very meager." Yet he was already displaying instincts markedly different from those of most young men starting a new family and professional life. In his spare time, for example, he volunteered as a social activist, building schools for the poor. At one fundraising event organized by the Andhra Mahasabha,[50] young Guruji became angry when not one of the wealthy attendees donated even a token sum to the cause.

"Nobody opened their mouth," he said. So Guruji opened his—and, completely on impulse, volunteered three months of his salary to the school-building project. "It was not that much money in absolute terms, nothing to write home about," he said. "But it meant a lot to me. It was three months of my annual salary, and I gave it away. What it meant in practical terms is that my wife and I would go two days a week without food. That's what it meant to us." And that is what they did until the donation was complete.

For Guruji, however, the experience was a revelation. "I felt a certain sadness about it, yes, but I was also extremely happy. It was a strange combination—a feeling of pride, I suppose, in having done something that nobody else had done. So there was pain, but there was also pleasure. There is something spiritual in that, I think. When it hurts so much to give, and yet still you choose to give—I think therein lies something of the essence of spirituality."

In a few years, children came. The couple had three daughters—"my three goddesses," as Guruji liked to call them: Anantalakshmi, born in 1961; Radha, in 1963; and Rama, in 1968. Between the births of Radha and Rama, in 1966, there was also heartbreak when Guruji and Amma lost their only son to medical complications shortly after his birth. Born in late August, the child died on September 7, coinciding that year with Janmashtami, the traditional birthday of Lord Krishna.

"Our little boy lived for all of 15 days and then left us," Guruji said. "My wife never even saw him. She had infectious hepatitis; he was born with jaundice—so the doctors

50 The Andhra Mahasabha was a progressive regional political organization that began as a subsidiary of the Indian National Congress and later allied with the Communist Party of India.

immediately separated them and took him to a different hospital." The young father was confused and dismayed by the staff's seeming indifference to the urgency of the crisis as the baby's condition deteriorated and death soon followed. "I had to take him in a small body bag and have him cremated," Guruji said. "I was very upset. I somehow felt that he was still alive. I kept asking myself afterward, 'Did I kill him?'"

Annapurna dealt with the loss in her own way. She and her sister-in-law Sundari Amma had both been pregnant together that year, and Sundari gave birth to a healthy son in December. "It is perhaps a testament to Amma's character that she did not become bitter after her own experience, but instead showered her love on the newest baby in the family," Radha said. "Then later in life, she had the opportunity to became intimately involved in raising and caring for [youngest daughter] Rama's two sons."

Guruji stoically put the entire episode down to karma. "There was a tie, a bond between my son and I, which had to be fulfilled," he explained. "That's how he came into my life."[51] Questioned about the nature of the bond, he referred back to the long conversation he'd had as a young man with Annapurna's grandfather, Gunturu Subbarao. "At the end of our discussion about theosophy that night he said, 'If I have to take a birth again, it should be to you.' So I think that was the debt to be repaid. I think Subbarao Garu fulfilled his *runanubabdha* and got liberated."

But the loss of Guruji's son also carried consequences in the Hindu social schema. "Well, it meant that my wife and I had three living daughters and no son," Guruji explained. "So my *gotra*[52] ends with me. Maybe that is also predestined, because no one will need to do *shraaddha* when I pass away."[53]

In any event, Guruji said, he was perfectly content with his family just as it was. "My daughters all married," he said. "Each of them had two children. They're happy with their families, and I'm happy with my grandchildren."[54]

ॐ
ह्रीं

For the first two decades of their marriage, Guruji's mother Lakshmi Narasayamma also lived with the family—an arrangement that suited Amma just fine. "She was a very active lady," she said. "She would do all the housework herself, which left me with a lot of free time!"

51 Guruji alternately used the term vadhbhanda, literally, "a bond of death," and runanubhanda, "a debt to be repaid," in describing his relationship with the infant boy.

52 Male lineage.

53 *Shraddha* is a Hindu ritual performed by a male child for his ancestors, in particular his deceased parents.

54 Anantalakshmi married Venkat Ram Pisipati; their children are daughter Pallavi and son Rishi Prasad. Radha married Balkumar Marthi; their children are daughter Matangi and son Kaushal. Rama married Prabhakar Kandarpa; they have two sons, Sthita Prajna and Viswajit. Radha noted, "After both my elder sister Ananta and I had daughters, many people at Devipuram commented that perhaps Guruji—due to his single-minded devotion to the Goddess—would leave only female descendants. As if to prove otherwise, his next four grandkids were all male!"

Once in the winter of 1969, Amma said, Guruji took his mother along to attend a scientific conference near Rishikesh in northern India. "She was so happy, because it meant she would get to visit some of the area's famous pilgrimage places along with her son," Amma recalled with a smile. "She got all geared up with warm clothing for the trip." Guruji also invited her to social events at the conference, such as formal dinners. "She would sit at the long table along with all the scientists!" Amma laughed. He also arranged for her to visit Lakshman Jhula, a famed suspension bridge spanning the roaring Ganges and offering spectacular vistas of the Himalayan foothills. The bathing *ghat* there was equipped then with iron rings, railings and chains for pilgrims to grasp for safety as they immersed into the holy river's powerful current.

"The other scientists were hesitant to go in because it was still too cold that time of year, and the water was flowing very forcefully," Amma said. Having come that far, however, Guruji's mother would not be deterred, and took the initiative to wade in first (as she single-mindedly immersed herself in the water, several scientists felt compelled to follow suit). But once in the water, the old woman discovered that the emotional pull of the Ganges could be as strong as its physical pull. Amma said, "She later told me that as she was taking the dip, holding onto these huge chains for protection, a thought crossed her mind: 'Maybe I will just let go now and float away with the blessed Ganges.' But then another immediately followed: 'No, it's an unfamiliar place and it would put my son through so much trouble'—and she desisted."

Lakshmi Narasayamma's active lifestyle would slow decisively a few years later when she suffered a paralytic stroke, crippling one side of her body. But she didn't let the disability stop her. "Through sheer will power, she did whatever she could to come out of it," Amma recalled. "She slowly taught herself to walk again, holding the walls for support. She would sift wheat flour with one hand, or sit and read her books, slowly turning the pages with one hand. She always found ways to keep herself busy."

Guruji's mother would remain an energetic, optimistic and integral part of the household until her passing in June 1977.[55]

Meanwhile, Guruji and Amma grew ever closer as a unit—both in worldly matters and, as time went on, in their spiritual pursuits. "They complement each other in

55 Sister-in-law Sundari Amma recalled Guruji sitting at his mother's bedside as she passed. Despite his lingering spiritual skepticism at the time, he offered her a sip of holy *tulasi* water, placed a calendar print of Shiva and Parvati where she could easily see it, and gently whispered, "Amma, look at the image. Focus your gaze on the divine."

many ways, like yin and yang," daughter Anantalakshmi observed. "For example, when we were kids growing up in Bombay in the 1960s, the public 'rationed distribution' system allowed each family mostly wheat, and only a tiny quantity of rice. So as a result, many people would buy their rice on the open [black] market and urge our parents to do the same."

Guruji, however, refused, even though it meant a decisive shift away from the family's familiar South Indian diet (in which rice, not wheat, dominated). "For my father, it was all about the principle involved," Anantalakshmi said. "So Mother supported him by making more *chapatis*, and preparing cracked wheat like rice so we could have it with *dal* and *sambar*, and so on."[56]

But while the pair generally worked in common cause, their personality differences were always clearly discernable. "My father typically favored a 'do-the-new' approach, whereas my mother tended to stick with her routines until whatever goals she had set for herself were completed—and only then would she take on new tasks," Anantalakshmi said.

Sometimes the interplay between husband and wife bordered on the comical. Guruji, for example, possessed no natural culinary talent but loved experimenting in the kitchen, trying to discover new flavors by "combining the most bizarre ingredients"—while often forgetting the most common ones, such as salt. "Dad would constantly pester us to sample his latest creations," Radha laughed. "Needless to say, we were less than enthusiastic to do so!"

Fortunately for the family, Annapurna was a natural in the kitchen. "Mother's cooking is perfect, ambrosial, despite her measurements being guesstimates," Anantalakshmi said. "On a few occasions, I've seen Daddy trying to bring a particularly good dish into some sort of standardization by asking her for the exact recipe with detailed quantities. But somehow that mystery always remained unresolved, because it could never get beyond my father's insistence on clear weights and measures, and my mother's inspired instincts!"

This same insistence on perfection would often exasperate Guruji's three daughters when they approached their father for help with homework, hoping to avail themselves

56 *Dal* refers to lentils, peas and other dried beans. *Sambar* is a lentil-based vegetable stew simmered in a tamarind broth. A popular staple of everyday South Indian cuisine, *sambar* is usually served with steamed rice and *dosas* (rice and lentil-based crepes).

of his formidable expertise in science and mathematics. "We'd go to Daddy, hoping to just get an answer quickly," Anantalakshmi said. "But instead we'd end up with a long discourse on the underlying principles—and no answer at all! He would always insist that we think it out for ourselves."

At the same time, Rama noted, the details of everyday life could sometimes prove a challenge for Guruji. "He would often forget what grade we were studying in, or forget to eat his lunch," she said.

Then there was the time he accidentally got off the elevator at TIFR Quarters on the wrong floor, walked to the door corresponding to his own and rang the doorbell. "As it turned out, it was the home of some family friends," Anantalakshmi said. "The lady of the house opened the door, and Guruji went in without looking up, sat down, picked up the newspapers and started reading. She brought him some coffee, which he accepted without question. Coffee and newspaper complete, his attention finally turned to his surroundings—and his first thought was, 'When did my wife change all the furnishings?'

"It was only then—a full 10 or 15 minutes after he entered that flat—that it dawned on him that this wasn't his home. He thanked the lady, made his way home and sheepishly recounted the tale to my mother," Anantalakshmi concluded. "Now one may think, 'Oh, that's just absentmindedness.' But how many of us can become so immersed in what we're doing that our surroundings don't even register? Is that absentmindedness or is it laser-like focus? Take your pick. But I would say that laser-like focus on the job at hand, whatever that may be, was and remained very intrinsic to Guruji."

Even as a householder, Guruji's behavior was perhaps atypical for a successful urban professional. "He had no apparent taste or desire for luxuries; he always seemed happy and satisfied with whatever he had," sister-in-law Sundari Amma recalled. "I never saw him behave with jealousy, anger or rudeness toward anyone. If someone spoke hurtfully to him, he simply remained silent or walked away."

As the child of such an individual, Anantalakshmi noted, one soon became accustomed to behavior that many people would consider unusual. "With our parents, and especially with Guruji—what he thinks, what he says, and what he does were aligned to a very great degree," Anantalakshmi explained. "Growing up in that sort of atmosphere, we did imbibe that idea at some level, and imagined it would be true of other people as well."

But while a Guruji upbringing sometimes made things difficult out in "the real world," it also provided a certain healthy perspective. Anantalakshmi said, "Hard as it was at first for us to digest that people don't always say what they think or do as they say, time also brought the wisdom that all the shades of the rainbow are required to make this a beautiful universe."

6 On Turning-Point Hill

Though he was based in Bombay, Guruji's work took him all over India, meeting with scientists, industrialists and intellectuals across the country. One seemingly typical trip in 1977 found him in Hyderabad, visiting the Electronics Corporation of India for discussions on mini-computer programs. Back in his hotel room near Nampally Station,[57] however, Guruji felt inexplicably restless. Having tossed and turned through several hours of fitful sleep, Guruji finally gave up and decided to step outside for some fresh air.

"I went out at about 4 a.m. and started walking aimlessly," he recalled. "It was quite cool. I eventually arrived at a stairway on a hill made by the Birlas, called Naubath Pahad.[58] There was a temple of Balaji glowing brightly on top;[59] on the way up there was a Hanuman Temple. My early childhood flashed by like a film reel in my mind's eye."

Guruji was reminded of the old Hanuman Temple opposite the Prabhat Talkies Theater in Vizag, where he used to go with his friends for *prasadam* as a child. He had never really frequented temples since those days, and now, in his mid-40s, he maintained no particular religious beliefs or practices.

"I was not exactly an atheist," he said. "Rather, I was neutral—I considered religion as 'not my domain.' I had developed, let us say, a highly questioning attitude toward it, almost bordering on the irreligious, to the point where I was unable to identify myself

57 Nampally Station is local parlance for Hyderabad Deccan Station.

58 Overlooking the city of Hyderabad, Naubath Pahad (one possible translation of which is, interestingly, "Turning-Point Hill") is home to the Birla Mandir, a 13-acre temple complex dedicated to Lord Venkateswara, a form of Vishnu. It is one of several modern temples financed by the Birla Foundation in cities across India, all known as Birla Mandirs.

59 Balaji is a popular appellation of Lord Venkateswara and, more importantly from Guruji's viewpoint, a form of the Goddess.

with any rituals or activities like that. I used to think, 'What is the need to believe in something that is a fact? You only need to *believe* in something if it is *not* a fact.' I also used to think, 'Why should I believe something that I don't experience? God is not verifiable! I don't see God, do I? So why should I believe in God?' Such was my attitude. Pure arrogance of science."

Amma recalled that when their daughter Radha was born in 1963, "she was a blue baby and Guruji's mother was afraid. She prayed to Lord Venkateswara, saying, 'If you make her well, I will come to Tirupati!'[60] Guruji got annoyed and said, 'Why do you always try to bargain with God?'[61] Even when his mother finally completed her promised visit to Tirupati almost 12 years later, Guruji was still not interested in entering the temple. But then, in 1977, Balaji himself called him inside..."

Indeed, Guruji suddenly felt almost as if he were being pushed from behind as he mounted the steps toward the brightly lit temple above. Halfway up, at the Hanuman Temple, "I took the vermillion, put it on my forehead and continued further up," he said. "It was 5:30 or 6 a.m. by that time; early morning, misty. Music was playing. There were, I think, four or five people ahead of me waiting for *darshan*.[62] An old man prostrated before Balaji—who is a female goddess in a male form; female on the inside, male on the outside[63]—and for some reason I was prompted to prostrate also. The old man's gesture acted as a trigger for me to do the same. It was quite unusual for me. I was not the type to prostrate before an icon, a symbol. I did it without consciously knowing what I was doing."

As he did, however, a sensation gripped him like nothing he had ever experienced before.

"I felt a thrill passing through me that lasted about 10 or 15 minutes, I think," he said. "I really lost all sense of time. You know how sometimes you get an experience of horripilation, where every hair stands on end? This thrill ran even deeper than that; it was something entirely new. Every atom in my body was thrilling. I was transported to a different plane of existence—an ecstatic state."

As he had in his first childhood vision, Guruji experienced the entire universe spinning rapidly around him in a broad vortex, steadily drawn into him at its center. Before he could even begin to process what was happening, Balaji appeared before him,

60 Guruji's mother was referencing the Venkateswara Temple in Tirumala, Tamil Nadu, primary seat of Lord Venkateswara.

61 Daughter Radha noted that Guruji apparently offended Lord Balaji by his comment: "For the rest of his life, if he sent any money to be placed in the *hundi* [donation fund] at Tirupati, he would promptly receive that exact amount back through someone else, as if the Lord were proving that he did not want Guruji's money!" she said.

62 Ritual viewing of a deity.

63 Here Guruji is expressing a distinctly Shakta view of Balaji, rather than the traditional Vaishnava understanding of the deity. Elsewhere Guruji affirmed, "It is well known by Shaktas that the inner form of Venkateswara is female."

saying in a soft but clear voice, "I am Lord Venkateswara; I am Bala, Balaji and Bala Tripurasundari."[64] Balaji then intoned:

purnamadah purnamidam
purnat purnamudachyate
purnasya purnamadaya
purnameva vashishyate

From the whole arises the whole,
From the complete arises the complete.
Deducting the whole from the whole,
The whole alone remains.[65]

When the vision ended, Guruji slowly stood and looked around himself, somewhat disoriented and only gradually realizing that less than half an hour had elapsed since he entered the sanctum. Nonetheless, he felt profoundly changed. Something revelatory had happened, some sort of epiphany—but he was at a loss to say exactly what. "If I told someone else about it, they might have shrugged it off, like, 'Come on, you must be kidding,'" he said. "But the experience was undeniable to me. I knew Balaji had come to me, and I considered it as *diksha*, a formal initiation. At that moment, it is fair to say, Bala became my first spiritual guru."

Lost in the wonder of the moment, Guruji walked out of the temple and slowly made his way back down the stairs to the street. "I made a mental note to myself," he said. "Yes, maybe I am missing something by not worrying about my religion and ignoring the spiritual aspects of life. I must look into it."

ॐ
ह्रीं

With the benefit of hindsight, many of Guruji's disciples today point to his experience at Balaji Temple as the pivotal moment that transformed him from scientist to spiritual teacher. Guruji did not entirely disagree. "Then and there," he would later affirm, "I decided that whatever life was left in me I should utilize for the welfare of everyone, and definitely not for destruction."

64 The final appellation, Bala Tripurasundari, usually refers in the Sri Vidya tradition to the child form of the goddess Lalita.

65 Balaji's statement comes from the *Brihadaranyaka Upanishad*, 5.1. The English translation is by Guruji. Despite its deep antiquity, the verse is in many ways a perfect opening of communication between God and a physicist. It basically lays out what is known to modern physics as the law of conservation of energy, stating that energy (or its equivalent in mass) can neither be created nor destroyed–that the sum of mass and energy in any system remains constant. Nothing more can be added, nor can anything be subtracted out. In Hindu spirituality, this "completeness" is the very essence of God and Ultimate Reality.

But at the time, there were few outward signs that any change had happened at all. "Strangely, there was nothing much," Amma said. When Guruji told her about the incident, "all I could think was, 'Oh, he did a full prostration to Balaji? That's odd. He would usually never do that.'"

Perhaps it is more accurate to say that the Balaji Temple experience marked the beginning of an internal shift that would gradually transform the way in which Guruji related to the world. "In some sense, it added fuel to the fire of an inward-looking process, which began around that time," he said. "So it did indeed mark a turning point in my life, from a search for truth in the external direction to a search for truth in an inward direction. Perhaps moments of enlightenment only really come when there is a deep conflict."

In the years that followed, Guruji would continue to experience frequent visions of Lord Balaji, albeit usually in the female form of the child goddess Bala Tripurasundari. But while these encounters would open his mind to vast depths of spiritual experience, Guruji said, his original vision at Hyderabad was the primary goad, intensifying his sense of dissatisfaction with his life and priorities as they then stood.

"At the Balaji Temple," he said, "I was given an experience—a jolt that made me question my attitudes. Why had I devoted so much time, passion and energy to my profession, and so little to my spiritual life? I thought, 'Why don't I investigate what is happening in my mind?'"

In a way, he reasoned, meditation was just another form of structured scientific observation, but with one major difference.

"Unlike in scientific investigation, the object wasn't something 'out there'; it was *me* I was observing," Guruji explained. "The *observer* is me—but the *observed* is also me. And the fact that I am observing would, in turn, make the observed observe me back. In other words, I have a say in what I am observing. The object and subject being the same, I can change the object even as the object is changing me."

For Guruji, the revelation was ultimately life-altering.

"It was quite a new feeling," he said. "It's not at all the way we generally interact with the outside world. It was more like a mirroring participation between the seer and the seen. It felt like, 'I am a part of the world, and the world a part of me. But how can the part also be the whole?' That bit was still bothering me. So I decided to explore my inner world."

In the days and weeks that followed, Guruji commenced a regular practice of meditation, usually sitting late at night after the family had gone to sleep, and continuing until long after midnight. As an initial goal he tried to reaccess the transcendent sound he remembered from childhood, and was both surprised and pleased when it returned almost at once—if anything, stronger than ever.

"I would sit up on my bed at night, meditating at 2 o'clock in the morning while my wife was sleeping next to me," he said. "I'd just listen to that humming sound coming from within me, which started out like the sound of a radio before the station comes on air, around 300 hertz, and then gradually went up into sharper frequencies, increasing in pitch as I observed it. I remembered hearing those sounds as a young boy, but now I realized that it wasn't just a single frequency—it was a spectrum of audible frequencies, passing over into visible experiences."

For the first two days of these meditations, "nothing much happened; a little calm and peace descended upon me." On the third night, however, he lost consciousness— then awoke to a sensation of terrifying disruption. "As I was waking from unconsciousness, there was suddenly a huge blast," Guruji recalled. "I felt as if a bomb had been placed in my heart, and that—with a tremendous noise and unbearably bright light—I had exploded into bits and pieces, every particle of my body thrown off to the ends of the galaxies."

The terrifying vision was, however, accompanied by what seemed almost certainly to be the message he had been seeking. "At that very moment I saw a sort of screen before me, upon which about 10 Sanskrit stanzas were written. But before I could read even half of the first line—I remembered only that it was '*Isavasyam idam sarvam*'[66]— it vanished, and I blanked out. When I woke up, I was really scared. I thought, 'How could such a dangerous explosion take place in meditation? What would happen to my wife and daughters if I died? Who would look after them?' Remember, I had lost my father at an early age, so I was thinking in those terms. And I decided then and there to stop all such dangerous activities."

66 A fragment meaning, roughly, "God is everywhere." The message is further explained in the next chapter.

The sheer intensity of his visions also made Guruji decide not to share them with his wife in any great detail; he did not want to worry her unnecessarily. As a result, Amma said, she initially underestimated the transformation her husband was undergoing—because outwardly, once again, he was simply not showing any significant changes at all.

"Yes, sometimes he would awake from his meditations and say he was afraid," she noted. "But I would usually tell him, 'Just drink a little water and try to go back to sleep.'"

7   A Dormant Volcano Awakens

Guruji's resolution to stop meditating didn't last long.

Just a few days after his alarming vision, he happened to visit the home of a TIFR colleague and fellow Andhra native, C. Radha Krishna Murthy, who maintained an extensive library of religious books, to which he had given Guruji permission to consult and borrow at will. Scanning the shelves that day, Guruji's eyes were drawn to an annotated edition of the *Isa Upanishad*.[67] When he opened the volume, he was astonished to discover that its opening lines completed the phrase he had seen in his recent vision: *"Isavasyam idam sarvam yat kimca jagatyam jagat"*—"All of the cosmos is inhabited, enveloped and protected by God."

Guruji was dumbfounded.

"My rational mind was somewhat shattered," he said. "How could I have already read a book that I had never seen before in my life? Was it something in my genes, that my mind was able to access that information? Step by step, my understanding that one must approach the truth only through rational processes was being shattered. I was beginning to realize that there were irrational, emotional, illogical, holistic ways of knowing the truth."

Almost immediately, he set aside his trepidations and commenced his sound meditations again. "They say that curiosity killed the cat, but being a scientist you are

67 The *Isa Upanishad* (c. 500–100 BCE) is one of the shortest *Upanishads*, consisting of 17 or 18 verses (depending on the revision) and constituting the final chapter of the *Shukla Yajurveda*.

curious—and curiosity overcame my fear," he explained. "I argued to myself: 'Well yes, I experienced an explosion of some sort, but I didn't die, did I? So why should I be afraid? Let me just try again and see what happens.'"

Once again, for the first two days nothing much happened. But on the third day he realized that something very unusual was taking place within him. It started with a "very peculiar, very pleasant tickling sensation at the base of my spine near the coccyx bone, and then something started moving upward. It felt a little warm but still very pleasant, almost sexual, and I heard the familiar 300 hertz sound in my heart. When it came up to my navel center I started seeing lights of various colors, and when it came to my heart center I was feeling very open, very loving and kind and compassionate."[68]

But as the sensation rose still further, it became more distressing. "As it reached my neck, the sound began to rise in volume and it suddenly became a roar—like a tornado wind or a huge torrent," he said. "It felt as if I was sitting on top of a volcano with the lava pushing out of it, and I too was being pushed out of 'me' with great force, a tremendous amount of force. I was being carried away by it to God knows where. And again I was scared—scared stiff. I didn't have any clue as to what was happening—what this tremendous current was or how to cope with the situation."

Overwhelmed by the powerful sensations flooding his body, Guruji grasped at the first prayer that came into his mind—a child's hymn to the goddess Saraswati, remembered from his youth:

saraswati namas tubhyam varade kama rupini,
vidyarambham karishyami, siddhir bhavatu me sada,
padma patra visalakshi, padma kesara varnini,
nityam padmalaya devi, sa mam patu saraswati

Saraswati, I bow to you. You give boons that fulfill my desires.
I am beginning my studies. May I attain the knowledge that I desire.
With eyes wide as lotus leaves, and colored like the pistils of lotuses,
You sit upon a lotus, too. Please protect me.[69]

68 Guruji is describing a spontaneous Kundalini Yoga meditation. The coccyx bone marks the approximate location of the *Muladhara Chakra*; the "pleasant, sexual" sensation indicates the *Swadhisthana Chakra*. The terms "navel center" and "heart center" overtly refer to the *Manipura* and *Anahata Chakras*. In the following paragraph, the neck corresponds to the *Vissudhi Chakra*, and the feeling of "being pushed out of myself" indicates movement toward the *Sahasrara*, located over the top of the skull.

69 Translation by Guruji. This prayer is traditionally recited by school children at the beginning of a new school year, or when undertaking a new course of study–as Guruji was undoubtedly about to do.

"I told her, 'Look, I have been praying to you all my life. In one form or another, I have been searching for truth. Why don't you come and help me now? I'm in trouble.' And she heard my prayer! Her lovely, smiling form appeared right in front of me—very beautiful, standing within a white lotus, wearing a white cotton sari and holding her *veena*."[70]

Guruji recounted the conversation that ensued:

"Why did you call me, Prahlada?" she asked. "What are you afraid of?"

"Don't you see?" he said. "I am in danger! Please help me!"

She smiled and said, "But I am giving you an experience of being outside yourself. Why not enjoy it?"

"Enjoy it?" he replied. "I can't take this kind of experience! I am dying!"

And at once the alarming sounds and sensations of his vision subsided.

"The volcano vanished," Guruji said. "I was flying in the sky peacefully, like a swan. I felt like a child in the lap of Saraswati."

"Don't worry," the goddess told him, as he gradually regained his composure. "The fear you feel is temporary. It will pass. After this, there will be a few more unpleasant experiences in your meditation—because there are memories stored in your genes, unknown to you, which must be worked through—but there will be many enjoyable experiences as well. Whenever you are afraid or have difficulty, just call me. I will come and take you out of danger. I am with you. Have no fear."

"That was the assurance given to me by Saraswati," Guruji said. "And thus did my friendship with the Goddess start happening; that is how I got connected to her."

And while he did indeed experience a few unpleasant meditations in the months that followed, he found himself less and less disturbed by them.

"Just as she predicted, there were some nightmarish experiences," he said. "For example, I saw my own body dismembered and cut into pieces. I saw people who were near and dear to me in mortal danger, and various natural disasters that caused a lot of damage. But with her help I was able to cope with these things. That's when I realized how very important it is to seek divine power for help in time of crisis.

"Even now, I still sometimes see very unpleasant things" he added. "Or sometimes I just get this unaccountable sense of fear, and no matter what I do I can't make it go away. In such cases all I can do is experience the feeling and eventually it goes away

70 Because Saraswati is the Hindu goddess of knowledge, music, arts, wisdom and learning, Guruji is suggesting that—despite his years of not maintaining an active spiritual practice—his dedication to the sciences, the acquisition and application of knowledge, were still a significant form of homage. The form he describes here is typical of Saraswati's iconographic appearance.

by itself. Maybe someday it won't go away, maybe someday it will kill me, but I'm not worried about death. And as Saraswati suggested, some of these things are doubtless connected with my own past." He smiled and then added, "Of course, others are more likely associated with some banal problem of the stomach—maybe hyperacidity—and could be easily corrected by eating more moderate and *sattvic* foods."

From this point forward, Guruji sat for meditation every day without fail. He found himself increasingly looking forward to his internal explorations. They gave him a deep sense of happiness that stayed with him throughout the more mundane hours of his workaday life.

"I started having beautiful and joyous experiences of a harmonious, joyful, creative nature," he said. "I was seeing light patterns, like the festival of lights that you see in the sky—exploding stars, beautiful patterns forming in various ways, lightning streaks going hither and thither."

At other times, various beings—both divine and not so divine—would appear and offer him weapons or *siddhis*.[71] "But Guruji never accepted these gifts, so to speak, from the gods," Amma said. "His goal was always very clear. His intention was not to gain power, but self-realization. He would never settle for these lesser things."

Almost always, Guruji's divine guide on his early inner journeys was Saraswati. In time, their encounters took on quasi-erotic undertones that at first made him uncomfortable. She began to call him "Hladini"—an androgynous appellation meaning literally "power of love," and strongly evoking *Puranic* stories of the divine couple Krishna and Radha.[72] According to Guruji's sister Suryalakshmi, things heated up quickly from there.

"One day when the children were still small, Saraswati actually asked Guruji to marry her," she recounted. "This wasn't any vision or a hallucination; she was sitting right in front of him talking, just like we are now! Guruji said no, of course, saying, 'I am already a married man with children!' but she kept repeating, 'Come on, marry me!' until finally he got fed up and said, 'Why don't I ask my wife and see what she says?' To his surprise, Saraswati immediately agreed."

71 Occult powers.

72 The Goddess would later appear to Guruji not as Saraswati, but as Hladini; that is, Radha herself.

So Guruji told Amma about his encounters with Saraswati and her strange demand, concluding, "Look, what can I say? This is what is happening. What should I do?"

The ever unflappable Amma replied, "If you want to, go ahead—but you can't leave me and the children."

"I won't leave," Guruji promised.

The next day, Suryalakshmi said, "Saraswati appeared to Guruji, gleefully saying, 'So your wife agreed!' and at that point she merged with him."

"That is how Saraswati became my mentor, my second divine guru," Guruji confirmed. "She would come in my meditation, while I was listening to the inner sounds. She would give me books to read in my meditation. And surprisingly, when I'd go to check in the Bombay University library, near the YWCA at Gateway of India, I'd find some of the same books I read with her, right there on the shelves in physical form."

Another interesting aspect of Guruji's early meditational experiences concerned explorations of his previous lives. Throughout his life, these experiences held a particular fascination for many, but Guruji—who was so often startlingly open about matters traditionally considered secret—would grow uncharacteristically reticent when asked about what he discovered.

"If I were a politician, I'd say, 'I would rather not answer this question!'" he laughed. "I have enough problems in *this* life; I don't want to worry about the past ones, too!"

In 1988, however, Guruji wrote a tantalizing third-person account of what Saraswati had revealed to him on the topic:

> She showed him some of his past lives—the good aspects, the bad aspects, the cruel aspects—as well as the various kinds of *tapas* (austerities) and *sadhana*s he had gone through. In his other lives, he had different names. The first few of them are Sanat Kumara,[73] Prahlada (devotee of Vishnu and son of Hiranyaka-sipu), etc., etc.

Haran Aiya added that another of his previous incarnations was the renowned medieval sage Sri Raghavendra Swami;[74] Guruji mentioned this in passing one day in the

73 Sanat Kumara is a *rishi* named in the *Chandogya Upanishad*. In Sanskrit, *Sanat Kumara* means "Eternal Youth." The final chapter of the *Mahabharata* states that Sanat Kumara incarnated as Pradyumna, Lord Krishna's son by Rukmini, to help advance the Divine Plan of Creation. On completion of his work, he returned to the divine realms, where he now serves as Lord of the Planets.

74 Raghavendra (1595-1671 CE), born Venkanna Bhatta in Mantralayam, Andhra Pradesh, was a renowned Hindu saint, philosopher and proponent of Dvaita philosophy proposed by Sri Madhvacharya. Contemporary images of the saint, incidentally, beat a striking resemblance to Guruji.

1980s, and Aiya still marvels at the memory. "It blew my mind away!" he said. "I was standing there in front of him and I said, 'Guruji, you never told me this before!' He shrugged and said 'Why is it important?' Amma was sitting next to him, and I asked her, 'Did he ever tell you this?' She said, 'No!' So there we were, both staring at him, and Guruji quietly said, 'Please, I don't want that to be publicized.' In fact, whenever I would stand up to introduce him to a crowd after that, he would glare at me with this look that said, 'Don't you dare!' So I would keep quiet."

Guruji did occasionally like to tell the story of having been, sometime in the 19th century, a *sannyasi* named Thyagisananda who lived in the holy city of Kashi (Varanasi). He recalled begging for food outside a merchant's palatial home. "I was almost exhausted, on the point of death," he said. "And the lady of the house came out bringing me food on a golden plate. I saw it, but I didn't eat it. It was too late. I died, right then and there." The woman, he said, was an earlier incarnation of his wife, Annapurna.

Some of Guruji's disciples told a more elaborate, romantic version of the story, in which the woman is not merely wealthy, but a princess, and the *sannyasi* does not die, but is nursed back to health by the woman, whereupon the two fall in love. Guruji dismisses such mythologizing, insisting that the real story is the simpler one, and that it's just a garden-variety case of karma in action. Because the wealthy woman failed to feed the *sannyasi* in time to avert his death, "she happens to feed him daily in this life, thereby finishing her *runanubandha*—or debt to be fulfilled," he said.

Over the years, Guruji added, he has explored "10 or 20" of his previous lives in varying degrees of detail—some ancient, some modern. The most recent would appear to predate his 1934 birth by no more than a decade or so ("Oddly, I was a soldier who died in a plane crash; I saw myself falling onto barbed wire..."). Some lives appeared as mere glimpses; others seemed entirely outside time ("One night, I experienced an entire lifetime in about three minutes of meditation").

Beyond such hints, Guruji rarely spoke of his past lives—in part because it might "appear to be egotistical," but also because most people's understanding of past-life regression is not sufficiently subtle to accurately interpret its meaning. He explained that "souls" consist of more generalized, less concentrated energy than do individual human beings; therefore, attempts to establish one-on-one correspondences in the sense of "*this* person used to be *that* person" are simply too imprecise and inaccurate to be useful. Even when one discrete individual "experiences" the life of another, he said, it is not necessarily an indication that the one actually "was," fully and completely, the other.

Finally, he notes, details of *his* past lives really aren't of much value to anyone other than himself. "It is much better to explore your own experiences than to simply hear about someone else's," he said.

ॐ

Meanwhile, Guruji's meditational journeys with Saraswati continued.

"She would take me to different places and times," he said. "I would hold her little finger like a child. We would walk on rainbows. Wherever she placed her foot, a lotus would appear. Such beautiful, beautiful times I had with Saraswati. She took me to places and civilizations in other worlds; she showed me unfamiliar life forms.[75] Always like a mother, ever smiling, ever happy and ever present at my beck and call. I would ask her questions and she would answer me."

He recounted some of these exchanges:

Q: What happens after I die?
A: You return to the elements. You become a spirit. Then you have the form of earth, water, fire, air, space and time.
Q: Why do you appear in human form?
A: You decide how you wish to see me, and I take that form out of the elements.
Q: How old are you?
A: Millions of years old.
Q: Then why do you appear so young?
A: We are really ageless beings. We can appear as any age—I can be nine, 15, 18, 33, whatever age you wish me to be, at any time.

"Such were my conversations with Saraswati," Guruji said. "I used to listen, enchanted, as she played on the *veena*. I was ecstatic. I would get really absorbed in it, listening for hours on end, deep in meditation—yet in physical time only a few minutes would pass! I used to ask myself, 'How can time dilatation occur when I am traveling at earth speeds? Am I Brahma?'"[76]

75   In the view of Shaktism and Sri Vidya, Guruji explained, the entire cosmos is the body of the Goddess, and thus its very *nature* is life, making the question "Is there life elsewhere in the universe?" slightly nonsensical: there is nothing *but* life—just not always in forms or at levels that the human senses can discern. Guruji noted, "There is definitely life in other places in the galaxy. It may not be life as we are used to, but there is life. In fact, there are other lifeforms co-existing with us right here on Earth and we don't know about them."

76   In Hindu cosmology, Brahma is Saraswati's consort.

Whatever the explanation, the music itself was divine.

"Sometimes I wished I had the ability to play the *veena* myself," he said. "I'd think, 'Why am I blessed enough to hear all of these wonderful musical extravaganzas, but not enough to be able to reproduce them for everyone's benefit?' Unfortunately, she never granted me that ability. Though once I saw her change form as she was playing—her head became my head, but the body remained hers."

When he inquired what this vision meant, she replied, "It means you are Saraswati."

"But how can that be?" he asked.

"Well, what is Saraswati?" she replied. "Saraswati is an order of *sannyasa*. You come from my lineage. So you will carry my name as a Guru."

"And that's how I got that part of my name," Guruji said. "It was given to me by her."[77]

Guruji questioned the Goddess further:

77 Guruji refers to his full Guru name, Sri Amritananda Natha Saraswati; the origin of "Sri Amritananda Natha" is explained in chapter 9.

Q: If I am to be a guru and someone asks me a question for which I don't know the answer, what should I do?

A: When a question is put to you, an answer may spring to you in your mind. If it doesn't, or it takes some time, understand that the solution is going to manifest in future, but not immediately. In any case, don't pretend you know all the answers. No one does. Not even me.

Q: Why can't you know the future?

A: The future is made by so many living beings together. So it is always somewhat hazy.

Q: Can I change my destiny?

A: Of course you can. But usually the environment plays a very large role in what is going to happen, not your actions alone. So while it may appear that you can know your destiny in a statistical sense but cannot change it, this is not necessarily so. In actuality, with an extraordinary effort that influences your environment, you *can* change your own and your environment's future.

One day Guruji asked Saraswati if he could somehow save the world from unnecessary travail by bringing advanced knowledge from the future back to the past. "Why can't I move forward in time, talk to a scientist yet to be born, and then bring his knowledge back to this time and help fast-forward things a little?" he asked.

The Goddess shrugged and replied, "Go ahead and try."

"So I went ahead," Guruji said. He located a spiritually receptive fellow physicist living a few centuries hence and the two held a "summit meeting" to discuss the future's scientific innovations. It didn't work.

"Once that fellow got talking, I couldn't understand anything he said!" Guruji marveled. He explained that even a physicist as great as Sir Isaac Newton would be completely out of his depth if suddenly confronted with Albert Einstein explaining relativity—unless Newton had first been briefed on the intervening centuries of scientific development.

Saraswati laughed and said, "You see, what you *can* know is directly proportional to what you know already. You've got to expand the container before you can increase its content. Which is why, in most cases, quantum leaps are not organically possible."

Remembering the incident, Guruji mused, "Just look at the new paradigms in the world today—the level of scientific cooperation that is necessary to understand genes, make hardware and software, build mega-structures or invent new forms of mathematics. Information drives action, and action drives information. This is the loop needed for expanding awareness, and it can happen only with integrity and cooperation between thousands of people. This is why cooperation, not competition, is the answer. Cooperation means surrendering a little sense of *credit for doing*, and shifts the focus to *results*."

The power of collective over individual action and achievement would, in time, become a recurrent theme in his teaching.

Not all of Guruji's meditational experiences involved Saraswati. And though he did not fully comprehend the import of these visions, their implications felt profound.

"For a few months, I saw cloud-like lights with bright colors dancing in front of me," he said. "I could not figure out who or what they were. Sometimes they were more like dancing points of light, discovering and locking themselves into patterns that made sense. I observed that, as time went on, they became sharper and more defined. It was as if by recognizing them I was forcing them into a shape of my liking. Perhaps they were other spirit forms who were trying to connect with me. My attention was giving them a shape."

Over time these images became increasingly concrete.

"As they took clearer shapes, I could recognize some beings from the past," he said. "They were mostly in the left side of my visual field. And I would recognize some geometric shapes in the right side of my visual field. I knew that those were future beings, higher in evolution than humans. The visions that were straight in front of me existed in the present, but in someplace far away. So in some sense, the past, present and future were mapped onto the left, middle and right fields of my view."

In years to come, such abstract visions would grow increasingly complex and occupy larger and larger swaths of Guruji's time in meditation. For now, they served mainly to convince him that he needed expert guidance.

8 The Wisest of Madmen

As his meditational experiences grew increasingly detailed and perplexing, Guruji made a visit to his family home in Visakhapatnam, which was still bustling with relatives and tenants. Among them was Annapurna Tatamma, an elderly but still-formidable relative of his father. An advanced *upasaka* of Bala Tripurasundari, Tatamma would often see the child goddess hiding among the flowers she picked to decorate the house, or following her around as she went about her daily chores. She also wrote a number of poems about Bala—some of which have survived and are, daughter Radha noted, "of sufficient quality to be set to music and sung."

A person so spiritually experienced, Guruji reflected, might be in a good position to advise him on how best to respond to his visions. And indeed, Tatamma listened with intense interest as Guruji narrated what he had seen. When he finished, she shook her head gravely and warned it was dangerous to navigate such deep and mysterious waters without guidance. "You mustn't meditate on your own anymore," she told him. "You must find a guru."

She offered to put him in touch with her own guru—a female adept of considerable renown in Vizag at the time—but added that she was a stickler for orthodoxy. Knowing his independent nature would chafe under such a teacher, Guruji politely declined. Then Gunturu Subrahmanyam, a maternal cousin of Amma, recommended his own

78 The name *Gurugaru*, like the name *Guruji*, means "Respected Teacher," *-garu* being a Telugu honorific in the same way that *-ji* is a Hindi honorific.

79 One who has acquired *siddhis* (occult powers) through *sadhana*.

80 A *prayoga*, in this context, is a ritual undertaken to achieve a specific, defined result.

81 This is his full title as cited by Guruji. Some disciples claim longer titles, such as "Swami Srilasri Swaprakasananda Tirtha Hamsa Avadhuta" or even "Swami Srilasri Swaprakasananda Natha Hamsa Avadhuta Tirtha Datta." However, Guruji noted, "*Srilasri* is invented. It is not of our *sampradaya*. It is of the Vaishnavite line."

guru—a unique figure who lived in the busy market town of Anakapalle, about 15 miles (23 kilometers) outside Vizag.

Then in his early 60s, "Anakapalle Gurugaru," as he was commonly known,[78] had been a religious prodigy since early childhood. Neither an educated man nor a conventionally benevolent holy figure, he was nonetheless reputed to be an accomplished *siddha*[79] and powerful Tantric adept whose prayers, blessings and *prayogas*[80] won striking results for those he chose to help. He was also possessed of a famously moody, capricious and unpredictable temperament.

"He was really a very simple person," Guruji said. "He was a renunciate and he knew the *mantra shastra* from the age of four or five. He never went to school. He was a vagabond. He spent all his money on various gurus and teachers, and had tried all kinds of stuff, both right and wrong." Gurugaru also presented a determinedly shocking physical appearance—skeletally thin and wild-eyed, with a halo of matted, grayish-yellow hair and a mad, cackling laugh.

"The first time you saw him, talked to him, heard him speak; the first time you saw his mannerisms—you could only think, 'This guy is certifiable,'" recalled Haran Aiya. "He had this crazy, disheveled look about him: his eyes always focused somewhere else, suddenly bursting out giggling for no apparent reason, going into these yogic poses. And when someone asked him a question, his eyes would fix on that person, unmoving, and he would start talking—the words just pouring out of him for an hour, an hour and a half, too fast for anybody to ever translate it!"

Gurugaru was also, despite his diminutive size, a physically powerful, even athletic individual. "When he'd visit a temple, he could run up a flight of a hundred steps without a problem," said Devi Parvati, an American woman who first met Gurugaru in the late 1980s. "He was very strong, too. He used to run up behind me sometimes and yell 'Parvati-ji!'—and whack me on the back so hard it practically knocked me over!"

ૐ

Formally titled Swami Swaprakasananda Tirtha Hamsa Avadhuta,[81] Anakapalle Gurugaru was born Narasimha Kodukula (Narasimha enters Guruji's life yet again) on July 31, 1915, to Mahalakshmi and Suribabu Kodukula, members of a "pious family known for its religiosity" in the village of Veduruparthi, Andhra Pradesh.

"Even as a child, he made his presence felt by all alike," A. Ramalinga Sastry, a longtime acquaintance, recalled years later. "Not because of his total disinterest in formal education, which he discontinued at the elementary level, or his obstinate mischief, but because of his habit of being in a deeply contemplative mood in opted solitude, going routinely into deep meditation most of the time, without any concern for the mundane."

Over the years, Gurugaru encountered many of the greatest spiritual teachers of his time and took initiation into any number of spiritual lineages. A hagiography circulated for years among his devotees recounts the rather jaw-dropping details:

During his 20th year, Sri Gurugaru received initiation from Sri Poornananda Yogi, a disciple of the Tibetan guru Maru Maharishi. He was introduced to Sri Vidya *upasana* by Sri Kesari Kameswara Rao of the Madhvacharya lineage.[82] In his 32nd year, he received initiation into [the goddess forms known as] the 10 Mahavidyas, Sri Rajarajeswari and Vanadurga, and [into the] *Saptasathi Chandi*.[83] He attained *purna diksha* [the highest initiation in Sri Vidya] from Sri Gnanananda Saraswathi of Anakapalle.

Traveling the length and breadth of India to enhance his spiritual knowledge, Sri Gurugaru mastered the 64 Tantras by the time he was 40 years old. By 43, he had learnt 70 million mantras[84] from the teachings of the 18 *peetams*[85] and many gurus. He spent a few years in Kashi [Varanasi] contemplating and analyzing the source of the mantras he had learned, greatly aided by Sri Dakshinamurthi Paramahamsa (1872–1954) of the Lalithanagar [section of] Visakhapatnam.

At the age of 58, he became a Vedic scholar with the grace of [the deity] Chintamani Mahavidyeswari. By 1980, in his 65th year, Sri Gurugaru felt the urge to renounce the material world and take up *sannyasa*.[86] To this end, he travelled to the Sri Bhadrakali Mahapeetam at Haridwar's Saptarishi Sarovar.[87] *Sanyasa Diksha* was showered on him by [Gurugaru's final guru] Srilasri Kalyanananda Bharati Tirtha Maharaj.[88] Years later, with his Guru's blessings, Sri Gurugaru took up the *avadhuta ashram*.[89]

82 According to another account, he was initiated into Sri Vidya by Sriman Brahmananda Nathaji.

83 Another name for the ancient "Shakta Bible," also known as the *Devi Mahatmyam*.

84 Traditionally given as the total number of all the mantras given to the world by God in the form of the primordial *Sada-Shiva*.

85 The 18 *Maha Shakti Peetams* are a group of major Goddess temples distributed throughout the Indian subcontinent.

86 Later-life renunciation within the Hindu scheme of *ashrams*, or life stages.

87 The Holy Pool of the Seven Sages temple in Haridwar, India, on the banks of the Ganges River.

88 Swami Kalyanananda Bharati Tirtha, originally from Andhra Pradesh, eventually settled in Haridwar, where Gurugaru met him. His guru, in turn, was Sri Rajrajeswarananda. These two figures are generally cited as the two gurus directly preceding Guruji in his *parampara*, or guru lineage.

89 That is, he fully withdrew from worldly involvement. The title *avadhuta* is important, indicating a self-realized renunciate, especially one "associated with the apparently crazy modes of behaviour of some paramahamsas, who dramatize the reversal of social norms, a behaviour characteristic of their spontaneous lifestyle."

"As the years rolled by [Gurugaru] attained saintly wisdom and became popularly known as Master Simhalu," Ramalinga noted. "People in difficulties flocked around him for solace and wise counsel." Despite his sometimes testy demeanor, Gurugaru shared his wisdom generously when he was in the right mood, initiating many more people into various secret mantras than was common in his day. But even more than his formidable spiritual credentials, it was Gurugaru's extraordinary personal devotion that won him the respect, admiration and loyalty of most ordinary people who encountered him.

"By treading an austere life path and being in penance most of the time, he imbibed the spark for mastering Vedanta and the *mantra shastra* by a self-study of Vedic literature," Ramalinga observed. "He came a long way by self-effort to be regarded as a self-illuminated and self-evolved person by all alike from far and wide."

Shreeram Balijepalli had known Gurugaru from earliest childhood. His father was one of the old master's first disciples and remained one for 60 years. Shreeram himself was born late in his parents' marriage, after an older brother perished tragically in an accident. His mother, who had passed menopause by that time, despaired of having another child and abandoned all belief in God.

"Gurugaru comforted my parents, and told them he saw Devi handing him a baby boy—me, apparently—who would be born to them soon," Shreeram said. He then gave the couple esoteric instructions to ingest certain mantrically energized foods, to undertake particular *sadhanas*—and nine months later Shreeram was born.

Growing up, Shreeram regarded Gurugaru as "my father, grandfather, guru and everything rolled into one," he said. "I used to play with his matted locks as a toddler. He would tell me, 'You are the Goddess's son!' Once as a small child I looked at a picture he kept of Goddess Rajarajeshwari and said to him in all innocence, 'But I don't even look like her!' He laughed aloud and said, "Well, damn it kid, you'd better believe me! You really *are* her son!"[90]

90 In Telugu, *"Champesavayya! Nuvvu naa maata nammu, nuvvu nijangaa Deviputruduve!"*

Of course, many who visited Gurugaru were not seeking mantras or transcendent knowledge, but rather material boons. "People used to bug him for favors—from transfers or promotions at a job to solving marital problems," Shreeram said. "Very few actually came for spiritual reasons."

That could be a big mistake, according to Guruji. "When you visit Gurugaru, don't ask for anything, because he'll give it to you," he would later advise visitors. "Even if it's not in your highest good, he'll give it to you—but there will be strings attached. You'll have to go through the karma of whatever it brings. Gurugaru is beyond good and evil, beyond right and wrong—such concepts don't even compute for him. So the best thing is to just go there, enjoy his energy, be there with him—but don't ask for anything."

When caught in a talkative mood, Gurugaru would occasionally hold forth on a variety of spiritual topics. "I have heard him give long—unending!—lectures in Sanskrit and Telugu, about how *pujas* should be done, the nature of fear, how scientists could tap into lightning to generate electricity, about his various spiritual experiences," one disciple said.

But more frequently, he would simply sit and stare back at his visitors. And that, according to Devi Parvati, was more than enough.

"When you were in his presence you really did feel this very, very powerful energy," she said. "In my experience, you never got discourses from Gurugaru; he just gave *darshan*, basically. That was it. To me he seemed totally non-intellectual, but he was deeply, utterly connected with the highest spiritual energy—and he would just totally bring it down."

Kathy Allen, a Sri Vidya practitioner from Connecticut and longtime disciple of Haran Aiya, received Gurugaru's *darshan* twice, both times in the old man's third-floor room at his daughter's home in Vizag.

"I remember his room clearly," Kathy said of a 1999 visit. "There were pictures of Dattatreya[91] hanging high near the ceiling in every direction; an orange wooden platform bed, which he seemed to never move from; and a little buzzer on the wall beside him, which he would ring for his cup of coffee. Gurugaru would sit on his bed, serene

91 The legendary divine founder of the Tantric lineages, Dattatreya is said to be the primordial guru–the combined form of the Hindu Trinity of Shiva, Vishnu and Brahma.

yet energetic, almost out-of-body—glowing this radiant amber glow, with a smile on his face, intensely staring at me. I had the feeling that, just by looking at me, he knew my past, present and future."

Noticing her interest in his Dattatreya images, Gurugaru explained that one of them was actually a photograph, not a painting. It had been created by chance, he said, when the photographer took a scenic photo of the mountains "not knowing that Dattatreya was standing before him until the photograph was developed and the deity's image became visible."

After Gurugaru briefly questioned Allen and her companions about their backgrounds and spiritual interests, "we sat silently and he intensely stared at us," she recalled. "I looked back into his eyes and tried to empty my mind and remain open to receiving the energy of the moment. I had no clue as to what he was doing or thinking. He made some quick movements with his hands, perhaps *mudras* that I did not recognize. He knew we did not want to leave, so he said something like, 'You can stay a little longer and meditate; this body you are looking at is nothing.' Eventually, though, he motioned for us to leave and we headed back down the narrow steps, through the small alley to the rickshaw and back to Devipuram. While I do not fully understand what happened that day, I have faith that this seemingly simple *darshan* of Gurugaru was a tremendous blessing."

In footage filmed by Netherlands-based videographer William Thomas in the mid-1990s, Gurugaru can be seen in all his strange glory, clad only in a loincloth, his large dark eyes disarmingly intense and penetrating. Staring into the camera and speaking in Telugu, he states that he has no attachment to anything, including his own body, that he gains his strength both from multiple temple deities and from the one formless, transcendent God. He adds that he has no ego left, and that neither praise nor abuse affects him.

Having learned about Gurugaru from Amma's cousin, Guruji was intrigued but hesitant to disturb the old master with a personal visit. So instead, he gave his relative a letter detailing some of the questions with which he was then struggling. They were:

- *How can one distinguish between a projection from within one's own mind and a real vision?*
- *Are visions produced by willfully thinking about them, or do they appear sponta-neously and one just happens to witness them?*
- *Do visions really open channels of communication with the divine, or are they just projections of the mind, like dreams?*
- *Are visions just a type of hallucination or are they more genuine than that?*
- *How do the experiences of sleep, death and* samadhi *differ from one another?*

Guruji also listed some of the books he had consulted in seeking answers to these ques-tions, and described a few of the visions he had experienced. He concluded, "What do you suggest I do next?" Amma's cousin brought the letter to Gurugaru, who read it and asked, "Who is this man? Before I respond to his questions, I want to meet him in person."

So Guruji traveled to Anakapalle and came to Gurugaru's home himself, respect-fully asking him, "Do you have answers I sought?"

Gurugaru replied simply, "Come back tomorrow at 4 a.m. And bathe first."

Somewhat put out—was this eccentric old character playing games with him?—Guruji nonetheless returned at the appointed hour. Ignoring Guruji's attempt at for-mal greetings, Gurugaru cut to the chase: "I want to give you something, some man-tras. Will you take them?"

Though momentarily taken aback, Guruji evenly replied, "I have not come here to take any mantras from you. I have come to seek answers to the questions I sent you. Will you answer them for me?"

"No," Gurugaru said. "I will not tell you the answers to your questions, but I do want to give you something. Will you take it?"

Guruji hesitated. If he said yes, he felt he "might be in trouble"—taking on a new responsibility without fully understanding its implications. On the other hand, if he said no, he could be "missing a once-in-a-lifetime opportunity." He was not sure what to do and he said so, asking the sage, "What does it mean if I accept these mantras? Will they do only good? Or can they also bring harm?"

"If they do anything at all, they will do only good," Gurugaru replied. "They will not harm you."

Guruji nodded, but remained concerned. He was already carrying considerable professional and familial obligations; he might not have time to chant the mantras regularly. So he asked, "If I take the mantras and I do not recite them, what will happen? Do they carry any compulsions or restrictions? If they do, I would rather not accept them."

"You don't have to worry about that," the old man replied. "If I give them to you, it means I will take care of you and that is enough."

With that assurance, Guruji said yes, he would accept the mantras.

Gurugaru gave him nine—Mahaganapati, Subramanya, Chandi, Surya, Dattatreya, Prasada Panchakshari, Bala Tripurasundari, Guru and Sowbhagya Vidya—at that one sitting. Afterward, Guruji inquired about the methods of recitation and other essential formalities of the mantras—such as time, place, number of repetitions per day, how many days, and so on.

"*Do as you will*," Gurugaru said, grinning and meeting Guruji's gaze steadily as he repeated the dying words of his father. "I wanted to teach you these mantras, and so I did. Use them when and as you see fit, or don't use them at all. Either way is fine with me. I place no restrictions on you. You are different from the others. Nothing is binding on you."

Surprised at the old guru's seeming indifference, Guruji said, "If I have questions, may I write to you?"

Gurugaru replied, "You won't need to write to me. You will find the answers to your questions by yourself. The mantras will give you the answers. They have a life of their own."

Guruji's spiritual development was rapidly accelerating: it was no longer confined to inner transformations, but had begun to spill over into his outer, workaday life. Even the usually cool-headed Amma, who had so far taken much of her husband's journey in stride, was growing increasingly concerned. "My reaction when he took the mantras from Anakapalle Gurugaru was, frankly, a little fear," she said. "I felt like, 'How could you do this without asking me?'"

In time, Amma would herself become a disciple of Gurugaru, and come to consider him as essentially a part of her extended family. Yet her initial reaction reveals much about the speedy and striking nature of the transformation that would soon change her husband's life, and her own, forever.

For his part, Guruji compared that first exchange with Gurugaru to the energy transfer he received at the Balaji temple in Hyderabad. But this *shaktipat*[92] from a human guru was qualitatively on a different level; its effect was much more dramatic and immediate. From that point forward, Guruji would very literally follow Gurugaru's advice in seeking answers from the mantras from the Goddess herself—a development that would decisively impact his own approach to decision-making, and to advising others.

"My guru gave me total freedom; how can I do any different?" he would tell them. "Use the mantras and rituals I teach you whenever and however you want. There is no requirement forcing you to somehow lead your life differently."

Indeed, Guruji extended this *laissez-faire* approach far beyond Gurugaru's original concept, applying it to a broad spectrum of spiritually related behaviors. Even vegetarianism, a virtually universal practice among traditional South Indian Brahmins, is not a prerequisite for Sri Vidya initiation according to Guruji. Though personally a lifelong vegetarian, he shrugged it off as a "cultural habit" of his family, caste and region—not a spiritual one.

"Non-vegetarians are eligible devotees, too," he said. "I used to argue that, out of the 10 avatars of Vishnu, only Vamana the Dwarf is a vegetarian Brahmin; all the others are non-vegetarians. So it is a case of vegetarian devotees worshiping a non-vegetarian god!" He laughed. "Why is this? Why can't a non-vegetarian devotee worship a non-vegetarian god or goddess? *Ahimsa*, is it? Non-violence? Vegetables like the *kushmanda*[93] live for a full year after being separated from the plant. They experience pain and pleasure too, even if they can't express it in terms we understand. *Himsa* [injury, harm] cannot be avoided. It is part of life. Life consumes life; that is the rule. We can't eat inorganics and live."

92 *Shaktipat*, denoting in Sanskrit "Descent of Grace," or "Influx of Divine Power," is an awakening that brings a person to the spiritual path. "Some people receive a very intense *shaktipat*, consisting often of a mystical experience of their oneness with all reality … or of energy shooting up their spine and exploding in their head, or of waves of bliss surging in their body, and so on. Others receive a *shaktipat* so subtle that it is almost imperceptible."

93 The *kushmanda* is the red pumpkin, which grows in abundance at Devipuram. "Even for a year after being separated from the mother plant, it does not rot and can still be eaten," Guruji noted.

It was a viewpoint fully consistent with Guruji's general disinterest in the mundane social markers of one's spiritual path—whether they concerned dress, diet or anything else. While he never rejected such practices outright, he did advise caution about attitudes and practices that emphasize divisions between people, or that act as "first you must do this" obstacles to the free exploration of one's spirituality. This philosophy even goes a long way toward explaining his own simple form of dress. "To put on distinctive religious garb and set oneself apart from the rest of mankind certainly flatters the vanity of one's tribe," he noted. "But is it spirituality?"

Physical austerity as a pathway to God drew a similar note of caution. "Asceticism is not a requirement for spiritual development," he said. "Austerities are as much of a waste of time as an overfull belly." When a sleekly muscled young male visitor to Devipuram once attempted to elicit Guruji's opinions on the benefits of advanced hatha yoga practices, Guruji laughed and replied, "You're talking to the wrong guy! I'm not really built for it!" When another expressed determination to undertake a strict spiritual fast, Guruji remarked, "It might be good for you, but only because you need to prove to yourself that you are capable of it."

The dos and don'ts of spirituality, he continually stressed, must come from within.

"All religions seem to preach that there are certain things you should or should not do," he said. "But who is to be the judge? I think that you, as a divine personality, should judge for yourself what you ought and ought not to be doing. Every conscious decision you make says something about the type of lifestyle you want to lead: whether you should or should not have sex, eat meat, drink alcohol, have coffee—whatever it may be, all the good things and bad things. You are the only person who can decide and tell yourself. Anything in moderation—just don't hurt yourself, don't hurt others and don't hurt the environment. Other than that, you are free to do what you want. This is the fundamental basis of all results in Tantra."

Our spiritual journey, Guruji taught, can only begin from where we are at this very moment. If any particular mode of eating, dressing or behaving inspires us, focuses us, gives us a sense of community, or makes us feel happier—then by all means, we should indulge as we see fit. What we should never do is allow such outward signifiers to function as a prerequisite (or substitute) for spirituality itself, or a vehicle for feeling superior to, or hostile toward, others who dress, eat or act differently.

"If a change has to happen, it will happen from within," Guruji said. "You will be guided by Devi herself. Who am I to decide for you? You have all the freedom in the universe."

श्री Sri Krishnamurthy.
(Sri Vidya Trust)

9 Setting the Stage

Returning to Bombay after his very eventful visit home, Guruji immersed himself in a new and demanding routine: though still a full-time scientist at TIFR, he began meditating deeply upon the mantras Gurugaru had given him, often for hours at a time—with results that quickly elevated his practice to a new level.

His initial approach was simple. In those days, Guruji kept a picture of the goddess Santoshi Maa[94] on his home altar, and would focus on the sword in her upper right hand while doing his *japa*, or mantra recitation. "As I was concentrating on the picture, the sword would somehow suddenly change to a garland of flowers," he said. "She was always smiling and putting that garland on my head."

Though he had neither prayed nor worshiped regularly for years, Guruji did grow up surrounded by the rhythm and spirit of Hindu ritual, absorbing it more or less by osmosis. And now the Goddess—via this image of Santoshi Mata—began teaching him more, answering his questions almost as soon as they arose in his mind, just as Gurugaru promised she would.

"I didn't know that much about external worship at the time," Guruji said. "I had never done much *puja* in my life. But at that point I started learning various things under her guidance—ways of doing the *pujas*, ways of reciting the mantras, the *Sri Sukta*, the *Purusha Sukta*; all these things I learned from her. She also taught me that one of

94 The goddess Santoshi Maa ("Mother of Contentment") is a relatively new addition to the Hindu pantheon. She became a pan-Indian phenomenon with the release of the 1975 Hindi film *Jai Santoshi Maa*, and her shrines soon proliferated across the country, particularly in North India. The movie was close to its height of popularity at this point in Guruji's life. Some Indian readers will find it surprising (even endearing) that a South Indian *sadhaka* of Guruji's depth and accomplishment would have begun his serious meditation practice with a "new" goddess form who was (and to this day remains) most popular among North Indian women.

the best ways of doing *puja* was to identify with your object of worship—because, she said, there is no distinction between the worshiper and the worshiped."

Guruji's changing mindset soon became apparent even to his colleagues.

"Once Sastry visited our home with his family," recalled college friend and TIFR colleague Dr. E.V.R. Rao. "We were talking on my balcony and surveying the view, when suddenly he told me he'd seen a vision to the northwest of a hilly wilderness area where Lord Venkateswara dwelled in sleeping mode—and this was years before Devipuram ever existed! Another time, I went to his house to discuss some professional issues I was having. He took me into his *puja* room, and asked me to repeat some mantras every day" to help resolve the problems.

Rao was never able to get into the habit, however, and Guruji let the matter drop. "As far as our relations were concerned, there was absolutely no change, no judgment," Rao said. "Whenever we got together, all throughout our lives, we'd talk about the old days and he'd tell me about his latest plans for Devipuram. He was never a formal guru to me, but to the end he remained my valued guide, philosopher and friend."

One Sunday morning, looking to connect with a wider community of spiritual seekers, Guruji took his family to the Yoga Shakti Mission on Napean Sea Road in Bombay. In those days, it was the city's premier gathering spot for the spiritually minded, offering yoga retreats, *puja* lessons and meditation classes. In addition, various swamis, yoga masters, mystical poets and religious thinkers would come and deliver "Sunshine Lectures," as they were called, on a wide variety of educational and inspirational topics.[95] It was at one of these Lectures that Guruji first met an accomplished *sadhaka* and guru named Sri B.S. Krishnamurthy, who was widely known and respected in Bombay circles as a devout, knowledgeable and deeply orthodox specialist in complex Vedic and Sri Vidya ritual.[96]

"Krishnamurthy Gurugaru was a short, jovial, almost baby-faced gentleman with twinkling eyes and a smiling countenance all the time," Guruji's daughter Radha affectionately recalled. "He loved to perform these really elaborate rituals—a *Navavarana Puja*[97] would go on for five or six hours! He had a deep, impressive, resonating voice,

95 The Mission, which now maintains international centers in London, New York and Miami, still hosts Sunshine Lectures and workshops on a regular basis.

96 Sri B.S. Krishnamurthy, the guru, should not be confused with Mr. Radha Krishna Murthy, Guruji's friend with a large spiritual library in Bombay, referenced in chapter 7.

97 Literally "Worship of the Nine Enclosures," the *Navavarana Puja* is one of the most important rituals in Sri Vidya practice.

and he sang *bhajans* and *kirtans*[98] very well. He would take a disciple's hand in his and give *shaktipat* with an intense, locking gaze of two or three minutes."

From their very first meeting, Krishnamurthy took a liking to Guruji—though he quickly understood that this unassuming, soft-spoken scientist was no typical house-holder seeking edifying lectures and lessons in *puja* technique. By this time, after all, Guruji was meditating nightly, reciting Gurugaru's mantras and steadily stoking their power. He also spent countless hours learning and performing *pujas*—not as a matter of grim personal discipline, but because he found genuine peace and joy in it. He was delving into arcane spiritual texts and exploring unimaginable universes—careening through past, present and future—with a goddess. He had begun to visibly glow with the intensity of his spiritual efforts.

So while Krishnamurthy understood that Guruji would glean very little from any Sunshine Lecture, he felt that this unusual man might be an ideal candidate for *delivering* one—and his instinct was squarely on the mark. Before long, Guruji's lectures were drawing large crowds. His clear-minded, unpretentious, often humorous presentations on *sadhana*, mantra, Sri Yantra, the *Lalita Sahasranama*, Kundalini Yoga and meditation technique were fresh, personal and original. Moreover, his status as a reality-grounded TIFR scientist—seemingly the polar opposite of a stereotypical starry-eyed mystic, with his casually erudite blending of science and spirituality—lent him a distinct curiosity appeal that differentiated him from other speakers on the Mission's roster.[99] For Guruji himself, it was a time of self-discovery, cultivating the seeds of his public life to come. Here was a man both finding his voice and realizing that he had something vital to say, honing his presentation and delivery style, refining his teaching technique—and growing accustomed to having an audience.

Noting Guruji's particular interest in the Goddess, Krishnamurthy began inviting him to accompany and assist in the performance of Sri Vidya rituals. "I learned the *Navavarana Puja* in the Dattatreya tradition, along with the 64 offerings and *mudras*,[100] by keenly watching Sri Krishnamurthy perform those rituals every evening," Guruji said. "Within a fairly short time, I too became adept at performing these more complex *pujas*."

Almost immediately, Guruji also began to display another lifelong spiritual preoccupation: an instinct toward simplification. The *pujas* and other rituals conducted by

98 A *bhajan* is a Hindu devotional song. A *kirtan* is a particular type of *bhajan*, characterized by call-and-response chanting.

99 Although some of Guruji's Sunshine Lectures at the Yoga Shakti Mission were reportedly recorded on cassette tapes, neither Guruji nor any of his closest associates, disciples or family members appeared to have copies at this late date.

100 Fundamental elements of advanced Sir Vidya ritual.

Krishnamurthy were rigidly orthodox and extremely elaborate, often lasting for hours (and not infrequently for days) on end. Guruji felt that busy working people—parents, breadwinners and homemakers—who might otherwise be interested in such spiritual pursuits, were undoubtedly being put off by the sheer time investment required.

So by referring to multiple ritual instruction books and scriptures, as well as his own meditational revelations, Guruji sat down and developed procedures for completing a full Goddess *puja* in between 90 and 120 minutes. Impressed by the thoughtfulness and precision of Guruji's research and the logic of his revisions, Krishnamurthy agreed to try. Sure enough, Guruji's approach was extremely well received by participants, and soon Sri Krishnamurthy was conducting their streamlined rituals for growing crowds, not just in Bombay but all over India. Krishmurthy was both astonished and impressed.

Not long afterward, when he was scheduled to conduct a traditional, four-day *yagna* at Mookambika Devi Temple in Kollur, Krishnamurthy invited Guruji and Amma to come and assist him. Guruji's work obligations at TIFR kept him away for most of the event, but he and Amma arrived in time for the *purnahuti*[101] on the final day. Immediately afterward, Krishnamurthy—without any prior warning—announced with great gravity that he had decided to accept Guruji and Amma as his disciples. He gave them both the Maha Shodashi mantra, the highest level of *purnadiksha*.[102]

Guruji said he recalled experiencing "no specific sensation" on this occasion "other than that it felt cold, like cool rain sprinkling down on a hot day." But on a more practical level—in light of his increasingly fruitful guru-disciple relationship with Anakapalle Gurugaru—he found himself in a quandary. "For a time, I was torn between these two gurus," Guruji said. "I was confused! Which one to accept? Two gurus, and both of them forced it on me! It was not a very comfortable predicament."

Daughter Anantalakshmi noted that the contrast between the two masters could not have been starker. "Krishnamurthy Gurugaru had a gentle, smiling demeanor— an aura of peace around him; basically, being near him was a comfort zone," she explained. "Whereas being near Anakapalle Gurugaru was more like a *dis*comfort zone. You had to constantly expect the unexpected. One moment he might be friendly and talkative, the next, surly and silent—then he'd dismiss you with a single word or phrase. But what an aura of power he emanated! So perhaps you could say this was a

101 *Purnahuti* or *Purna Ahuti* means "complete offering" and usually involves offering nine types of grain, *ghee* and other substances into a sacrificial fire while chanting prescribed mantras. It is one of the last steps in a *puja*.

102 *Purnadiksha* is "complete initiation," the highest level of *diksha*, implying qualification to become a guru oneself and take on *shishyas* (disciples) of one's own.

case of two very different *sorts* of gurus—one to keep you balanced, and the other to shake you up and snap you out of whatever it was that needed snapping!"

The situation came to a head soon afterward when Guruji traveled to Anakapalle and told Gurugaru all that had transpired with Krishnamurthy.

Gurugaru listened to his student's account patiently, then cackled loudly, scoffing, "Maha Shodashi by itself isn't even *purnadiksha*! You need the *mahavakyas* too![103] But anyway it doesn't matter, because I am going to give you *purnadiksha* my way." He sprinkled some water on Guruji's head, gave him the Maha Shodashi mantra and the *mahavakyas*, and removed the *diksha* name given by Sri Krishnamurthy—whereupon he renamed Guruji "Sri Amritananda Natha Saraswati."[104]

The "*diksha* war" simmered for another few months, according to daughter Radha: "When Guruji told Krishnamurthy about Gurugaru's action, he responded, "Who is he to give you *Mahavakyas*?!"—and he *also* gave Guruji the *mahavakyas*. And the competition to become Guruji's guru was taken to a new level!"

In the end, however, Gurugaru easily won the day. A deeply unconventional *sadhaka*, *siddha* and yogic prodigy, utterly dismissive of outward social niceties and expectations, he was in many ways Guruji's perfect match as friend, guide and guru, giving him free, "do as you will" latitude in developing his own powerful and personal spiritual practice. Krishnamurthy, on the other hand, remained—despite his respect for Guruji's innovations—a stickler for the strict, ritualistic "methods and methodologies" for which he was justly renowned. Guruji was ultimately too subjective and intuitive a practitioner to be satisfied with that sort of teacher; moreover, his *sadhana* was advancing prodigiously—arguably outstripping Krishnamurthy's own.

In the months and years that followed, Guruji and Krishnamurthy gradually grew apart.[105] While Krishnamurthy would remain in contact with Guruji, occasionally attending and participating in major events at Devipuram, the guru-disciple relationship was decisively over. "I had found the simpler yogi to be my real guru," Guruji said.

Their affection was mutual, and it was always clear that Guruji held an honored place in Gurugaru's esteem. Sometimes, for example, Gurugaru would sit alone in his room, meditating for hours while long queues of supplicants sweltered in the

103 The *Mahavakyas* are the four "Great Sayings" of the *Upanishads*.

104 For many years a document circulated among some disciples, claiming that Gurugaru later "promoted" Guruji to the status of "Maha Mandaleswara," giving him the extended *dikshanama*, *Advaita Amritananda Paramahamsa Parivraajaka Acharya Digambara Avadhuta Athivarnami Srilasri Maha Mandaleshwara*. Asked about this assertion, Guruji smiled and replied that the extended name was "both threateningly long and a product of flowery exaggeration. My full, given *dikshanama* is Amritananda Natha Saraswati. The rest was all added in by overzealous disciples."

105 Guruji wrote of himself in 1988 that he "belongs to the Natha Sampradaya, who follow Avadhuta Dattatreya as the founder of the Divya Kaula order. Other luminaries in the line of Gurus are Gorakshanath, Lahiri Mahasaya, Yogananda, Sivananda, Trailingaswami, Ramakrishna Paramahamsa, Shirdi Sai Baba, Satya Sai Baba and Nityananda (Guru of Muktananda), to name a few."

heat outside waiting to offer donations, narrate problems, and seek prayers, advice and blessings.

"He wouldn't see any of them," Guruji said. "He'd tell them 'Go away! Get out of here!' But with me it was always different. He'd say, 'Ah Sastry, it's you! Come in! Sit down!'"

Why the special status? Guruji shrugged.

"Maybe he knew I didn't have any money, so I wouldn't try to offer him anything," he replied. "But at the same time he knew I wasn't going to ask him for anything either. Maybe he knew that I just came to see him because I liked him."

ॐ ह्रीं

106 *Bhavas* are modes of devotion in Indian Tantric traditions, *pashu* means "bound," that is, an ordinary human or beginning Tantric practitioner. *Veera* indicates a "heroic" or intermediate Tantric practitioner. *Divya* means "supreme" or "heavenly," denoting the most advanced of Tantric practitioners.

Guruji's affinity for Gurugaru extended well beyond the realm of personal resonance. Both Gurugaru and Krishnamurthy, he explained, "belonged to the Kaulachara Dattatreya tradition, so either way I belonged to that tradition. Within it, however, there are three *bhavas* called *pashu*, *veera* and *divya*.[106] The *pashu* knows the *shastra* but is doubtful about practice of any of the *panchamakaras*, or Five Ms.[107] The *veera* practices the Five Ms. The *divya* has no need for an external *shakti*; his *shakti* is Kundalini, which is fully internal." While "Krishnamurthy-ji had a wide knowledge of scriptures, and could recite the Vedas beautifully, he was a Kaula of the *veera* order," Guruji said. "I later learned that I had finished my *veera sadhana* in earlier lives."

Anakapalle Gurugaru, on the other hand, "was a yogi of the *siddha* order," meaning that "he did practice the Five Ms earlier in his life, but after taking the *sannyasa* order he stopped them. He became what he himself used to call an '*Upanishad Kaula*,' which meant the same thing as *divya bhava*—that is, one who has no further need to use the Five Ms."

107 The Five Ms refers to the taboo-breaking *panchamakara* ("five substances") used in certain Tantric rituals and usually identified as *matsya* (fish), *mamsa* (meat), *mudra* (parched grain), *madya* (alcoholic drink) and *maithuna* (sexual intercourse), though more and less transgressive substitutes exist for each item. See also "Introduction: The World of Sri Vidya" in *The Goddess and the Guru, Volume II.*

In terms of spiritual evolution then, Gurugaru made the most sense as a teacher and guide for Guruji. "He was a *siddha*, meaning his words always used to come true," Guruji said. "He never insisted on surrender from his disciples. He never misbehaved with women that I know of. So I veered toward him," ultimately concluding that "my true guru was Swami Swaprakasananda"—that is, Anakapalle Gurugaru.

ॐ ह्रीं

Sri Krishnamurthy passed away in the early hours of Varalakshmi Vratam, the Goddess's fast day, on August 27, 2004. While his role in Guruji's spiritual development was ultimately fleeting, his legacy as an essential catalyst to action remained strong and significant. "I learned many things from him, for which I am ever grateful," Guruji said. "Whenever we met, I would pay my respects for the knowledge he imparted to me."

After all, it was during their association that Dr. N. Prahlada Sastry, scientist, first became Sri Amritananda Natha Saraswati, guru and teacher. The Sunshine Lectures that Krishnamurthy enabled gave Guruji his first serious platform for sharing his ideas and experiences, while also demonstrating a significant public interest in his brand of open, simplified, demystified spirituality. Finally, Krishnamurthy's ritual guidance provided Guruji with hours of hands-on practice, while also inspiring a deeper sense of how these intricate practices might be made more effective and accessible for modern householders in a fast-accelerating world.

The stage had been set.

A Sri Yantra drawn by Guruji in 1979 as the cover for the so-called *Lusaka Notes*, published during his time in Africa.
(Sri Vidya Trust)

10 Into the Heart of Africa

Even as his spiritual credentials and reputation grew, Guruji still faced a towering dilemma in the mundane world: he remained a layman, a scientist and an employee of TIFR—and that organization's focus was increasingly shifting from pure scientific research to applied military technology. In his everyday work, Guruji was now tasked with the development of defensive nuclear weaponry.

The situation had evolved gradually through the 1970s, as India's political tensions—with neighboring Pakistan and China, in particular—grew hotter. In response to General Zia ul-Huq's 1977 military coup in Pakistan, India sharply ramped up its nuclear-response capabilities and TIFR was tapped to support the government's efforts. As he found himself ever more immersed in defense-related projects, Guruji began to question their morality.

"I asked myself, is it really so important to create weapons of destruction?" he said. "Even though the goal is to eliminate threats and defend my country from its enemies, is it really valid to cause harm and suffering among innocent civilians, to destroy fertile lands and wipe out vast fortunes and *crores* worth of investments?[108] And when that kind of destruction can occur at the click of a button, should I really make myself a partner in the crime? I went into the sciences because I wanted to do something good for society—but is this good? Is this what I'm supposed to be doing? Using creative

108 A *crore* is 10 million in Indian English.

energy for destructive purposes? Shouldn't such massive personal effort be expended to *save* lives rather than end them?"

Nonetheless, TIFR's confidence in Guruji's ability to get the job done remained absolute. He gained steadily in authority and prestige, and was soon leading air defense initiatives with a team of 40-plus scientists working under Dr. P.V.S. Rao—even as his doubts grew stronger by the day.

Reflecting on his Brahmin heritage, and the caste's traditional focus on priestly activity and teaching, Guruji mused, "If Lord Krishna was here today, he would tell me, 'Don't fight, go and teach!' Air Missile Defense and things like that, creating atomic weapons—it was just not in my blood, and ultimately I rebelled against it."

Yet the practical implications of rebellion presented a dilemma for a conscientious family man with a wife and three teenage daughters depending on him for their livelihoods. Could he somehow maintain the status quo of his work and family life while also addressing his concerns over the increasingly violent nature of his research—and simultaneously finding a way to pursue his expanding spiritual explorations? The possibility seemed increasingly doubtful.

Temporary respite came when Guruji was offered a two-year visiting professorship teaching quantum mechanics and relativity theory at the University of Zambia, in the capital city of Lusaka. Considering the opportunity a blessing in very thin disguise, Guruji took a long sabbatical from TIFR and headed for Africa with his family. "I saw this assignment as a chance to get away from all that defense work and take a fresh look at myself from far away," he said.

The Republic of Zambia, a landlocked nation in south-central Africa, was a British colony from the mid-19th century until it won its independence in 1964. In the ensuing decades, it struggled to build a functional modern infrastructure and an educated workforce. To that end, Prime Minister Kenneth Kaunda, who would lead the country until 1991, founded the University of Zambia in 1966, with just 312 students. By the time Guruji arrived a dozen years later, enrollment stood at more than 4,000 (today the figure exceeds 12,000).

While it was cultivating a home-grown talent pool for the future, Zambia in the 1960s and '70s also had an immediate need for boots-on-the-ground experts with advanced degrees and professional credentials, who could get the country moving in the present. A significant portion of that demand was met through a partnership with the Indian Technical and Economic Cooperation Programme, which sent thousands of Indian experts to Zambia in fields ranging from banking and engineering to agriculture and industry, medicine, education and more.

Among them was Wijayaharan Aiya, a Sri Lankan architect who had migrated to India in order to escape increasing discrimination against members of the ethnic Tamil minority at home.[109] Aiya and his wife Sakuntala arrived in Lusaka in late 1970.

Beyond his professional work, Aiya was a lifelong spiritual seeker with a mastery of extremely specialized and complex ritual ceremonies—a skill that placed him in great demand within Lusaka's burgeoning Hindu community. Soon after settling in Lusaka, Aiya "began performing public *pujas* every Friday," for which "Sakuntala would cook huge quantities of food to feed the guests as well as numerous children from the neighboring apartments."

"Over time, these *pujas* became rather large gatherings, with quite a number of families," Aiya said. "Before long, they began to look like a cross-section of India: there were Bengalis, Marathis, Gujaratis, Punjabis, people from Madhya Pradesh. One day a knowledgeable gentleman named Dr. Ramaswamy, from the southern state of Kerala, started bringing *his* friends, and slowly the *pujas* took on the features of organized worship in South India."

But while Aiya's primary sectarian affiliation was the Tamil Shaivism imbibed from his first teacher—Srilasri Sivasatchidananda Mataji, a female guru in Sri Lanka—he also harbored a deep ambition to revive a centuries-old family tradition of Sri Vidya goddess worship, which had been broken just 50 years earlier. Aiya explained:

> Worship of the Devi, the Divine Mother, had been in my family for at least six generations, but it was discontinued during my grandfather's time when he lost his only daughter. She died during *Navratri*, the Mother's festival, in 1918 when

109 Systematic, institutional discrimination against ethnic Tamil Sri Lankans by the majority Sinhalese created a tense social standoff that would, in July 1983, erupt into the Sri Lankan Civil War, which raged for more than a quarter century, ending only in 2009.

she was only 16 years old, and my grandfather just couldn't take it. He told the Mother, "I have been doing *puja* to you all these years, but no more. You took the light away from my home, so I will not light another lamp for you."

I was only a kid when I first heard this story, maybe 10 years old. But it didn't sound right to me—when somebody dies, you stop worshiping? Why should something that has been in place for six generations be allowed to just die out? I thought, "Maybe when I'm older, I'll restart this tradition." So in my early 20s I began looking for someone to teach me the *Lalita Sahasranama*, one of the most important prayers to the Divine Mother. In fact, I asked my first guru, who had initiated me into Subramanya worship, if she would teach it to me.

"How old are you right now?" she asked me.

"21," I said.

She replied, "Hmm, 21 and he wants to learn the *Lalita Sahasranama*! What do you think this is? Go finish your studies, get a job, get married, have children. Then come back to me and I'll teach it to you."

Well, I couldn't help thinking, "This woman is already 68 years old; by the time I finish all of that, she'll be long gone!" She looked at me and laughed. "All right, you rascal, I know what you're thinking!" Then in a more sober voice she added, "The desire to learn this has been planted in your mind, so when you are ready—even if you are in the middle of nowhere, on a deserted island, in any godforsaken place—somebody will appear and teach it to you. Take it from me."

One day in Lusaka, Aiya recounted this bit of personal history to his friend Balasubrah-manyam, a senior Brahmin colloquially known in the community as "Balu." An ethnic Tamil like Aiya, Balu was in his mid-60s at the time (Aiya was in his 30s) and served as chief engineer at the Zambia Electricity Transmission Company, the state-owned power corporation. When Aiya finished his tale, he wistfully added, "So here I am, 6,000 miles from home in Africa. Who is going to teach me the *Lalita Sahasranama* now? I guess the time is still not right."

In a soft voice, Balu replied, "*I know the Sahasranama*. My grandfather taught it to me, and I will teach it to you."

Fueled by an enthusiasm built up over decades of waiting, Aiya's tutelage was head-spinningly rapid. It began just a few days later, during *Shivaratri* observances,[110] when Balu led him through five full recitations of the lengthy hymn in a single all-night sitting. The next day Aiya acquired a portable tape recorder and began listening to the *Sahasranama* day and night—at work, at home, while driving. "Within one week I committed the whole thing to memory," he said. "I mastered it. And soon afterward we began including the *Lalita Sahasranama* in our Friday *pujas* at the house."

That development drew the attention of Brahmins in the community, who were unaccustomed to—and not necessarily pleased by—the spectacle of a non-Brahmin chanting the venerable prayer. "Whenever I'd turn around and look there would be new faces at our *pujas* all the time, people I had never seen before," Aiya recalled. "Some came out of simple curiosity—to see if I was doing a good job of it, or just chopping up and murdering the thing. But still others came because they were genuinely interested in what was going on."

Among those more open-minded souls was Dr. Ramaswamy, then dean of engineering at the University of Zambia and a close friend of Balu. One day he arrived at Aiya's *puja* with a companion in tow—a new colleague from the physics department, visiting from India. It was, of course, Guruji, who remembers being distinctly impressed by what he saw and felt.

"Haran was already quite a respected teacher by the time I met him," Guruji recalled. "He was singing *bhajans* of Satya Sai Baba; they had a very active group going on there in Lusaka. I thought to myself, 'There is true devotion among the people here. Here's a place resonant with vibrations of a divine personality; here the Devi is present in her full glory. Here there is the possibility of achieving *shaktipat* by way of spreading happiness and joy to many people.'"[111]

The sense of burgeoning potential flowed in both directions. During the *puja*, Aiya watched as Guruji displayed the corresponding hand *mudras*—a telltale sign of the Sri Vidya adept—and his mind reeled with hope. "I remember thinking, 'If I ask him, and if he can initiate me into Sri Vidya, then maybe I can revive the great tradition of Devi worship that used to be in my family before," he said.

110   *Maha Shivratri* is a major annual Hindu festival honoring the Supreme God Shiva, said to be the day he married the Goddess in the form of Parvati. Devotees generally stay awake all night in worship. The *Shivratri* Aiya refers to occurred on Tuesday, March 7, 1978.

111   For the full story of their meeting in Aiya's own words, see his foreword to this volume.

After the *puja*, Balu introduced Aiya to Guruji, and the two of them conversed briefly—Guruji complimented Aiya on the *puja*, but suggested a few minor changes in pronunciation and technique. Aiya listened carefully and noted the corrections, but said very little—Guruji's presence disarmed him entirely.

Later that night, after the *puja* attendees dispersed, Aiya talked to Balu (who had already known Guruji for some time through Dr. Ramaswamy) and learned a bit more about this unusual physicist—including the fact that both Anakapalle Gurugaru and Sri Krishnamurthy had given him *purnadiksha*, thereby authorizing him to become a guru to others. Even at this early date, scholar Corinne Dempsey observed, Guruji had already acquired "a reputation for both spiritual precocity and unconventional thinking."

So Aiya asked Balu, as a close friend and as a Brahmin, whether it would be appropriate to approach Guruji and ask for initiation. Balu replied there was no harm in asking, and arranged for the two men to meet privately a few days later. When Aiya made his request, Guruji immediately agreed, brushing off the Brahmin/non-Brahmin distinction as irrelevant. The only question was when the *diksha* should take place. Aiya recalled:

> We walked into the living room where Balu was sitting with Guruji's wife, Annapurna. Guruji said, "Anu"—that's what he called her—"can you bring the *panchangam*, the almanac? I am going to give Haran initiation; we just need to decide on the date." But in the brief interval it took for her to go and retrieve the almanac, he changed his mind and said, "Oh, why bother with formalities? Let me just ask her directly."
>
> And he sat down and closed his eyes. His body was so still, not a muscle flickering anywhere. I thought, "Oh my God, after all this Mother is going to tell him, 'Don't give this fellow anything! Chase him out of here! End of story!'" Those two minutes he spent in meditation were the longest, most difficult two minutes of my life!

But he finally opened his eyes and said, "All right, I'll come to you on *purnima* day, the full moon, this coming 5th of October [1979]. It's a Friday, a very great and auspicious day. I'll give you initiation then." And that was it. On the appointed day, my wife and I prepared everything and waited for him. Guruji arrived exactly at noon, and did *puja* until eight in the evening. It was 1:34 p.m. when he gave me the mantras.

After that, I wasn't sure of the appropriate guru *dakshina*—how to repay him for the initiation.[112] So I asked him outright and he replied, "Whatever I have given to you, you must give to others, without regard to their caste, creed, gender or ethnicity. That is the only *dakshina* I want from you."

"When Haran came to see me and asked me, very hesitantly, for initiation into Sri Vidya, I gladly accepted him as my spiritual son," Guruji said.[113] In all, he initiated Aiya and Sakuntala Amma into 16 Sri Vidya mantras, including the Maha Shodashi, and later taught them "the intricacies of performing *Sri Chakra Navavarana Puja* according to the Dattatreya tradition." Aiya, for his part, displayed a nearly insatiable depth of curiosity over every nuance and subtlety of Sri Vidya liturgy.

"When I met Haran, he was a live wire!" Guruji said years later, joking about the intensity of those months together in Lusaka. "I made the fundamental mistake of trying to correct some errors in his pronunciation, and the next thing you know I had become his guru! That was a real problem! If I hadn't made that error, I would probably have been an ordinary person today!"

As the relationship and collaboration between Aiya and Guruji deepened, the problem of Brahmin prejudice, such as it was, soon faded as well. "Guruji never discussed it with me, but I heard through the grapevine that a few of the Brahmins actually confronted him on the issue," Aiya confided. "Guruji Amma told me later that she had never seen him so angry! After that, no one had the courage to confront him again."

But they were still watching Aiya. What would he do with this long-exclusively-Brahmin knowledge? Would it have any effect at all on this presumptuous man and his ever-more-popular *puja* gatherings?

112 *Guru dakshina* is a traditional form of reciprocity between a student and teacher; a formal expression of acknowledgment, respect and thanks. The "repayment" is rarely monetary; it more commonly takes the form of a special task the teacher wants his or her student to accomplish. Guruji's statement to Haran Aiya is best understood in this way.

113 Guruji later confided to Aiya that he had seen 28 members of the Lusaka community who would become his disciples–"some were Brahmins, some were not"–in meditation long before he left for Africa.

"Well, in two months' time, they saw the change taking place in me," Aiya said. "Because when deep change begins to take place inside a person, it's going to manifest on the outside as well. And they started thinking, 'My God, maybe this fellow really *got* something! What if we missed the bus?' And quietly—one by one by one—they too went and asked Guruji for initiation. And Guruji, with no hesitation whatsoever, gave it to them."

A rich period of spiritual common purpose ensued, which Balu would later credit to the Goddess's grace in bringing Guruji to Africa:

> How else can one explain the fact that the many who so aspired, in this far-off city of Lusaka and this far-off land of Zambia, found their Guru at the right time? And what is more, [that] the Guru came to Zambia, unbeknown to the *shishyas*-to-be, as if in search of them. One can only say *She* willed [it] and things happened. ... The acceptance of any[one, regardless of caste] as a *shishya* and an *upasaka*, and the Mantras which were to be given, were all as revealed to *Guruji* by *Sri Devi*. Blessed indeed are those who were thus initiated in Lusaka![114]

Aiya's daughter Saru, though only a child of seven at the time, fondly remembers one of her first encounters with Guruji. "My most vivid early memory of him took place at his home in Zambia," she said. "Any time Aiya went over there he'd bring me along. That day Guruji was in his shrine room, just finishing a *Navavarana Puja*, and all I could see was this beautiful red fruit—some sort of African plum, I think—sitting under the little pedestal where he kept his Meru. I kept staring at it while he and my father were talking; for some reason I thought it was the most beautiful fruit I'd ever seen. And Guruji must have noticed because, as we were leaving, he leaned down and handed me that fruit, saying, 'Here, this is for you.' I still think it was the most delicious thing I ever tasted!"

On any number of levels, Guruji was getting an on-the-job crash course in spiritual leadership. He was invited to perform weddings, something he'd never done before. He was asked to consecrate an idol of Lalita Devi, another ritual he had never performed. He became a driving force in the founding of Sri Lakshmi Narayana Temple—Zambia's first Hindu temple, in Lusaka—and played a pivotal role in establishing the Amman Temple in the smaller city of Kafue, 30 miles away through remote grasslands teeming with elephants, lions and hippopotamuses. Both temples still thrive today—and three decades after their founding, a newspaper story on the Kafue Temple still noted Guruji's and Haran Aiya's contribution:

> In 1979, ten devotees constructed a hall to meet the needs of devotees visiting the temple. ... On the suggestion of Mr. Vijaya Haran [sic] and Dr. N. Prahlada Sastri [sic], a Professor at the University of Zambia, who were expounding Lalitha worship, it was God's will that Lalitha Ambigai (or Kanchi Kamakshi) be installed in the temple sanctum. The deity [was] specially made in India. The duo [Guruji and Aiya] visited India and brought the deity specially made of five-metal alloy [i.e., *panchaloha*] in Madras. At the installation of Lalitha Ambigai, along with a Maha Meru, on Masi Maham day in February 1980, it was suggested that her sons, Ganesh and Skanda, accompany the mother. Mr. N. Gananadha volunteered and brought the two deities, [also] made of *pancha loham* [sic], from Jaffna, Sri Lanka. On 13th September 1980, Dr. N.P. Sastri installed Ganesh and Skanda at the temple.

Guruji accomplished all these tasks, he said, by following Gurugaru's advice and directly asking the Goddess to instruct him. "I only learned the mantras from my guru," he said. "Their inner meanings, their deeper meanings—and the deeper aspects of how to conduct the *pujas* and such things—these were all taught to me directly by Lady Saraswati."

It was autumn of 1979 when Guruji and Aiya first met. The next spring Aiya's contract with the Zambian government reached its end, and he left for the United States to take a new position with an architectural firm in Rochester, NY. Shortly thereafter, Guruji completed his visiting professorship and returned to India. But the pair's six months together in Lusaka were transformative. "It's hard to believe that it all happened in such a short period of time," Saru said. "In my mind, those days were like a golden age—they seemed to go on forever."

Guruji's family shared the distinct impression that they were experiencing a precious moment. "Our time in Zambia entailed so many firsts for me," said daughter Radha. "It was my first time flying, my first time living in a new country, seeing so many new sights, peoples and cultures. It was such an exciting time, too, being drawn into the magical web of Haran Aiya's *pujas* and music and enthralling stories."

No one, however, was as deeply affected as Aiya himself. "That brief time completely changed my life, the life of my family, and the lives of everyone around me at that time," he said. "Everything took on new dimensions, extraordinary depth; in the realm of *puja*, we understood more and more of what we were chanting and why. Everything completely changed."

Aiya later told a fellow disciple that just before he left Lusaka for the United States, "he prostrated to Guruji, who cupped his feet on Aiya's head and imparted to him much of his energy. In Aiya's words, *that* is what changed everything for him."

During his months in Lusaka, Guruji had recommenced his practice of delivering weekly "Sunshine Lectures"—only now they were hosted at Aiya's home. "I lectured on various topics connected with my experiences," he said. "On the Sri Vidya, Kundalini Yoga, Tantra and various other aspects, including the *Dasa Mahavidyas*—the 10 Great Paths to Liberation."[115] The *Mahavidya* lectures were, in fact, collected into a now-coveted, limited-run book—usually referred to as the *Lusaka Notes*—that was personally illustrated by Guruji himself and privately published in Zambia in 1980.

On April 26, 1980, "Aiya, his wife and their young daughter [Saru] immigrated to the United States, commissioned with blessings from Guruji to spread the secret teachings of Sri Vidya," Dempsey wrote. In the years that followed, "Aiya, conveniently armed with the personality of a maverick, one for whom elitism is particularly irksome, began teaching students from all walks of life. His eventual establishment of an elaborate, ritual-centered temple"—at first named the Kanchi Peetham and housed in the garage of his Rochester home, now known as Sri Rajarajeshwari Peetham, and spread over a

115 Material from a number of these lectures is included in *The Goddess and the Guru, Volume II*. Most of the Lusaka "Sunshine Lectures" were recorded but the cassettes remain untranscribed in a private collection.

sprawling parcel in the rural suburb of Rush—"emerged as part of a natural progression. From this point in Aiya's life, obstacles were less daunting and openings plentiful."

For Guruji as well, Lusaka marked a pivotal new beginning. "Bombay was, for him, more about meditating, acquiring knowledge and learning some ritual from Sri Krishnamurthy," daughter Rama said. "It was during our stay in Zambia that Guruji's *own* approach to ritual practice really began to evolve."

श्री The back cover of
the *Lusaka Notes*, drawn
by Guruji in 1979.
(Sri Vidya Trust)

11   A Path Fraught with Danger

Guruji's sojourn in Zambia was transformative on multiple levels. As a distinguished visiting university professor, he enjoyed an excellent salary, liberal benefits and the high social status of a renowned nuclear physicist. Almost as a bonus, the posting had also afforded him an escape, at least temporarily, from the missile defense work that so troubled him at TIFR, as well as an opportunity to immerse himself in the pure scientific theory, research and teaching that he loved best.

At the same time, it was in Lusaka that Guruji first truly came into his own as a spiritual leader and a guru. While he had already begun this transition before ever leaving Bombay—lecturing widely, performing scores of *pujas* and taking on a modest number of disciples—it was in Africa that Guruji first became the center of a large and growing spiritual community; that his teachings began to be preserved, distributed and treasured; that he was first called upon to preside over large *pujas, homas* [fire rituals] and other events; and that he directly participated in the establishment of a temple.

He had, in other words, become a full-fledged guru with a large and growing flock of *shishyas*—including, interestingly in light of his increasingly peace-oriented mission, several members of the Indian military.

"My brother Prasad Rao and his wife Sundari became my first disciples in Bombay," Guruji recalled.[116] "Then came Wing Commander Mehta from the Indian Air Force. A few persons like him—from squadron leaders to combat pilots—were posted right there at TIFR to provide input to the research staff. Then in Lusaka, there was Dr. Ramaswamy and Dr. Balasubrahmanyam and his wife. Then Wijayaharan and Sakuntala. Then about 30 or so more in Lusaka, Kafue and Mufulira, all in Zambia."

Asked what it was like to become Guruji's first disciple, Sundari Amma was charmingly self-effacing. It happened in June of 1978, she said, when the family gathered to observe the first anniversary of Guruji's mother's passing.

"Guruji was sitting in his *puja* room when he suddenly called out, 'Sundari, come here; I want to give you mantra *diksha*,'" she recalled. "I was such an ignoramus then—I hardly knew what a guru was or what mantras were! So I actually yelled back, 'I'm busy making coffee!' That's how foolish I was! But his grace and fervor for teaching were such that he asked Amma to come into the kitchen and take over so I could go in and learn. And that's what I did. He initiated me into all the Sri Vidya mantras that day, from Ganapati all the way up to Maha Shodashi. He even wrote them down for me! And that's how I became his first disciple—from there, all the others followed!"[117]

They followed indeed, their number expanding steadily—even exponentially—on an almost daily basis. Significantly, many who took initiation during this crucial early period went on to establish affiliated shrines and temples in Canada, Australia and England. "The Sri Vidya *upasana* which was imparted to these people spread from this starting point to various other countries," said Guruji. "Today you see *peetams* established in all these countries, and who knows how many more places in times to come—because the real *peetam* is inside every person, if only they could realize it."

Guruji also transformed physically during his African sojourn. He slimmed noticeably and fully grew out his familiar white beard (though it was more salt-and-pepper in those days), while also adopting the simple "cotton shirt and *dhoti*" dress style that would become his signature. (Prior to that, he had generally remained clean-shaven and dressed in a more Western fashion, at least in his professional life.)

117 Sundari Amma later came to enjoy considerable renown for her Bombay *satsangs*, in which she shared Guruji's teachings with a generation of urban, middle-class women. She observed: "To many people like me, leading a narrow life up until then, Guruji revealed the possibilities of the human existence. In Bombay, people praise me for my *satsangs*. But I simply took Guruji's words, which were revelations from Devi herself, and repeated them like a tape recorder! So of course the *satsangs* were good–but the credit is his, not mine."

Guruji's African experience was also highly satisfying in terms of his own *sadhana*. Time and again his meditations yielded stunning visions and revelatory interactions with the Goddess. With each new encounter, he felt more compelled to share what he learned with as many people as wanted to hear it. During this time, the Goddess appeared less often in the form of Saraswati and more frequently as Sri Bala Tripurasundari; that is, Goddess Lalita in the form of a nine-year-old girl. And it was in this guise that she began urging him to leave his job at TIFR and fully devote himself to her service.

"Why do you need that job?" Bala would ask him. "You have attained a high level of spiritual practice that can no longer be confined by your professional status. Quit your job and stay with me. I will provide everything you need."

"That sounds so good," Guruji had to admit. "You have infused me with your being. You have taught me the sacred scriptures. You have shown me many worlds. I am giving your mantras to all who seek them. Performing *pujas* has become my way of life. But I am not a rich man. If I abandon my only livelihood, then what will I do? What about my responsibilities in the world? Who will feed my family? My daughters are still young and their education is not yet complete."

"Don't be silly," the Goddess replied. "Are you their caretaker or am I? They are *my* family. *I* am the Mother. *I* am the provider. And *you* also are in my care. Nothing bad will happen to any of you, I assure you. You are safe and sound in my arms."

So it was in this altered state of body and mind that Guruji guardedly returned to his job of more than two decades. Yet for TIFR it was business as usual: Sastry the scientist was unceremoniously reassigned to the Air Defense Division, and thrust immediately back into the very same dilemma he had gone to Africa to escape.

Committed to amicably working out a solution with his employers, Guruji met with senior administrators and painstakingly detailed the reasons for his reluctance to remain involved in missile development. In a *dénouement* surely hinting at Bala's play, the famously employee-friendly TIFR proved singularly unable to accommodate one of its most senior scientists. And indeed, Guruji conceded that perhaps nothing short of such intransigence would have sufficed to push him out of a job in which he had excelled and found intellectual fulfillment for years. "Yes, the challenges we faced there were immense," he acknowledged. "Yet I liked and enjoyed those challenges. I would never have left such an organization but for my own peace-loving nature."

Following internal procedure to the letter, Guruji formally appealed to TIFR's governing board for a transfer to a pure research position. Again, the result was counter-intuitive: his appeal was completely ignored; there was no response at all—and that snub was the final straw. He went home and told Amma, "I don't want to continue in this job any longer. I'm going to resign."

He explained, "I didn't tell anyone of my decision except for my wife. Because if I had talked to anybody else they would have said, 'What are you thinking? You're leaving a comfy job and a nice home? Things are going great for you!' But for me it was a moral decision, and Amma was perhaps the only one who would have understood that."

And she did. "If you don't want to stay, then don't stay," she told him. "Whether you have a job or not, you know your responsibilities. You'll share what you have and we'll make do. Whatever you decide, I am with you. Wherever you are happy, the children and I will be happy too. If you want to go into the jungle, we'll come there with you."

Amma later confided to daughter Radha that "when Guruji took the momentous decision to quit his job, it was like a veil of *maya* shrouded her and she could not even contemplate any obstacles. From that time on, it became her mission in life to help realize Guruji's vision."

Thus reassured, Guruji returned to TIFR to make his final stand. "I told them that I wanted to go back to pure physics," he said. "I didn't want anything to do with applications involving any kind of destruction—no way! They replied, 'Sorry, but you are too valuable in this role. We just can't let you go back to pure research.'

"So I said, 'To hell with your job, then. I quit.'"

And so the deed was done. After an exemplary 25 years of professional service at TIFR, Guruji formally resigned: his course was set. Yet the heady rush of freedom that accompanied this decisive break was tempered by its stark implications for his family.

"I had three *lakhs*," he said.[118] "Two *lakhs* from selling my house in Bombay and one *lakh* in total savings. So I knew at least that we wouldn't have to go and beg. We could manage to survive."

Still, it was a leap of faith far beyond any he had ever attempted. He split the funds into five equal parts: one for each of his three children, one for the Divine Mother, and the last for himself and Amma. Not surprisingly, most of their friends and relatives considered the move extremely ill-advised. "In the Indian context, marrying three daughters is a big responsibility," one longtime disciple explained. "Clearly, any conventional person who heard of this decision would have thought that Guruji was being foolish and irresponsible."

But Guruji and Amma were past worrying over petty judgments. Leaving the comfort and security of their established Bombay life behind, the family packed up and returned to Guruji's family home in Vizag.

It was 1981. He was 47 years old.

The family's move to Visakhapatnam from cosmopolitan Bombay certainly entailed major lifestyle changes: money would be tighter, living standards less modern, social expectations and dress codes a bit more conservative. However, the daughters of the house had never been particularly pampered or spoiled by their upbringing in India's splashy commercial and entertainment capital. True to his own parents' example, Guruji had always leaned toward "simple living and high thinking," Radha noted. "There were never any luxuries to speak of in Bombay anyway," Rama added. "We were always a simple family—new clothes bought only when necessary; even a birthday or a festival didn't necessarily warrant new clothes."

The teenagers were further weaned off Bombay's comforts during their two years abroad in Zambia, so there was no particular sense of trauma or dislocation. "It was all a big adventure," Radha shrugged. "We never really thought of the move to Vizag as destabilizing our lives in any way. I guess the enormity of the decision didn't really occur to us. Home was wherever our parents were, and that was all that mattered."

In many ways, in fact, the return to Vizag—which they had frequently visited during holidays and school breaks anyway—felt more like a family reunion than anything

118 Guruji is referring to money; i.e., he had ₹300,000, about US$40,000 at 1980 exchange rates, equivalent to about US$125,000 in terms of 2016 buying power. A *lakh* is 100,000 in Indian English.

119 Brother Nishtala Venkata Prasada Rao married Maheshwari (also called Sundari Amma); they had three children, son Srinivas, son Subba Rao and daughter Sri Vidya.

120 Guruji's sister Suryalakshmi married Ramalinga Swamy Gunturu (now deceased); they had four sons, Vijaya Subba Rao (now deceased), Narasimha Rao, Bhaskar and Gopala Krishna.

else. Guruji's younger brother Prasad Rao had himself moved back to the house a few years earlier.[119] Also resident there was the formidable Annapurna Tatamma, Guruji's widowed paternal aunt who had originally advised him to find a guru, and whom Anantalakshmi remembers as a "strong, independent and inspiring woman." Guruji's sister Suryalakshmi, who lived nearby with her husband and children, completed the family circle.[120]

"For the next three years we all lived together, and it was a great time for us cousins," Radha said. "My mom and my aunt [Prasad Rao's wife Sundari] complemented each other very well. Amma would do the cooking and my aunt would manage us at mealtimes, help us with our studies and generally maintain order."

The house's inner courtyard was its nerve center, dominated by a large mural of a clipper ship (painted by the artistic Radha in honor of her uncle Prasad Rao, who was in the marine shipping business). "It was always busy there," she said. Family, friends, tenants and neighbors would gravitate to the courtyard for "spiritual discussions, storytelling, music and dance, or just general gossip. I remember that when Guruji would begin one of his discourses, his childhood friend Mr. Avadhani—a Kali *bhakta* himself—would call out to the household, 'Prahlada is scattering pearls! Make haste and gather them!'"

The household was constantly abuzz with activity. "Innumerable social events, rituals, weddings and so on, were conducted in the house," Radha said.

"And dance!" Rama added. "Radha and our uncle's daughter Srividya were classical dancers, and among the tenants there was a lady dance teacher—so the house was always reverberating to the beats and melodies of dance lessons and practice sessions!"

On warm nights, the terrace atop the house provided a breezy, comfortable spot for socializing, reading, studying—or, in Guruji's case, more mystical endeavors. One hot summer evening, as the family carried their bamboo mats up the stairs to the roof to sleep under the stars, Guruji turned around and asked, "What day is it today?" Someone replied "*Chavithi*"[121]—to which he responded, "Ah, then no wonder Ganapati is leading the way!"

"He said he'd caught a glimpse of Lord Ganesh, with his trunk and large tummy, lumbering up the steps ahead of us all!" Radha recalled. Others saw mysterious visions at the house as well. Once Annapurna Tatamma, during evening prayers, saw

121 *Vinayaka Chavithi* or *Ganesh Chaturthi* is the Hindu festival celebrating the birth of Lord Ganesh (Ganapati or Vinayaka) as the son of the god Shiva and the goddess Parvati.

the shimmering image of a voluptuous woman richly decked in ornaments and veils, standing beside Guruji as he performed *aarti*.[122] On another occasion, a visitor who came to pick up a *yantra* from Guruji entered the house with his two young daughters and was later spotted by several people leaving the house with an otherworldly third young girl in tow.

Even for non-family, paying tenants, "the house was very lucky," Radha said. "Most of them moved on to their own homes." Anantalakshmi agreed that "whoever came to live there seemed to prosper, which is a truly wonderful thing."

In the midst of all this, Guruji—having made the professional leap from science to spirituality—plunged into his new vocation with a highly focused energy and gusto. The Goddess wanted him, he reasoned: now she had him. The question was: what next?

"I didn't want to go to the cinema; I didn't want anything," he said. "Nothing really interested me except going inside myself and meditating." Opening to the resultant inner flow, he listened continuously for direction, trying to divine exactly why the Goddess—still frequently visiting in the nine-year-old form of Bala Tripurasundari—had so urgently pressured him to leave TIFR and the material trappings of his successful professional life in Bombay.

With steadily increasing resolution and confidence, Guruji quickly began establishing a name for himself in his hometown—just as he had done at the Yoga Shakti Mission in Bombay, and among the South Asian expatriates in Lusaka. He again resurrected his "Sunshine Lectures," holding sessions in the house's courtyard every Sunday and drawing ever larger crowds.

He also hosted group recitations of the *Lalita Sahasranama*, led performances of the complex and intricate *Navavarana Puja*, and conducted other, mainly Goddess-related rituals on request for all comers. Straightforward though his efforts may appear today, they were decidedly revolutionary in the India of a generation ago (and would still seem so to many today). Sri Vidya was, once again, essentially a secret religious practice—basically impenetrable to anyone not either born into a particular Brahmin sub-caste or blessed by initiation and instruction from one of the practice's elusive gurus. Scholar Corinne Dempsey explained:

122 *Aarti* is a Hindu religious ritual, a part of *puja*, in which light from a lamp lit with wicks soaked in *ghee* (purified butter) or camphor, is offered to the deity.

From a theological perspective, the protection of Sri Vidya knowledge has to do with its potency. Many adepts object to the public mention of the main fifteen-syllable Sri Vidya mantra [i.e. the Panchadasi mantra], be it written or spoken, since its power is such that to utter it is "to enunciate the source of power that creates, maintains, then destroys the universe." Practitioners rightfully fear that misuse by the uninitiated could be particularly dangerous. When considering the issue of initiation, however, it seems that secrecy may have as much to do with caste as with theology. Although it is understandable that powerful, potentially dangerous, religious knowledge be handled by those with proper training, why is it so difficult—under traditional circumstances—to receive this training in the first place?

A partial response to this question [is] that as knowledge becomes scarce, its value increases, as does the perceived power of those possessing this knowledge. Secrecy, value, and power are thus intimately connected. ... [T]he Smarta Brahman community,[123] the segment of society typically associated with Sri Vidya, [has historically guarded] the tradition as a means for maintaining the privilege of their own community. The Smarta community's assumed exclusive access to specialized Sri Vidya knowledge helps them continue to claim ritual virtuosity during modern times, as well, and furthermore supports conservative understandings of caste and gender roles. Naturally there are Sri Vidya *upasakas* who defy caste values and gender distinctions, depending on lineage and individual inclination, but ... few in South India dare to do so.

123 Smarta Brahmin is the Hindu caste and community into which Guruji was born.

Guruji, of course, was resolutely among those who *did* dare. But while his efforts in opening Sri Vidya to a wider audience may have disrupted traditional forms of transmission, they never represented a conscious or focused effort to "break the Brahmin monopoly." In Guruji's mind, caste differences were but another man-made distinction, not unlike vegetarianism and non-vegetarianism; that is, a form of social labeling that served mainly to distract aspirants from the serious business of *sadhana*. "I was trying to shed my Brahmin 'brand' and embrace a more inclusive caste," Guruji said. "The caste of all human beings who aspire to, and are therefore eligible for, spiritual *sadhana*."

In a brochure from this period, Guruji stated that his goal was to bring "yoga and meditation within the reach of all, to promote social harmony between similar and dissimilar cultures of the world," and to spread "learning and worship, permitting access to one and all without any discrimination of caste, color or creed."

In another pamphlet he wrote that Sri Vidya's Goddess had counterparts around the world: "Hindus call her Gayatri, Christians call her the Virgin Mary, Buddhists call her the Compassion, Sufis call her the Movement; other ancient religions simply call her Mother Earth. She is our source, our sustenance and our end. She is Kundalini, the power moving us toward the unity of all life."

And since Sri Vidya arguably represented the planet's most ancient, fully developed and historically uninterrupted form of Goddess worship, Guruji felt his best contribution would be to "bring about an awareness of and interest in the minds of people about the *Sri Chakra Puja* and Devi *pujas*" as a means of spiritual advancement independent of one's faith or belief system.

In sum, Guruji ultimately spread knowledge of Sri Vidya not because he harbored any broad social agenda, but because he saw no sense in secrecy. He had witnessed and experienced the practice's power to effect personal and social empowerment and transformation. He had found bliss and liberation in its practice, and wanted to help others access the same sort of happiness, power and creative energy. In a world of isolation and alienation, he felt that Sri Vidya offered people a way to connect and find their common source. In a world beset with division and violence, it encouraged love and mutual respect.

The idea that such a positive and altruistic practice could somehow threaten either personal or societal stability struck him as patently absurd.

"Sri Vidya means 'sacred learning,'" Guruji explained during a talk in mid-1980s, in a fairly early explanation of his approach. "It is a large body of rituals held secret for ages, restricted only to priests because of the immense powers that the learning unfolds with practice. The idea [of the tradition's secrecy] was that destructive powers should be not be made available to minds lacking discipline and compassion."

These "destructive powers" involved pure *shakti*, the uncontrolled energy believed to be at play in the direct worship of the Goddess—as opposed to the "safer," more modulated energy involved in approaching her indirectly as the subordinate consort of a male god. It was (and still widely is) believed that "goddesses bear a seemly, auspicious demeanor when they are subjected to the will of their husbands or consorts—that is, when they serve within the [socially and cosmically safe and predictable] structures that their spouses provide." Direct worship of the Goddess, by contrast, meant invoking dangerous "powers of illusion, natural forces, and energy in a pure form, beyond the control of any governing, restraining structure."

As a result, the practice of Sri Vidya came to be seen as "fraught with danger." Indeed, it was popularly believed "that the worship of Śrī-chakra is elaborate, complex and hazardous, and very few people would venture to undertake it," as one scholar-practitioner noted in the 1980s. Another scholar of the period observed, "Even today, the Dravidian-speaking sections of southern India give evidence—through puberty rites, menstrual taboos, and widow restrictions—of greater concern for controlling and containing female powers than do the Indo-Aryan linguistic regions of the north," another observed.

These human "female restrictions" were both implicitly and explicitly extended to the Divine Feminine—with the result that direct worship of the Mother Goddess came to be considered a risky undertaking best confined to temples and solitary ascetics. Since any inadvertent ritual error or innocent mispronunciation of a mantra could invite disaster, even devout householders avoided Sri Vidya practice at home.

This then was the social and religious context within which Guruji first began promulgating his comparatively radical philosophy of openness and inclusion. "There was so much fear of worshiping the Mother in those days," his sister Suryalakshmi recalled. "Not just fear of performing rituals like *Sri Chakra Puja*; people were scared to even read a hymn like the *Sri Lalita Sahasranama*. They were afraid it would cause disruption in their lives."

Without ridiculing or dismissing these deeply ingrained superstitions, Guruji argued that they were based on social prejudice and chauvinism, not spiritual truth.

"Guru Dattatreya was given to Atri, a sage, and his wife Anasuya,"[124] he said, "which indicates that one *can* be a householder and still do *sadhana*. He was openly ritualistic and a great Tantric. He taught the worship of Shakti to people from all classes. His system was called *Kaula*,[125] meaning 'total'—internal as well as external worship."

Accordingly, Guruji's teachings in Vizag during this period display repeated reassurances and deep compassion toward his students, especially women. He went out of his way to assure them that the Divine Mother would never seek to harm them, that they were all her children and she sought only to love and protect them. "People used to stream in throughout the day to listen to him," Sundari Amma recalled. "He would sweep away their fear and apprehension, and awaken within them new enthusiasm, devotion and faith."

For example, just before Guruji left for Africa, Sundari Amma's mother told him she was worried her daughter was practicing Sri Vidya in his absence. "What if something goes amiss in the *pujas* or mantra *japa* while you are away?" she asked him. Guruji took the elder woman's hands in his own and replied, "Dear lady, do not worry about your daughter. If she makes any mistakes I will absorb them and give over to her whatever merits she receives. The Divine Mother's grace is with us, so what do we have to fear?" Noted Sundari Amma, "This image of the guru offering my mother *abhaya*—absolving her from fear—holds a special place in my heart."

Suryalakshmi added, "He taught people as a *satguru*[126]—as 'one who dispels the darkness'—that the Goddess is a gentle mother, loving, kind, doting, and compassionate. He taught them that it was okay to read and recite her hymns and prayers, to keep a Sri Chakra in their home, to do *puja* to Rajarajeswari, Kali, Saraswati—to all of these goddesses and more."

Guruji gradually instilled confidence in his followers that anyone could pray to the Divine Mother—whenever, wherever and however they wished. And in time, with his encouragement and Amma's example, more and more women (and men) began actively participating in his *pujas* and recitations. Before long, many were independently organizing and leading recitations, prayers, rituals and other homages to the Goddess on their own.

124 In the *Ramayana*, Anasuya was the wife of an ancient Indian rishi named Atri. She lived with her husband in a small hermitage on the southern edge of the forest of Chitrakuta. Known for her piety, austerities and devotion, she had attained miraculous powers though her religious practices. When Sita and Rama visited her during their exile, she was exceptionally kind and respectful. In return, they granted her the blessing of giving birth to Lord Dattatreya, the primordial divine guru who encompasses the trinity of Brahma, Vishnu and Shiva.

125 The meaning of *Kaula* is further discussed in "Introduction: The World of Sri Vidya" in *The Goddess and the Guru, Volume II*.

126 *Satguru*, or *sadguru*, means a "true guru," or advanced spiritual preceptor, as distinguished from other forms of gurus such as music instructors, scriptural teachers, parents and so on.

127 Smt. A.B. Bala Kondala Rao is "one of the prime disciples of Guru Vempati Chinna Sathyam" of Chennai, and has been for nearly 50 years "a guiding light and an inspirational beacon in the field of Kuchipudi the world over."

128 Roxanne Kamayani Gupta is a classical Indian dancer, scholar of comparative religion and Indian culture, and yoga teacher who took initiation in Sri Vidya from Guruji in 1988. She first traveled to India in 1973 to study dance and became deeply involved with Indian spirituality. She is also an initiate of Kriya and hatha yoga and has been teaching yoga since 1974. She conducted her Ph.D. research in Banaras on the Kina Rami Aghoris, a radical Tantric sect. The author of *A Yoga of Indian Classical Dance: The Yogini's Mirror* as well as several scholarly publications, she is also the founder of Surya Namaskar for World Peace.

129 A central Sri Vidya scripture narrating the mythological exploits of the goddesses Lalita Tripurasundari and Bala Tripurasundari.

130 Balakka's finished ballet, titled *Lalitha Parameshwari* (Supreme Goddess Lalita) enjoyed a successful U.S. premiere in September 2016.

One prominent example involved the renowned classical Kuchipudi dancer, Smt. A.B. Bala Kondala Rao. "Balakka," as she is widely known, has performed around the world but remains based in Visakhapatnam, where she founded the Kuchipudi Kalakendra dance school.[127]

Balakka first met Guruji in the 1980s and, while she never took formal *diksha* from him, she "was inspired by him and Devipuram to compose many dances and even full-length dramas on the theme of the Goddess," said Roxanne Kamayani Gupta, an American religious scholar and herself one of Balakka's dance disciples.[128] "This emphasis on the Goddess is a recent development in the Kuchipudi dance-drama tradition, which for the past several hundred years has concentrated mainly on stories related to Lord Krishna."

At one point, Balakka decided to create a ballet based on stories from the *Lalitopakhyana*.[129] In working out the choreography, she consulted with Guruji to ensure that her work reflected authentic Sri Vidya tradition, and he designed a simplified Sri Chakra for use in a pivotal episode of the performance. Gupta explained the "extraordinary" experience that followed:

Balakka has her own creative process while composing dances and dramas, but this one was very different: she found that she could not concentrate on anything mundane. She was in an altered state of consciousness and couldn't sleep at night due to the intense energy moving through her body. It was almost more than she could bear. Again she went to Guruji for advice, and he told her to undertake a *Sri Chakra Puja* to pacify the goddess. Performed on the actual Sri Chakra Guruji designed for the drama, it was a breathtaking ritual undertaken by Balakka and all her disciples. The *puja* not only calmed the Goddess's energy within Balakka, it infused the dance space with its blessings. "I didn't want to remove it," she said. "I just wanted to spend time meditating there." Following Guruji's advice, her Lalita ballet came to fruition and was hailed by audiences and critics alike as a sublime experience, akin to a living *darshan* of the Goddess.[130]

This episode, Gupta noted, "just goes to further show how profoundly Guruji has changed the spiritual landscape of Vizag and its environs, infusing it with the Goddess's energy."

ॐ
ह्रीं

But while compassion, openness and nonjudgment have loomed large in Guruji's teachings from the beginning, he rarely allowed himself similar latitude or leniency in his personal spiritual practice.

"Partially because of his background, Guruji did operate in a mode of exceptional freedom," explained longtime disciple Alok Baveja, a professor of business management at Rutgers University. "He flourished under freedom and, by his nature, he wanted his disciples to enjoy the same level of freedom. But in his personal *sadhana*, he was always extremely disciplined. Not expecting others to do disciplined *sadhana* doesn't mean that he himself was not disciplined."

Especially in those early years, few would have made the mistake of assuming so.

Guruji in the 1980s was a formidable, even slightly intimidating figure with a powerful, focused gaze that hinted at an intensity, passion and force of will that he rarely displayed in later years. By the early 2000s, Guruji was projecting a much warmer, more grandfatherly personality, becoming almost disarmingly casual and approachable. It became common to hear visitors and disciples refer to him in fond diminutives involving terms such as "cute," "sweet" and even "like an Indian Santa Claus."

"When you looked at Guruji in the last 10 years of his life, he just seemed like this nice old guy, in the usual, next-door-neighbor sort of a way," said Megha Chatterjee, a New Delhi journalist based in Toronto. "You really had to keep reminding yourself, 'Wait a minute, he was this important nuclear scientist! He's a guru; thousands of people come and fall at his feet!'"

And this was, in many ways, exactly how Guruji liked it—this sort of humble accessibility helped defuse people's self-consciousness and self-doubts, removing some of the primary barriers to spiritual practice. But at the same time, it could also lead them to underestimate the depth and breadth of his accomplishment.

"He does seem very unassuming nowadays," said Balasingam Janahan, or "Jana," a business executive based in Irvine, CA, and a seasoned Vedic priest for the area's

Hindu community. "He basically dismisses a lot of his own spiritual achievements and downplays a lot of the abilities that he used to share with us. But back then, you immediately knew there was something very unusual about him. He wasn't so famous yet, but he had an extremely charismatic, even magnetic personality. His eyes had an almost hypnotic intensity."

This "stricter" version of Guruji emerged most strongly when he worked with disciples displaying high aptitude, or promise as teachers themselves. "Let me tell you unequivocally, Guruji in those days was not the way he is now," Jana said. "You almost wouldn't recognize him as the same Guruji that I first met in the 1980s."

Haran Aiya, however, argued that—despite appearances to the contrary—Guruji remained essentially the same. "He really never changed," Aiya said. "It may sometimes have appeared on the surface that he was stricter in the beginning and gradually became more permissive and open with the passage of time—but in truth, he didn't change. He simply measured what should be given to different people in different times and circumstances. Remember, 'Sri Matre Namah'—'the one who measures'—is the first name in the Lalita Sahasranama."

Jana conceded that, even in the early days, Guruji modulated his approach to suit the capacity of his audience. "Yes, he always kind of knew the level of people he was dealing with," he said. "In later times, he left it to individual students to make their own choices about sadhana once they were initiated. But back then, he would tell you his orders exactly. He would give precise directions on how you must do this and do that, detailed to the minutest point."

Jana was still a teenager when Guruji taught him his first puja, the Mahanyasam.[131] "He was a very strict teacher, with a very intense manner," he said. "He actually got short with me at a couple of points, to the extent that I felt kind of bad; I thought I was upsetting him." When Guruji noticed his student's distress, however, he explained, "No Jana, I am not angry at all. The reason I am hard on you is because I know you can do better, and I want you to get this exactly right."

"In those days," Jana added, "once you were initiated as Guruji's disciple—particularly if he saw you as a someone who could pass along his teachings—he would always check to make sure you were chanting the mantra, the number of times you were chanting it, the placement of your concentration—he would nurture you along

131 A ritual to Lord Shiva involving nyasa, the manual placement of divine energy into the worshiper's body.

every step of the way. And he would follow up frequently, asking questions about how your *sadhana* was progressing. Even when he was away, he would keep in touch by letters or ask you to call once in a while and bring him up to date on your *sadhana*."

Even novices sometimes enjoyed a high level of one-on-one attention. "During Guruji's first visit to Toronto, I explained that I didn't know Sanskrit," recalled Sundhara Arasaratnam, a retired management consultant in Newmarket, Ontario. "I was worried I wasn't pronouncing the mantras correctly. Instead of pointing me to 'teach-yourself' books, he sat down beside me and patiently taught me the basic Sanskrit letters—the vowels and the sets of consonants. Then he made a beautiful drawing that showed the locations of the chakras in our body, and how the Sanskrit letters map onto each of those chakras."

As time went on and the number of Guruji's disciples grew larger and too diverse for such personalized attention, he would create audio-visual aids enabling individuals at every level of knowledge and ability to practice at their own level, in their own time. While he continued teaching to groups throughout his life, Guruji's individual encounters became much more casual and relaxed.

"I asked him one time why he changed his approach like that and he told me, 'I want everyone to be able to feel comfortable coming to me, and to think of me more as a friend than as a teacher,'" Jana said. "And that's a really good explanation of what he did. Rather than always being the one who's teaching and telling people things, he wanted to share in others' knowledge as well. That is how he managed to work with people at so many different levels of knowledge. He always kept himself more or less at the same level as whoever he was talking with."

That included the very young. It was not uncommon at Devipuram to find Guruji sitting in the shade with a group of local village children, leading them through practice chants of the Sanskrit syllabary, as teachers have done in India for thousands of years.

"He has always had a unique way with children," noted Sriganesh Madhvanath (known as SriG), an early disciple who now lives in New York. "He has a deep understanding of the gift that children have for play and creative work, still uncorrupted by worldly convention and experience. He once joked to me that the difference between children and adults is that, when given a choice, children choose to play, and adults choose to eat!"

One summer, Guruji was staying with SriG in Bangalore for a few days, and trying to lose a few pounds by drinking vegetable smoothies. He thrilled SriG's then 11-year-old daughter by placing her in charge of their preparation. "He asked her to come up with a health drink of her choice every day by blending together any combination of raw vegetables she found in the kitchen—and he would drink whatever she came up with," SriG laughed.

On another occasion he challenged SriG's then nine-year-old son, who loved playing computer games, to brainstorm a gaming concept that would introduce players to the goddesses of the Sri Chakra. "My son came up with an idea where each goddess posed questions to three characters. If they were answered correctly the goddess would grant them a *siddhi*, or mystical power. Guruji was delighted and had my son formally present his work to everyone at the next *satsang*.[132] I can't think of an instance where my son felt more encouraged for his creative efforts."

132 A *satsang* is a spiritual discourse or sacred gathering; in this particular case a large gathering of Guruji's Bangalore disciples with Guruji presiding.

12 It Wasn't Meant for Them

Guruji had been in Visakhapatnam for about a year when the Goddess appeared to him with orders that would definitely shift the course of his life. Once again taking the child form of Bala Tripurasundari, she demanded, "*Nannagaru, naaku illu kattandi!* Father, build a home for me."

"A home?!" Guruji replied, laughing aloud. "Have you mistaken me for a king or a *zamindar*?[133] I am just a common man. I barely have a proper home myself anymore! How am I supposed to get one built for you?"

"Who says you don't have a home?" Bala answered him. "Is not what is mine also yours?"

"Fair enough!" Guruji replied. "Yours may be mine, mine may be yours. But it's a matter of resources—where would I ever find the money? I am sorry Mother, but I cannot build you a home. Perhaps you'll find someone better qualified than me to do this work."

"No, you'll build one for me," she said. "It has to be done by you, and no one else. You'll be able to build it soon."

Amma recalled, "In those days, Guruji was spending hours in meditation, and she kept telling him, '*Nannagaru, gudi kattu!*'[134] She used to show him images of old temples in his mind and ask, 'Should it be more like this? Or more like that?'"

133 Wealthy landowner

134 Father, build me a temple

135 A vast temple complex in Cambodia, Angkor Wat is the largest religious monument in the world, with a site measuring 162.6 hectares.

"She was showing me some very complicated designs—like Angkor Wat[135] and stuff like that," Guruji explained. "I told her, 'I can't handle that kind of a thing. Show me something simpler!'" And a few days later, she showed Guruji what he immediately recognized as the definitive vision of his home for the Goddess: a beautiful, modestly sized temple in the precise shape of a Sri Chakra Meru, fully populated with *yoginis* at every level, and Lalita, the Divine Mother herself, holding court at its pinnacle. Rousing himself from meditation, Guruji sat and drew a detailed sketch of the apparition, titling it *Manidveepa*—literally, "The Isle of Jewels"—the Goddess's heavenly abode in *Puranic* lore.

He took the sketch to a carpenter and commissioned a wooden model to be built. A few weeks later, it was complete. Constructed of wood and brass, and quite sizable at three-feet square and a foot-and-a-half high, the model detailed seven levels of the Sri Meru, complete with carefully cut lotus petals and triangles as well as miniature doors, windows, railings and stairways. Satisfied, Guruji took the model home, placed it in his shrine room, and asked Bala how she wished him to consecrate it.

The instructions she gave were very specific: Guruji would lead a holy pilgrimage, what she termed a *Ratha-Yatra*, or chariot procession, through the city to the seashore. But in this case Guruji himself would be the "chariot," walking barefoot while carrying the temple model on his head at the front of a procession of 108 *suvasinis*—married women, each representing an aspect of the Goddess—continuously reciting the *Lalita Sahasranama*. Upon reaching the shore, the procession would board a fleet of boats and cross the harbor by sea.

Its final destination was a place called Sagara Giri—literally, "Ocean Mount," a prominent hill in Visakhapatnam's Outer Harbour area on a rocky headland known as Dolphin's Nose, which juts dramatically into the Bay of Bengal at 358 meters (1,175 feet) above sea level. Near its summit, the stately white Kanaka Durga Temple commands a sweeping view of the city and the sea. Upon reaching this holy sanctuary of the Divine Mother, participants in the procession led by Guruji would conduct an elaborate *Sri Chakra Puja*.

The *Sagara Giri Durga Teppotsavam* ("Ocean Mount Floating Durga Festival") would begin promptly at 6 a.m. on Sunday, October 17, 1982—the first day of *Navratri*, and a moment astrologically designated as *abhijit prijith*,[136] meaning that any effort

136 Flawless.

undertaken at that time would reach successful fruition. News of the event spread through Guruji's fast-expanding network of disciples and supporters; old-fashioned word-of-mouth carried the announcement even further afield. For good measure, leaflets were also scattered across Vizag. Within days, 108 women had volunteered to serve as *suvasinis* and chant throughout the procession.

Meanwhile, the Visakhapatnam Port Trust agreed to provide motorized transport boats to move participants from the city to the temple and back. Everything was falling into place perfectly—until the weather took a turn for the worse.

The skies grew ominously dark on the morning of Friday, October 15, and by afternoon a light rain had begun to fall. As Saturday morning dawned, the rain was pounding down hard and seemingly getting worse by the hour. By the time night fell on the eve of the Sunday procession, the Nishtala household was bursting with friends and relatives engaged in last-minute preparations. But rain was whipping the house in ferocious sheets driven by howling winds.

"This isn't going to happen," Guruji's brother Prasad Rao said as he grimly stared out at the weather. "No one is going to come. We'll have to reschedule."

"It doesn't matter," Guruji replied. "All 108 of the *suvasinis* are inside me anyway. I will complete the procession alone."

More bad news followed, however. Port officials called to report that the boats reserved for the event had swamped in the rain. Their engines were waterlogged and they would not be available for the event.

"Then we'll row," Guruji replied, unmoved.

Yet the situation continued to disintegrate.

As the night wore on, the power failed, plunging the crowded house into darkness. Amma had just finished laying out the ingredients for a massive batch of *laddus*[137] for the event. As she stood pondering what to do next, Guruji's sister Suryalakshmi lit a lantern and said, "Come on, let's get to work," and the two carried on their preparations in a dry, narrow passageway of the house.

Still the rain showed no sign of letting up. Guruji—who had been sitting by a window, glowering moodily out into the darkness—suddenly rose, entered the shrine room

137 Ball-shaped sweets.

138 "The system was located as a depression over west central Bay of Bengal at 0300 UTC of 15 October, with its centre near 15.5 deg. N, 86.5 deg. E, about 500 km south-east of Kakinada. ... The depression moved in a northwesterly direction [toward Visakhapatnam] and rapidly intensified into a severe cyclonic storm by the 16th early morning. ... [The] storm lay close to the coast on the 16th night, [and then] weakened rapidly. ... Fairly widespread heavy to very heavy rain was reported from the three northern coastal districts. ... The greatest amounts were recorded over the coastal areas of Visakhapatnam district with Bheemunipatnam [30 miles north of Visakhapatnam] recording an exceptionally heavy rain of 54 cm [21.25 inches]."

139 "Generally, the average 24-hour rainfall for the city is just 4–5 mm. But in the last 24 hours, the city received 101.4 mm of rainfall, something that has happened almost [three] decades after the massive rainfall that reported on October 17, 1982, when the city received 371.2 mm [14.61 inches] rainfall only in 24 hours."

140 The shehnai is a double-reed conical oboe of India, frequently played on auspicious occasions, such as weddings and temple festivities.

141 A "monument to hospitality," Turner's Choultry (built in 1892) is a rooming house for travelers.

and emerged again carrying the temple model. As everyone stared, he silently walked out into the courtyard and unceremoniously left the little temple sitting in the rain. Then he came back inside and sat down again. Whether by coincidence or miracle, the rain stopped completely within 15 minutes. Saying a quick prayer of thanks to the Divine Mother, Guruji carried the model back into the shrine room and went to bed.

That punishing *Navratri*-eve rainfall remains to this day Vizag's heaviest on record. Remembered by meteorologists as the Kakinada Severe Cyclonic Storm of 15–18 October 1982,[138] the storm dumped some "371.2 mm [14.6 inches] of rainfall [in only] 24 hours," between Friday and Saturday, October 16 and 17, before weakening suddenly and going out to sea.[139]

Under brooding gray skies, still drizzling rain and filled with whirling dark clouds, Guruji arose early the next morning, bathed, dressed and stepped outside. A few but far from all of the *suvasinis* and musicians had arrived. With the help of Prasad Rao, Guruji—bare-chested and barefoot as instructed—carried the model outside and hoisted it atop his head. A clarion blast of *shehnais*[140] announced the commencement of the event, and the small procession set off through the puddled streets toward the beach, amid a growing swell of women's voices chanting the *Lalita Sahasranama*. Hearing the commotion, people from around the neighborhood—most of whom had assumed the event was canceled—hurriedly dressed and ran to catch up. Before the procession reached the shore, all 108 *suvasinis* had arrived, and the ranks of participants were steadily swelling with disciples, friends, supporters and strangers alike.

Prasad Rao recalled, "We started from Turner's Choultry"[141]—a Visakhapatnam landmark located adjacent to the Nishtala family home—"and went onward to the ferry point for crossing over the channel, halting at all the temples along the way to offer coconuts and *haldi kumkum*, seeking the blessings of their respective deities."

Upon reaching the vast expanse of the Visakhapatnam waterfront, the participants boarded the nonmotorized replacement boats supplied by the Port Authority, with manual rowers sitting at the ready. The *suvasinis* were distributed between several boats; another carried Guruji, still carrying the temple model atop his head. Despite slow progress through choppy waves, still churning from the storm, "the procession eventually arrived safely at Sagara Giri without any untoward incidents," Prasad Rao said. When all had alighted, the procession began its slow ascent up the hill, with the women still chanting *Lalita Sahasranama* continuously.

Upon finally reaching the Durga temple, Guruji climbed onto the *simha vahanam*—a life-size statue of Goddess Durga's lion mount outside—and sat upon it as Suryalakshmi performed a preliminary blessing, breaking a coconut, lighting camphor and offering *aarti*. Then Guruji dismounted, carefully removed the model from his head, and—with the help of several participants—carried it into the Durga temple, whereupon the ritual began in earnest.

"Every negative thought was erased from our minds as Guruji performed the *Sri Chakra Puja*," Prasad Rao said. "In fact, I recall that at one point Mr. Pudipeddi Lakshmana Murthy"—an elderly disciple of Anakapalle Gurugaru—"had a vision of Durga shining within Guruji and he fell at Guruji's feet chanting Durga *stotras*. Guruji blessed him with *shaktipat*."

When the ceremony ended hours later, the sweets prepared the night before by Amma and Suryalakshmi and offered to the Goddess were distributed to all as *prasadam*. Just before sunset, the procession descended the hill to return to the city. "We were pleasantly surprised to see that the port staff had re-commissioned the power launches; they were all lined up at the embarkation point," Prasad Rao noted. The Sri Meru model was left behind as a gift for the temple and Guruji returned home, satisfied that the Goddess's wish had been fulfilled.

A few days later, however, a Kanaka Durga Temple trustee noticed the model during a routine tour and told the head priest, "It's fine for people to come and perform *pujas* here, but they need to take their things when they're done. They can't leave this here." Informed of this response, Guruji returned to the temple, retrieved the model and brought it home again. When Amma saw it back in the shrine room, she exclaimed, "What happened? Wasn't this a gift to the temple? What harm was it doing?"

"Don't worry," Guruji replied, thoughtfully regarding the miniature temple. "It seems it wasn't meant for them." Indeed, it appeared that the Divine Mother did not want him to hand off this vision of her "home" to anyone other than him.

श्री Vedic priest Sri Vemakoti Krishnayaji with the "cinema goddess" during the *Maha Devi Yagna*, Visakhapatnam, 1983. Guruji's handwritten titling can be seen below.
(Sri Vidya Trust)

13   The Cinema Goddess

Barely six months after the Sagara Giri procession, Bala appeared to Guruji again and revealed the reason why the temple model had been returned to him: because it was precisely that—a model. Now, she said, it was time to commence construction of a real-life temple based on its design.[142]

Guruji protested that, aside from having completed the Durga temple procession, none of his material circumstances had really changed: he still lacked the land, labor and funds to carry out any such building project. "If you wish it to happen," he told her, "I'm afraid you will have to make it happen yourself."

"Come on now, is this why you left your job? So you could sit around talking like that?" she replied. "This is my *sankalpa*, not yours.[143] You are just the doer. You should consider it a blessing that I chose you for this work."

"Of course I do!" Guruji said. "You know very well that I have always honored you and followed your wishes. But you also know that I have a family to take care of."

"Your children are my responsibility," Bala said once again. "Your future is my responsibility. Those who place their trust in me are always in safe hands."

"Then how do you want me to proceed?" he asked.

Bala instructed him to arrange a *Maha Devi Yagna*, an elaborate, 16-day Vedic fire ritual dedicated to the Goddess. She specifically cited the 610th name of the *Lalita*

142   Though many assert that the model was buried under the foundation stone of the Sri Meru temple, Guruji clarified this is not the case. After its return to their home, he said, he and Amma "kept shifting the model to different rooms, but–partially due to water damage–it did not last long." Like so many other things in life, he said, "it was there for some time, but not forever."

143   *Sankalpa* means a conception, idea or intention formed in the heart or mind, or a solemn vow or determination to perform or carry out that desire or intention.

144 Years later, Guruji would write in *Understanding Sri Chakra Puja*: "The nine-year-old form of Balaji is my Guru. It was she who demanded that the Sri Meru temple be built, and she who got it done."

145 The phrase *Avarana Devathas* here means basically the same thing as *Khadgamala Devis*, referring collectively to the deities who inhabit the nine enclosures of the Meru.

146 The four Vedas are the *Rig*, *Sama*, *Yajur* and *Atharva* Vedas, the foundational scriptures of Hinduism. The four ways of learning about God are *karma yoga* (selfless action), *jnana yoga* (philosophical research and wisdom), *raja yoga* (physical exercises and meditation), and *bhakti yoga* (devotional service).

147 Guruji is referring to the subtle energy centers of Kundalini Yoga, which are visualized as lotuses having various numbers of petals. The *Muladhara* is the lowest, foundational "root" center, and has four petals.

148 Guruji is using the British-Indian method of counting floors, in which the U.S. first floor is the British ground floor, the U.S. second floor is the British first floor, etc. Thus, by the U.S. system, Guruji contemplates a seven-story, not a six-story structure.

Sahasranama: "*Pratipan mukhya rakanta thithi mandala pujita*"—expressing her preference to be worshiped during the cycle of 15 *tithis* or lunar days beginning with *Pratipada*, roughly from the full moon to the new moon.

"Very well," said Guruji. "It will be done."[144]

He realized, however, that before he could inspire others to be enthusiastic about the temple, he needed to convey more precisely how it would look in real life. A fragment from Guruji's writings of this period lays out his ambitious early conception, similar to yet strikingly different from the structure that finally emerged a decade later:

> The temple will be 108 feet square and 72 feet high, like a rising pyramid. There will be 108 Sri Merus installed in the temple, one each under the foot of every *Avarana Devatha*.[145] At the ground level the temple will have four entrances, representing the four Vedas and the four main modes of learning about God.[146] These also represent the four petals of the *Muladhara Chakra*.[147] In this level will be four enclosures—the ten *siddhis*, eight divine furies and ten *mudra shaktis* will be installed here. In the next enclosure, the 16 lunar *kalas* and in the third enclosure the eight powers of erotic love, Goddess Rati Devi, will be installed. The first floor of the temple represents the 14 worlds and the second floor represents 16 deities including the five senses and five motor organs. At the third-floor level, we find ten more deities; namely, the five subtle senses and five elemental states of the world. At the fourth floor level, the eight forms of Saraswati will be installed. At the fifth floor level, the *Shaktis* Saraswati, Lakshmi and Parvati are to be installed, along with Lalita Rajarajeswari at the sixth level.
>
> Thus the entire construction of the temple is a massive task of constructing six floors,[148] which will require enormous funds. In this structure, the installation of 108 deities and 108 Meru *Prastharas* is by itself a magnificent task requiring very high standards of sculpture, architecture and spiritual strength. A very rough estimate of the structural cost works out to around ₹50 *lakhs* [about US$1.25 million at the time].

Yet as Guruji began working out plans for this unprecedented Devi temple, many of his closest supporters worried that even his proposed *Devi Yagna* was a case of too much, too soon. "When he announced his intention to perform the *yagna*, Guruji's friends and relatives expressed deep concern," said Prasad Rao. "Frankly, we doubted the feasibility of a ritual of this nature and magnitude. We were well aware that Guruji had very meager funds to draw upon and virtually no organizational backup."

Confronting his brother, Prasad Rao asked, "Are we really in a position to bear all the expenses associated with a *Sri Devi Yagna*? Why do we have to do it right now? You've already made a magnificent attempt with the Sagara Giri ceremony. That's enough for now. Let's wait a bit and hold this *Devi Yagna* some other time."

Cynical though such sentiments appear in retrospect, they seemed more than reasonable at the time. As complex as the Sagara Giri event had been to organize and execute, a full *yagna* would require vastly more in terms of time, financial resources, planning, ritual knowledge and sheer manpower.

And even Guruji himself had no idea of how to begin.

So he made inquiries and soon learned of a priest named Sri Vemakoti Krishnayaji, who headed a small temple to the sun god Surya in the nearby village of Parvathipuram, and was said to be a specialist in complex Vedic *yagna*s. Guruji decided to pay him a visit.

Upon hearing Guruji's story, Krishnayaji readily agreed to perform the ceremony and immediately began listing off the various requirements: the offerings would have to be performed by a team of qualified *ritwiks*[149]—Krishnayaji could supply those; then there would have to be group chants—not only of the *Lalita Sahasranama* but also of the *Vishnu Sahasranama*.[150] The actual *pujas* to the Goddess would involve *kumkum*[151] offerings—by married women only, of course; no widows...

"Wait a minute," Guruji interrupted. "No widows? Why not?"

"It simply isn't done," Krishnayaji replied. "Those are the rules."

"Rules!" Guruji scoffed. "Who comes up with rules like that? And why do these rules always seem to involve the haves taking something else away from the have-nots? The have-nots are in far greater need of prayer, are they not?"

149 Vedic priests.

150 "The Thousand Names of Vishnu," one of the most sacred and commonly chanted *stotras*, or devotional hymns, in Hinduism.

151 Red turmeric.

"Those are fine sentiments, Dr. Sastry," Krishnayaji replied. "But it is not the way things are done. If you insist on having widows participate in the *kumkum archana*, then I am afraid I cannot help you."

Guruji thanked him for his time and left. He felt overwhelmed by the endless procedural strictures piled atop the more mundane challenges of locating a place in which to hold the event and then somehow sourcing the money to pay for it all. He wanted to obey the Goddess's request, but saw no way forward. Surrendering to her will, he decided to simply wait and see what happened.

A few days later, as if on cue, Krishnayaji appeared at his doorstep. Guruji, surprised, invited him in. "Well, you win," the priest said with a smile. "You have a powerful will, my friend. The Goddess appeared in my dreams and chided me for my inflexible stance on widows." He laughed. "She actually called me a stick in the mud! So here I am. I'll manage the priests and oversee the ritual components; you take care of the rest, all right?"

Guruji assented and the work began.

The first step was selecting a site. After numerous inquiries, he finally turned to Simhachalam, Visakhapatnam's renowned temple to Lord Narasimha and always one of Guruji's favorite places of worship. Though the temple dates back a thousand years, its administrators had only recently completed construction of a new *mandapam*—essentially a large function hall for special events—less than a mile from the Nishtala family home. When Guruji approached temple trustees about his *Devi Yagna*, they decided it would be the perfect event to inaugurate the new facility (which was auspiciously named—"by coincidence or providence," Rama noted—the *Prahlada Kalyana Mandapam* or Prahlada Prayer Hall). The starting date for the *yagna* would be Wednesday, April 27, 1983.

A venue secured, Guruji next set about finding a suitable image of the Goddess to install as the event's centerpiece. Having collected price estimates from several area sculptors and merchants, however, Guruji realized that he lacked anything close to the money or time required for such a commission. As usual, he turned to the Goddess for advice.

"I recall it was a Friday and we were all gathered at Guruji's place reciting *Sri Lalita Sahasranama* in the prayer room," Prasad Rao said. "Guruji was deep in meditation when all of a sudden his eyes snapped open and he asked, 'Where is the Parameswari Cinema Hall?' One of his devotees immediately volunteered to bring him there."

It turned out that the cinema was, at the time, showing a hit Telugu devotional film called *Raja Rajeswari Mahatmyam*,[152] which had been playing to packed houses across Andhra Pradesh for several weeks. In order to enhance the "divine mood" during the film's run, the theatre's proprietor had installed a plaster statue of the goddess in the lobby, surrounding her with ersatz offerings of fruit, burning lamps, camphor and incense.

Guruji, accompanied by Amma and the devotee, arrived in an auto-rickshaw and went inside to find the goddess statue standing before them. It was fairly large and quite graceful; with a few small touch-ups, Guruji reckoned, it would be perfect. He told the proprietor about the upcoming *Devi Yagna* and asked if he would be willing to donate the statue for the event. Honored by the request, the cinema owner readily agreed.

When the film's run ended shortly thereafter, Guruji and Amma returned with a group of disciples to retrieve the goddess and transport her to the *mandapam*. Attracted by the joyful cheers as the party carefully loaded the goddess into her own auto-rickshaw, a passing group of professional musicians offered to provide a musical escort.

"I didn't call any musicians, did you?" Guruji asked Amma.

"Why would we need to ask?" she replied. "The Divine Mother wanted them, so here they are! Let's go!"

And with a blare of *shehnais*, the impromptu procession made its way to the prayer hall. As part of the ongoing publicity efforts for the *yagna*, Guruji hired another vehicle to ply the streets of Vizag for several days preceding the event, blaring an announcement pre-recorded in the sweet voice of his then eight-year-old niece Srividya—Prasad Rao and Sundari Amma's daughter—as a fitting stand-in for Bala Tripurasundari, at whose insistence the entire event had been arranged.

152 The 1982 devotional film *Raja Rajeswari Mahatmyam* ("In Praise of the Empress of Emperors") was indeed a hit movie in Telugu-speaking markets that year. But while the film occasionally appears on YouTube and a DVD is listed in some Indian library catalogs, no complete bibliographic reference has been located.

The grand *Devi Yagna* opened under a shimmering full moon on April 27, with 108 *ritwiks* led by Vemakoti Krishnayaji performing rituals for each of the 18 *Maha Shakti Peetams*. The festivities would continue nonstop for the next 16 days until the new moon arrived on May 12—and it was a big hit with the populace. "The whole city of Visakhapatnam was agog with devotion," Mrs. Neti Sitadevi wrote in a Telugu biography of Guruji. Before the event ended, "more than a *lakh* people visited and prayed and offered obeisance at the feet of the Goddess."

As the days passed, the buzzing devotional energy in the *mandapam* became ever more palpable. Rituals commenced at 5 a.m. and ended late in the evening, with a 360-wick *aarti* offered to the erstwhile "cinema goddess" to close each day's ceremonies. The several delicious meals served each day attracted less devotionally minded visitors, as did the classical dance, vocal and instrumental performances sprinkled throughout the program along with learned religious and philosophical discourses.

Then there was the ritual; a kaleidoscopic array of ritual—from ancient Vedic chants to modern devotional hymns; from simple *kumkum archanas* to hours-long *Navavarana Pujas*. Some were performed by the *ritwiks*, some by Guruji and Amma, still others by members of the public. After a recitation of the *Lalita Sahasranama* in the afternoon, *puja* would be offered to 18 *suvasinis* representing presiding deities of the *Maha Shakti Peetams*. Still later, a *kumari puja* was offered to the children in attendance.

At the conclusion of each day's events, "the 108 *ritwiks* would recite the *Mantra Pushpam*,"[153] an ancient Vedic hymn, Radha recalled. "The whole hall reverberated with melodious chants, touching one's being to the core."

One day an old beggar woman appeared and asked Guruji to perform a *puja* to her. Without hesitation he invited her to sit down, and—with utmost devotion—performed a full *suvasini puja* to her. He later told Amma, who was at his side throughout the *puja*, "These are the situations in which the Goddess takes the liberty of testing us. She may come in any form or guise. No one can be ignored or disrespected during this grand event."

On the 16th day, when the *Maha Devi Yagna* reached its finale, the Goddess's image was carried—accompanied by 18 *kalasa*,[154] again representing the *Maha Shakti Peetams*—in a final great procession to the sea. "The city turned out to bid an

153 The *Mantra Pushpam* ("Flower Mantra") is an ancient Vedic hymn recited when offering flowers to the deities at the end of a *puja*. Part of the *Taittiriya Aranyaka* of the *Upanishads*, the hymn speaks of the unlimited benefits to be gained through esoteric spiritual knowledge.

154 "When a pot is filled with water or other nourishing liquid, along with leaves or flowers or fruits or grains, then it is called *kalasa*. This *kalasa* indicates the womb of the goddess that gives forth life in the form of leaves, flowers, etc. ... [I]ts present-day relevance in ritual observations cannot be stressed enough, as there is rarely a household or village ritual to the goddess that is performed without it. ... The notion of the pot as the representation of the goddess can be traced to proto-historic Andhra [Pradesh in India]."

emotional farewell to the Goddess who had become so dear to them," Sitadevi observed. "With heavy hearts, the procession's participants submerged her into the sea, where she bobbed up three final times—as if she too were heartbroken to part with her devotees—before finally disappearing beneath the waves."[155]

With that, Guruji and Amma themselves waded into the surf—in an act of *avabrith snanam,* or release from a vow fulfilled—before returning to the Simhachalam *mandapam* for a concluding *puja.* The final cost of the event was ₹70,000, an expense advanced solely by Guruji from his savings. But when donations from the *yagna* were tallied, the total collected came to ₹73,000. Thanking the Divine Mother, Guruji deposited the balance into a trust account opened on her behalf, which he named the Sri Vidya Trust.

Reflecting on the event years later, Amma observed, "The *Devi Yagna* is really where Devipuram began. The rest, as they say, is history."

▽

155 "The act of taking a clay idol to a nearby water body and immersing it has a great spiritual meaning. . . . After its worshipable stay on the earth, it finally merges back with the elements. Though the idol is gone, [the deity] lives forever! And that story is the same for the true being, the soul, too. It is in this spirit and fervour that the immersion is celebrated all over India."

The Kamakhya *yoni* shrine discovered by Guruji on a rural hillside at Dongalamarri ("Thicket of Thieves") on Sunday, July 24, 1983.
(William Thomas)

14   The Jingling of Anklets

Each evening following the final *aarti* at the *Maha Devi Yagna*, Guruji would address the gathered worshipers, telling them about his meditational experiences and the Devi's apparent desire for him to build her a temple. After one such narration—on the third day of the grand *Devi Yagna*, April 29, 1983—he was approached by a man named Putrevu Baburao who, along with his brothers, owned a cashew plantation in a rural outpost of Visakhapatnam District. Rather uninvitingly called Dongalamarri ("Thicket of Thieves"), the plot was located near the village of Narapadu, between the towns of Anakapalle and Sabbavaram, some 33 kilometers (20 miles) inland from Vizag.[156]

After receiving Guruji's blessing, Baburao lingered to chat, noting that he was inspired by Guruji's vision for a Goddess temple. Apparently on impulse, he abruptly offered to donate three acres of his plantation to serve as a home for the structure. Guruji thanked him politely but demurred. He was already actively scouting locations closer to the city—one serious contender being a hilly parcel just a few miles north of Visakhapatnam, near the beautiful palm and mango-fringed shores of Rushikonda Beach. The land Baburao was describing, by contrast, sounded too remote for significant development.

156 "In revenue records, the place was called Dongalamarri Sitaramapuram Agraharam," explained daughter Rama–*dongalu* meaning "thieves" in Telugu; *marri* referring to the massive banyan trees that grew there in profusion. "It is said that some thieves used to hide in the thicket of trees near the road and loot the travelers, hence the name." (The rest of the name is decidedly less threatening: *agraharam* evokes a secluded woodland place for Brahmin study; and *Seetaramapura*, the legendary abode of Lord Rama and his queen Sita.)

Baburao, however, was adamant. "At least pay a visit before you turn me down," he pleaded. "And truthfully, I would be most grateful if you'd accept my gift right this moment."

So Guruji tentatively accepted—and in so doing, he changed the path of his own and thousands of other lives.

One day soon after the excitement of the *yagna* and its aftermath had subsided, Guruji took a moped from Vizag to inspect the Putrevu land. As he observed the passing countryside, he couldn't deny its natural beauty—the sharp, angular hills of the Eastern Ghats towering over lush green stands of palm and watery rice paddies that extended for miles in every direction. Rural women strolled along the roadside, gracefully balancing bundles and pots atop their heads; turbaned farmers whistled and flicked long switches as they herded buffalo to graze.

Yet it was also a harsh and underdeveloped terrain. The Putrevu plantation was particularly remote, accessible only by a narrow, rocky footpath overgrown with brambles and thorns. The donated parcel consisted mainly of cashew trees and hilly scrub-forest, surrounded by dramatic hills jutting abruptly from the landscape. Gnarly trees and thickets grew tangled and wild in the rust-red soil particular to the region. No human beings were to be seen save an occasional subsistence herder or farmer.

Overall, it was a lot to process. "Keep in mind, Guruji grew up in the city," Suryalakshmi said. "Our family had always lived in cities; we'd never had much real contact with the countryside. So when Guruji saw this place, it was a real dilemma—you know, what kind of place is this? No water, no anything. Why would the Mother have chosen such a place?"

Nonetheless, Guruji returned to the parcel again a few days later, and once more a day or two after that—roaming and exploring, not quite sure what he was looking for, stopping at times to pray for guidance, occasionally sitting to meditate—trying to fathom the purpose of the Goddess's gift. Not much happened at first, but with each visit he felt more certain that the site was "her own choice," he said. Yet at the same time, he was still "looking for confirmation that this was indeed the site designated for building a temple according to her wishes."

One day as he climbed the western slope of one of the parcel's steep hills, he spotted something unusual—a large, roughly oval-shaped expanse of exposed rocky ledge, gently curving and about nine feet wide, with a triangular six-foot crevice at its center. The formation was "very similar to that of the Kamakhya Peetam in Assam," Guruji recalled.[157] "It had obviously been cut by human hands a long time ago to resemble a woman's thighs, with a triangular depression that had the distinctive features of the *yoni*, a woman's genitals."[158] Crystal-clear water trickled out of the crevice in a small rivulet.

Thrilled to find such an unambiguous sign of the Goddess's presence—not to mention a natural spring watering the otherwise dry parcel—Guruji knelt and took a sip of the water from his palms. It tasted sweet and pleasant. He decided to offer thanks to the Goddess, first washing his feet with the water and then sitting upon the rock to perform mantra *japa*. The energy was excellent, even extraordinary. He took careful note of the *yoni*'s location so that he could easily find it again. From that day, it became the focal point of his visits.

"I thought it was a good place to start," he shrugged. "I would come especially to sit there and meditate upon this *yoni*. Such formations are held sacred by us Shaktas as symbols of the abundant procreative power of the Divine Mother. And any time I went there for meditation, I'd always feel happy."

It was on one of these visits to the forgotten Goddess shrine that a transformative encounter took place. The date was Sunday, July 24, 1983, the height of summer and the day of the *Guru Purnima*[159] full moon. Almost as soon as he had settled into his meditation posture, Guruji felt powerful vibrations radiating upward through his body and began slipping into a deep trance-like state.

"It was 12 noon," he recalled. "It was hot; the sun was beating down—but then it suddenly felt cool. I heard the jingling sound of anklets. I opened my eyes and saw a light coming out of my heart and forming itself into a huge ball of light in front of me. It gradually condensed into an incredibly beautiful female figure, her skin like flashes of lightning or electric pulses in constant motion. She was shining like a jewel and all bedecked in bridal attire."

"I am Kamakhya," she told him. "Will you do *puja* to me?"

157 The Kamakhya Peetam, in Guwahati, is a Hindu temple dedicated to the goddess Kamakhya, Assam. By far India's most famous Tantric pilgrimage center, its inner sanctum, called the *garbhagriha*, is a rock fissure in an underground cave: "The *garbhagriha* is small, dark and reached by narrow steep stone steps. Inside the cave there is a sheet of stone that slopes downwards from both sides meeting in a *yoni*-like depression some 10 inches deep. This hollow is constantly filled with water from an underground perennial spring. It is the vulva-shaped depression that is worshiped as the goddess Kamakhya herself and considered as most important *peetam* (abode) of the Devi."

158 *Yoni* is a Sanskrit term meaning "vagina" or "womb." It refers to an explicit or abstract representation of *Shakti* or *Devi*, the Goddess as the creative force that embodies and animates the cosmos. Conveying the sense of a source, origin point, or place of divine passage, it is considered the feminine counterpart to the *linga*.

159 Guru *Purnima* is a major Hindu festival nurturing spiritual and academic teachers. It falls on the day of the Full moon (*Purnima*) in the Hindu month of *Ashadh* (June-July).

160 This part of the relevation stayed with Guruji. "He is not at all tied up with the concept of having all vessels and ingredients available to execute *pujas*," a long-time disciple revealed. "He once explained to me the most powerful tool is your own visualization."

161 "Worship with the *Pancatattva* generally takes place in a Cakra or circle composed of men and women, Sādhakas and Sādhikas … sitting in a circle, the Śakti being on the Sādhaka's left. Hence it is called Cakrapūjā [the circle ritual]. … The intention of this ritual, when rightly understood, is … to regulate natural appetite, to curb it, to lift it from the trough of mere animality; and by associating it with religious worship, to effect a passage from the state of desire of the ignorant Paśu to the completed Divyabhāva in which there is desirelessness."

162 For Guruji's full account of experience, see the essay "What Kamakhya Told Amrita," in *The Goddess and the Guru, Volume II.*

163 In medieval Kaula Tantric practice, rituals focused on Shiva's wrathful form as Bhairava sometimes employed a practice known as *Bhairavi Chakra*, employing the taboo-breaking *panchamakara* or Five Ms.

Awestruck, Guruji replied, "What a blessing! What higher fortune could I have than to do *puja* to you?" Then motioning around himself, he added, "But as you see, I don't have any articles for *puja*."

She smiled and said, "I will visualize them and they will come to you."[160]

"Once I agreed to do *puja*, she did a couple of things," Guruji continued. "First, she removed her ornaments, which were her only clothing, without inhibition. However, as this used to be the custom in India in ancient times it did not really surprise me. I was used to seeing nude goddesses in meditation. What *did* seem strange was that she then bowed down to my feet. I was stunned and asked her, 'What does this mean?'

"She said, 'I am the world. You are going to be a Guru in my lineage. The world is going to bow down at the feet of the Guru. Those people who worship me will bow down to you. I am in all of them. You will promote *yoni* and *lingam pujas*, and also the worship of paired female and male energies to manifest new orders of consciousness through circle rituals.[161] You will be a *Kaula*, meaning you will worship all—female, male and paired energies.'[162]

What happened next was even more unexpected.

"She opened up to me," Guruji said. "Now, I was familiar with the idea of nude worship in the *Bhairavi Chakras*,[163] so I could accept its sacredness and power to invoke higher lifeforms through the congregation of egoless people in circles. Yet the idea of physically interacting with a divine power was totally new to me. As she promised, I would seek the articles of *puja* and they would manifest by her grace. When it came to bathing her, I asked her for water. She stared up into the sky and clouds gathered over us and then burst, and we were drenched in rain. I did *puja* to all of her limbs until she was satisfied.

"Then she embraced me and told me I would feel this embrace always," he concluded. "And with that she vanished back into the triangular pit in the rock. But how true it was! Whenever I was alone, I could always feel her gentle love play within me."

An erotically charged experience, to be sure—and one completely consistent with that aspect of the Goddess known as Kamakhya. "*Kama* means 'desire,'" Guruji explained. "Any desire, but more commonly sexual desire. *Akhya* means 'name.' So she is the name, the root cause, the very *womb* of the desire to manifest. She is the pleasure driven by the pairing of opposites, and she is also the ecstasy in music and dance. She ignites one life from another by coupling two lives, a sperm and an egg, to produce a new life."

In years to come, shades of Kamakhya's eroticism would profoundly influence Guruji's aesthetic choices in developing Devipuram, and deeply inform his writing and teachings as well. Yet despite Kamakhya's antiquity in Indian philosophy and tradition, these choices would draw almost equal measures of ridicule and condemnation from the secular mainstream, and moral outrage and censure from self-appointed guardians of tradition and morality.

All of that, however, still lay far in the future. For now, Guruji was content to simply meditate alone at this remote Kamakhya shrine.

During one session soon after his powerful initial vision, Kamakhya returned in the form of "a devastatingly beautiful girl of 16 years," and told Guruji, "I am the blissful state of Goddess Bhairavi, residing here in the form of Kamakhya. Lord Shiva dwells in this place too, as its guardian.[164] His natural presence here is special and auspicious. You will build a temple to him atop this very hill!"

Then speaking of the *yoni* formation itself she said, "This crevice, shaped like the triangle within the *Muladhara Chakra*,[165] evokes the Universal Womb. Its waters have alchemical powers and you will find me here blessing all with success, and bestowing love upon everyone. Together with Lord Shiva, I create and sustain life. We are here to help you."

Guruji understood this vision to mean that the Goddess expected him to build two temples upon this hill—one at the very top dedicated to Shiva, and another at the *yoni*-shaped ledge itself on the slope, dedicated to Kamakhya "in her *digamber* (naked) form."

But did Bala seek these temples instead of the Sri Meru she had shown him earlier? Or in addition to it? He simply wasn't sure yet.

During another meditation at the *yoni*, Guruji felt himself swept backward through time. He saw a magnificent *yagna* being performed on the very spot where he sat, but judging by the participants' dress, speech and manners, he understood that the event was taking place at least two centuries earlier. Kamakhya seemed to be showing him an

164 Bhairavi is the fierce consort of Bhairava, a fearsome form of Lord Shiva, who dwells in cremation grounds. The exact term she used was *kshetrapalaka*, or guardian deity.

165 A subtle energy center located under the base of the spinal column in Kundalini Yoga.

166 The *Sama Veda*, dating back to about 1700 BCE, is the third of the four Vedas. It is one of the core scriptures of Hinduism, along with the *Rig Veda*, *Yajur Veda* and *Atharva Veda*.

167 Final offerings.

168 As elucidated by Guruji, Nadabindu Kaladhari is a divine form whose manifestation shows "that Sound and Form are one and the same. When the Primordial Sound (*Nada*) is struck, the Primordial Point (*Bindu*) commences the manifestation of Space (*Desha*) and Time (*Kala*)."

169 A three-dimensional, pyramidal form of the Sri Chakra diagram, cast in *panchaloha*, an alloy of five metals (gold, silver, brass, copper and iron) that is considered extremely auspicious for holy objects.

170 Guruji elaborated: "The Chatura Ayatana (Four Directional Deities) are Ganapati at *nairuti* (southwest), Vishnu at *vayu* (northwest), Surya at *ishanya* (northeast) and Shiva at *agni* (southeast). These four symbols, taken together with the *bindu* (Devi), represent the *Shakti Pancha Ayatanam* ("Five Seats of Shakti"). Thus, people doing *Shakti Pancha Ayatana puja* need not obtain each of the idols individually; the Meru itself contains them all."

171 A type of Sri Chakra characterized by the ratios Guruji describes here. He added that he designed the Sri Meru Nilayam temple based on the same configuration.

episode from the history of her shrine—were these the people who originally sculpted the *yoni*? Or simply the last ones who worshiped here? They seemed to be performing a rare and unusual sort of *yagna* as well, Guruji noted, employing chants from the *Sama Veda* rather than the more commonly used *Rig Veda*.[166]

As he contemplated the scene, his point of view suddenly shifted. Instead of merely observing the *yagna*, he was now at its center—inside the *kunda* or fire pit itself. "I had the experience of lying on this *peetam* with flames emanating from my body while four priests performed a *homa*," he said. "During *purnahuti*,[167] I felt a heavy object about the size of a fist being placed on my heart."

As the *rishis* continued their chant, the Goddess materialized above Guruji "in the form of Nadabindu Kaladhari"[168] and a deafening voice filled the heavens. "I am the Power! I am the Source! I am the Womb of the Universe! I am the Universal Mother!"

Kamakhya then transformed back into her more familiar form and told Guruji that a precious relic of the *yagna* he had just witnessed remained buried at the *peetam*: a Meru *yantra*—the very same object, in fact, that he had felt placed upon his chest in the fire. She instructed him to retrieve the Meru and install it in the sanctum of the Shiva temple he would build atop the hill. Guruji then awoke from his meditation, sitting alone again on the *yoni* in the present day.

"I was shaken," he said. Even experienced centuries later through a meditative state, the revelation's intensity packed an emotional impact that seemed "beyond all limits." He immediately rushed to narrate the experience to Anakapalle Gurugaru, who advised, "Well, do as she said! Dig at that very spot." Guruji returned with a couple of laborers, who dug to a depth of about two and a half feet before unearthing a small, scorched metal pyramid.

"It was a *panchaloha*[169] *yantra* of a unique design like none I had ever seen before," Guruji said. A mere two and a half inches square and an inch and a quarter high, the object was nonetheless fascinating in its details. "It resembled a typical Maha Meru, but with some significant differences. A Sri Chakra is always considered to encompass the *Shakti Pancha Ayatanam*—the Five Seats of Shakti.[170] But this Meru differed from most Sri Chakra Merus to such an extent that I don't really know whether it can be called a conventional Meru at all. It was a based on a *Kailasha Prastara*[171] with an almost hemispherical shape and a radius height equal to half of its base width.

"But since I found it at the same place where I had *darshan* of Goddess Kamakhya, I attach great significance to it," he continued. "The Meru I found had several extra diamond-shaped plates inserted above each of the star shapes, having 14, 10, 10 and 8 corners respectively. The diamond-shaped plates have no *puja* relevance; they serve simply to show the separation between one star and the next, demarcating the triangles from the undefined areas, which seemed so much more logical. But it *was* unusual. On the other hand, the accuracy—three lines joined without forming triangles—was very good. This characteristic does qualify to make it a good Sri Chakra."[172]

Yet even as Guruji the mystic unquestioningly embraced his extraordinary experiences with the Goddess Kamakhya, Sastry the scientist continued to question its nature. "It's sort of like that scene in the movie *Contact*," he said, "where Jodie Foster speaks of her entire experience in spiritual terms—but when she is finally asked, 'Do you believe in God?' she says, 'I can't.'"[173]

"Even now I often wonder: what was it exactly that happened to me at Kamakhya? Was it a real experience? Was it a trance? Was it a hallucination? One thing that's absolutely true is that I had the experience, not only at that moment but repeatedly for 11 years afterwards"—that is, over the entire period that it would take to complete the temple constructions at Devipuram. "So it's like this: I can't prove it and I can't disprove it—but it was true to me. It could have been a very lucid dream; I do not deny it. But to me it was an open-eyed experience. That's all I can say. Anything more than that—well, you could not know unless you were able to get into me, to get inside my experience. Because for me no proof is required for that experience. Reality does not need proof, and it is reality to me. It was a spiritual reckoning through meditation."

In accordance with Kamakhya's wishes, then, Guruji resolved to commence construction of the two temples on the hill, financing them at least initially through the meager overage from the *Maha Devi Yagna*, which sat waiting in the Sri Vidya Trust account, and augmented, once again, by Guruji's personal savings.

172 The Meru retrieved by Guruji received worship at the Sivalaya Temple and later Kamakhya Peetam for many years, but Guruji eventually reinterred it under Kamakhya, where he first found it. Good photographs of the Meru are now frustratingly difficult to come by (many of Guruji's own early photos of Devipuram have been lost). The image reproduced in this volume was taken by a devotee in 2001, shortly before the Meru was reburied. While its angle and resolution do not clearly show the extra plates Guruji mentioned, both Amma and Suryalakshmi positively identified it as the Meru Guruji found at Kamakhya.

173 Guruji refers to a scene involving a Congressional committee hearing on whether astrophysicist Ellie Arroway (Jodie Foster) is an appropriate representative of the human race to make first contact with an alien race. A committee member asks, "Do you believe in God, Dr. Arroway?" Arroway responds, "As a scientist I ... *we* rely on empirical evidence, and in this matter I don't believe there is data either way." The committee member then asks, "So your answer would be that you do not believe in God?" Arroway responds, "I don't understand the relevance of the question."

I have considered the alternative of building a few guest rooms. instead of the temple.
Right now the need is not urgent. And we have to live down with a stigma that we are not building the temple. I believe this is the best course.
Any visitors can stay with me in my house in Vizag; and visit Devipuram for a few days. Some bare amenities are there. I am arranging for my sister to live there, so that food won't be a problem. This bath is not essential; for bath, the pump house will do. After the temple is made, if any money is left (very very doubtful - it won't be enough) we will build a couple of toilets. We have started work on foundations for pillars. The hope is to complete work by June.

15　Temples Raised by Woman Power

To build a temple from scratch, even under the best of circumstances, presents a daunting array of technical, practical and spiritual challenges. In the absence of funds, materials, labor or congregants, it would seem little more than a dream. Place all of those problems in a remote, uninhabited wilderness without significant roads or infrastructure—no running water, no electricity, no telephone, no nearby shops or markets, no emergency services—and "extremely unlikely" begins to seem the optimal assessment. Add the natural hazards of the local environment—snakes, scorpions, stinging insects, clouds of mosquitoes—and the word "impossible" comes to mind.

Asked how he nonetheless found the will to forge ahead, Guruji laughed and said, "I was mad then—and I still am!"

That might also have been the impression of a pair of local village women who witnessed the first glimmering of Devipuram's birth one fateful morning as they sat grazing cattle on a scrubby hillside. Their casual gossip was suddenly interrupted by a most peculiar sight—a distinguished, white-bearded city gentleman, calmly and purposefully marching up the slope with a single large brick perched atop his head. He nodded a friendly greeting as he passed, and continued on up the hill. After a few minutes he descended again, only to reappear a short time later carrying yet another brick. Here (though the curious women could hardly have guessed it at the time) was a man with a dream, a vision—but also a man in need of a plan. While thinking through the myriad challenges surrounding this new project, he was keeping himself busy by at least making a start of things.

But more focused construction efforts would soon have to begin.

In preparation, Guruji dipped into the Sri Vidya Trust account and used the funds to have a deep well drilled near the southeast corner of the parcel (the area now occupied by the Ashram that Guruji and Amma would one day call home). A water-storage tank was erected and a one-room thatched hut built over the electric water pump and its generator, becoming a basecamp for almost every aspect of the project.

"On the entire parcel of land we had just that one hut," Suryalakshmi recalled. "The well cap was there and we'd go there to cook, sleep, bathe, store materials—'Devipuram Circus' we used to call it.[174] It was always being transformed to suit the needs of the moment."

Primitive latrines were dug a judicious distance from the Circus. "We were pretty much unfazed about having to use open-air toilets at Devipuram," Radha noted. "Because to be fair, we really suffered no lack of privacy. In those days there was nobody around for miles—and people could be heard coming long before they were seen."

Even Guruji admitted that life at Devipuram in those days could be an occasionally hair-raising experience. With no electricity, the nights were profoundly dark and silent but for the sometimes alarming noises of the surrounding forest. "I wouldn't say I was ever afraid," he said, "but there *were* times when I got a little worried. I could hear things creeping and slithering in the dark—on the dirt floor below me, in the thatched roof above. And I would say to Devi, 'I hope you know I cannot perform any of these tasks for you unless you keep me alive!'"

Even more unnerving than the natural threats were those of the supernatural variety.

One dark, moonless night, Guruji was walking back to the hut when he sensed a dark mass speeding rapidly toward him—it hit him in the lower abdomen ("the navel-genital area," he said), toppling him to the ground and momentarily knocking the wind out of him but doing no serious harm. The creature, he explained, was not an animal but a *pishacha*, a minor demon. "Just because we cannot see these beings who dwell on different planes than we do, it is arrogant to assume that they do not exist," he added with a shrug.

174 The name meant "circus" in the old British sense of a busy hub or central meeting point (such as Picadilly Circus), not in the sense of an entertainment spectacle or a frenzied, disordered situation.

Throughout the rest of their life together, Guruji and Amma would enjoy regaling visitors from around the world with stories about those early days at Devipuram. In the beginning, however, that happy outcome had yet to be written and there was no guarantee (or even likelihood) of success.

"The first time I went to that place with Guruji, there was only the water tank and one or two thatched huts, that's all—absolutely nothing else," Aiya recalled. "I remember thinking, 'What has he bitten off for himself this time? It's going to be a Herculean task to build this thing up!' But the next time I visited, the temples were already going up and I knew he was going to complete this task—that's when I understood the sheer willpower that was making it all happen. And I don't mean just Guruji's will alone; I mean the Devi herself was willing it to manifest. Of this, I never had any doubt in my mind."

From the outset, professional architects and builders were beyond Guruji's reach, mainly because their rates were too high. "The architectural drawings alone would have cost ₹50,000," daughter Rama noted. "It was just too expensive, so the thought of assigning the building tasks to external firms was quickly shelved."

Instead, Guruji invested in a do-it-yourself book on construction.

The land was also too far from nearby towns and too difficult to access from the main road. So Guruji, of necessity, turned to local villagers to carry out the work—and since the menfolk were more often occupied with outside jobs, it was usually the women who ended up dominating the work crews, despite the heavy physical labor involved. "In the beginning, there were four or five very young women who worked as laborers," Aiya recalled. "Some of them were barely out of their teens at the time. And Guruji worked right there alongside them. He would mix the concrete with them and carry the concrete up the ladders, just like an ordinary laborer."

Of course, he was by no means an ordinary laborer—but he was, despite his spiritual predilections, a realist and a pragmatist.

"My biggest problem at Devipuram has always been manpower," Guruji explained. "Since this place was a jungle, far from the city, I could not convince anybody to come here—and really, it's not fair to expect city people to leave everything and come here.

But that is how I came to realize the potential of the local people. From the beginning, it was mainly 'woman power' that built and sustained this place."

In many ways, in fact, woman power was Guruji's greatest advantage. On the mundane level, the girls' impoverished rural upbringings had, in real and quantifiable ways, made them smarter, more intuitive workers—trained by lifetimes of shortage and "making do," they were highly skilled at finding novel, creative solutions to difficult problems in the absence of sufficient materials and resources.

On the spiritual level, growing up immersed in the Goddess-drenched folk practices of Andhra Pradesh led the women to accept the Tantric features of Devipuram's temples as natural and unremarkable. Neither *yonis* nor *lingams* perturbed them in the least; they displayed a frank and organic *bhakti*, or devotion, free from the inhibitions and prudery sometimes displayed by more sophisticated, educated urban visitors.

"What takes us intellectuals a long time to get, these village girls got quite simply and easily," Guruji said. "They knew how to go with the flow. They had no inhibitions or fear. What I was able to pay them was nothing compared to the service they offered; it was Devi herself who brought those gems here." He treated them accordingly, with a level of respect and deference that they had almost certainly never experienced before in their lives.

"In the evening, after the day's work was through, he would invite the girls to sit down, and he would wash their feet and do *puja* to their feet," remembered Sundhara Arasaratnam, the Toronto management consultant, who spent time with Guruji at Devipuram during those formative days. "Guruji would say, 'They are, each of them, embodiments of the Mother. It is the Devi herself who is helping me build these temples.' When it came time to distribute wages, if he had 10 girls working there, he would bring pay for 11; they would each get a little extra. The bonus, according to Guruji, was for the invisible 11th worker, who was the Devi herself."

Indeed, it was these young builders who gave the place its name by referring to the once-forlorn "Thicket of Thieves" as *Devi Talligudi* ("Goddess Shrine"), the local name for the ancient Kamakhya *yoni*. *Devi Talligudi* was subsequently Sanskritized to *Devipuram* ("The Goddess's Abode"), the title it retains to this day.

Some of the women who contributed so much to building Devipuram can still be found worshiping there today, often with grown children and grandchildren in tow.

When he wasn't at work on a building site, Guruji could often be found reviewing plans and preparing for the multitude of jobs that lay ahead. One early disciple recalled making a long spiritual pilgrimage to Devipuram, only to find Guruji deeply absorbed in the niceties of concrete construction—and in no particular mood to discuss more transcendent matters.

Devipuram's first two temples arose from the jungle almost simultaneously—the one on the hilltop called Sivalaya (*Shiva-alaya*, or "Abode of Shiva"), and the one at the *yoni* called Kamakhya Peetam ("Seat of Kamakhya"). Both structures were necessarily uncomplicated in design. Kamakhya consists of a single, large rectangular room built over the *yoni* ledge; Sivalaya is slightly larger with several rooms and an open floor plan.

Construction conditions were difficult and the work arduous. The stairway that now ascends the hill from Kamakhya to Sivalaya did not yet exist, so workers had to scale the steep, rugged terrain multiple times per day, lugging needed tools and materials along with them.

And before construction of Sivalaya could even begin, the craggy stone peak of the hill required leveling. Dynamite would have been the choice of most professional excavators, but Guruji lacked not only the funds and expertise for that, but also the will: he did not wish to inflict such extreme violence upon nature in the name of constructing a temple. In his view, the entire parcel was the Goddess's body, to be treated with due reverence and respect. So after conducting a *Praja Yagna* ritual for the minerals, plants, animals and spirits who might be disturbed or displaced by the temple project, Guruji enlisted residents from two nearby villages to carry out the task by hand. "I still remember the rocks being manually broken atop the hill," Suryalakshmi said. "So many villagers were involved—initially the people from Ammulapalem were organized; later people from Balijapalem came in as well. In all, it took about two months."

Once a sufficiently level surface was achieved, work on the temple itself began in earnest. The structure, sheltering a massive *yoni-lingam* in strikingly anthropomorphic form, would eventually be enhanced by a shaded patio and a rooftop terrace featuring a large Sri Meru, all overlooking the spectacular green hills and valleys that spread to the horizon in every direction—while also, Guruji added on a practical note, "affording the temple complex some degree of visibility from the road."

Meanwhile, halfway down the hill, the small, freshwater spring and rustic *yoni* shrine where Guruji had seen his transformative vision of Kamakhya were also being expanded and developed. Walls began to rise around the ledge, and a roof was installed.

Yet Haran Aiya's daughter Saru recalled being much more awestruck by the original *yoni* formation when she saw it as a young teenager. "It was nothing like what's there now; you wouldn't even recognize it," she said. "No concrete work had been done yet, so you could still see the actual boulders that Guruji found, the exact place where he meditated and saw Kamakhya—and the *yoni* they formed was so unbelievable, so graphic! If you knew what you were looking at you would say, 'Holy cow, am I really seeing this?'"

As part of the temple construction, the *yoni* crevice that Guruji discovered had been largely covered, shaped, defined and somewhat abstracted by stone and concrete work. "I believe he stylized it to the point where it is now, precisely because the way he found it—the way it had been for the people who did the *homa* there centuries ago— was just too graphic," Saru said. "I remember thinking it was a shame to cover it up. I asked Guruji why that was necessary, and he told me that it just hit too close to home, that people nowadays just couldn't handle that kind of thing, they couldn't accept it."

But while Saru understood Guruji's decision, she still felt something was lost in the translation.

"In a sense, I think it undermined the validity of it, the historic continuity," she said. "Because if you're seeing it right in front of your eyes, how can you question it? It's there—*she's* there. But when you cover it and show just that small portion that can be seen today, the original 'wow!' impact is lost. From the structure that's there today, you can't even envision how it used to look. But even though I was only 13 at the time, I was fortunate enough to have seen it, and I'd like to document that—I want people to know what it was like before."

Yet Guruji would have to argue for years that the "explicit" *yoni-lingams* worshiped at Devipuram were not mere products of his imagination or innovation, but in fact unimaginably ancient archetypes in India, stretching from the mists of prehistory well into the Common Era. And recent scholarship bears him out on this point.

"Goddess religion predates both *Brahmanic* and Buddhist forms in Andhra," said Professor Sree Padma Holt of Bowdoin College, who grew up in Visakhapatnam and is today a leading expert on the history and archaeology of goddess religion in India.[175] She noted that the area's earliest surviving goddess figures[176] began appearing in the historical record of Andhra Pradesh in the last few centuries before the Common Era, including "a few life-size stone images of the fertility goddess [that] started emerging for regular worship."

For centuries, these images were invariably nude, emphasizing the Goddess's creative and fertility aspects, both human and agricultural—and replete with scenes of her "giving birth, prominently displaying her vulva, simply being portrayed in a naked youthful form, or holding a child," all of which presentations can be readily found today at Devipuram.

As the centuries passed, however, and more patriarchal schools of Shaiva and Vaishnava Hinduism grew in popularity, the Goddess's nudity came to be viewed with increasing disfavor, a view that only intensified under the medieval Muslim rulers and Christian colonizers who followed. Sree Padma explained:

> The goddess as *sakti* dominated the religious culture prior to the prevalence of the *Brahmanic* pantheon of deities. When the three main deities, Brahma, Vishnu and Siva, arrived to share the religious space, they needed to derive resources from the goddess. [Accordingly,] symbols intrinsic to the fertility and *gramadevata*[177] cult evolved into the anthropomorphic shape of subordinated goddesses. The *purnakumbha*,[178] *srivatsa*,[179] and lotus became chaste and devoted anthropomorphized spouses to Siva, Vishnu and Brahma; that is, as Parvati, Lakshmi and Saraswati, respectively. The role of these goddesses served to promote the ideology that focused on the ultimate power attributed to these gods, as well as the patriarchal value system legitimized by that power. ... [Moreover,

175 Dr. Sree Padma Holt received her M.A. in Archæology, M.A. in History, and Ph.D. in History and Archæology from Guruji's *alma mater*, Andhra University in Visakhapatnam. Since 1998, she has been on the faculty at Bowdoin College in Brunswick, ME. Her academic research involves women and goddesses in Hindu tradition and ancient Indian history.

176 Sree Padma notes, "The prehistoric goddess, in spite of her changed identities, continues to retain some basic qualities and remains relevant as a goddess independent of Brahmanic, Buddhist, and Jaina identities throughout history. Taking into account the primary nature of this prehistoric goddess, I refer to her as 'fertility goddess.'"

177 *Gramadevata* is a Sanskrit term literally meaning "village deity," and denotes the presiding, guardian or patron deity of a Hindu village, town or city. In many South Indian villages, these deities were goddesses rather than gods.

178 The *purnakumbha*, or "overflowing pot," was a ubiquitous symbol of the Goddess in ancient India.

179 *Srivatsas* are auspicious geometrical designs, usually drawn by women and used to bless homes and temples with the Goddess's presence.

the Goddess was] admitted as part of the pantheon of *Brahmanic* deities only after being properly clothed.

In the more Goddess-focused regions of India, however—prominently including the Visakhapatnam district of Andhra Pradesh, where Devipuram is located and Guruji was raised—this subordination of the Goddess did not run very deep. Indeed, it "remained something of a mere theological veneer within the context of the newly emerging urban temple religion," Sree Padma noted. Nude fertility goddesses continued to enjoy widespread popular worship in outlying rural settlements and villages.

In the cities, however, concentrated worship of the Goddess was driven at least partially underground—one result of which was the emergence of increasingly powerful (and secretive) forms of Tantric worship. As Sree Padma explained, "Experiencing competition from each other and also from the continued strength of *gramadevata* worship and the more recently established cult of *Mahadevi*,[180] Saiva and Vaishnava clerics" reacted by reviving the ancient Goddess in powerful, esoteric guises; namely, the "fierce forms of independent goddesses as Tantric deities."[181]

Guruji often referred to these historical developments in defending Devipuram's imagery, and indeed they provide an illuminating prism through which to better appreciate the emergence of Sri Vidya—as well as the controversial iconography at Devipuram.

Slowly but surely, Guruji hoped, he could help Indian society recover some of this vast reservoir of forgotten lore and practice, one visitor at a time. And the task was indeed significant. As religious scholar Christopher Wallis explained:

Indian culture underwent a kind of reset, a reboot, with the Muslim conquest and then British conquest. There was such a contraction of Indian religion; so much knowledge and wisdom was forgotten and lost that the religion became a simplified version of itself, centered on the temple culture; people going to temple, not for spirituality but essentially for good luck. This is a big problem, because the nature of the Indian tradition is that it asserts that the religion is eternal, *Sanatana Dharma*. This phrase is misleading, because it implies that

180 The Great Goddess. Sree Padma is referring to the emergence of the more mainstream Goddess cults of the Shakta school of Hinduism.

181 Sree Padma elaborated that *non*-subordinated goddess forms remained so largely through the power of royal patronage, which over the centuries resulted in some fiercely independent *gramadevatas*, such as Durga and Kali, who are both rural and tribal in origin. These eventually made "exalted appearances in Sanskrit compositions" and enjoyed "liturgical worship in Brahmanic temples as powerful warrior goddesses." Sree Padma explained that this phenomenon led to the emergence of *Mahadevi* being "equated with *prakriti*, *sakti* and *maya* … [a view that] continues to hold sway today [even] among educated and middle-caste people who may have distanced themselves from *gramadevata* worship."

166

"our dharma, our religion has been unchanging throughout time," [when] in fact it has changed enormously. But if you believe it's unchanging, then you do not go back and look for the knowledge that has been lost. And what we see in modern India is people who know a little bit about [religion, but] think that they know everything—which is, as Abhinavagupta says, the worst form of ignorance. [Because] if you know a little bit, but think that it's all that there is to know, [then] you are not open to more; you don't go looking for more. ... That's why we have thousands of [ancient Hindu religious] scriptures, but nobody in modern India is reading them and there is no interest in them.

One result of this lost knowledge is that today the "portrayal of fertility goddesses in naked form [has become] a rare phenomenon," Sree Padma stated. Very few nude idols are made anymore, and their original symbolism has largely been lost to history—though "some of the naked stone images of the goddess [from] past centuries are still in worship." In that sense, Sri Padma said, "the worship of a naked female form as the fertility goddess is both ancient and current." But in modern times, nude goddess forms have been largely relegated to prayers for healthy childbirth and children's welfare, not the broader, more elevated spiritual aspirations that they once encompassed.

This shift away from holistic goddess culture is evident not just in classical Indian sculpture, but in ancient Sanskrit literature, most prominently that of the celebrated Kalidasa (c. 400 CE):

Kalidasa wrote about sex, romance and the feminine form with a frankness, elegance and erotic charge that was common in Sanskrit poetry in the golden age, but is astonishing in today's Indian context. The sophistication of language is never overtaken by the sheer exuberance of the pleasure—and Kalidasa, being a courtier, knew how to woo and win with style. Yoga has survived with minimal change from Kalidasa's age but sexual attitudes have become tragically regressive and puritanical. In today's India, Kalidasa would be instantly at home in a temple but lost in social intercourse. Sex has become the great unmentionable and Indians have become God's Frozen People. The *Kumarasambhavam* [Kalidasa's breathtakingly beautiful and influential retelling of the Shiva-Parvati love story] is a living testament to how much endures unchanged in India, and also to how much has been lost to the cruelties of history.

One of Guruji's larger goals at Devipuram was to recover and reconnect with that older wisdom. Still, the imagery he developed for the job was undeniably provocative.

Despite his considerable "toning down" of Kamakhya's original *yoni* shrine, the enhanced stonework still vividly evoked human female genitalia. Moreover, Guruji considerably upped the ante by adding a Shiva *lingam* that rose out of the *yoni*—and not the sort of smooth, abstract pillar typical to most Hindu temples, but an explicitly anthropomorphic rendering of the human male genitalia.

Again, none of this would have been a surprise to Indians a thousand years ago: the ubiquity of nude goddesses and anthropomorphic *lingams* is thoroughly documented in modern museums and art books. For most critics, the real problem with Devipuram's *yoni*s and *lingam*s was not the imagery itself so much as its *currency*. These icons were *not* museum relics safely rooted in the ancient past: they were brand new, "in your face" and offered for worship. And as such, they ventured into an area of fraught sensitivity in both East and West—the elusive, dimly understood, largely indefinable realm of Tantra.[182]

182 Specific to Sri Vidya and Guruji's teachings, see "Introduction: The World of Sri Vidya" in *The Goddess and the Guru, Volume II.*

The *Oxford English Dictionary* offers an academically sound starting point: in authentic Hindu usage, the term "Tantra" refers to either a "mystical or magical text, dating from the 7th century or earlier" or a religious practice derived from such a text, involving "adherence to the doctrines or principles of the tantras, involving mantras, meditation, yoga, and ritual." In fact, Sri Vidya is the last surviving school of authentic Hindu Tantra. However, "the term tantra and the tantric traditions of Hinduism ... have been subjected to a great deal of misunderstanding in both India and the West." While adherents generally understand their practices as "paths to liberation," popular viewpoints focus on "the relatively widespread associations of the tantric traditions with sorcery and libertine sexuality."

For many urban, educated Indians arriving at Devipuram, Sree Padma explained, the message conveyed by the temples' vivid sexual imagery is that, "clearly, some kind of Tantric stuff is going on here." That impression would only be reinforced by more subtle indicators, such as Guruji's "putting women in the higher place, opening [Sri Vidya practice] to non-Brahmins—he really has a lot of Tantric elements at play here," she said.

And in today's India, that's a breeding ground for controversy.[183]

Of course, Devipuram's core audience—namely, initiates of Sri Vidya and other Shakta lineages (that is, Goddess-centered schools of Hinduism)—readily saw beyond any so-called "indecency," and understood the profound messages being conveyed by the temple imagery. The sophisticated exegesis of Sri Vidya and other Tantric traditions, as Sree Padma noted, has long since overlaid its primordially "sexual" surfaces with more complex layers of philosophical and ritual significance.

In general, Guruji added, the young tended to be more open-minded than their elders, and villagers more receptive than urbanites, seeing only the natural processes of life, growth and death where more "sophisticated" city dwellers spied impropriety, degeneracy and scandal.

Sree Padma explained that villagers and other rural dwellers are typically driven more by pure faith and much less by "the imagery as such, or what it conveys. If they believe in a particular place, they will go there and pray. Naked goddesses are still widely worshiped in the villages, especially by women seeking children. So if people go to a shrine and then go home and say, 'I went there when I was in trouble, and it really helped me,' the word gets around and more people go there. It doesn't really matter what the imagery is, in that sense."

Guruji's personal association with Devipuram was also pivotal for many rural devotees, she added. "Because he has earned the respect of the local communities and he is helpful to them, they think, 'He's a good man, so whatever he started here must be good too,'" Sree Padma said. "They don't judge him; if there is a shrine and it has all the typical Hindu symbols—the *swastika*,[184] the Goddess and so on—they don't think twice. They go there and worship."

Devipuram's most vocal critics, by contrast, tended to be urban dwellers steeped in the modern mainstream of Hindu tradition but not specifically knowledgeable about

183 A fuller discussion of the Tantra controversy appears in chapter 24, "The Powerhouse of Devipuram." See also *The Goddess and the Guru, Volume II.*

184 Her reference, of course, is to the *swastika* in its original and primary Hindu context as an ancient symbol of auspiciousness.

(or sympathetic to) Sri Vidya philosophy and practice. In the years ahead, they would create many a crisis for Guruji and Devipuram. But for now, both were far too remote and unknown to have yet attracted the censure of their ever-vigilant moral glare.

On Friday, November 11, 1983, just a week after Diwali and Lakshmi *puja*, and with the first two temples complete, Guruji formally registered the land gifted by the Putrevu brothers. That weekend—following a three-day *yagna* presided over by a newly retained caretaker priest, Buchiramayya Vajjhulu—the two temples were consecrated on the same day: first Sivalaya (since Shiva is the *kshetrapalaka*, or guardian deity of Devipuram), and then Kamakhya Peetam.

The event was decidedly low-key, with only about 35 local villagers in attendance. Amma recalled that as the ceremony began "there was a heavy downpour, which miraculously fell only on temple hill, nowhere else in Devipuram." Guruji and the presiding priest declared this to be a very good omen indeed. When the priest later insisted that both she and Guruji climb to the roof of temple for part of the ritual, Amma remembers only "a swaying-ladder, wet-silk-sari, heart-in-my-mouth experience."

By the time they moved on to Kamakhya Peetam,[185] the rain had grown so fierce that attendees and hired musicians alike had vanished. "So for the Kamakhya consecration it was just the priest, Guruji and I, and the elements," Amma said. At the very moment the ceremony ended, so did the rain.

And with that gesture of divine approval, Devipuram was officially open for worship.

185 The full name of the temple, as consecrated, is the Kamakhya Digambara Avadhuta Peetham.

16   The Chorus of a Thousand Voices

Devipuram's new status as a functioning place of worship, however, did not immediately translate to worshipers. Though word was gradually spreading through surrounding towns and villages about the erstwhile scientist and his unusual temples, both Guruji and Devipuram remained largely unknown beyond a close, still relatively small circle of friends, disciples and well-wishers. As a result, the hard-to-access temples were usually quite empty of visitors.

"At that point nobody even knew there was a place called Devipuram," recalled Alok Baveja, the Rutgers professor. "Today, there's a Devipuram bus stop. You go to the airport in Vizag and any taxi will take you directly there. But to find it back then you had to take a bus way out into this rural area, sit next to the driver and literally say, 'Stop here!' Then you got off in the middle of nowhere and took a walk through the jungle."

Once there, however, the experience could be magical. One might find Guruji working on a construction project, conversing with a visiting disciple, or conducting a *puja* in one of the temples. The setting was completely idyllic, and many who took the trouble to make the journey in those early days found themselves rewarded with large doses of Guruji's undivided time and attention.

"At night, Guruji and I would pull our cots into the open air and sleep out there, looking up at the stars and talking about everything," Alok said. On one such evening he musingly asked Guruji, "If the same souls are always being reborn, and yet the population of Earth is continually increasing, then where do the souls come from to fill all of those new bodies?"

Guruji lay silently for a while in the darkness and then answered, "But you are assuming that souls operate *in quanta*—as units."

"It was an answer that required me to think more," Alok said. "And that, it seems to me, is the role of a guru. He'll throw something at you that makes you think a little deeper, expand yourself."

One day Alok watched Guruji perform a two-hour *Navavarana Puja* for a poor, elderly woman who had come to pray at the Kamakhya Peetam. "As the *puja* finished, I could see the beaming smile of gratitude on this woman's face," he recalled. "She prostrated at Guruji's feet and then opened a knot at the end of her sari, carefully took out a five-*paise* coin and gave it to him. Guruji accepted that money with a reverence that seemed to me extraordinary."[186]

Upon her departure, Guruji carefully laid the coin in front of the shrine's deity, explaining to Alok, "This woman walked a long distance on foot to come here. What she has given to us are Devi's very precious blessings." As he left the temple, he added, "It is only with the blessings of such people that Devipuram will come up."

186 A *paisa* is 1/100 of an Indian rupee; a fraction of one U.S. cent.

ॐ
ह्रीं

On another occasion, Alok had the rare privilege of watching Swami Swaprakasananda—Guruji's beloved Anakapalle Gurugaru—perform a *puja* at Kamakhya. He happened to be visiting the Ashram one evening when a young woman arrived and narrated a marital difficulty. "I remember Gurugaru was sitting on a chair with Guruji on the floor near his feet," Alok said. When the woman finished, Guruji rose and suggested that they all walk to Kamakhya and perform a *homa* for her.

Upon their arrival, it became clear that Gurugaru rather than Guruji was going to lead the ritual. "It was one of the most extraordinary *homas* I have ever attended," Alok said. The *peetam* was pitch black, with no light except for that of the sacrificial fire itself. Gurugaru began chanting the opening mantras, and soon entered a trance-like state. Alok tried to figure out the ritual being performed, but it quickly became clear that Gurugaru was following no established sequence at all. "It was all completely spontaneous, almost wild," Alok said. "His chants and actions seemed totally random. He was throwing *kumkum* into the fire, rocking like a madman, his eyes closed, seemingly chanting whatever came into his head, without any apparent rhyme or reason. To me, at least, it seemed totally chaotic."

Yet the darkened temple was soon abuzz with a powerful, pervasive energy; the young woman at the *homa*'s focus seemed transformed in the dim firelight. "There is no question in my mind that whatever he was doing was highly effective," Alok said. He glanced over to see Guruji's reaction; he was calmly observing Gurugaru and easily following along with no apparent confusion or surprise.

"But for me the whole thing was beyond belief," Alok said. "I was literally shaking. I had never seen anything like it in my life."

By now Guruji was splitting his time between the temples and his home in Vizag—generally spending Monday through Thursday in the city, and Friday through Sunday at Devipuram. With the Sivalaya and Kamakhya temples complete, Buchiramayya Vajjhulu, the new chief priest, was conducting daily *pujas* and generally keeping the property occupied to ward off potential troublemakers. Buchiramayya, however, only held that position for a few months before he grew weary of the isolation and decided to move on.

One day, while discussing the situation with his sister Suryalakshmi—his first and always most steadfast supporter—Guruji suddenly asked if she might consider taking Buchiramayya's place.

"But I am not qualified!" she protested. "I don't know how to do anything except for the *Sri Sukta Puja*."

"Then do that," Guruji replied. "Do what you know."

Suryalakshmi consulted with her husband, who agreed to support her in her desire to volunteer at Devipuram for a while. "I had other responsibilities but my brother needed help, so I tried to balance my obligations—or rather, she did; the Goddess did. Because really, what did I do? Whatever I did for him, it was she who made it possible."

Suryalakshmi's temporary stay at Devipuram eventually stretched into an adventure lasting nearly six years. Her husband joined her whenever possible, and Guruji was almost always present on weekends, providing an excellent opportunity for the sister and brother to rekindle their close childhood friendship as he taught her the things a temple priestess would need to know. "He used to have me read along with him in performing rituals, and would slowly explain them to me: 'Okay, you do this *puja* like this, that *abhishekam* like that,'" she said.

As she grew more ritually skilled he told her, "Sister, people will be traveling here from faraway places. So don't keep strict temple hours; perform *pujas* for them whenever they come, whomever they may be. Let them all leave happy."

"Without fail," Suryalakshmi said, "I followed his words."

The siblings also discussed philosophical matters at length. "What is the meaning of life? What is death? What is fear? What is night? What is Kundalini and how does it rise? What are chakras? He used to explain all these things to me," Suryalakshmi recalled. "We'd sit down after dinner and talk until long past midnight, into the early hours of the dawn. He was my brother, yes, but he was also my *manasika guru*.[187] He was a teacher at heart. He taught me everything."

Suryalakshmi remembers Guruji's special affection for Kamakhya Peetam during those long, quiet days: "He used to go there often to do *puja* and *japa* and receive her *darshan*." Indeed, Guruji's focus and commitment during those formative years was such that he typically performed a three-hour *puja* routine each day at Kamakhya—90 minutes for a *Navavarana Puja*, and 90 minutes for chanting the *Devi Mahatmyam*.

Some years later, after the building tasks at Devipuram wound down, he also taught some of the women who helped construct the temple. "He trained so many village girls to perform *pujas* and recite the mantras with perfect pronunciation," daughter Rama noted. "*Lalita Navavarana*, *Lalita Sahasranama*, *Trishati Ashtottaram*, *Khadgamala*, the *Panch Suktas*, including the *Rudram*, the *Kalavahana* and *Triveni Kalpam*, as well as Varahi, *Syama* and Ganapati rituals, *Bala Puja* and more..."

Once again, Guruji came away impressed by their natural aptitude. "These girls came from poor, traditionally low-caste backgrounds," he explained. "But if you went and saw how they did the *pujas*, how they dressed the goddess, you could see the love and fun with which they did everything, always giggling and laughing, really enjoying

187 A *manasika guru* is one who teaches the disciple or student any knowledge or skill, not necessarily spiritual in nature. It is more a term of respect, regard and affection than a formal title. When a disciple accepts someone as *manasika guru*, the guru need not even know that he or she is considered as such.

the process. This is precisely the sort of energy she loves. Nothing made Devi happier than having these girls as her priestesses."

In 2013, American documentary filmmaker Julianne Reynolds profiled one of these village girls, named Leela, "loving her simplicity, innocence and absence of pride." In the process, Reynolds learned that Leela had originally "wanted to live a much simpler life. She never set out to learn Sri Vidya *pujas*, but her mother got her the job at Devipuram, and she found that it gave her a sense of purpose and ownership. Guruji himself taught her this ancient wisdom, and she took to it with a butterfly's grace."

When both her husband and Guruji were away on other business, Suryalakshmi would often find herself alone at Devipuram for days on end, with no phone, electricity, running water or transportation. So she filled her days with *pujas*, cleaning and maintaining the temple premises, enjoying the area's pristine natural beauty—and, at night, stargazing.

"I was only afraid for the first couple of days there by myself," she recalled. "With that jungle and all of those cashew trees, who knew what kind of snakes and insects might be around? But then I'd listen and I could hear the sound of buses and trucks passing on the main road off in the distance, and birds were singing everywhere. And I thought, with so much life all around me how can I say I'm alone? That made my fear go away, at least most of the time."

More often, the phenomena she witnessed at Devipuram filled her with wonder. On several occasions while chanting the *Lalita Sahasranama*, she heard a chorus of voices join her. "It would suddenly feel as if a thousand *suvasinis* were reciting along with me, even though there wasn't another soul in sight. It was as if the voices were coming from the cashew trees, from nature itself, from all around me. Even now my heart beats faster as I remember it."

One night Suryalakshmi was sleeping by her fire in the Devipuram Circus hut when she was awakened by a rustling sound in the doorway at three or four in the morning. As she sat up, peering into the darkness, a young girl of eight or nine years old stepped into the flickering firelight. Her hair was plaited in long braids and she wore a simple skirt and blouse, both white. "Are you afraid to be alone here, Grandmother?" the girl asked with a smile.

"I am not alone," Suryalakshmi replied, struggling to keep her composure. "You are with me, no? So there are two of us."

"That's right," the girl replied. "I am with you."

"Well, I am glad you are here," said Suryalakshmi. "But all the same, tell me, who are you? Why did you come to visit me?"

"I am just me," the girl answered. "And I came to keep you company."

"Very good," Suryalakshmi said. "So you can be my company and I will be yours."

"No, I will be your company," the girl replied mysteriously. "I give company to one and all."

"As you wish," Suryalakshmi said.

The girl stayed the entire night, sleeping beside Suryalakshmi and holding her hand. "I will never forget her touch," Suryalakshmi said.

At dawn, however, she awoke abruptly to find her visitor gone. Stepping outside, she spotted her walking off into the nearby jungle and followed, calling for her to wait—but the girl kept walking without turning around. Suryalakshmi caught up with her again at a clearing in the woods, and saw her for the first time in full daylight.[188] She was remarkably beautiful and graceful, with a very dark complexion and no jewelry at all. Feeling a rush of elation Suryalakshmi uttered, "Shyama!"[189] The girl smiled and vanished before her eyes. Though Suryalakshmi called and searched through the area for some time, there was no further sign of her.

When Guruji arrived that Friday, Suryalakshmi excitedly narrated her experience. "Who else could it have been but the Goddess herself?" he replied. When she later related the event to Anakapalle Gurugaru, the old renunciate enthusiastically agreed, adding with his distinctive cackle, "See what good hands you are in?"

Yet there were frightening moments as well. One day, Suryalakshmi heard a commotion brewing near the foot of the temple hill. Descending to investigate, she found an angry confrontation taking place between the Putrevu brothers, who had donated the land, and a group of men from the local Gavara tribe, which owned an adjacent

188 The clearing was in fact the site that was then being prepared for construction of the Sri Meru Nilayam temple.

189 "Dark-skinned one," an appellation of one of the Goddess's primary forms in South India.

parcel of cashew groves. The Gavaras were upset by the construction taking place at Devipuram, fearing that it would harm the land's agricultural value and threaten their livelihood.

"They were shouting, 'How could you gift away these lands?'" Suryalakshmi said. But at that very moment, the same young girl who had visited her in the night stepped out of the forest, again wearing braids with a long white skirt and blouse.

The girl asked the men, "Why are you fighting? I want to come and live here. Why do you object?" The men were momentarily silenced with surprise at the appearance of this strange little girl.

"None of them realized it was the Devi, of course," Suryalakshmi said, "but they were startled. You could feel an otherworldly force and strength radiating from her. And just like that everyone immediately calmed down and began discussing matters in a friendly way."

She saw the mysterious girl on another occasion in the form of an apparition towering "nine feet tall, wearing a green sari with a red border and following me." When Suryalakshmi looked up in awe, the girl smiled and said, "See? I am always protecting you," then vanished again. Suryalakshmi's years at Devipuram were peppered with such events, which she always interpreted as the Goddess helping to boost her faith and keep loneliness and fear at bay.

"I'll tell you this," she said. "If not for the Mother's grace there wouldn't be anything there at Devipuram. With her grace, there is everything you see. In playing my part, I might have done well or not. But I served her truly."

श्री Guruji and Amma during
the Prathista of Sahasrakshi, Devipuram, 1990.
(Sri Vidya Trust)

17 You're Asking for Trouble

Even while Sivalaya and Kamakhya Peetam were still being constructed, Guruji's attention had already shifted to his third and most ambitious project yet—the unprecedented Sri Chakra–shaped temple known as the Sri Meru Nilayam or the Sahasrakshi Meru Temple, which would, 11 years later, become the iconic centerpiece of Devipuram.

The structure's genesis lay in one of Guruji's earliest encounters with Kamakhya, during a monsoon downpour. "She took me by the hand and we walked through the rain to the place where the Sri Chakra temple stands today," he said. "She told me to build it like a pyramid, and fill it with all the attendant Khadgamala deities installed in their places and receiving *puja* every day. At its center would be the main deity Lalita Maha Tripurasundari sitting atop Shiva, creating new worlds of higher harmonies. She said, '*Sarve Jana Sukhino Bhavantu!* May they bring happiness to one and all!' She told me, 'I am the Mother and this temple will be my child.'"

Since that stunning encounter, Guruji had periodically pondered the logistics such a project would entail—but the proliferation of complications at every level quickly became overwhelming, and he would set it aside to deal with more pressing concerns. He would surely take up the matter of the Sri Chakra temple one of these days, he thought, just not today. Not right now.

That state of affairs continued for only a few months, however, before Bala began bringing up the topic again and again. Guruji recalled, "She would come to me in the form of a little girl and ask, 'Daddy, when are you going to build a house for me?'

"I'd say, 'A house! What house?'

"She would say, 'You know what house.'

"So finally I thought, 'You know, maybe I'll try to build this thing after all.'"

He went to see Gurugaru in Anakapalle, describing both Bala's demands and his inclination to take up the project.[190] Gurugaru, however, balked. "No, no, no!" he said. "Don't go near this, Sastry; it's dangerous! You're asking for trouble. It's a huge project and you may very well find yourself unable to manage it. She'll drive you crazy!"

Guruji nodded thoughtfully and set the idea aside again. But a week or so later, Bala appeared once more, asking, "So when are you going to build me my house?"

Once more, Guruji took the matter to Gurugaru.

"And once again he said, 'Don't touch it; it's a bad business. You're setting yourself up for failure.' I asked him why and he said, 'Look Sastry, this isn't any ordinary structure. She wants you to build a Sri Chakra—many have tried before you, but none have ever succeeded.'"

After listing off a few such failed attempts—including one by no less a figure than Vidyaranya, renowned high priest to Harihara Raya I and Bukka Raya I, founders of the Vijayanagar Empire in the 14th century—Gurugaru added, "Consider this too: such an endeavor would be a big distraction from your *sadhana*. Take my word for it. Don't go near this."

Guruji nodded, bowed in *namaskaram* and returned to Devipuram.

Upon Bala's next appearance, he told her of his guru's response. She replied, "Okay, write down these stanzas and bring them to him." So Guruji noted down the Sanskrit verses. He then took the message to Gurugaru, who read it and went into meditation for a long time. Upon opening his eyes, he delivered his verdict: "Well it seems you are destined to do this, Sastry. I think you will complete it."[191]

And with that he poured a little water into Guruji's hands and said, "Go ahead and start building."

190 Guruji always sought the advice and permission of Anakapalle Gurugaru before any major undertaking, beginning with the 1982 Sagara Giri procession and including both of the temples built earlier at Devipuram.

191 Guruji shared these stanzas, but requested that they not be published and remain "a divine secret forever."

"Balaji was so relentless," Amma recalled of that period. "But once Anakapalle Gurugaru also realized that it was her *sankalpa*, he gave his blessings to the project and said, 'I will give all my *tapas shakti*[192] to you to complete it successfully.'"

॥
श्री॥

The next steps were determining the exact site for the temple, clearing and leveling it for construction, and plotting and marking the base coordinates. This Guruji did himself with great precision, using reference coordinates supplied by Kamakhya in meditation. "He marked all the points using poles and jute twine," Suryalakshmi said.

When workers began digging at the center point indicated by Guruji, they unearthed yet another surprise—this time a large underground silo apparently used to store cashews in olden times. Inside stood a two-foot-high Shiva *lingam* from some long-ago harvest *puja*, still decorated with three horizontal lines drawn in sandalwood paste. "So we discovered that Lord Shiva had been guarding the future site of the Sri Meru temple for all those years," Suryalakshmi said, "until it was ready to become the Mother's residence."

In meditation, Bala instructed Guruji to place a copper *yantra* of Matsya, Lord Vishnu's fish avatar, under the foundation stone at the center point of the temple.[193] On the night before the foundation stone was laid, it was to be consecrated by Guruji by chanting the Gayatri mantra 1,008 times.[194] The ceremony was planned accordingly.

Then things got complicated. Delivery of the *yantra* was delayed; it did not arrive until the night before the ceremony. Guruji was tired, but determined to proceed according to plan. As he sat to begin chanting, however, Kamakhya appeared and instructed him to increase the number of recitations upward from 1,008 to "two *crore*"[195] in order to spiritually supercharge the site.

Guruji was at a loss—the ceremony had already been arranged, an astrologically auspicious date selected, guests invited. But it would be physically impossible for him to complete so many recitations by morning—indeed it could take months or longer. The event would have to be scrapped and rescheduled. "Very well," he told Kamakhya, surrendering to her will. "As you wish." And since he had already begun chanting anyway, he decided to continue for a while and at least make a start. But at precisely that moment he felt himself transported with her to "some celestial plane."

192 Gurugaru's *tapas shakti* would be whatever power he had obtained through his spiritual austerities.

193 Guruji explained, "*Matsya* is a Tantric *mudra as well*. It signifies the upward travel of the *ojas* to the *bindu*, showering us with bliss of *amrita*."

194 The Gayatri mantra is one of Hinduism's oldest and most venerated Vedic hymns, drawn from the *Rig Veda*.

195 20 million.

"There she was before me, smiling in all her grace with her beautiful, lotus-petal eyes," he said. "And she told me, 'Sit and watch.'" As he did so, the cosmos seemed to spread out before him, a vast shimmering Sri Chakra filling its entirety. Within the intersections of the Chakra he saw 108 gatherings of a thousand *rishis* each, all of them chanting the Gayatri mantra simultaneously. The music of their voices, he said, filled the universe with "a deep, wave-like roar." Between them all, they easily completed the 20 million recitations, whereupon the vision faded. Guruji opened his eyes and looked around. Day was dawning; all the preliminary mantras were complete. The laying of the foundation stone would be completed on schedule after all.

"You see, she had given me a task that was impossible to accomplish in the given time," Guruji observed. "She wanted to test whether I would accept it or not. But when I did, she arranged everything without my having to make any effort."

The ceremony took place at high noon on Sunday, October 16, 1983, Vijaya Dashami, the day following the ninth night of *Navratri*. (Interestingly, this was a full month before the consecration of Sivalaya and Kamakhya, though the Meru temple was still more than a decade away from completion.)

The stone was laid as part of a solemn *sankhusthapana* or groundbreaking ceremony, which was supposed to have been presided over by a prominent local Brahmin politician. The politician, however, was running "late, very late," Anantalakshmi said. On hand and ready, however, were two local members of lower, "scheduled" castes—a female revenue officer named Sudha Rani and a male disciple of Guruji named Malleswara Rao.

When it became clear that that the politician would be a no-show, Guruji invited these two to fulfill his ceremonial role: Sudha Rani positioning the Matsya *yantra* over the foundation stone and Malleswara Rao cementing it into place. After they completed the task, the Brahmin belatedly arrived and—seeing that his job had already been completed—offered to read his prepared remarks anyway. His topic expanded upon a Telugu proverb, "The fortune of a stone, a place and a man cannot be foreseen."[196] Considering that the speaker's tardiness had elevated two members of scheduled castes into a role reserved for a Brahmin, Guruji observed, the proverb served to underscore that the Goddess "has no preference for any particular caste."

196 "The fortune of a stone, a place and a man cannot be foreseen. The first may be formed into an idol and worshiped; the second may be cultivated and made fruitful; and the third may become wealthy and be raised to a position of influence."

Long before construction began in earnest, Guruji had realized that the three-acre parcel donated by the Putrevu brothers was not large enough to accommodate the Meru temple. "Part of the temple site shown to me by the Devi was not included in the donated land—it was partly on that parcel, but partly outside. So to complete the Meru as she instructed, I needed to buy another piece of land." The funds in the Sri Vidya Trust account had been largely depleted in building the two smaller temples, so again Guruji dipped into his and Amma's personal savings in order to complete the transaction. It was yet another leap of faith.

"Being a scientist, I do still lack faith at times," Guruji said. "But she has guided me through every step. She told me once, 'Lack of faith is not an impediment to your progress. You must question at every step. Never take my word for granted. Test it out, and check the truth of it.' And she keeps testing me to this day, testing how steadfast I am. My God, the number of tests she puts you through is unimaginable. She'll take you right up to the last minute to test whether you're going to stand on your faith. And that's exactly when you have to stand firm, because only then will she give it to you."

In late 1986 Guruji would complete the purchase of an additional 10 acres of land adjacent to the original parcel, bringing the total size of Devipuram to slightly more than 13 acres.

In his initial conceptualization of the Meru temple, Guruji took as inspiration both the Sagara Giri model and the Meru he had unearthed at Kamakhya.

But in trying to realize that concept in brick and mortar, his first challenge was working out its enormously complex geometry, painstakingly recreating its 44 angles and nine enclosures, and then projecting them upward into a life-size, three-dimensional structure. And as he delved deeper into the specifics of the design, it became increasingly plain that his initial concept was both too big and too impractical.[197]

"The complication was that if each of the Meru's *avaranas* were built as one floor high—thus nine floors in all—the space at the *bindu sthanam* would be very, very small," daughter Rama explained. "So to maintain a sense of the Meru, Guruji allowed

197 Guruji's earliest conception involved a 108-foot-high structure. A later, 72-foot version is described in chapter 13. Guruji completed the temple in 1994, and as of this writing the structure at Devipuram still remains the largest Meru in the world.

a slight height distinction for the *srusthi* (creation) and *laya* (destruction) enclosures, while the *sthiti* (preservation) enclosure was accorded more space—hence the floors for the fourth, fifth and sixth *avaranas*."

While maintaining the 2:1 height/width dimensions of the Kamakhya Meru, the structure would be scaled to two of Hinduism's most sacred numbers: 108 feet wide by 54 feet high. That height comprised three stories totaling 30 feet, plus the dome *garbhalaya*[198] at 18 feet and the *kalasam*, or spire, at six feet, all centered precisely above the foundation stone.

198 The *garbhalaya* (womb chamber) or *bindu sthanam* (central point) are both terms designating the *sanctum sanctorum*, where the main temple deity resides.

In the end, the design would work, but the mental labor had been immense—and the physical construction would clearly be slow and painstaking. "It was no mean task," Guruji said, shaking his head. "It took four years—from 1984 until 1988—just to see to the accuracy of the geometry of the *yantra* on the ground. But I was helped at every stage of construction by Kamakhya, who acted as my consultant throughout. Whenever I was in doubt, I would ask a question and she would answer, always in embrace."

And so the Meru began to materialize, with Guruji providing designs, work assignments and technical guidance, and area villagers serving as day laborers. Word of Devipuram's ambitious new construction project was spreading. "So many young people came to help build it all," Suryalakshmi recalled. As they worked, she would busy herself preparing a hearty vegetarian lunch for the workers. "They seemed very appreciative that I made it and served it to them myself," she recalled.

One day while touring the construction site with Alok, Guruji motioned toward a handmade ladder rising precariously from the ground and spanning the temple's skeletal frame toward the partially constructed dome. He told Alok to climb up and have a look around.

"So I climbed," Alok said, despite a lifelong fear of heights. "The ladder was shaking all the way and so was I. Guruji shouted up, 'Don't worry! It will hold you; I've climbed it many times!' And as I got higher up and looked around, I began to understand why he wanted me to go up there. He wanted me to see—to *realize*—for myself just how difficult it had been to put everything together. When you're in the middle of a jungle, when your labor is unskilled, when you don't have the money—when all you have is your vision."

Remarkably, Alok added, Guruji projected absolutely no sense of attachment to the project. He seemed to be watching Devipuram rise and expand with the same curiosity and fascination as any other onlooker. "Guruji always made it clear that the ownership of Devipuram did not reside with him," he said. "In fact, I would always joke with him, saying, 'Devipuram was constructed not because of but *despite* your poor management skills!'

"For me, the fact that this place is here at all is sufficient proof that the Goddess exists!'"

A drawing sketched by Guruji while explaining Sri Vidya worship to a disciple.

(Sundhara Arasaratnam)

18   Stringing a Garland of Swords

By the end of 1988, after years of painstaking design and off-and-on construction—progress generally fluctuating on some combination of donor largesse and Guruji's physical availability—the primary frame of the Sri Meru temple was nearing completion. Yet an equally daunting task still lay ahead: to populate it with sculptures that embodied the myriad deities of Sri Vidya ritual practice, more than a hundred of them in all. Once again, the task was almost overwhelming in its scope.

In Sri Vidya cosmology, the *Navavarana*—the "nine enclosures" or tiers of the Meru—is populated by a group of female deities (*devis* or *yoginis*) totaling 108 in all, each representing a discrete aspect or power of the Goddess. Collectively, they are sometimes referred to as the *Khadgamala Devis* (literally, "Goddesses of the Garland of Swords"), after a popular teaching hymn that enumerates all of their names.[199] For centuries, these goddesses have been worshiped by Sri Vidya adherents with a complex series of mantric, meditational and ritual practices by which the devotee mentally circumambulates and ascends successive levels of the Meru, paying homage to each goddess along the way, meditationally absorbing and assimilating her before moving on to the next.

But while the technique was ancient, most of these primarily meditational deities had never been represented in physical form in a temple setting.[200] Unlike most Hindu

199   See "Introduction: The World of Sri Vidya" in *The Goddess and the Guru, Volume II.*

200   While most of the *Khadgamala Devis* are esoteric meditational goddesses, exclusive to Sri Vidya practice, a few—such as Mahalakshmi and Varahi, for example—are known in broader Hindu practice. In the case of these goddesses already possessing established *dhyanas*, Guruji also based his iconography on their canonical descriptions.

deities, they have no *dhyana* descriptions—that is, as essentially secret, esoteric goddesses, they never possessed the canonical physical descriptions that generally help artists and devotees to envision what a given Hindu god or goddess "looks like" based on experiential testimony of the *rishis*. In the absence of such precedents, Guruji asked the Goddess how to begin.

"Meditate and they will appear to you," she told him. "They will play games with you, but don't run away from their erotic play—that is how they transmit their powers.'"

At this point, it is worth noting, a *third* form of the Goddess had begun communicating with Guruji about the temple. Rather than Bala or Kamakhya, "during this phase it was Hladini—more familiarly known as Radha, lover of Lord Krishna—who spoke to me," he said. "So over the entire period of construction, I had a total of three divine mentors: first Bala, then Kamakhya and finally Hladini."[201]

ॐ
ह्रीं

In accordance with the Goddess's instructions, Guruji began systematically meditating on each successive *Khadgamala* goddess. Hladini herself would take the form of each, while Guruji carefully noted "her form, posture and weapons," and then described them to a professional sculptor. The innate artistic abilities he displayed in childhood came in handy during this process. "As she revealed each goddess to me, I would translate those visions to the sculptor in words and drawings, and he would then use these descriptions to create concrete castings," Guruji said.

Guruji found this visualization process to be immensely enjoyable, often spending hours in meditation for a single *devi*. "I saw how her perfect creative potential manifested itself in each of her different aspects, in each varying image of her beauty, all in three dimensions," he said. "Each one unique, each perfect in her own way."

The sculptor who gave life to these visions was Sri Gopalachari, an experienced temple artist from Kuppam, halfway between Bangalore and Chennai. Gopalachari took up residence at Devipuram while he completed the work. "My vision accounted for about 80 percent of each image you see depicted in the temple," Guruji said. "The remaining 20 percent was the vision of Gopalachari"—whom Guruji initiated and trained in Sri Vidya especially for the purpose.

201 Hladini is an androgynous appellation meaning literally, "the power of love," drawn from Puranic stories of the divine couple Krishna and Radha, and used to refer to both. Saraswati had for a time referred to Guruji as Hladini. In the *Blue Book* later published by Guruji, he listed Hladini in his Guru lineage alongside Anakapalle Gurugaru, implying that she was Swaprakasananda's *Shakti*.

"I wanted their skin color, eyes, attire—their entire forms—to be as real as they could be, so as to help *sadhakas* feel their presence," Guruji said. He added with a smile, "Some said I should not have made them so sexually provocative. But if they could have seen what I saw, they'd be surprised at how much I downplayed the provocativeness of their true forms! I am just sorry I couldn't perfectly capture them exactly as they were—alas, that would have taken thousands of lives of overwork! Maybe someday we'll be able to see each other's visions in real time by recording our thought waves from a million angles and then collating them into a coherent picture using supercomputers. But until then, we have only the statements of people such as myself who try to describe our experiences."

And for many, that was enough. "Thousands of visitors have reported seeing the *devis* walking and dancing, alive on the premises of the Sri Meru temple," Guruji said with satisfaction.

One was Swethambari Koteshwara Rao, a landscape and interior designer from Secunderabad, who confided that she first saw this "deeper aspect" of the Meru deities about a decade ago.

"There's much more to those *devis* than Guruji ever revealed on the surface; there are deeper layers in each of them," Swethambari said. "They are so much more alive and ecstatic than Guruji has shown in the physical idols. You'll laugh, but I've actually heard them talking to one other and to me too; whispering, giggling, blushing, fluttering their eyelids—more playful than schoolgirls! They dwell in a *sukshma loka*, or subtle sphere, that coincides exactly with the temple structure. I have witnessed it. Guruji knew all about these layers, of course, but—for reasons known to him alone— he never brought them out for the public. Yet one time when I shared my experiences with him, he said the world had come a long way since the Sri Meru was built, and that more and more people were maturing and ripening sufficiently to witness the unfolding of these deeper layers."

Unfortunately, such subtleties were lost upon many. Critics once again condemned the nude and often erotically posed *Khadgamala Devi* sculptures, just as they had censured the *murtis* of the Kamakhya and Sivalaya temples.[202]

Yet in terms of traditional Indian iconography, none were particularly shocking. "They are not even nude, technically speaking," Sree Padma noted. "They are clothed.

202 See chapter 24, "The Power-house of Devipuram."

189

Historically women in India either didn't wear any upper garment, or else just a piece of fabric tied around the breasts but not entirely covering them. That is entirely consistent with tradition; a lot of goddesses are shown like that."

For his part, Guruji was past worrying over public perceptions.

"By this time, a divide had formed between the value system that society had imposed upon me and the value system that I had been taught by the Goddess and had started believing in," he said. "They clashed. As soon as I began seeing everybody as a part of me, the concept of being ashamed or shaming others—'I am nude! You are nude!'—ceased to exist for me. And this can be very hard for one's society, or for one's family, to accept. They may think, 'This person must be depraved!' And however much you try to tell them, 'Look, you don't understand...,' it's still really hard for them to accept."

Over the next seven years, from 1988 until 1994, the Meru gradually filled with *Khadgamala Devi* sculptures. Ninety were Gopalachari's near-life-size figures, crafted in cement mortar and painted in bright enamels. Seventy of these were arranged at ground level with many housed under their own roofs, creating a series of mini-shrines within the Meru grounds. Another 20 were positioned on the first and second levels above the ground. Then came a number of smaller bronze deities as one approached the top.

Clarifying the correspondence between the temple layout and the design of a typical Meru icon, daughter Radha noted, "The ground floor consists of the *bhupura* (i.e., the outer three lines housing the 10 *siddhis*, eight *matrikas*, and 10 *mudra shaktis*), the 16-petaled lotus, the eight-petaled lotus, and the *devis* of the 14-cornered figure. The first floor [U.S. second floor] contains the *devis* of outer 10-triangle figure, and the second floor [U.S. third floor] houses the *devis* of the inner 10-triangle figure. The highest point, at the dome, houses the eight *vagdevis*, the *trikona* and the *bindu*." (In addition to this array, there are several invisible *devis* "hidden in the three lines of the *bhupura*," Guruji noted.)

At the focal point of the temple, sitting in regal splendor within the dome, was a magnificent (and completely traditional) black granite sculpture of Devipuram's main deity, Sri Sahasrakshi Rajarajeswari. An important form of Lalita Tripurasundari in temple worship,[203] Sahasrakshi symbolically contains, subsumes and transcends all of the Meru's other deities.

Her monumental *vigraha* had been created to Guruji's precise specifications by Sri Netranandam, a well-known *shilpi*, or hereditary religious sculptor, from the famed temple city of Tirupati, 500 miles (800 kilometers) to the south.[204] Netranandam's Sahasrakshi carries a noose and an elephant goad in her two upper hands, flower arrows and a sugar cane bow in her lower two hands. She is seated atop (generally understood to mean "in sexual union with") the prone figure of her consort Kameshwara, one of Lord Shiva's most handsome and alluring forms. Her right leg is tucked up and her left foot hanging down, indicating her "left" or Tantric orientation.[205] It took Netranandam three months to complete the sculpture, which would become the first deity installed and consecrated in the Meru, via a formal *prana-prathista* ceremony.[206]

In fact, shortly before the *Prathista*, Guruji personally transported the massive sculpture to Devipuram on a marathon pickup-and-delivery adventure with his son-in-law Prabhakar, husband of youngest daughter Rama.

"We drove her all the way from Tirupati in a Maruti van," Guruji recalled. The precarious drive back to Devipuram took an entire sweltering day that taxed the vehicle's engine, suspension system and human occupants to the limit.[207] "The tires were getting hot, too," he said. "We were worried whether one might burst, because we had no usable spare."

Sahasrakshi finally did arrive safely in Devipuram with van and drivers intact, but a larger task still lay ahead—to raise the six-foot, 650-kilogram (1,433-pound) sculpture some 50 feet to the peak of the Sri Meru without the aid of a crane or other motorized assistance (luxuries that still remained beyond the reach and means of the remote temple complex). This arduous lift was carried out manually on Wednesday, May 9, 1990, a full-moon day just weeks before the formal *Prathista* ceremony.

"We built chain lifts to take her up the first two floors," Guruji said—and that was the easy part. "The third and final floors were the most difficult," he continued. "She

203 The literal meaning of Sahasrakshi is "She With a Thousand Eyes," figuratively understood as "the All-Seeing." *Rajarajeswari* means "Empress of Emperors." This omniscient regent is the supreme *anthropomorphic* manifestation of Sri Vidya's highest deity, Sri Lalita Tripurasundari. Lalita herself manifests mainly in the form of Sri Chakra and her mantras. For further details, see *The Goddess and the Guru, Volume II*.

204 A *shilpi* is a sculptor highly trained in *vastu* (the Indian predecessor science to *feng shui*). Shilpis sculpt temple deities to extremely precise mathematical specifications that also correspond to the dimensions and orientation of the temples in which they are seated. Some say that one needs to learn from a *shilpi* master to really understand the icons of India.

205 Shiva's size in the sculpture is notably smaller than that of Devi, to the extent that it seems out of proportion at first glance. Guruji states that this design is intentional, "because Devi, due to her dynamic nature, appears much 'bigger' than the static Siva. In other words, her influence on our perception is far greater."

206 *Prana-prathista* means "Installment of the Life Force," and indicates the ritual by which a stone sculpture is infused with the spirit of a deity and rendered ready for worship.

207 The Maruti Omni van–a popular vehicle manufactured by Maruti Suzuki India Limited–was powered by a 796 cubic centimeter (49 cubic inch) inline-four engine that would have been seriously challenged by a moving job of this magnitude.

had to be lifted by hand by six people. I was worried that somebody would be mortally hurt!"

The stairway, which had been designed—like the rest of the temple—by Guruji alone, was precisely wide enough to accommodate the statue's base. However, the structure's capacity to bear the weight of the statue was still strictly theoretical. "Keep in mind, I wasn't a civil engineer," Guruji said. "We simply didn't know whether the stairs would take the load."

They did, though the job was massive. It took three grueling hours for the six laborers to carry the sculpture up the final 10 feet. When they reached the narrow top floor, a dozen more workers joined them in lifting the sculpture onto the concrete plinth that had been prepared to receive it.[208] "That was the final test," Guruji said. "Would the slab I built take the load of the sculpture plus about 18 people?"

Again, it did. "When we had finally placed her in position, everyone heaved a sigh of relief!" he said.

As the sun sank toward the western horizon, Guruji performed a brief *laghu prathista*—a simplified, "light" consecration prayer in advance of the elaborate formal ritual to come—and as the full moon rose at dusk, the gathered devotees were rewarded with a view that seemed to clearly express divine pleasure with their efforts.

"It was the perfect time—6 p.m. exactly," Guruji said. "The sun was setting in the west; the full moon was rising in the east: sun, moon and Devi were all exactly aligned."

ॐ
ह्रीं

The formal *Prathista* ceremony began a couple of weeks later on the new moon day of Thursday, May 24, and continued for 11 days until Monday, June 4, 1990. The spring weather was typically hot and dry and the sun was relentless, with temperatures hovering around 100°F (38°C).

Sundhara Arasaratnam, who traveled from Toronto with Haran Aiya to take part in the festivities, remembers his impression upon seeing Devipuram for the first time. "I knew that it was still under development, but I was taken aback," he said. "It was *very* desolate, dry and bushy. There were no proper roads, just dirt footpaths strewn with thorns, shrubs and sharp stones. But there were also birds singing, cows lowing, cashew and palm leaves rustling in the hot breeze."

208 These were not all Hindu workers, but representatives of several other faiths as well, Amma noted.

And of course there were humans. "Everywhere around me people were working, readying the temple for the *Prathista*—I could hear work instructions being called out, carpenters thudding hammers, women walking elegantly by with building materials balanced on their heads. Everywhere I was met with welcoming smiles—all Guruji's golden influence, I think. Everyone seemed happy and harmonious. And as I settled in, a sense of absolute contentment sank into me as well."

Soon after his arrival, Sundhara climbed alone to the peak of the Meru temple. "I could see the mountains to the west and the Sivalaya temple and Kamakhya Peetam to the north," he said. "Beyond Sivalaya were more cashew plantations and coconut groves. To the south there were teak plantations and, just past them, some small village dwellings. And yet this remote area was gradually being transformed into a spiritual teaching establishment!"

By this time, the all-purpose thatched hut once known as Devipuram Circus had been replaced by the ground floor of the Ashram where Guruji and Amma resided. "There was a concrete roof in place with plans to build more flats on top," Sundhara said. "Guruji occupied the first flat on the north side of the building and the other three rooms were for people permanently residing there and helping him."

As the sun rose on the first day of the *Prathista*, loudspeakers broadcast the Gayatri mantra and hymns of praise as Gurugaru patrolled the edges of the property, reciting mantras to ward away poisonous snakes and insects. A new *homa kunda*[209] had been constructed in an open, thatched-roofed structure directly under the eastward-facing visage of Sahasrakshi at the top of the Meru.

209 Ritual fire pit.

The master of ceremonies was once again Krishnayaji—the same priest who had, more than a decade earlier, presided over the grand *Devi Yagna* in Visakhapatnam. He was accompanied by five trained Vedic priests, or *ritwiks*. "They took their place in the ceremonial hut and commenced the preliminaries," Sundhara recalled. "Sahasrakshi's eyes were covered with a soft cloth, the idea being that, over the course of the *Prathista* ceremony, the energy from her eyes would become too intense. Then Guruji and Amma arrived and took their seats as well, both of them emanating a strong golden aura—it was as if Shiva and Shakti themselves had come to preside in person."

The *kalasa* pots were installed and the initial rituals began—*Maha Nyasa*, followed by the *Pancha Sukta* and other *pujas*. And as the Vedic ceremonies proceeded in the *homa kunda* shed, Tantric *pujas* were conducted at Sivalaya and Kamakhya Peetam. Activities paused at 2 p.m., allowing for lunch and a nap in the heat of the day. At six in the evening, participants reconvened around the *homa kunda* to chant the *Lalita Sahasranama*, followed by devotional singing and then a philosophical talk by Guruji. The *ritwiks* assembled a *Maha-lingam* from 1,008 smaller *lingams*, and performed additional rounds of *pujas*. Each day's events were capped by classical dance and music performances.[210] Variations of this routine were repeated over all 11 days of the event, as more and more people poured in from surrounding villages and towns.

The event's grand finale took place on Monday, June 4, 1990. "By then the strength of the crowd was a good 5,000," Sundhara said. "People came in waves despite the limited transportation facilities and the intense sun and heat."

The *Prathista* culminated with the *abhishekam*, or ritual bathing of Sahasrakshi in the waters of the *kalasa*, fully energized after 11 days of prayer and chanting. "The *prana*[211] was invoked into her by Guruji," Sundhara recounted. "She was dressed like a bride and all the *upacharas*[212] were offered to her. The cloth covering her eyes was removed, and the full *aarti* was offered to her with *naivedhya*.[213] The *bali* was cooked rice and pumpkin, broken in front of her, then red *kumkum* spattered over on top of it."[214]

It is said that if all the rituals of a *Prathista* are performed correctly, then at their conclusion some envoy of the five elements—earth, water, fire, air or ether—will appear and forcefully make their presence known.

"And that's exactly what happened," Sundhara said. "The scorching noontime sun was suddenly obscured by dark clouds, and a huge thunderstorm rolled in with gale-force winds and torrential rains soaking the parched earth to mud.

"A group of us were standing on the second floor of the Meru temple, listening to the loud croaking of frogs and chirping of birds and letting the drenching rain cool us off from the heat of the previous few days. And that's when I noticed Guruji standing outside the Ashram, smiling up at us all. He looked so happy! It was a memory for a lifetime."

210 Srividya, Radha noted, was "born just after my aunt [Sundari Amma, Guruji's first disciple] watched the blockbuster movie *Jai Santoshi Maa*, and she named 'Srividya' after the Goddess's manifestation in Guruji's life!"

211 Life energy.

212 *Upacharas* are various ritual services–denoting the sort of love and respect shown to an honored guest–that are offered to the deity in worship.

213 *Naivedhya* is food offered to the deity as part of a worship ritual, before the offerer eats or distributes it.

214 *Bali* is historically an animal sacrifice associated with some sects of Shaktism, but in most modern practice–as in this instance–is performed with a vegetable substitute.

Those who attended the *Prathista* also got an early taste of Guruji's unique and personal approach to temple worship. Atypically, there were no priests or other "gatekeepers" standing between the worshipers and the worshiped: no altars, and no restrictions based on caste, gender or religion. It was a hands-on temple, and everyone was welcome to participate in *pujas* and freely interact with the deities of their choice.

"In most other temples, the deity sculptures are far away," Guruji explained. "You can't touch them; often you can't even *see* them. But at Devipuram you can walk up and touch them, get to know them, literally shake hands with them! That's our specialty: the deities are not kept far away in guarded towers. They are all fully accessible to all, and that accessibility is an important part of the experience. I want people to come and enjoy spirituality in resonance with nature, so that their finer instincts come to the fore.

"That was the vision I had."

A few days after the *Prathista* ceremony, Guruji invited a small group of family and friends to accompany him and Amma on a picnic at the Simhachalam temple outside Vizag.

"It was one of Guruji's favorite haunts; he used to go there a lot," said Jana, the Irvine-based businessman, who was 19 at the time. When they arrived at the temple, Guruji took him aside. "He told everyone else to go on to the main sanctum—you know, 'We'll meet up later,'" Jana recalled. "But he told me to stay with him, saying, 'Come on, there's someone I want you to meet.'"

Guruji deftly navigated his way through a small back corridor into an open-air courtyard within the temple walls. There he approached a small hut, a retreat for saints. He knocked on the gate, calling out, "Gurugaru! Gurugaru!"[215] And after a few minutes, an elderly man came limping angrily toward the gate. His hair hung past his waist in long, matted dreadlocks—still quite black though his bushy beard was gray; he wore only a red *dhoti* and no shirt. "Who's there? Who's bothering me?" he snapped, squinting against the sun as he approached. Then a few steps away his expression softened and his face lit up with recognition. "Ah!" he said. "Sastry Garu, it's you! Come around to the front, I'll let you in."

215 Guruji uses the term "Gurugaru" here not as a reference to Anakapalle Gurugaru, but simply as a Telugu honorific meaning "Respected Teacher."

As they walked from the gate to the door, Jana whispered, "Who is he?"

"He is a very old saint," Guruji said. "Some say over 400 years old. My grandfather knew him well and used to come and see him."

The elderly Swami was, in fact, one of India's more legendary modern religious figures, known as the Saint of Simhachalam or *Jatala Sadhu*, the Dreadlocked Ascetic. During his lifetime, the Saint was visited by some of India's most prominent leaders—including Prime Minister Indira Gandhi, and Presidents Varahagiri Venkata Giri and Giani Zail Singh. He was for a time associated with the famed saint Sai Baba of Shirdi (1838–1918), and is reputed to have given his blessings to Lakshmibai, the legendary Rani of Jhansi (1828–1858), a towering figure in India's First War of Independence. A pamphlet published by a Hyderabad shrine dedicated to his memory offers the surprising details of his life:

> Swamiji was born around A.D. 1550, the eighth child to his parents. He is accredited by medical tests conducted by qualified doctors of the All India Institute Of Medical Sciences (AIIMS) in New Delhi, to have lived for more than 400 years. By the standards of modern day science, this may look impossible but by his own narration of the past to his devotees, the Swamiji has expressed personal familiarity with events spanning over four centuries and this evidence is borne out by many documents. He came to the holy and pious Simhachalam around 1850, at the time of the foreigners' onslaught [i.e., the period leading up to the First War of Independence from Great Britain]. During his stay at Simhachalam, four generations of families served him. At the time of coming to Simhachalam, he was naked but for the long, matted hair [i.e., dreadlocks] hanging over his body. Subsequently, he started wearing a saffron *dhoti*.

To readers of Tantra-related literature, the Saint of Simhachalam may be more familiar as "Junior Guru Maharaj," a pseudonym bestowed by Robert Svoboda in his 1986 book, *Aghora: At the Left Hand of God*, wherein the guru called Vimalananda relates an interesting episode from the Saint's life:

If I tell you his origin, you won't believe me. When Lord Curzon was Viceroy of India at the turn of the century, archaeological excavations were going on in the state of Orissa, and in a cave in one hill they discovered the perfectly preserved body of an old sadhu. Someone thought to call a man from the Jagannath temple in Puri who knew about samadhi and such things, and after massage, and oil rubs, and I don't know what else he was able to bring the sadhu down from his samadhi and back into consciousness of the world. That sadhu is my Junior Guru Maharaj. I have met people who have known him ever since then and they say his looks have not changed in the least up to the present day, except that in some places his hair has grayed.

Vimalananda adds that at "first glance he didn't look like much to me," but that he soon realized, "Yes, this man has some power!" He later learned that "after being dug out of that cave" the old saint had "spent twelve years on the branch of a tree doing *japa*, never touching the ground even once." Moreover he was "still doing his *sadhana* every day" during his narration, which takes place in the 1970s and '80s. "You see, he has done terrific *sadhana* all his life. He has done such penances that … there is no one in India, and that means in the world, to beat him at doing penances."

When Jana and Guruji arrived at the hut's front door, the old Saint pulled them inside, and slammed the door shut behind them after casting a grimace at the gaggle of pilgrims waiting outside. "People who knew who he was were camping out in front of his home in those days," Jana said. "They just wanted to get a glimpse of him; they were trying to get his *darshan*."[216]

The Saint led them into his quarters and there sat cross-legged atop his cot, which was cluttered with "bottles of Thums Up and Limca soda pop, and newspapers," Jana said. "You couldn't even see the mattress. He seemed to be a hoarder; he kept a lot of things piled on the bed and just sat on top of them."

Guruji and the old man were soon comparing notes on various arcane details of meditation and ritual technique while Jana looked on, mystified. "The Saint was a

216 *Darshan* here meaning an audience with the Saint.

very, very intense person," he said. "His eyes were startling and crystal clear." Finally, the old man seemed to notice Jana.

"Did you want to ask me anything?" he said, abruptly.

Still shocked by Guruji's revelation of the Saint's age, Jana stammered, "How old are you?"

"I don't know," the Saint replied.

His mind blank, Jana blurted, "Can I take your photo to show people back home?"

"No," he said and abruptly returned to his conversation with Guruji.

"Sastry Garu," the old man said toward the end of the exchange, "I'd like to speak with you about something. A few months ago, I took a [karmic] load off of someone, and it came to me in the form of a cold, with phlegm and a fever. I've been unable to shake it off; it's still lingering in my body."

Guruji said, "Give me your hand." Taking the old man's palm in his, he locked eyes with him for a moment, and then said, "Okay." He released the Saint's hand; that was all.

"The Saint thanked him glowingly, looking at him with such love," Jana said.

"Please, let me give something to you in return," he told Guruji.

"I don't need anything," Guruji replied.

The old man hesitated for a moment and then, turning to Jana, said, "Come here and do *namaskaram* to me."

"So I did, and he touched me," Jana recalled. "And that touch was so electric, such an inexplicable feeling. I know that he passed something on to me. I was just in shock."

A few minutes later, Guruji took his leave of the Saint, and led Jana by the hand back into the main sanctum of Simhachalam, where he suddenly stopped just before rejoining the others, and gave him a mantra, completing the Saint's gift. "He told me to keep it, that it would always be there to protect me," Jana said. "I share this story only because I want to emphasize that Guruji was never an ordinary person, by any means. I want people to know his true intensity. Even someone of this Saint's caliber explicitly acknowledged how powerful he was."

Years later, Jana met Svoboda, the author of *Aghora*, and related his experience with Guruji and the Saint. Svoboda was skeptical.

"In order to test me, he asked me things like, 'Where did you meet him? What does he look like? What was particular about him?'" Jana said. "When I was able to answer with full conviction and accuracy, he finally affirmed that his 'Junior Guru Maharaj' was indeed the Saint whom I had met. And when I told him how he was affiliated with Guruji—that he was actually Guruji's good friend—Svoboda was quite shocked because this guru did not receive a lot of people; not just anyone could go and see him. He was only able to vibrate at a certain level, and would only receive people to whom he could relate on that vibratory level."

In 2015, nearly three decades after *Aghora*'s publication, Svoboda confirmed that it was indeed "Jatala Sadhu who appears in the *Aghora* books as 'Junior Guru Maharaj.'" He elaborated:

> I met Jatala Sadhu in early 1982, introduced to him by his disciple Vimalananda. Thereafter I visited him at his ashram at Simhachalam once (occasionally twice) each year until he left this earth eleven years later. Each visit lasted for three days, which was his limit for guests from the outside world, and I felt extraordinarily fortunate to have been allowed that long. Guru Maharaj (which is how I always addressed him) was intensely intolerant of almost everyone, and at least once daily during my stay I would be treated to the spectacle of some pilgrim coming to his door hoping for permission to come into his presence only to be loudly told '*Po re!*' (Telugu for 'Go on!' or 'Git!'). Should such would-be devotees attempt to insist, importune or beg, Guru Maharaj would shout at them with greater volume, and if they still refused to move on he would pick up whatever was handy (a banana, a coconut, a rock) and throw it vigorously in the miscreant's direction. That would do the trick. ... Whatever may be the veracity behind claims ... for his longevity ... I can personally testify to the fact that he was indeed very, *very* old.

Guruji added that the Saint was also very close to Anakapalle Gurugaru, who once told him, "The Saint of Simhachalam gave me *Sanyasa Diksha*, and I in turn gave him

217 In other words, Anakapalle Gurugaru received formal initiation into the renunciate's life from the Saint of Simhachalam, and as *dakshina* offered the Saint the highest level of initiation into Sri Vidya *upasana*.

218 Guruji reflects upon the meaning of this exchange in the epilogue of this book.

219 *Mrita Sanjeevani* is most famously mentioned in the epic *Ramayana*, when Lord Rama's brother Lakshmana is mortally wounded, and Lord Hanuman is dispatched by Rama to bring *Sanjeevani* from the mountain Dronagiri in the Himalayas. When he reaches the mountain, however, Hanuman is unable to identify the herb—so he lifts the entire mountain and brings it to Rama.

220 The Marwaris or Marwadis are a nomadic people originating in Rajasthan.

221 Holy basil, or *tulasi* (*Ocimum tenuiflorum*), is an aromatic plant in the family *Lamiaceae*, which is native to the Indian subcontinent.

Maha Shodashi."[217] The two *sannyasis* remained close friends; Guruji remembered once seeing the Saint greet Gurugaru by affectionately rubbing his head and saying, "*Pichi, Pichi, Pichi!*"—Telugu for "You're mad, mad, mad!" Though mystified at the time, Guruji would vividly recall this exchange in the final months of his life and give it great significance.[219]

Guruji affirmed to another disciple, William Thomas, an American living in the Netherlands, that the Saint might indeed have been over four centuries old. "Guruji told me his great-grandfather had told his father how he used to sit on the Saint's knee when he was a little boy—so by his family's recollections alone, they could verify his age to be at least around 200 years old."

When Thomas met the Saint shortly before the old man died in the early '90s, he was lying on his bed. "I remember it was difficult to look him in the eyes," Thomas said. "I had never seen anyone with such intense eyes; they were like burning coals. There was something unnatural about him, though not in a bad way. He really seemed like a being from another world or dimension. I have never met anyone like him since."

Guruji said that, for a long time, the Saint maintained a garden of extremely rare medicinal herbs—including *Mrita Sanjeevani*, a legendary plant that reputedly possesses the power to revive the dead.[219] He once witnessed the herb in action when a Marwari widow arrived at the Saint's retreat with the body of her newly deceased husband in tow.[220] "She was wailing and saying, 'Is there no one in this holy place who can bring my husband back to life?'" Guruji recalled. "The Saint came out, held the root of the *Sanjeevani* to the corpse's nose, and the Marwari gentleman woke up from death."

Guruji experienced a somewhat less dramatic use of the herb garden on another occasion, when he was visiting the Saint with Anakapalle Gurugaru. The conversation had been dragging on for hours, and Guruji was growing impatient. "I felt hungry so I kept nudging my guru, like 'Come on, let's go get something to eat!' Well, when the Saint noticed me doing this, he went and plucked two *tulasi* leaves from his garden.[221] He gave one to each of us, saying 'Eat it!' We did, and our hunger disappeared."

This mystical horticultural treasure was, unfortunately, lost a few years later when "some jealous soul set fire to his garden of invaluable herbs," Guruji noted. And resilient though he was, the ancient Saint of Simhachalam himself finally passed on as well, leaving this world on June 5, 1993, at a reputed age of around 443. His *samadhi* can still be visited in the Simhachalam Uphills.

🕉 Amma attends to the bookkeeping for Devi-puram, mid-1990s.
(Sri Vidya Trust)

19　The Backbone of Devipuram

As Devipuram's development consumed increasing slabs of Guruji's time, it fell to his wife Annapurna—by then known simply as "Amma" to most—to maintain some semblance of normalcy, routine and stability in their lives. That task became infinitely more challenging when she and Guruji shifted their primary residence from the family home in Vizag to the Ashram at Devipuram.

In the ensuing years, she became a ubiquitous presence there, greeting and conversing with visitors, inquiring after their comfort and making any necessary accommodations (for example, reducing spice levels for those who found the Andhra fare served in the canteen too fiery). Yet she remained, in many ways, an enigma. "Until you really get to know her, just a little snippet here and there is all she'll say; that's it—otherwise, no news," said Haran Aiya.

Yet it is not uncommon to hear disciples and visitors debate the precise nature of her role in Guruji's life and work. "Amma is very difficult to understand," said Smt. Satyavati, a Mumbai housewife who befriended Amma in the mid-1980s and has been a close confidante for more than 30 years. "Essentially you should realize that she was the compassion behind Guruji. She was the strength behind him."

Ahalya Arasaratnam, a Toronto businesswoman, concurred: "Guruji himself on many occasions called Amma his guru—the energy, the *shakti*, behind all that happens with him. Without her, he said, there is no life."

Certainly any account of Guruji's life or of Devipuram itself would be incomplete without a consideration of Amma's incalculable contribution. "The whole of Devipuram depends upon her for so much of its everyday, normal functioning," said a former staff member at the temple complex, who asked to remain anonymous. "If Guruji was the life-force of Devipuram, then Guruji Amma was its backbone." He elaborated:

> She was a project manager and administrator of the highest caliber—systematic and streamlined. It was she who assigned eight hours of work to staff members every day. She maintained the accounts. She answered the phones. She decided the daily menu in the canteen, measured out the ingredients and gave them to the cook. She divided up the flowers every day for the different shrines. And if Guruji ever asked for any document or record—even if it was 10 years old— Amma would go into the storage room and return with the requested materials within minutes. She knew where everything was.

Yet Alok noted that Amma's multiple roles illuminated another essential truth about Devipuram—and about Guruji himself.

"The point is really not how well Amma performed these accounting and management tasks," he said. "The point is that she is *not* a trained accountant or manager; she did it all as per her understanding. She was in a position where she *had* to manage accounts and take on all these tasks, not unlike how Guruji's sister *had* to become a priestess, or unskilled village women *had* to become the builders, or Guruji *had* to become the architect.

"In many ways, this has been the underlying story of Devipuram from the beginning, and it was the root cause of Guruji's difficulties," Alok explained. "He never forced anybody to come to Devipuram; he never promised them, 'This would be good for you.' To the contrary, he told them to do what was best for them. And when the person wasn't sure what was best, he would help them by providing his meditative intuition—which often meant telling them not to stay at Devipuram."

Those who know the couple best say Amma's most important role in Guruji's life was as a sounding board and reality check for his idealistic dreams. If Guruji was the accelerator pedal, in other words, forever racing forward with new projects and initiatives, Amma often found herself obliged to be the brake, keeping those projects within the realm of the possible—and within budget.

"Amma was always trying to make the best use of available resources and minimize waste," said daughter Radha. "She strived at all costs to maintain harmony, which allowed Guruji to focus on bigger-picture concerns."

"Many a time, Guruji was all about the grand plans and magnificent visions," daughter Anantalakshmi added. "When that happened, Amma would go through a threefold process. First, if the plan was too ambitious or timing not quite right, she expressed her views to Guruji, generally in private." Having had her say, Amma then left him to decide the matter in meditation—this was the second step, "the 'letting go' phase, saying, 'The Goddess will take care.'"

If Guruji determined the plan should go forward, "then Amma went into hands-on, back-office planning and detailing mode, to see how best that vision could be achieved," Anantalakshmi concluded. "She never became overwhelmed in the face of inevitable obstacles; she always met them with wit and wisdom. Guruji knew this about her, which is one reason why he was always able to remain so cool and calm."

The same yin-and-yang quality that was notable in the couple's earliest years together found its full fruition at Devipuram. Even a casual day visitor would quickly realize that Amma was Guruji's most tireless protector and guardian—whether helping prepare for an elaborate *puja*, managing workforce and budget issues, or providing input and counterbalance on the more controversial erotic elements in the temples. Consequently she was often perceived, positively or negatively, as Guruji's "gatekeeper"—her "sharp eye and sharper hearing always catching the subtle nuances in the body language and mannerisms of everyone around her."

"Amma was fiercely protective of Guruji," Radha elaborated. "She was absolutely impervious to being misunderstood or misinterpreted by those seeking to sway him in one direction or another. She stood her ground, often fighting an uphill battle to arrive at a practical approach to the frequently idealistic plans floated by Guruji, though she always trusted him implicitly and shared his vision and goals."

Alok recalled the time he was relaxing at a lecture by Guruji, neither taking notes nor taping it, but just letting the words wash over him. Amma noticed this and whispered, in a scolding tone that was only half in jest, "What kind of disciple are you? Do you already know everything that Guruji is talking about? That is Saraswati Devi speaking—and you're not even recording it?"

The depth of Amma's reverence for Guruji sometimes obscured the fact that she was an advanced and experienced Sri Vidya *upasaka* in her own right. "She would never miss her daily *pujas*," the former staff member noted. "She has regularly chanted the *Durga Saptashati* for the past 30 years or more." And when caught in the right mood, Amma will occasionally share her own extraordinary premonitions of Devipuram in the years before it was built. In one such vision, she told me:

> I saw an old man sitting in front of me, very old, maybe 80 or 90 years old. He asked me to come to him, and when I did he initiated me with the *Gayatri Mantra*. So I went ahead and did that japam, and after a time I saw a hill rising before me, a big hill, and at the top I saw a giant snake's hood and the snake gazing down at me. Its body came down the hill and its tail rested way down on the ground below. The tail was down here, the snake up there. I felt very small. That vision came in, I think, 1978 or '79. A few years later, the first time that I came to Devipuram, I saw that very same hill here, and I remembered it. It was the very same one from my vision.

"They say that marriage is made in heaven and, in this case, it is true," Alok observed. "Theirs is a perfect match because, for a person of Guruji's spiritual depth, you need an equal partner—and she is more than equal, in my experience."

Amma's reverence for Guruji, it must be noted, was fully reciprocated. Though usually subtle and understated, there were times when his regard was on open display—for example, on Amma's birthdays, when he would often perform public *pujas* to her as the Goddess incarnate. In the late 1980s, Alok witnessed such a ritual on their wedding anniversary. It began when Guruji unexpectedly announced to a small group that had gathered for a morning *puja*, "I would now like to offer my love by worshiping my wife." Alok recalled:

> That *puja* was one of the most moving experiences I have ever had in my life. The love with which Guruji worshiped Amma that day is hard to describe. After the invocation, Amma closed her eyes and sat unmoving for the entire length of the *puja*. When the ritual was over, Amma still did not move. As I looked at her, I realized that she was not conscious of her environment. Guruji told us that Amma was in a "higher state" and that we should not disturb her. But when she remained in that state for some time without showing any sign of coming out of it, Guruji placed her head in his lap. He lovingly stroked her hair, repeatedly calling "Anu, Anu..." Guruji then asked me to take a coconut, go outside, and break it, which I did. Guruji took the broken coconut and put *kumkum* on it and placed it near Amma. Slowly she started to show signs of conscious awareness, and finally she opened her eyes. Guruji asked me to stay with her and not leave her alone until she was fully conscious. And soon Amma was back to her usual self again.

"It was a moment when I saw how a true spiritual marriage really unfolds," Alok concluded. "Guruji once mentioned to me that the purpose of his life is to show that spirituality and worldly life can coexist—and not only coexist, but that each can actually help the other, that they can support one another to build something even better."

"It is not much discussed, but theirs was a great love story," scholar Roxanne Gupta added. "Amma loved him so; she lived for him. And Guruji quite certainly felt the same way."

Guruji himself was, of course, fully aware that people were curious—and sometimes impatient—about Amma and her role in his life. But he made his position on the matter very clear.

"Sometimes people tell me, 'You shouldn't let Amma control you! You should stand up for your independence!'" he said. "What nonsense. I have lived with her for over 50 years. We know each other inside out. We have three children and six grandchildren together. I'm there for my wife and she is there for me. Why would I turn away? For the sake of what? Because she controls me a little?"—he shook his head and laughed—"Who *doesn't* control me? *Everybody* tries to control me! So just because she tries to control me too now and then, I should run away? No."

He paused and then allowed, "Okay, so maybe I sacrifice a little freedom. So what? That's the trade-off. I value our relationship as an important part of Tantric spirituality. You live in the spirit and yet you live in the world, you see? If you try to live strictly on an existential level, you're essentially operating in a vacuum—no affections, nothing to bond to; nowhere to ground yourself. In my opinion, cultivating a place of belonging is equally important. And the partial loss or restriction of freedom that comes with it is just part of the game. In fact, I think it can be valuable.

"So that is one of the messages I have tried to convey in this life," Guruji concluded. "You don't have to leave your family; you don't have to run away from your worldly life in order to be spiritual.[222] You can find it wherever you are, whatever the circumstances. You can be in prison, scheduled to be hanged within the next half an hour—and still practice detachment. I want people to realize that their spirit is always free, even if they consent to limit that much-needed freedom in their everyday lives. If you can learn to both exercise your freedom *and* cope with your limitations—accepting them lovingly and caringly—then you will always be okay."

222 This is, like many of Guruji's teachings, an ancient but largely forgotten Indian ideal. For the renowned classical Sanskrit poet Kalidasa (c. 400 CE), "the sacred and secular were not divisions that rendered life boring but a unity to be embraced with verve and grace….This ability to maintain a spiritual consciousness in the midst of abundant and pleasant lives was a characteristic of ancient India and Kalidasa was its most representative voice."

20   Points of Connectivity

Guruji traveled widely and frequently during his long years of constructing the Sri Meru temple—and it was during this period that his reputation first began to spread beyond India, particularly in the United States and Canada.

In those days before cell phones and instant messaging, life on the road brought him welcome respite from the relentless pressures and demands of building Devipuram, while also offering a chance to do what he loved best—to teach, write, meet new people and cultivate his own spiritual practice. Guruji's primary North American basecamp was the home of Haran Aiya, the beloved "spiritual son" of his Zambia days. Tucked away on a leafy suburban side street at 33 Park Circle in Rochester, NY, the house's attached garage did double-duty as a popular Devi temple.

Guruji and Amma first arrived in Rochester in June 1988, with daughter Radha, then 22, in tow. Amma had been actively seeking a "suitable alliance" for her middle child when Guruji calmly announced that "Radha's husband is in the United States, and that is where her marriage will take place." His prediction came true when Radha met Balkumar Marthi—a young Indian microbiologist with a Ph.D. from the University of Delaware, then working with the U.S. Environmental Protection Agency in Oregon—while attending a Thanksgiving feast in Boston.

Their wedding was celebrated in full-on South Indian style on May 21, 1989, at Aiya's home—with closed-circuit video feeds set up for the numerous attendees unable to squeeze into the tiny temple itself. Friends and family from across the United States and India (including Guruji's old Andhra University classmate, Kandula Sitaram Sastry, by then a physics professor at the University of Massachusetts at Amherst) descended on Rochester for days of celebration and ritual, as well as classical music and dance.

As he became better known and the size of his international audience expanded, Guruji for the first time began explicitly speaking of his "mission"—to the extent that his relaxed, non-doctrinal approach could be called that—as one of "democratizing" Sri Vidya and Tantra, making their personal and societal benefits freely available to an increasingly broad public. "Sri Vidya *upasana* brought me great happiness," he said. "I wanted to show people that they too could have access to such happiness. So I would ask Devi, 'How can I share this happiness with others?' She would show me visions of how to do it, and I would follow her instructions."

However, American and Canadian audiences—whether second-generation Indians or non-Indian whites, blacks and Asians—proved considerably less inclined to accept such statements at face value, and much more likely to press for details and specifics. Adjusting to expectations, Guruji obliged: "My goals, based on my visions of the Devi," he told a Rochester audience in 1988, "are to explain the why and how of Sri Vidya ritual in ancient and modern times, and to bring scientific enquiry to bear on the spiritual empowerment techniques of Sri Vidya." Questioned further, he also mentioned a desire "to preserve and promote the feminine qualities of beauty, kindness and creativity; to empower women and children; and to teach the ageless role of *Eros* in Indian music, temple dance and sculpture."

Non-Indian admirers would occasionally marvel at the strangeness of seeing this unambiguously masculine, white-bearded figure—looking for all the world like a Old Testament Patriarch right out of the Sistine Chapel—referred to by South Asian devotees as an embodiment of the Goddess, and preaching a profoundly feminine spiritual vision.

Scholar Roxanne Gupta explained that this seeming contradiction was in many ways the essence of his attraction. "Guruji possessed a highly developed feminine side, but he was not at all effeminate," she said. "A large part of his appeal was that he *got* that; he *embodied* that ideal—of a masculinity not comprised of violence and domination. He was totally in touch with the feminine, but in a way that enabled him to relate better to women rather than reject them. That too was an important part of his message."

Still, Guruji would bristle when Westerners attempted to pigeonhole him as a "spiritual feminist."

"He hated that!" Gupta noted. "He felt it would only alienate men. Indians in general tend not to like the term 'feminism'; it's often construed there as meaning 'women rule over men,' and that was never Guruji's idea. He was much more about not wanting *either* side to be dominant, about *healing* the relationship between the masculine and the feminine, both within and without."

Regarding his "democratization" of a previously secret religious sect, "Guruji's one-pointed endeavor was always to demystify Sri Vidya and make this sacred path accessible to all children of the Mother," said Mrs. Sriganesh Madhvanath (more commonly known as SriG Amma), a longtime friend, disciple and fellow nuclear physicist whose association with Guruji dated back to his TIFR days.[223]

In an academic study of Guruji's approach, Gupta actually coined a term—"de-esotericization"—to describe this phenomenon, in the process placing Guruji squarely within a growing worldwide trend "by which formerly secret traditions become popularized in the context of globalism."

"De-esotericization is related to a general breaking down of barriers that impede information flow across all kinds of boundaries—geographic, political, and those related to gender, caste, class and ethnicity," Gupta elaborated. "Books, videotapes, seminars and CDs now offer information, and even initiation, into esoteric Tantric practices that were once highly guarded secret visualizations and practices controlled through transmission lineages."

223 The late Smt. Gnanapurani Madhvanath (1934–2014) was known to her friends as Gnana and to most of her acquaintances as SriG Amma. She was a pioneering physicist who joined the Bhabha Atomic Research Centre in 1957 as one of its first female researchers. She knew Guruji as a professional associate during this period, when he was still a scientist at TIFR. SriG Amma later did research at the University of California at Berkeley, before leaving her career to start a family. She settled in Buffalo, NY, in 1992, and became deeply involved with Aiya's Rochester temple, transliterating, translating and editing countless Sanskrit, Tamil and English texts. She relocated to Bangalore in 2005, where she passed on April 9, 2014. Guruji and Amma stayed with her during the week before her death.

Gupta acknowledged that Guruji's subtly radical attempts to popularize Sri Vidya did not go unchallenged within the tradition itself. Quite the contrary, more conservative practitioners continually questioned the legitimacy of Guruji's efforts. They complained that his lack of secrecy, his openness to other traditions, and his free mixing of eclectic influences (from nuclear physics to Reiki) created an ungainly, unholy hybrid that was no longer truly Sri Vidya at all.

> Some argue that because his vision grows out of both an "eastern" traditional and "western" scientific background, Amritananda's worldview is not reflective of the "real" Sri Vidya. [In fact] his worldview is global insofar as he actively seeks to compare Sri Vidya to other "alternative" healing and spiritual methods from around the world—[incorporating such influences] as Brahminical esotericism, quantum physics, the Hindu diaspora, New Age sexual therapeutics, and women's empowerment—to find common grounds for comparison. In synthesizing information from various sources, his explanations of Sri Vidya emerge as cross and counter-cultural hybridizations. Some might say that the "purity" of the Sri Vidya tradition—if there ever was such a thing—has become tainted, or at least highly colored, in the process of translation. Put another way, de-esotericization and popularization of a once–highly "secret" tradition raises questions regarding authenticity for scholarly and other outside observers of the tradition.

Indeed, Guruji's open-minded ease with hybridization often surprised even Western seekers—many of whom had, after all, sought him out precisely because he was an acknowledged guru in an ancient, authentic Hindu lineage, and his teachings carried a corresponding authority. But Guruji was not interested in preserving some abstract conception of "purity" for its own sake—his criteria for any practice always focused primarily on the question of what worked and why.

Thus, among the arcane Sanskrit scriptures, palm-leaf manuscripts, Tantras, commentaries and *paddhatis* that cluttered his bookshelves at Devipuram, one could also discover an eclectic mix of Western titles, including Carl Rogers' *On Becoming a Person: A Therapist's View of Psychotherapy*, Marianne Williamson's *A Return to Love*, Margot

Anand's *The Art of Everyday Ecstasy*, Stephen Covey's *The 7 Habits of Highly Effective People* and Neale Donald Walsch's *Conversations with God*, not to mention Mikao Usui's *Original Reiki Handbook*; Brian Greene's popular primer on quantum physics, *The Fabric of the Cosmos*; Sri Aurobindo's epic blank-verse poem *Savitri*, based on the theology of the *Mahabharata*; and a scattering of books on various world shamanic traditions.

"Guruji was always looking for 'points of connectivity'—and these tended to make any 'points of disconnection' largely irrelevant to him," Alok said. "To a large extent, this approach accounted for his ability to connect with people from all kinds of different backgrounds and viewpoints. It also helps explain his diverse interests—in spirituality and religion, science, meditation, social work, housing, women's issues, computers and multimedia, dance, music, [alternative] medicine, and so on."

Yet none of these influences necessarily undermined the authenticity of his teachings, Gupta argued. "Insofar as Amritananda consciously understands and succeeds in justifying what he does according to the logic of Sri Vidya, these adaptations must be understood (by those of us studying the tradition from outside) as developing within Sri Vidya, a living tradition which is in the process of re-defining itself in a post-modern age," she said.

Because at the end of the day, Guruji filtered *all* of these diverse influences through a worldview that was ultimately aligned with and rooted in Hindu philosophy and practice in general, in order to discover and synthesize methods of spiritual development that worked. "The key metric for Guruji was always experiential validation," Alok said. "Any techniques he adapted were backed squarely by his own experience, and had the goal of replicating that experience for others."

During that first American tour in 1988, Guruji and Amma were invited to stay for a few days at the Himalayan Institute, Swami Rama's mountaintop Ashram in Honesdale, Pennsylvania. "Swami Rama was away, but had left instructions that Guruji and his party be given VIP treatment," said Sundhara, who accompanied them on the visit. One day while browsing in the Ashram's bookstore, Guruji handed Sundhara a volume and said, "You should have a look at this."

His interest piqued, Sundhara purchased the book, brought it back to his room and began flipping through it. "To be honest, I was totally lost; it was way over my head," he recalled. "So I glanced through the contents page and saw a chapter on Sri Vidya. That being the path Guruji teaches, I turned to that chapter and started reading. It referred to Sri Vidya as the highest form of Goddess worship and said that, within this tradition, the ultimate form of *japa* is called *Aksha Mala*, and the ultimate form of meditation is called *Bindu Bhedana*."[224]

Curious, Sundhara approached Guruji that evening and asked him, "What is *Aksha Mala*?"

"He looked at me with some surprise and said, 'It is a closely guarded secret,'" Sundhara recounted. "So I left it at that, and didn't dare ask him anything more."

A few days later, however, during *Guru Purnima* celebrations at Haran Aiya's house, Guruji delivered a long lecture on ritual technique and, upon concluding, said with a smile, "If anyone wants to hear more, come back after midnight." Most attendees laughed, taking the comment merely as a self-deprecating joke about the length of his talk, and went home. But Sundhara and a handful of others stayed to see what might happen.

Sure enough, shortly after midnight Guruji returned to the now almost empty room carrying a flip chart. "He went on to explain the entire *Aksha Mala* method in detail—how one maps the letters onto oneself during *japa*, how one can map every ritual onto his or herself," Sundhara marveled. "It was a classic example of Guruji breaking all traditions and divulging 'hidden' secrets for the benefit of everyone who truly desired to know."

So after another couple of days had passed, Sundhara decided to press Guruji on the book's other reference. "I collected some courage and asked him, 'What is the *Bindu Bhedana*?'" he recalled. "And again Guruji gave me a stern look and said, 'Where did you get that term?' I said, 'It's from the Swami Rama book you handed me!' Again Guruji said nothing more, and again I dared not pursue the matter further."

But about a week later, when Sundhara returned to Aiya's Park Circle temple to attend some weekend *pujas*, Guruji quietly pulled him aside and handed him two cassette tapes. "Here you are," he said. "The *Bindu Bhedana*."[225]

224 Both are advanced forms of meditation in Sri Vidya. While knowledge of the techniques is now trickling down to a larger number of spiritual practitioners, just a generation ago (the incident described here took place in 1988) such an open transmission of these traditions would have seemed completely unprecedented—thus the disciple's astonished reactions.

225 A recent article evocatively describes *Bindu Bhedana* as follows: "We've all heard of near-death experiences [in which] people tell us they experienced themselves leaving their body and moving towards a brilliant white light. Entering that light is the mysterious experience the yogis call bindu bhedana, which is one of the most important practices advanced yogis undertake. They don't wait to die to enter the light—they spend their whole lives basking in its illumination. In deep meditation (which to some degree mimics the experience of death physiologically), yogis connect with the light while they're still in their bodies, and in this way they become channels for the flow of its healing, enlightening power into the world."

"I froze," said Sundhara. "Another secret, guarded for centuries, and Guruji decided to open it up to me—and then to the world! Because later on, Guruji loaded both the *Akasha Mala* and the *Bindu Bhedana* tapes onto the Devipuram website as MP3 sound files. Around the same time, he also taped the entire *Devi Mahatmyam* in his own voice to help anyone who cared to learn it."[226]

To those who balked at such blatantly public mass-shares of formerly inaccessible knowledge, Guruji replied with a shrug. "Just because it's out there doesn't mean everyone will see it," he said. "But those who yearn to know will find it and learn it."

Some of Guruji's most public examples of de-esotericization took place while participating in the large-scale ritual events favored by Haran Aiya, whose infectious enthusiasm and intense reverence for his guru—together with his colorful narrations from Guruji's life and teachings—had already elevated Guruji to the status of an all-in-one holy man, folk hero and quasi-celebrity within the close-knit Rochester temple community.

"One of the ways Aiya deflects the guru-wonderworker limelight [from himself] is to extol the powerful capabilities of his own guru, Guruji," explained scholar Corinne Dempsey in an in-depth study of Aiya's temple in the early 2000s. "I have heard Aiya on a number of occasions remark that Guruji, who appears to have accumulated extraordinary *siddhis* through his extensive Sri Vidya practice, has no need for the elaborate rituals Aiya promotes and performs. Guruji's powers are such, according to Aiya, that 'all he has to do is touch you' for your desires to be realized." Dempsey continued:

> The only time Aiya asked me to turn off the tape recorder during an interview session was when he described in detail one of the more spectacular feats he witnessed Guruji perform. Guruji himself does not want people to know the extent of his abilities, and Aiya is trying to be a good disciple. ... But people, Aiya included, do talk freely about the 'lesser' miracles Guruji performs. Barbara, a devotee in her late thirties ... told me of such an instance. During the 1999 [*Guru Purnima* observance] in late July, an annual festival for honoring one's guru and guru lineage, Guruji and his wife were in the United States and came to Rush for

the festivities. They arrived ceremoniously in a devotee's van, and were greeted by a large group who waited, barefoot, on the parking lot in front of the temple. Barbara was among them: "So I was out here with this whole crowd of people and standing on this pavement, lifting one foot at a time, trying to cool them off because it was terribly hot. And he comes up in the van and gets out, and it feels like the pavement got cold, or like it cooled down and was tolerable. And I turned to the lady next to me and—she said it first, she said, 'Is it my imagination or did the ground just cool?' I said, 'It's not your imagination because I was about to ask you.'"

Aiya recounted another curious phenomenon during the same visit. A congregant had prepared his backyard to host a full-scale *yagna*, installing a specially constructed *homa kunda* and a marquee, hiring a Vedic priest, and preparing food for scores of visitors. But when the day of the big event finally arrived, torrential rains scuttled his plans.

"It was pouring—I mean, pouring cats and dogs," Aiya said. As the gathered guests peered glumly out from under the marquee, "Guruji sat looking at the *homa kunda* with no expression. Then suddenly he stood and quietly walked into the house. We couldn't see him; we didn't know what he was doing. But a few minutes later he came back and very casually sat down again."

Within minutes, Aiya said, "it was as though somebody had turned off the tap. It stopped raining. Then I noticed that if you looked around at about a 50-foot radius, outside that radius it was still pouring! But inside it, nothing. So I quietly nudged [the host] and told him, 'You know, something's happened here.'"[227] Catching a glimpse of Aiya's inquiring expression, Guruji quickly turned and disappeared into the crowd. On the drive home later on, however, Aiya asked him what about the incident.

Guruji said, "Well, this poor gentleman went through so much trouble to give the people some benefit from this *homa*. How could we just let all of his efforts go to waste?"

"Yes, yes, we know all that," Aiya pressed him. "But what did you *do*?"

Guruji shrugged and said, "I used a *Brahmastra*"—a celestial missile from Hindu mythology, said to have been forged by Lord Brahma. He declined to discuss the matter further.

"And that was just one occasion," Aiya concluded. "One place."

227 The parallels to Guruji's actions during the deluge the night before the Sagara Giri procession are difficult to ignore.

ॐ
ह्रीं

In 1989, Gupta was a Ph.D. candidate at Syracuse University and working as outreach coordinator at the school's South Asia Center. "One day I was invited to speak to a religious studies class about goddess worship in India," she recalled. "I spoke mostly about how many living female spiritual teachers in India were worshiped as living goddesses." As an example, she mentioned Mother Meera, an Indian saint who happened to be visiting nearby Geneva, NY, at that time.[228]

After her talk, Gupta was approached by a young man of Indian descent who enthused, "You should meet my mother! She is also a Goddess devotee!"

"Sure, I would love to meet her, where is she?" Gupta replied politely, expecting to hear the name of some distant town in India. Instead the student replied, "She's right next door. She works in the library."

"I was taken aback," Gupta said. "There was something about this young man's energy that made me say, 'Well, then let's go meet her right now!'"

Gupta and the mother immediately hit it off. "You are very lucky," the woman told her. "My Guru is coming to my house this very night. You are welcome to come and meet him." Gupta took down the address and drove there after work.

"I entered the house and there was Guruji sitting alone," she recalled. "Amma was resting in an adjacent room. From the first moment I saw him I felt both spiritually intrigued and very much at ease. I received two mantras from him that same day, and I never asked him for another in all the years after that." Later in the evening Haran Aiya arrived at the house as well.

"So I hit the sacred trifecta!" Gupta smiled. "Guruji, Amma and Haran, all in one day! It was the beginning of a beautiful, lifelong relationship that has been one of the greatest blessings of my life."

Over the course of the evening, Gupta mentioned the local presence of Mother Meera, the saint she had discussed in her lecture earlier in the day—and Guruji expressed a desire to go and receive her *darshan*.

"This blew my mind," Gupta said. "Who ever heard of a male guru willing to publicly touch the feet of a living woman? Many gurus are so status-conscious that their egos would rarely allow them to meet, let alone bow down to another guru!"

228 Mother Meera, born Kamala Reddy in Madanapalle, Andhra Pradesh, in 1960, is believed by her devotees to be an avatar of the Goddess. Originally associated with the Sri Aurobindo Ashram in Pondicherry, India, she has lived in Germany since the early 1980s. She still regularly appears to give *darshan* there, and frequently visits the United States and Canada. Mother Meera's Geneva, NY, *darshan* was hosted by author Andrew Harvey, then a professor of literature at Hobart and William Smith Colleges. Harvey had a complex relationship with Meera and would go on to write two books about her: the first, *Hidden Journey* (1991) praises her as an avatar and guru; the second, *The Sun at Midnight* (2002) attempts to discredit her.

But Guruji was adamant, and a few days later Gupta took him and Amma to see her.

"Mother Meera did not talk," Guruji recalled of the *darshan*. "There was pin-drop silence in the room. She held my face close to her navel and I just felt peace, a very motherly feeling."

For Gupta, it was "a moving experience to watch Guruji bow down, then look up and lock eyes with Mother Meera. It was a sight I will never forget, one that brings tears to my eyes even now."

21 A Goddess in Upstate New York

In the summer of 1990, Aiya was contacted by an American woman named Devi Parvati, who was at that time the sole remaining priest of the Rajarajeswari Peetam in Stroudsburg, Pennsylvania.[229]

A small Sri Vidya temple founded in 1968 amid the rolling Pocono Mountains, the sanctuary had fallen into debt and disuse following the death of its founding swami.[230] Tasked with settling its closure, Devi Parvati was struggling to find an appropriate home for the temple's spectacular black granite Rajarajeswari *murti*—along with a massive *Shiva-lingam*, a large idol of Lord Ganesh and a number of other sizable bronze deities. She particularly feared that the Rajarajeshwari sculpture might be auctioned off by the Internal Revenue Service in a tax sale, that "somebody might buy it and put it in their garden as a centerpiece, or that it might end up in a museum," Aiya recalled. "I'm not kidding, she was concerned!"

In her distress, Devi Parvati recalled the summer day two years earlier, in 1988, when Guruji, Amma, Radha and a few others had unexpectedly visited the Stroudsburg temple during their first U.S. tour. Though they stayed just a few hours, Guruji made a deep impression on her and the two exchanged contact information. Now she steeled herself and called him in India, offering the temple outright for his use as a U.S.

229 Devi Parvati (Dombkowski) founded the Hindu Heritage Summer Camp, teaching Hindu philosophy and religious practices to children of Indian immigrants to the U.S. Based in Pennsylvania and New York during the period described in this chapter, she now resides in Calgary, Alberta.

230 Though they share the same name, the Rajarajeswari Peetam in Stroudsburg, PA, was unrelated to Haran Aiya's Rajarajeswari Peetam in Rochester, NY.

base of operations. Guruji politely declined, explaining that Rajarajeswari's intended home was Haran Aiya's temple in Rochester, a four-hour drive to the north.

When Devi Parvati visited Aiya a few weeks later to inform him of Guruji's statement, he was both incredulous and grateful, feeling that he had been presented "with an opportunity of many lifetimes." He immediately called Guruji, who confirmed, "If the Divine Mother wants to come to your house, who are we to say no? Let her come!"

The transfer happened four months later on Saturday, January 19, 1991, a crisp winter day with temperatures hovering just a few degrees above freezing. By fortuitous coincidence, Guruji and Amma were back in the United States, visiting their daughter Radha and her husband Balkumar, who were living in Portland, OR, and awaiting (at literally any moment) the arrival of their first child.

But when Aiya called and asked him to preside over the deconsecration of the Pennsylvania temple, the transfer of its *murtis* and their re-installation in Rochester, Guruji immediately booked a Thursday flight to New York, promising an incredulous Amma and Radha he would be back in Portland by Sunday. "Guruji gave me a wink before he left," Radha recalled, "as if he knew the baby's arrival was imminent. But anyway, Amma was there with me."

On Friday afternoon, Guruji, Aiya and a small group of Rochester congregants arrived at the Stroudsburg *peetam* and were soon hammering together wooden crates to carry the precious cargo. Later that night, Devi Parvati entered the temple sanctum for a farewell *puja* to Rajarajeshwari and found Guruji sitting in front of her. "He said hello; we exchanged a few words," she recalled, "and then he very quietly stood and said, 'Come and stand here.'" Devi Parvati stood at the spot he indicated, very close to Rajarajeswari, and Guruji placed his hand on her head. "He chanted, not for a long time," she recalled. "There was no ritual. It seemed very informal." Then he said "Here, hold this"—and Devi Parvati felt a strange sensation enter and spread throughout her body.

Guruji explained that he had temporarily transferred the *murti*'s energy into her for safekeeping during the move. "He said, 'You'll carry her energy to Rochester and then

1 The Sri Meru temple
at Devipuram, 2011.
(William Thomas)

2 Aerial view of the Sri Meru
temple, showing its unique
Sri Chakra configuration.
(Sri Vidya Trust)

3 Modern-day Visakhapatnam, as seen from Kailasagiri Park. The Dolphin's Nose headland can be seen to the far right. (Dreamstime)

4 The thousand-year old Simhachalam temple, just north of Visakhapatnam. (Dreamstime)

5 Guruji and his mother,
Lakshmi Narasayamma, c. 1935.
(Sri Vidya Trust)

6 Nishtala Narasimha Rao,
Guruji's father, c. 1950.
(Sri Vidya Trust)

7 Guruji's birthplace and
childhood home, shortly
before its 2001 demolition.
(Sri Vidya Trust)

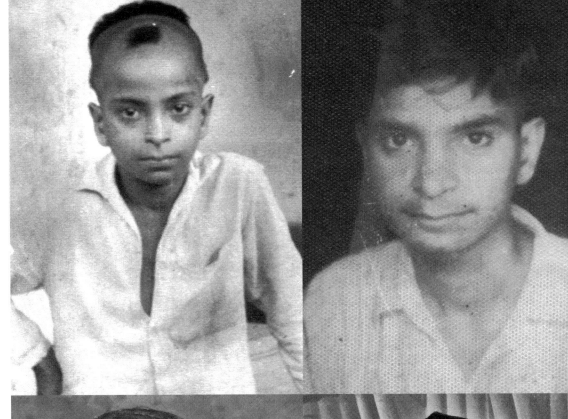

8 Guruji after his *upanayanam* head-shaving ceremony. (Sri Vidya Trust)

9 Guruji as a boy, photographed by his father. (Sri Vidya Trust)

10 Guruji's student ID photo from Andhra University. (Sri Vidya Trust)

11 Guruji upon graduating with his master's degree from Andhra University. (Sri Vidya Trust)

12 Swami Jnanananda
as a young man.
(Sri Rama Jnana Mandir
Publication League, U.S.A.)

13 Swami Jnanananda
as Guruji knew him.
(Sri Rama Jnana
Mandir Publication
League, U.S.A.)

14 Dr. Homi Bhabha, founder
of the Tata Institute of
Fundamental Research (TIFR).
(Public domain, via
Wikimedia Commons)

15 Guruji as a young
TIFR scientist.
(Sri Vidya Trust)

16 Guruji and Amma at the time of their marriage, "a happy union, through which much worldly good would be achieved." (Sri Vidya Trust)

17 Amma with daughter
Radha, c. 1964.
(Sri Vidya Trust)

18 The TIFR against the
Bombay skyline.
(TIFR)

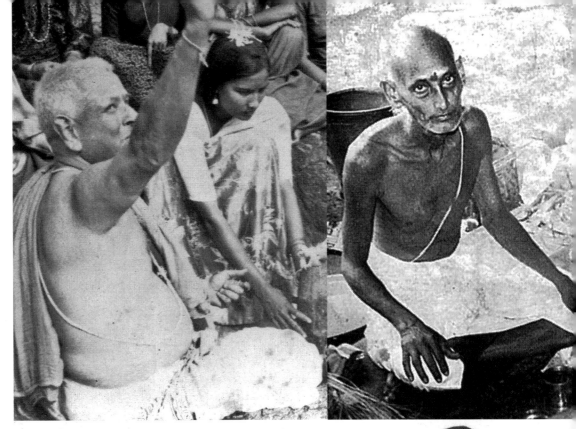

19 Sri B.S. Krishnamurthy performing a Shiva *puja*.
(Sri Vidya Trust)

20 Anakapalle Gurugaru, as he was when Guruji first met him.
(Sri Vidya Trust)

21 Guruji as family man, with Amma and (left to right) daughters Rama, Radha and Anantalakshmi. Bombay, c. 1974.
(Sri Vidya Trust)

22 Birla Mandir temple, Hyderabad, the site of Guruji's transformative vision of Lord Venkateswara. (Karthik Easvur / Wikimedia Commons)

23 Guruji and Amma on the rooftop terrace of their Visakhapatnam home with daughters (left to right) Radha, Rama and Anantalakshmi, and nephews, c. 1986. (Sri Vidya Trust)

24 Guruji in the mid-
1980s with his "spiritual
son," Haran Aiya.
(Pamela Lang)

25 A lighthearted moment:
Amma, Guruji, Haran
Aiya and Sakuntala.
(Pamela Lang)

26   Guruji with Meru model atop his head for the *Sagara Giri Durga* procession, October 17, 1982. (Sri Vidya Trust)

27   The *Maha Devi Yagna*, Visakhapatnam, May 1983. The "cinema goddess" at center; Vemakoti Krishnayaji stands second from the left in white; Amma is at the far right. (Sri Vidya Trust)

28 The Goddess Kamakhya. "A huge ball of light gradually condensed into an incredibly beautiful female figure, her skin like flashes of lightning, shining like a jewel and bedecked in bridal attire." (Darla Teagarden)

29 The *yoni* shrine as it
was discovered by Guruji,
shown during excavations
before construction of the
Kamakhya Peetam began.
(William Thomas)

30 A rare photograph of
the Meru unearthed by
Guruji at the *yoni* shrine;
the gold devotional figures
were placed on it by a
visitor seeking blessings.
(Arra Aravindhan)

31 Local villagers building
the Sivalaya temple,
Devipuram, 1983.
(Sri Vidya Trust)

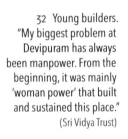

32 Young builders.
"My biggest problem at
Devipuram has always
been manpower. From the
beginning, it was mainly
'woman power' that built
and sustained this place."
(Sri Vidya Trust)

33 Guruji atop the Sivalaya temple, 1984.
(Sri Vidya Trust)

34 Guruji overseeing preparation of the Sivalaya temple building site, 1983.
(Sri Vidya Trust)

35 Guruji's sister
Suryalakshmi while living
alone at Devipuram, 1986.
(Sri Vidya Trust)

36 Amma at Kamakhya
Peetam, mid-1980s.
(Sri Vidya Trust)

37 Bala Tripurasundari. "The nine-year-old form of Balaji is my Guru. It was she who demanded that the Sri Meru temple be built, and she who got it done."
(Painting by Michael Bowden)

38 Guruji sits atop Sivalaya's hill as the frame of the Sri Meru temple rises below; the Ashram and water tower are visible at far left.
(Sri Vidya Trust)

39 The foundation of the Sri Meru temple, with Kamakhya Peetam and the Sivalaya temple in the background.
(Sri Vidya Trust)

40 Manually raising the 1,400-pound Sahasrakshi *murti* to the peak of the Sri Meru temple.
(Sri Vidya Trust)

41 The *Prana Prathista* of Sahasrakshi.
(Sri Vidya Trust)

42 Unfinished goddess statues slowly fill the unfinished frame of the temple.
(Sri Vidya Trust)

43 The black granite Devi *murti* "rescued" by Guruji, Haran Aiya and Devi Parvati, now at home in Sri Rajarajeswari Peetam, Rush, NY.
(Vilas Ankolekar / Sri Vidya Temple Society)

44 Guruji and Devi Parvati atop Sivalaya, 1994.
(Devi Parvati Dombkowski)

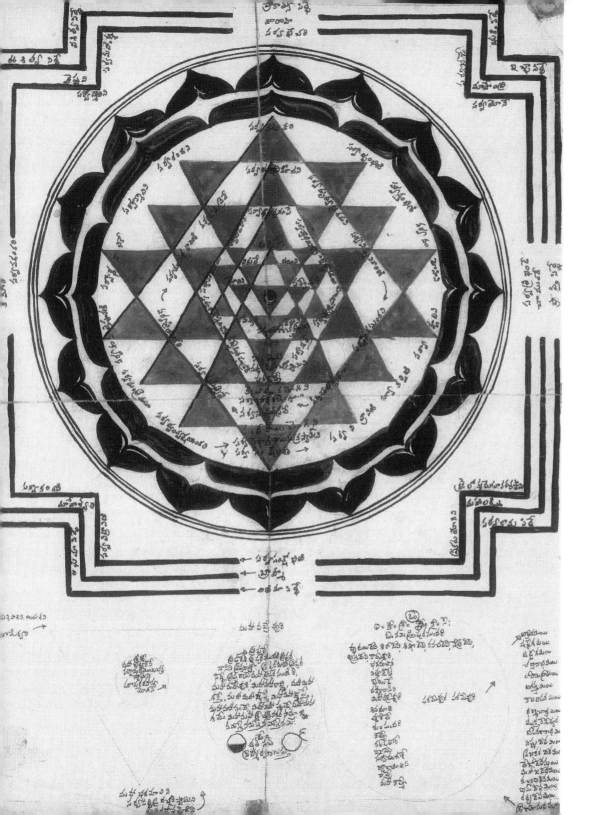

45 A Sri Yantra drawn, painted and (tentatively) labeled by Guruji in the late 1980s, and preserved by Amma ever since. (Sri Vidya Trust)

46 Guruji, Gurugaru and
Haran Aiya at the *Maha
Kumbha Abhishekam*, 1994.
(Sri Vidya Trust)

47 Guruji officiating at the
Maha Kumbha Abhishekam.
(Sri Vidya Trust)

48 The Saint of Simhachalam,
also known as Jatala Sadhu.
(Sri Rama Viswambharadas
Adhyathmika Seva Sangam)

49 (A) Guruji balances nine brass *kalasa* atop his head immediately preceding the light phenomenon.
(Sri Vidya Trust)

50 (C) The light vanishes into the distance.
(Sri Vidya Trust)

51 (B) Strange light phenomenon captured by *Times of India* photographer Mickey Menon during the *Maha Kumbha Abhishekam* of Devipuram on February 25, 1994.
(Sri Vidya Trust)

52 The *Khadgamala Devi* Sarva Samkshobhini ("she who agitates all") at the Sri Meru temple, late 1990s.
(Sri Vidya Trust)

53 A Tantric *Kalavahana Puja* at Kamakhya Peetam.
(Julianne Reynolds)

54 The *yoni* shrine at
Kamakhya Peetam as
it appears today.
(Julianne Reynolds)

55 An anthropomorphic
lingam at Sivalaya temple.
(Giri Ratna Singh)

56 The altar in Guruji's study near Boston, MA.
(Michael Bowden)

57 Guruji performing a *puja* to Amma as the Goddess, April 2007.
(Sri Vidya Trust)

58 The Devipuram Meru.
(Sri Vidya Trust)

59 Guruji visiting Haran
Aiya at Rush, NY, 2003.
(Sri Vidya Trust)

60 Guruji in a New
England Patriots cap
performs a *Sri Chakra Puja*
at Oyster River High School,
Durham, NH, 2003.
(Subbarao Kompella)

61 Indian followers: crowds line up for *darshan* of Guruji and Amma in Hyderabad, 2013. (Sri Vidya Trust)

62 International followers: chatting with a group of Western yoga practitioners at Devipuram, 2014. (Oleg Zinkovetsky)

63 Guruji's biological family: here Guruji and Amma are joined by their three daughters and sons-in-law and six grandchildren, as well as Guruji's brother Prasad Rao and his wife, Sundari, 2014. (Sri Vidya Trust)

64 Guruji's *vasudaiva kutumbakam* or "global family" of disciples and devotees; Guruji and Amma preside over a *Siri Jyoti Puja* at Devipuram, 2014. (Oleg Zinkovetsky)

65 Devastated: Devipuram in the aftermath of Cyclone Hudhud, October 2014.
(Sri Vidya Trust)

66 Green again: Devipuram one year later, October 2015.
(Julianne Reynolds)

67 This memorial sculpture and Guruji's remains now reside in the Guru Dhyana Mandiram at Devipuram.
(Sri Vidya Trust)

68 The scorched Sri Chakra Meru used in Guruji's cremation as he had requested.
(Julianne Reynolds)

69 At rest. Guruji's body in repose at Devipuram, October 12, 2015, the day before his cremation.
(Sri Vidya Trust)

70 A mid-1990s devotional image showing Guruji seated on the *yoni* at Kamakhya Peetam.
(Sri Vidya Trust)

we'll take it out and put it back into her once we arrive there,'" Devi Parvati recalled. "I said, 'Wow, why me? How can I do this?'"

Guruji replied, "You are the Goddess. There's no reason why not."

Early Saturday morning, the temple was formally deconsecrated, its *kalasa*, or holy spires, removed from the roof, and its *murtis* packed into a moving van. By early afternoon the Rochester contingent had set off on the long drive back to Aiya's home, proceeding carefully along the wintry roads. Oblivious to it all, Devi Parvati sat happily slumped in the back seat of a devotee's car. "I was in an altered state!" she said. "I was completely euphoric, totally in bliss for the whole day!"

The party arrived at Aiya's temple at seven in the evening, and immediately commenced the long ritual of *prana-prathista*—re-establishing the deity's energy in the image—which they finally completed around 1 a.m. Even after Guruji returned Rajarajeswari's energy to the *murti*, Devi Parvati remained disoriented. "It took me a long time to ground myself back into my body," she said. "Sitting through the rituals, I was still very spaced out. I just sat in meditation through pretty much the whole thing."

And with that, Rajarajeswari and her entourage established in their new home in Rochester—where they remain to this day. Guruji, meanwhile, caught a flight back to Portland, where he had just become a grandfather for the second time. "Our daughter was born exactly halfway between removing the *kalasa* at Stroudsburg and installing Rajarajeswari at Rochester," Radha said. "It was so special and auspicious! We named her Matangi—and only later found out that the day she was born was also Vasant Panchami, the special day for worshiping Saraswati."[231]

During his international travels, Guruji often found himself at the center of attention, conducting rituals, teaching *pujas*, initiating disciples, delivering lectures, presiding over weddings, visiting devotees in their homes, and more. The one element that seemed perennially absent from his agenda was fundraising. Time and again, those who encountered him in those days remarked that—for a man in the midst of constructing an ambitious temple complex—Guruji seemed singularly unconcerned about money.

231 Matangi is a primary Tantric form of Saraswati. She is also called Shyamala, Meenakshi, Mantrini and more, and is considered one of Lalita Tripurasundari's three most fundamental manifestations (along with Rajarajeshwari and Varahi).

This apparent indifference certainly didn't indicate any hidden sources of wealth—the need for capital existed, without a doubt. It was simply that Guruji was content to leave the matter in the Goddess's hands.

"He didn't have money, you see?" Aiya said. "Just nothing! Whatever people gave from here and there—that is what slowly brought Devipuram up. But Guruji never opened his mouth and said anything like, 'I am building a temple, please donate.' His attitude was, 'If somebody feels that they should offer something, they will offer it.' Guruji was never the sort of person who is after money, that much I will tell you. Even now he is like that."

But people remained curious about the funding sources for Devipuram, and so in the mid-1990s, Guruji wrote a brief statement:

> What are the sources of funds for Devipuram? Sri Amritananda has many disciples in many countries all over the world. Through them, on an average, he is getting about 40% of the funds. From his devotees and friends in cities throughout India, and the local population who are connected with Devipuram in one way or another, he is getting about 60% of the funds. The non-formal education programs are being sponsored in part by the Indian government. Sri Vidya Trust is a non-profit organization.
>
> Sri Amritananda has given his all to Devi and he has been working without taking any wages except food. He lives in the guest house [Ashram] built by him at his own cost. A part of the guest house is given for people who want to come and stay and is offered free to them for their stay. If anyone gives anything to Guruji, even saying that it is for his personal use, he is giving it as much as possible to the Trust's activities.[232]

232 During interviews for this book, Guruji waved off further discussion of finances.

Jana noted that it was, in fact, Aiya who was most responsible for raising Devipuram building funds in North America. "Haran Aiya did a lot of work to get those things going," he said. "He didn't let Guruji even think about it. As a disciple, he took that duty into his own hands. But it's true, Guruji couldn't be bothered about money—he couldn't have cared less. Why? If you asked him he would say, 'Why worry? Devi will take care of the whole building of the temple.' Simple as that. Since it was an intent that she had put out there, he simply knew that it was going to materialize."

Sister-in-law Sundari Amma related another exchange with Guruji that reveals even more about his ambivalence toward money and its temptations.

> Guruji, his brother, Amma and myself were travelling by Jeep on a pilgrimage to Arasavilli.[233] Guruji had his eyes closed, meditating. As we approached Srikakulam, he suddenly opened his eyes, saying that a *yakshini*[234] had just appeared to him and revealed a spot nearby where there was a buried treasure! Being young at the time, I immediately said, "Well, we need money to build the temple! Most people can only donate, at best, ₹100 or ₹50. So let's go retrieve this treasure and use it!" But Guruji laughed and said, "That's not how it works. To commit money won in a lottery is not true commitment. I will have to work hard—and many thousands of others will have to expend their labor too. This temple will be built by mitigating the karmic debts accumulated over many lifetimes of those who traverse the path along with me. And in return we will build a temple within the heart of every person who comes here. For that, we do not need money!"

But while the economics of temple construction did not loom large in Guruji's consciousness, his educational mission remained central.

"Building the temple was always a secondary concern when Guruji was in the United States," Jana said. "It was always there in the background, but he was a lot more interested in building a strong core group of devotees who really wanted to learn in depth about Sri Vidya *sadhana*. His mission back then was basically to find people to whom he could teach this knowledge—and who could then teach it to others. He used to say, 'I want to find a few stones that I can polish into diamonds.'"

Nonetheless, Guruji's broader interest in de-esotericization dictated that—while expert *sadhakas* would be instrumental in teaching his ritual innovations of Sri Vidya—ordinary worshipers should not feel put off or intimidated by the complexity and sophistication of the practice at its highest levels. On the contrary, he wanted

233 That is, to the Surya Narayana Swami Temple in Arasavilli, about 120 kilometers (75 miles) north of Vizag.

234 *Yakshinis* are minor female deities, believed to be attendees of Kubera, the Hindu god of wealth. Often depicted in art as exceptionally beautiful and voluptuous, yakshinis are said to guard treasures hidden in the earth.

everyone who approached him, regardless of their knowledge or ability, to understand that this vital connection—to the Goddess, to Sri Vidya *upasana*, to him personally—could be achieved and enjoyed by one and all.

One weekend evening at Park Circle, after the day's *pujas* and rituals were over, an intimate gathering of 15 or 20 people was relaxing—informally chatting, telling stories, laughing and having fun. Contentedly settling into the mood, Guruji said, "You know, there's only one thing missing here tonight." The group turned to him, wondering what mysterious truth the guru was about to impart: What exactly *was* missing from this pleasant gathering?

"Potato chips!" Guruji responded with a smile. Amid laughter and exclamations of agreement, a bag of chips was located and a full bowl set out for everyone to share. "You know, it's not a coincidence that we are all sitting here like this, chatting and enjoying ourselves," Guruji said to a disciple sitting next to him, as the hum of conversation resumed. "This has always been the vision. I don't want to be sitting on a pedestal. I want to be fully accessible, like a friend." He then added, motioning toward his heart, "The *Anahata Chakra*[235] is pulling us in; let us go inside and enjoy it for some time." And he sat back to fully savor the gathering.

On the California leg of his U.S. visit, Guruji encountered a woman who was suffering from severe anxiety issues, almost bordering on obsessive-compulsive disorder. She had found herself paralyzed by the idea that even when she walked on the grass or along a sidewalk, she was killing innocent insects and even microscopic creatures. The situation had grown so acute that she was spending most of her time indoors. In the midst of a crowded ritual gathering, Guruji suddenly approached her, held out his hand and said, "Come on, let's take a walk."

The woman tried to explain the intense fears she associated with "taking a walk," but he replied, "Don't worry. I will protect you and them both, and the Goddess will protect us all." So she joined him, and as they walked she felt compelled to spill out all of her fears and anxieties—experiencing a great wave of peace and relief as Guruji silently listened and nodded.

235 In Kundalini Yoga, the *Anahata Chakra* or "Heart Center" is the fourth primary chakra, associated with a calm, serene, compassionate energy, devoid of violence.

"Even Jain and Buddhist monks are like that," he told her when she was through. "They don't like to step on insects or breathe in microbes. But you also have to live your life. You have to move forward. You can't always avoid these situations, so you have to just say a prayer—something simple like, 'This is not intentional; please forgive me'—before you step outside. And then stop worrying about it. And remember, I am always with you. So if any creature is harmed, it is I who will take on the karmic consequences, not you."

Did she believe that Guruji really had the ability to extend such protections?

"Of course," said the woman, whose fears and compulsions have not returned since. "But I don't think that was the most important thing about our walk. For me, what meant much more was the very fact that on that day—in the middle of a major *puja*, with so many important people present—he took the time to notice that I was in trouble and cared enough to try to help me feel better again. That for me was the essence of Guruji—always compassionate, always patient, never judging. He truly embodied all of those qualities."

When Guruji needed a longer-term escape from the relentless demands of his U.S. schedule, he sought anonymity in, of all places, the northeastern U.S. city of Boston, Massachusetts—more specifically the gritty, working-class suburb of Somerville, which directly abutted the more posh environs of Cambridge, home to Harvard University and the Massachusetts Institute of Technology. There he would disappear for weeks at a time, living in a nondescript inner-city duplex, spending hours each day in meditation and worship before a spectacular home altar tucked discreetly into an attic alcove. The home belonged to a Sri Lankan Tamil immigrant family, the Janahans (parents of Jana, who had accompanied Guruji on a visit to the Saint of Simhachalam).

"Guruji liked staying in Boston because he could find solitude there," Jana said. "Every now and then he needed peace and silence to get into a purer state of mind and attune to higher knowledge. He found my parents' shrine room very conducive for that."

Between 1988 and 1992, Guruji made several extended visits to their home where— half a world away from the Devipuram construction site, and several hundred miles

225

removed from the noise and crowds that attended most of his North American appearances—Guruji would read, study and write prodigiously: philosophical tracts, lecture notes and ritual instruction books. He also paid occasional social calls to old scientific colleagues who were now teaching and conducting research in the academic halls of nearby Cambridge. In their company, discussing the latest developments in quantum mechanics and astrophysics, Guruji was able to become Dr. Sastry again for a while.

As a high-school student with his summers off, Jana enjoyed the luxury of almost unlimited free time with Guruji. "Sometimes he would come upstairs early in the morning, and we would just sit and talk for hours in the shrine room," Jana recalled. "He taught me so many *pujas*, and told me stories about his life and experiences with the Devi."

Then one day, Guruji announced to Jana that the Goddess had given them a new task: to write a comprehensive guide to Sri Vidya worship. "The Divine Mother is asking me to create a *puja-paddhati*,"[236] he said. "I will get the flow of knowledge from her and dictate it, and you will transcribe it."

Though personal computing was still in its infancy at the time, Jana managed to source an IBM 286 from a cousin for the task. Having set it up in the attic, he and Guruji went to work. "Each morning, Guruji would go into meditation, and then I would type whatever he dictated on the 286," Jana recalled. "It was a very intimate situation. He would close his eyes for an extended period of time, then open them and begin speaking while I typed." Jana would correct, format and print the dictations in the afternoons while Guruji attended to phone calls, visitors and other business—and then "the next morning I'd bring it to him to review. Our routine kept going like that for weeks."

The first fruit of their collaboration was a slim volume called the *Sri Sukta Sodasa-Upachara Puja*, a relatively compact ritual based on an ancient Vedic hymn to Lakshmi. Having found their rhythm with that project, the pair launched almost immediately into a guide to the full *Navavarana Puja*[237] itself, probably the single most significant Sri Vidya ritual.

236 A ritual instruction book.

237 The "Ritual of the Nine Enclosures" of the Sri Chakra.

Each day, Guruji would awaken hours before dawn to bathe, meditate and prepare for the day's work.

"He had a discipline of waking up at 2 o'clock in the morning," Jana explained. "He would finish his daily mantra meditation and then do a *Sri Chakra Puja*, which would take him about two hours. He wanted to make everything as simple as possible, and he had already spent several years perfecting the techniques in his own *sadhana*. After seeing the results, he told me he felt this was the most effective methodology to use."

The comprehensive guide that resulted is still revered and widely circulated among Guruji's and Haran Aiya's disciples and beyond. Most commonly referred to as the *Blue Book*, it was privately published by Aiya's Rochester temple in August 1988 (sporting the distinctive blue cover that gave it its name). Complex though it can be, the volume in fact reflects Guruji's vastly streamlined and simplified version of the full traditional ritual—"opening the gateway," as one user phrased it, "to completing the *Sri Chakra Puja* in 60 minutes, while not compromising any of its benefits and conforming to the guidelines [set out in] the *Parashurama Kalpa Sutra*."[238]

The *Blue Book* remained a living work in progress for many years, as Guruji constantly scribbled additional notes, edits, corrections, clarifications, improved transliterations, explanatory diagrams and hand-drawn illustrations into scores of disciples' copies, many of which subsequently found their way into a number of variant "corrected" editions that have appeared over the years.

As the work approached its 25th anniversary in 2013, Guruji asked a disciple to, in her words, "consolidate his work to provide a comprehensive view and thorough understanding of the *Sri Chakra Puja*."

Having collected and collated years' worth of editorial notations, discourses, writing and audio recordings expounding upon the *Blue Book*'s contents, the disciple (who requested anonymity) then corrected and standardized the volume's Sanskrit diacritical marks. In all, her work spanned several years and comprised no fewer than "253 distinct editorial rounds" (!) with Guruji. The resulting volume, *A Jewel from My Mother's Crown*, was published in 2015.

238 A medieval guidebook to Sri Vidya practice that remains a primary source in Guruji's lineage.

While in Toronto, Guruji was contacted by the founder and chief administrator of a major Hindu temple there, who asked him to organize a ritual to boost the congregation's energy.[239]

"Guruji agreed immediately," Sundhara recalled. "He performed a *Rudra Homa* that lasted 11 days. It was the first time that I or anyone else there had ever witnessed such a ceremony." Rather than presiding as a high priest over the ancient Vedic fire sacrifice, dedicated to Shiva's most primal form, Guruji got almost everyone at the temple to join in, learning and performing the ritual along with him. Then he kicked it up another notch.

"On the final day, there must have been about 300 people in attendance," Sundhara said. "Guruji gave a brief talk and then spontaneously announced that he wanted to initiate everyone present into Sri Vidya. I was dumbfounded at his openness, but he went ahead and asked them all to repeat after him as he recited the Ganapati, Subramanyam and Bala Tripurasundari mantras." Next he began reciting the Sowbhagya Panchadasi[240] mantra, but abruptly stopped halfway, staring at the front row and not continuing further. After a moment's pause, Guruji thanked the assembled worshipers, bowed in *namaste* and returned to his seat.

On the drive home, Sundhara asked Guruji why he decided to initiate so many. "He replied that, during his speech, Anakapalle Gurugaru and the Goddess Lalita were sitting in the front row listening, just like any other attendee—but at the end they told him, 'Well, give them all some mantras!' So Guruji complied and gave Ganapati. He then looked at Gurugaru and Lalita again and they said, "Go on, give more!" So he gave Subramanyam. "Go on, go on!" they urged him, so he gave Bala.

"But just as he was about to give Panchadasi, he said, Lalita rose and covered his mouth with her hands, indicating that was enough for the time being," Sundhara said. "So he stopped."

ॐ
ह्रीं

On another occasion, Guruji was invited by a prominent Shaiva priest from the western United States to visit his temple and discuss his vision for Devipuram and the rising Sri Meru Nilayam.[241] Guruji was pleased to comply, but as he began explaining his policy of granting Sri Vidya *diksha* to all who asked, the Swami balked. "But how can you know if they are qualified to receive it?" he demanded. "For example, what would you do if someone just walked up to you on the street and said, 'Give me some mantras'?"

Without hesitation, Guruji replied, "I would give them."

In fact, he continued, precisely such an event had only recently occurred when he was making a flight connection in Germany. Out of the blue, a European gentleman suddenly approached Guruji and asked him for *diksha*. Sprinkling him with water from an airport fountain, Guruji happily gave it. "The very fact that his request was so unlikely was reason enough to conclude that some sort of divine intention was involved," Guruji explained. "Only those who are ready to receive the mantras will arrive at the particular place and time where they are being offered—so I feel it is only right to give when I am asked."

Later, after Guruji and the priest had clashed on issues ranging from the nudity of deities to the openness of the temple to non-Brahmins and non-initiates, it became clear that there would be no meeting of the minds. The Swami, knowing a lost cause when he saw one, politely took his leave.

Guruji's demanding North American schedule took an unexpected toll in April 1991, when he suffered a massive heart attack in New York.

Earlier that morning, he and Amma had been visiting a disciple in Scarsdale, NY, just north of New York City, when "Guruji became very restless," Amma recalled. "He said he wanted to go to his son"—that is, back to Haran Aiya's home in Rochester, more than 300 miles away. He would not be dissuaded, and the couple drove there, arriving at Aiya's place around 5 p.m. Guruji was preoccupied and uncomfortable during the entire journey, but insisted on spending time with the crowd of devotees that was waiting to greet him.

"As always, there were so many people gathered to talk with him," Amma said. "He was replying to their questions, but he was definitely not at ease. He even became a bit short with some of them. I could tell he wasn't feeling too well."

In the midst of it all, Guruji suddenly lost consciousness and "slid off the sofa into a heap on the floor," Amma said. An ambulance was called, and Amma began assigning tasks to those present. "Everyone was very concerned and some of them started screaming and crying," Radha said. "But Amma was very firm. She told them to rub Guruji's feet and hands and remain calm. Soon the ambulance arrived and he was taken to the hospital."

But the situation was grave. Within moments of arriving at Genesee Hospital in Rochester, Guruji suffered yet another attack but was again stabilized.[242]

"The doctors said he would be okay if he survived through the next few hours past midnight," Radha said. Aiya and a longtime disciple, Dr. Vishwanathan, remained at the hospital to await news. Meanwhile, "Amma came back to the house and led everyone present in a continuous chanting of the Panchadasi mantra." A few hours later, Aiya called to report that Guruji was stable and out of danger.

The next day Aiya returned to the hospital, bracing himself for the shock of seeing his old friend and guru stretched out helpless, connected to tubes and machines. When he entered the ICU, however, "I felt like I'd walked in on a party," he said, laughing at the memory. "There was Guruji, sitting upright in bed, merrily holding court. Half of the nurses and residents in the hospital were gathered around him. He was telling stories and they were all laughing and smiling, completely captivated by him!"

"I've never met a real guru before!" one nurse told Aiya. "Can we keep him?"

Punning on Genesee Hospital's name, Guruji quipped, "Look Haran, I've had my rebirth in Genesis!"

No sooner had the medical crisis subsided, however, than a financial one ensued—as Guruji learned firsthand that America is a very expensive country to get sick in. "Guruji did not have medical insurance, and the treatment ran huge bills," Alok said—to the tune of about US$45,000, according to Guruji's recollection.

"Aiya's Rochester disciples took up a collection to help pay the bill," Alok said. "But I remember Guruji saying, 'Let's just pray that Devi takes care of this and puts no financial burden on anyone.'" And indeed she did not. Dr. Vishwanathan used his medical wherewithal to negotiate the cost down with great success: the Indian-born heart surgeon agreed to forgo his fee altogether; the hospital itself waived some other portions of the bill. The remaining expenses were met by various community service organizations after they sent social workers out to interview Guruji.

In the end, the funds donated by Aiya's disciples—which would have been more than sufficient to cover the full bill—were not needed at all. Rather than distributing refunds, however, several of them suggested that the money instead be donated toward the construction of Devipuram.

Guruji refused.

So instead the donors agreed to deposit the funds into a special account as seed money toward what would become, eight years later, Haran Aiya's much-expanded Sri Rajarajeshwari Peetam at its present home of Rush, NY.

"Despite the impression of some, Guruji isn't some kind of superhuman," Alok said recently. "In fact, what I really relished about him is the fact that he was a normal human being, with the same limitations and failings as the rest of us. To assume that Guruji never got sick, or felt down or upset about things—that's not correct."

He recalled the time when a woman asked Guruji to counsel her and her husband when they were experiencing serious marital difficulties. The attempt was a debacle—the husband became hostile, openly insulting Guruji and mocking the entire attempt.

"Soon after this, Guruji and I went out for an evening stroll," Alok said. "He seemed quite dejected. He told me that he really wanted to see this couple live happily together. It was clear that the encounter was weighing on his mind and making him feel quite down."

All at once, however, Guruji stopped his ruminations and said "*Chod do!*" (Hindi for "Leave it!" or "Let it go!") Then he looked up at the sky and intoned, "I am unlimited! I am the cosmos!"[243]

"This seemingly simple affirmation changed the whole atmosphere," Alok recalled. "A dramatic shift took place. Guruji was his usual self once again. He then turned to me and said, 'If you look at *bhakti yoga*, *jnana yoga* or any of these practices, there is only one underlying principle that makes them work—and that is *vairagya*, detachment. The ability to detach and let go when needed is *very, very, very* important.'

"Whenever needed," Alok concluded, "Guruji was able to connect with the cosmic force and not be limited by all the things that we as humans typically suffer

243 While advising a devotee in distress, Guruji once recommended using another Hindi expression with similar meaning: "You know there is a great phrase used in India—'*chalta hai*' ['so it goes' or 'it's fine']. When things are not working out, as they often don't in India, we say '*chalta hai*' and keep moving. This is our *maha-mantra* for letting go. Whenever you feel like things are not going as you wish, just say '*chalta hai*' a few times, and almost immediately you will feel better, you'll see. If only we could combine the effort and focus of the Western mindset with the '*chalta hai*' attitude of India, all of our lives could be great."

from—pain, pleasure, all of that. For me, that is really where he really contributed to our evolution and growth as human and spiritual beings. He showed us a benchmark. He showed us a way it can be done."

22 An Impossible Dream Comes True

As 1993 drew to a close, the colossal task of building the Devipuram temples—initiated a full decade earlier, following Guruji's first visions of the goddess Kamakhya—was finally nearing completion. The moment had arrived to consecrate the Sri Meru temple, and Devipuram as a whole, as a living center of worship, by way of the ceremony known as the *Maha Kumbha Abhishekam*, or "grand ritual bathing," of the temple.

Dating back to the early centuries of the Common Era, when modern Indian temple practice first began to take shape, the *Maha Kumbha Abhishekam* is based on the concept of breathing life into a temple by invoking and harnessing the presiding deity's divine *prana*, or spiritual energy, within the structure's precincts. This is achieved via the ritual chanting of mantras and other ancient prayer formulas, the vibrations of which are absorbed into a series of specially prepared pots or vessels—the *kalasa*, usually made of brass or earthenware—filled with holy water and surrounding the ritual enclosure. At the end of the ritual series, the energized water is poured over the temple and its deity. A description published by Aiya's Rochester temple further explains:

> *Kumbha abhishekam* is a general term for the grand celebration and series of purification rituals that are done [following] the construction or major renovation of a temple. It's traditionally performed every 12 years, at which time any

repairs are also commissioned. "*Kumbha*" refers to the highest peak of the temple, which receives *abhishekam* [ritual bathing] at the culmination of the festival. A full *kalasam* (or many *kalasa*, as is often the case) is charged with mantras and *pujas* for several days. On the final day of the observance, the *murti* and/or actual temple itself receives the *abhishekam* of all the *kalasa* used throughout the festival. The remaining water is then sprinkled throughout the property.

This pattern of events, and the methods of worship [used] will vary from temple to temple—for example, *bhajans*, *homas*, chanting or any combination of *pujas* can be performed. But the one thing that always takes place at a proper *kumbha abhishekam* is the charging or recharging of the deity and the surrounding environment.

The Hindu belief is that it's not enough to just build a temple. It must also be maintained, both physically and spiritually. This strict and regular maintenance schedule is a major reason why so many Hindu temples have lasted centuries and are still in use today. A *kumbha abhishekam* is also a community-building activity by its very nature—so many people are needed to coordinate the different parts that the event naturally draws hundreds of devotees who are connected to the temple.

Sri Meru Nilayam's *kumbha abhishekam* was scheduled to take place on Wednesday, February 23, through Friday, February 25—corresponding to the period from *Vijaya Ekadashi* to the *Magha* full moon that year.[244] Even as the big event rapidly approached, however, a tremendous amount of work remained to be completed.

"If you had seen Devipuram even two weeks before the function, you would never have believed it would be possible to accomplish what got done in that short duration of time," said Devi Parvati, who spent six months living and working at Devipuram during the lead-up to the consecration ceremony. The job was formidable, to say the least: while temple construction had been the focus of Guruji's efforts, most other infrastructure remained primitive.

"The approach road to Devipuram was one big pothole," Devi Parvati recalled. "It rattled your teeth to drive in, and I always wondered if this would be the time that the road would totally demolish our Jeep! There were workers all along the road digging

244 Spanning the three days preceding the *Magha* full moon, *Vijaya Ekadashi* begins on the 11th day of a lunar fortnight in the Hindu calendar system, and is dedicated to Lord Vishnu and Goddess Lakshmi. In the *Skanda Purana*, Lord Krishna states, "This *Ekadashi* obliterates all kinds of sinful reactions and demoniac influences that may be affecting the spirit soul." *Magha* is the 11th month of the Hindu calendar, corresponding with January-February.

trenches for water runoff. They were just beginning to even out the road in front of Kamakhya Peetam, and there was still a kilometer of road left to finish."

Nor were the structures within Devipuram particularly accessible. "There were as yet no steps to either Kamakhya Peetam or to Sivalaya at the top of the hill," Devi Parvati said. "People had to climb up the tough, rocky hill with great care. Meanwhile, construction of guest bathroom and toilet facilities also had yet to begin."

Astonishingly, however, the entire daunting array of tasks was completed on schedule.

"One would feel 'There is so much left to do!' and then, almost overnight, things would just kind of get completed," said Guruji's son-in-law Venkatram Pisipati (Anantalakshmi's husband), who took charge of constructing the approach road. "The story would just keep repeating like that, over and over."

Devi Parvati had a similar impression. "As soon as Guruji voiced what was needed, time and time again that person or thing would simply show up," she said. "I tried to capture the essence of Devipuram with my camera, but it was impossible to do, because each week things kept shifting and changing. Watching Devipuram grow—and where the resources, people and money came from that allowed each new phase to develop—was in itself miraculous. For all of us, this preparation period was a perfect lesson in trust, trusting that the Mother was taking care of us in every way possible."

Devi Parvati had come to Devipuram in hopes that her long experience running a small Hindu temple in the United States could prove useful. It did not. "I didn't know the prevailing business culture, plus I'm a woman, plus I don't speak Telugu—so I really couldn't help with the temple planning as much as I would have liked," she said.

But the trip was far from wasted. While she was there, Guruji undertook to teach her the *Sri Chakra Puja*. As they proceeded, Devi Parvati would ask him increasingly in-depth questions, and Guruji would patiently respond with explanations that she found both beautiful and enlightening. She suggested turning their conversations into an English-language book that might eventually reach a far wider public. Guruji enthusiastically agreed, and thus was born his most comprehensive philosophical work—the straightforwardly titled (though never quite completed) guide known as

245 *Understanding Sri Chakra Puja* should not be confused with the *Blue Book*. For more than two decades, an incomplete, unedited manuscript of *Understanding Sri Chakra Puja* has circulated among devotees. In 2011, a disciple had a small batch privately published in paperback form. Sometimes called the "Red Book," its entire press run was placed in the Devipuram bookshop and quickly disappeared. Surviving copies are rare and coveted (Guruji himself appeared to have only one). Guruji's edited, augmented and resequenced version of the text's philosophical portions appears in *The Goddess and the Guru, Volume II*.

Understanding Sri Chakra Puja, written in the autumn and winter of 1993–1994.[245] As noted in its prologue:

> There are millions of people in the world today who perform *Sri Chakra Puja*, but very few of them understand the meanings of the mantras and procedures; why they are being done; what is a good way of doing things. … It is the author's belief that an attempt [to explain these things] has not been made before—at least not in a book that is accessible to all.
>
> Its genesis occurred when Sri Devi inspired Her devotee, Devi Parvati, to begin systematically questioning Amrita at Devipuram, India, with the object of making his replies available for the benefit of every devotee of Sri Vidya. Devi Parvati would ask Amrita questions and tape his answers; then she would painstakingly transcribe and type what was said, and Amrita would review and refine the results.

"Working on the book with Guruji was so powerful," Devi Parvati recalled. "He was teaching me step by step. He wanted to get into things in depth. So I would take detailed notes and type them up on the computer each day, then Guruji would go over them to make sure everything was correct. I really wanted to be of help, you know? And that kind of became my job during my stay there."

As an experienced priestess, Devi Parvati found the ritual aspects of the book easy enough to follow. Her biggest difficulties came, she said, when Guruji brought physics into his philosophical musings. "Sometimes he would get way out in space, using scientific terminology that was really hard for me to understand," she said. "I'd have to stop him and say, 'Guruji, what does that even *mean*?' So when you read the manuscript, you can see places where it gets very scientific and other places where it doesn't. But overall, we tried to keep it as concrete as we could. "

On most evenings in those days before the Sri Meru temple opened, Guruji used to walk up to the large Meru atop Sivalaya and meet with visitors and disciples. "That was one of the things I loved the most," Devi Parvati recalled. "We would sit and meditate and talk as the sun went down. Studying Sri Vidya in that environment was a wonderful experience—and very *rustic*. There were so many times when the power would be cut for the whole day, and at night we'd have one lantern, which everyone would kind of congregate around outside. Other days, the water supply would be the issue—there were just *so* many issues then! It could be really hard. But it was also such a beautiful place; I mean, there were times when I really felt that learning Sri Vidya in this corner of India a thousand years ago wouldn't have been much different."

As the *Maha Kumbha Abhishekam* loomed ever closer, however, there were countless more pressing matters to attend to.

For the *kalasa* to be used during the consecration of the temple, Guruji chose nine brass pots in graduated sizes—each representing one successive *avarana*, or enclosure, of the Sri Chakra. During the three days of the ceremony, these *kalasa* would be kept in a structure called the *Yagna Shala*—literally, "sacrificial chamber"—wherein the primary *homas* would be performed during the event.

The *Yagna Shala* was another brand-new addition at Devipuram—a large, earth-and-concrete dome completed just two weeks before the consecration ceremonies began, and modeled on an ecologically and financially practical design Guruji had developed for use in local villages.[246]

"The structure is still used regularly to this day for *havans* and *yagnas*," Sundhara observed. "It has eight differently shaped fire pits to invoke different energies during the execution of the *yagnas*." Inside, however, the heat and smoke from these fire pits remain minimal: they are drawn upward by the curvature of the 16-foot-high structure, and vented out the top. All around the dome, large, arched openings fitted with grates had been added, allowing those outside to sit around the entire circumference of the dome with a good view of the proceedings taking place within.

In addition to the *kalasa*, all moveable deities from the Sri Meru temple—including the *utsava murti*[247] and the *Prathama Meru*,[248] along with the smaller, metal *Khadgamala* deities—were also transferred to the *Yagna Shala* for the duration of the event.

246 Dome houses were one of Guruji's social initiatives. See chapter 23.

247 A small processional image of Sahasrakshi, through which the deity can leave the temple without the need of moving her massive stone *vigraha* in the sanctum.

248 A Sri Vidya temple's primary ritual yantra.

From the beginning, there were indications that attendance at the *Maha Kumbha Abhishekam* would be massive. Tremendous buzz was building in the villages surrounding Devipuram, as well as in Vizag and its environs. Meanwhile, longtime disciples from Mumbai, Bangalore, Hyderabad and other major cities were also spreading the word. In addition, devotees from the United States, Canada and Europe had long since booked their tickets to India. An appeal for volunteers to help Devipuram's small staff manage the myriad moving parts of the *Kumbha Abhishekam* was wildly successful—but even their numbers were daunting: close to 700 would be performing various tasks during the event and staying at Devipuram for its full duration.

One glaring absence was Anakapalle Gurugaru, who again excused himself (as he had from Sahasrakshi's *Prathista*) on the grounds that—as a *sannyasi*—it would be inappropriate for him to attend a celebration held primarily by and for householders. But he did send his handwritten blessings for the event,[249] and would make a brief appearance on its final day. And in his visits during the lead-up to the *abhishekam*, Gurugaru was in a festive mood, making lighthearted mischief wherever he went.

"He was a character and a half!" Devi Parvati remembered with a laugh. "When he'd come to visit Devipuram, he would sneak into the Meru and leave some tricks behind. I never figured out exactly what he did, but later Guruji and I would be walking through the temple and suddenly he'd stop and say, 'Hmm, Gurugaru did something here; I'd better fix that.' It would be some totally etheric and energetic mischief; it had nothing to do with the physical world—but Guruji would have to stop and etherically shift and change it."

Still, the relationship between Guruji and his chosen guru remained warm and affectionate. "Gurugaru was really just a happy-go-lucky guy," Devi Parvati said. "Guruji always knew how to take him. When he got up to his tricks, Guruji just took it with a grain of salt. At those moments, if Gurugaru suggested that Guruji do or try something, Guruji would just say, 'Mm-hm' and completely ignore him."

As a bright, balmy morning dawned on Wednesday, February 23, the *Maha Kumbha Abhishekam* formally began with the rhythmic reverberations of Vedic chants echoing across Devipuram. Following a light breakfast, the fire rituals that would energize

249 Signing himself Swami Avadhuta, Gurugaru wrote: "Near Anakapalle is Devipuram. It has been decided to perform *Kumbha Abhishekam* to Sahasrakshi Rajarajeswari. This place is built by Sri Prahlada Sastry, Guruji. He is my dear disciple. This great function will be completed conquering all directions and obstacles with the Grace of Dattatreya. Our blessings have been completely given for this."

the *kalasa* commenced at 9 a.m. sharp, continued until noon, then recommenced at 3 p.m., never stopping until 8 p.m.

Once again, the presiding priest was Sri Vemakoti Krishnayaji, who had performed both the grand *Devi Yagna* in 1983 and Sahasrakshi's *Prana-Prathista* in 1990. When Guruji invited him to perform the ceremony, Krishnayaji enthusiastically accepted, halving his usual fee and bringing along 10 *ritwiks*[250] instead of the five Guruji had requested—as well as piles of additional ritual supplies to make the ceremonies as spectacular and comprehensive as possible. (Krishnayaji would return to Devipuram again later that year to lead 12 *ritwiks* in one hundred recitations of the *Devi Mahatmyam* during that October's *Navratri* observances.)

250 Assistant priestess.

Notably tall and regal in bearing, Sri Krishnayaji was "always an imposing sight," Devi Parvati observed, "with his heavy, 22-karat gold earrings and ruby-encrusted arm bracelets glittering in the sun as he walked to and from the *Yagna Shala* each day." Guruji and Amma, however, remained the event's main attractions—their presence an indispensable requirement at virtually every *homa* from morning until night.

Throughout that first day, steady streams of visitors kept pouring in until thousands filled Devipuram's grounds. And though the crowds were constantly straining to see (or preferably touch) Guruji and Amma, the ritual's energy dynamics simply did not allow that sort of interaction. "Because of the intensity of the power generated by the *homas*, neither Guruji nor Amma was supposed to touch anyone until the *Kumbha Abhishekam* was complete," Devi Parvati explained. To help ensure this level of separation, an *ad hoc* "Guruji Committee" was formed.

"Our job was to surround Guruji and Amma as they moved to and from the *Yagna Shala* and other places, and to protect or insulate them a bit from the earnest devotees and pilgrims, who all wanted *darshan* and to touch Guruji's feet," said Devi Parvati, who served on the committee. "It felt a little like being a bodyguard to a rock star!"

Inside the Sri Meru Nilayam temple itself, the rest of the *Khadgamala Devis* were worshiped each morning with multiple *Sri Chakra Navavarana Pujas* performed simultaneously by 108 devotees. Visitors who wished to learn the *puja* for themselves were invited to sit beside a devotee and follow along. Meanwhile in the *bindu sthanam* at the top of the temple, a select group of *sadhakas* from Aiya's New York temple sat reciting prayers and hymns to Sri Sahasrakshi Rajarajeswari.

In the afternoons, visitors could attend any of numerous other *pujas* taking place around Devipuram, or relax to uplifting *bhajans* performed by Haran Aiya and other talented vocalists. In the evenings, there were classical dance recitals as well as Carnatic instrumental and vocal performances until 11 p.m.

As the second day of the festival dawned, even larger crowds streamed into Devipuram. Keeping this massive influx of visitors fed was a tremendous logistical challenge in itself. "One of the most difficult jobs to orchestrate was serving those thousands of people three meals, coffee and snacks daily," Devi Parvati noted. But thanks to the towering stacks of donated rice, pulses and vegetables, together with an efficiently organized system of meal vouchers and the help of several hundred volunteers, "it was performed with surprising ease," she said.

By Friday, February 25, the day of the *Magha* full moon and the final day of the *abhishekam*, the largest crowds yet—estimates generally ranged between 10,000 and 20,000—surged into Devipuram to witness the festival's culminating event, the ritual bathing of the temple.

Following morning *pujas*, everyone who had participated in the *homas* gathered to carry the *kalasa* and deities from the *Yagna Shala* back up to the top of the Sri Meru temple. Guruji and Amma led the stately procession, each carrying *kalasa*, along with Anakapalle Gurugaru (who made a rare public appearance for the event). They were followed by Sri Krishnayaji and his *ritwiks*. Next came Sri Chaitanyananda Natha (Haran Aiya) and his wife Sakuntala, carrying the temple's *Prathama Meru*; then came the rest of the principal participants, each of them bearing one of the metal *Khadgamala Devis* or other smaller deity figures. Guruji gave Devi Parvati the privilege of carrying Sahasrakshi's *utsava murti*,[251] which otherwise rested in the temple's peak at the main stone deity's feet.

251 Processional image.

"The crowd had to be restricted to ensure that the temple structure would not become overloaded," said Sundhara, who was also part of the procession. "Guruji and Amma, Gurugaru, the *ritwiks*, Haran Aiya and Amma, all sat in a circle around the main sanctum at the top, while Guruji invoked life into each level of the temple—it was just enthralling!"

Having reached Sahasrakshi's home at the top of the temple, members of the procession mounted a specially constructed scaffold one by one, carrying their *kalasa* even further upward to the very tip of the *bindu*. There Guruji stacked the nine pots into a conical tower, which he then—with the help of other officiants—hoisted onto his head, to create what Devi Parvati termed "an antenna for the energy generated in the temple to move through," and momentarily bring the full height of the structure to 63 feet.

At that very moment a streak of bright white light—some say it looked like a Shiva *lingam*—flashed across the cloudless blue sky, momentarily engulfing those at the top of the temple, and then streaked away again. The vast crowd reacted with a collective gasp; a *Times of India* photographer, Mickey Menon of Bombay, happened to catch the sequence on film. Later published with the caption, "Unexplained light drenching the dome and those on it at the precise moment of the *Maha Kumbha Abhishekam*," the images gave birth to yet another mystical tale surrounding Devipuram and its founder.

Inevitably, despite the thousands of eyewitnesses, some have since claimed that the photos must either be altered fakes or else reflect some sort of glare-induced anomaly in their exposure. Both possibilities, however, seem unlikely.

"If you look carefully at the photos, the white light is cloud-like and parts of it are transparent, going right through the spire on top of the Meru," said William Thomas, a design professor in Rotterdam who was present at the event. "In my opinion, this is not a photographic artifact but a real, phenomenal sight. I was there to witness it. You can also see it coming and going through the set of photos. It's really remarkable."

It's worth noting that many people on the Meru itself did not see the light effect. Haran Aiya, for example, says he did not; Guruji said he did. Devi Parvati did not see the light, but noted that—with or without mysterious phenomena—it was "a most exciting and powerful sight" just to see Guruji standing with the *kalasa* atop his head as "the crowds roared with delight." Guruji said he barely heard the cheers. "I forgot myself in the moment," he said. "I was just contemplating the light beam that had bathed the *kalasa*. I just sort of let myself merge into the happiness of that light." Sri Krishnayaji and his *ritwiks*, meanwhile, showered red flowers over the pots, over the top of the temple, and then over Guruji, Amma, Sri Chaitanyananda Natha and Amma—and then doused all of them in the turmeric-dyed water from the *kalasa*.

("Guruji's beard and hair were yellow for days afterwards!" Devi Parvati laughingly recalled.) The ceremony now complete, all participants descended from the scaffolding and entered the *sanctum sanctorum* for a final round of prayers to thank Sri Sahasrakshi Rajarajeswari for the successful completion of the *abhishekam*.

And with that, the Sri Meru Nilayam temple was officially opened to the public.

"Everyone was ecstatic and filled with divine energy," Devi Parvati said. "As we withdrew from the sanctum, we could see and hear the countless thousands of pilgrims all around the temple, applauding and shouting, crying and laughing, all of them happy that they had witnessed and participated in such a unique and inspiring event. Throughout the day, the lines of pilgrims waiting to receive the blessings of Sri Sahasrakshi Rajarajeswari never dwindled, as thousands upon thousands of people moved through the Sri Meru Nilayam for a quick glimpse and *darshan* of her radiant *murti* in the *bindu sthanam*."

Cultural programs continued through the afternoon and evening—a highlight being a classical Kuchipudi dance performance by Guruji's niece Srividya and Roxanne Kamayani Gupta. For the next three hours, Guruji and Amma—finally free to mix and socialize with visitors now that the ceremonies were over—joyfully made themselves available to all. "They were physically exhausted, but you could find them throughout the rest of the afternoon and evening giving *darshan* to any and all who came for their blessings," Devi Parvati said. "Guruji was just glowing—laughing and joking and giving them all his undivided love and attention."

His reaction was hardly surprising. This day, after all, marked the validation of his seemingly impossible dream, the culmination of more than a decade of toil, planning and prayer, problems and possibilities, daunting obstacles and unimaginable bliss—of almost singlehandedly ensuring that this day would someday come to pass.

But as the hour grew later and Guruji and Amma began to fade with exhaustion, Mrs. Pragna Parekh arrived from the kitchen and insisted that they come with her and rest for a while.

She had kept dinner warm.

23   Beyond Temple Walls

At long last, the strange and beautiful temples of Devipuram had come into physical, brick-and-mortar existence. They were no longer merely one man's quixotic and eccentric visions, known to few and visited by even fewer. The completed temple complex now belonged to the world, and its fame—or, some would say, infamy—was very quickly spreading.

"Devipuram exists for all of us now, wherever we live on the planet, not just for Guruji anymore," Devi Parvati observed at the time. "It's a place where we can all come to uplift our spirits and nourish our minds and hearts through worship, ritual, meditation, yoga, music, dance and the arts. It is a place dedicated to serving God through helping and serving one's fellow living beings, a place dedicated to helping us mold our lives into joyful divinity—a place where we can all become the Mother Goddess herself."

As the flow of visitors and devotees steadily increased in the months following the *abhishekam*, the refinement of the roads and grounds continually improved. Shady groves of trees grew thicker, flower and vegetable gardens thrived, and Devipuram became ever more lush, green and attractive to visitors. One dramatic addition from this period was the *Simhadwaram*, or "Lion's Gate"—a high, ornate arch marking the formal entry to Devipuram, framing the Sri Meru Nilayam at the end of an elegant, palm-lined approach.[252]

Yet for Guruji himself, the completion of the Devipuram temples was accompanied by a distinct feeling of loss. Some of this, to be sure, was simply the sense of anticlimax that follows the achievement of any goal or quest that has long provided the guiding principle of one's life. But there were also more specific causes. For soon after the *Maha Kumbha Abhishekam*, Guruji experienced a permanent shift from the way he had interacted with the Mother Goddess for more than a decade—one that ostensibly brought her even closer to him, but still *felt* like a separation. It was a change he began to sense almost the moment Sri Meru Nilayam was opened to the public.

"After I finished the temple in 1994 and it began attracting more and more people, the Goddess started moving more and more away from me," Guruji said. The situation became undeniably clear when the radiant Hladini—his longtime confidante, advisor and model for the *Khadgamala Devis* and myriad other construction details at Devipuram—appeared for what would be her final visit. "Don't expect to see me in my human form anymore," she told him. "From now on you will see me in everyone you meet. You will see my beauty everywhere."

Rather than experiencing any sense of joy at this development, Guruji felt little short of abandoned. "It evoked a great sadness in me," he said, "because it meant I would not be able to converse with her as I used to. It meant I would not be able to see her as frequently as I liked."

Observing his downcast reaction, Hladini explained, "For all this time you've been experiencing me as different from you, separate from you. Well, you should know that I am *not* separate from you, and you need not ask me questions anymore—ask *yourself* the question and then answer it yourself. When you ask the question, you're you. When you answer it, you're me. There is no distinction. I will see the world through your eyes, and appreciate that whatever you are seeing is also me, and also you. I will be like a mirror, mirroring you to you. We won't be different anymore. I will come as a thought, indistinguishable from your own thoughts, for we are one."[253]

"And that," Guruji said, "was the final instruction given to me by her."

253 Guruji would later use
Hladini's phrase, "We are One," in
abbreviated form, as Devipuram's
first independent Web domain
name.

244

ॐ
ह्रीं

But even as his vivid anthropomorphic visions of the Goddess began to fade, Guruji's other meditative experiences remained vivid and fruitful.

For example, "Sometimes I used to see a continuous pattern of heavy brocade, like a moving fold in a silken sari decorated with fine threads of gold and silver, with glimmering threads of light all along it," he said. "Different points would catch the light. The glow would linger for a little while, then it would become dull. Miles and miles of this fabric—it just kept going on and on, never repeating. Each thread in the brocade was alive, a universe in itself, extending to infinity. The slight curvatures in the fabric were like the warps in the multidimensional space–time continuum grid that physicists talk about. I was also reminded of the saint Kabir, who used to compare God to a weaver weaving the fabric of the cosmos. And I saw another parallel in a famous scriptural description of Lakshmi:[254]

> *hiranya varnam harinim suvaarna rajata srajam,*
> *chandram hiranmayim lakshmim jatavedo mamavaha.*"[255]

Guruji explained: "This means, 'Golden-hued consort of Hari, She is made of fine gold and silver threads. She is cool, radiating golden abundance, Lakshmi. May the procreative fire bring her to me.' It's an extremely popular Vedic prayer for bringing abundance into every home, but I think it also encodes a beautiful experience of Kamala-Lakshmi. She is the wealth of the all-pervasive Vishnu—that is Hari—and this prayer describes that cosmic abundance. I think that perhaps it is a seer's vision of the threads in a fabric as a metaphor describing the surface of the cosmos."

Guruji further observed that the droning hum which had characterized and presaged many of his earlier visions was completely absent. "All of these new experiences were silent spectacles," he said, speculating that he had possibly passed out of the frequency of audio waves, and into the visual frequency range. "The unstruck sound ceased to be; my body was totally relaxed, my mind was alert, but only seeing in wonder whatever was happening. Perhaps it was precisely these conditions that enabled such visions to manifest."

254 The Hindu goddess of wealth and abundance.

255 This is the first verse of the *Sri Sukta*, a hymn contained in the *Rig Veda*. It is the most ancient known hymn to the goddess Lakshmi, dating to pre-Buddhist times.

ह्री

In another abstract series of visions, the cosmos manifested not as a fabric, but as an infinite series of globular shapes that—over several years of meditational observation—gradually resolved into "pixelating discs." He would "see circles with a sharp glow around the edges," Guruji said. "They were all the same size. They filled my entire field of vision. They were actually uniformly bright globes, but when viewed from the side the center glow would show much less, and the periphery would seem brighter. I was reminded of Fresnel interference rings in optics."[256]

256   Fresnel zones are groups of radially symmetric rings of light or matter waves.

Upon even closer inspection, each of the globes contained what appeared to be a living being. "I could see one meditating, Buddha-like figure within each of the spheres," Guruji said. "It was as if they were creating these halos around themselves. The globes were closely packed in a planar array[257]—it couldn't have been a three-dimensional array, because the globes would have intersected. But what were they? Were they different worlds being created by other people in deep meditation?"

257   In telecommunications and radar, a planar array is a multi-part antenna in which all of the elements are in a single plane.

Eventually he realized that he could enter any one of these globes as a gateway to "a totally new universe." He sensed that the Devi was showing him "the genetic code of the cosmos," but felt he never fully grasped her message.

This globular theme first emerged as a repeating pattern in his meditations beginning in around 1990. "I only observed them when I was totally relaxed," he said. "They never came on demand, only unexpectedly, suddenly." By the time the Devipuram temples were complete, he had seen them "about 18 times or so."

"Their sharpness gradually diminished at the edges, more colors entered into them, and they became bright discs, all the same size," he said. "There were patterns in them, not unlike color-blindness test patterns. They would linger for a few minutes and then become grainy pixels, crumbling and disappearing altogether. I tried to figure them out, but again, I could not."

He was, however, able to interact with the discs just as he had interacted and conversed with the Goddess in his earlier meditative experiences. "I realized that, through my volition, I was able to give a direction to what I was observing," he explained. "I did an experiment once: I tried to grab a disk and throw it—and I found that I could do that. But what it did, I don't know. Afterward, I felt sorry for having done it, because it seemed so unfair that I—a mere earthly creature—should have interfered with a divine plan. It created a void in the pattern! Was I a demon, destroying some particular universe? Or was it a discus of Vishnu aimed *against* a demon? I still do not know."

Other visions ranged from the lovely—involving "various types of asymmetrical floral designs of perfect beauty"—to the frustrating; for example, a series of books whose content continually shifted. "Every time I would focus on a certain passage to read it, the content would change," he said. "I eventually got quite fed up with deciphering these changing books. How could printed matter change? I had no clue."[258]

It was during this perplexing transitional period that Guruji first encountered a young woman who would eventually become his first and only disciple to fully "replicate" his encounter with the Goddess at Kamakhya Peetam. Along the way, she and Guruji would become lifelong friends and her explorations would provide him with validation and encouragement at a time when he had ceased to experience such visions himself.

Yet their first encounter certainly did not presage any such lofty outcomes. Sunita Medepalli was an 18-year-old orphan from Bombay, living with her aunt and uncle in Hyderabad.[259] She was shy, physically frail and somewhat sickly. She was not interested in romance or marriage; it was "pure, unconditional love" that she sought. Her aunt was a religious woman who taught her many *pujas*, prayers and hymns; Sunita enjoyed these activities as "one way of keeping my mind at peace, which it was lacking." Her favorites were always Goddess-oriented.

One of her aunt's friends, Anandamayi Aunty, was a disciple of Guruji. One day Sunita saw his photo on the woman's altar and felt a profound urge to meet him in person. That opportunity came a few months later, when Guruji and Amma came to stay with Anandamayi. She hosted a *puja* and reception for them, and Sunita watched Guruji from the back of the room. She was struck by his genuine, friendly manner and simple mode of dress—to her, he didn't "look like" a guru—but she could not bring herself to approach. As they left the event, Sunita turned for a final glance at Guruji and found, to her astonishment, that he was looking intently back at her.

258 Guruji's final thoughts on these "changing text" visions are contained in the epilogue.

259 Sunita Medepalli was with Guruji the day he died. She passed away herself on August 25, 2016, as this book was being prepared for publication.

"There was a very bright light shining in between his eyebrows, which was focused toward the space between *my* eyebrows," and she "suddenly felt some heat at that particular spot," she said. "Later, I came to know that it was the *Ajna Chakra*."[260]

At another *puja* two days later, Sunita again found herself too shy to approach Guruji. But as he and Amma were leaving she thought, 'How I wish this man would bless me with his hand on top of my head!' As if on command, Guruji immediately turned to her and did exactly that. Looking back, Sunita said, "I was never the same person again after that touch. It was the beginning of a new life deep inside me."

A few years later in 1996, while a college student in Hyderabad, she finally visited Devipuram. She loved the Kamakhya and Sri Meru temples, but was primarily attracted to Sahasrakshi at the Sri Meru's peak. In her prayers, Sunita asked the Goddess to let her come and live in Devipuram someday.

In the short term, no such thing happened. Sunita completed her B.A. in economics and moved back to her childhood home of Bombay (by then formally renamed Mumbai). She continued to meditate with a photo of Guruji—and finally plucked up the courage to speak with him in person during a reception in the city. She recalled:

> I asked him whether I was eligible to do meditation. He smiled and said, "Anybody can do it. It's supposed to be good for cultivating a calm and a peaceful mind." I asked him whether there was any particular procedure he recommended, and he asked if I had received any mantras. When I answered no, he immediately gave me Panchadasi. He had me repeat it three times after him and then told me to close my eyes and chant it whenever I sat down for meditation. With that I touched his feet, and once again experienced heat and vibration.

Sunita took up a serious meditation practice and—besides a generally enhanced sense of calm centeredness—she also began to experience detailed interactions between herself and Guruji and Amma in "astral bodies," teaching her various *pujas*.

One day when Guruji was visiting Mumbai, Sunita told him about her growing "obsession" with moving to Devipuram. He told her, "Then pack up and come." Over the objections of her friends and family she did so almost immediately, arriving at Devipuram on December 16, 1997, and slipping quickly into its slow-paced flow—helping Amma with her chores and then meditating for hours at the Sri Meru and Kamakhya temples. "And then each morning I would go walking with Guruji, and he would answer my questions, if I had any," she said.

A few months into her stay, on March 9, 1998, Sunita's experiences at Kamakhya Peetam abruptly jumped to a new level of intensity. "The moment I entered meditation I sensed somebody coming into the room," she said. "A black shadow in the form of a woman entered first into me and then into Guruji's photograph in front of me. I sensed myself separating from my body as this woman took my hand and pulled me along with her. I wondered who she was and where she was taking me."

Finally the figure spoke, identifying herself as the Goddess Kamakhya and saying, "It is because of me that you have come to this place. It was upon my instructions that Guruji built this temple. There is no difference between him and me."

Kamakhya asked Sunita to begin meditating nightly in the temple, from midnight until dawn. "I will be waiting for you," the Goddess said with a smile. As Sunita began doing so, Kamakhya's form grew more distinct. "I could see her standing with one hand on her hip, laughing, full of jewelry, asking me what I wanted." As she had once promised Guruji, Kamakhya also told Sunita, "You will be able to sense my presence whenever you are alone. That is how I intend to be with you. You needn't worry."

Also mirroring Guruji's experiences, their interactions soon grew more erotic in nature. Kamakhya explained, "There is a difference between pure passion and love, and lustful passion and love. When I make love to you or anyone else, the emotion of love is pure because it is free from all other kinds of desire and lust: you feel as if you are simply loving yourself."

Sunita's visions continued in this vein for several months. The sheer similarity of their experiences struck Guruji as a powerful vindication; as a scientist, it was gratifying to see his "experimental results" being replicated at last. As a spiritual leader, he wondered if perhaps Kamakhya had chosen Sunita to be his successor; he began to speak of appointing her as new *peetadhipathi*, or "pontiff," of Devipuram.[261]

But it was not to be.

261 A *peetadhipathi* is the senior religious member of a Hindu temple, generally empowered to act as the sole authority and legal representative of the temple.

"Sunita was highly experienced in the meditative sphere," Alok ventured. "But in terms of maturity, charisma, ritual skills and so on, she really didn't have the wherewithal to be a pontiff." Nonetheless she remained at Devipuram for about five more years before personal circumstances finally compelled her to leave. Later relocating to Vizag, she remained a close spiritual friend of Guruji literally into his final hours.

Even while cultivating such spiritual mentorships and continuing to develop his personal *sadhana*, Guruji remained fully engaged with the outer world, often impressing visitors with his ability to focus entirely on whatever person or topic happened to come before him. Though somewhat hyperbolic, one disciple's paean to Guruji during this period captures the impression he made on many who encountered him:

> He is a scientist, a perfectionist, a walking encyclopedia. If you ask him how an aircraft's landing gear works, you'll get an answer detailed down to the last nut and bolt. If you ask him about the practical application of the Fourier Transform in mathematics, he'll explain it to you. But above all he is an authority on Sri Vidya and Tantra. If you ask him about the deepest significance of Maha Shodasi Mantra, he'll draw a few diagrams and explain it to you as if you were a kid in first grade and he was teaching you addition and subtraction.

Of course, Guruji would probably have been the first to assert that he was no expert on either landing gears or the Fourier Transform—but he *did* possess a vivid intellectual curiosity and he *was* remarkably well-read and well-informed, conversing with ease and enthusiasm on an extraordinarily diverse array of topics.

"One day we were chatting and I asked Guruji, 'Is the universe elliptical like a *banalinga*?'" Sundhara recalled.[262] "Guruji went silent for a couple of minutes, then took a piece of paper and explained in basic coordinate geometry theory why it probably *is* elliptical. It was amazing to watch him simplify this aspect of cosmology in a way almost anyone could understand."

On another occasion, he mused that ordinary reality as we perceive it is probably akin to a simple hologram, liable to collapse at any moment. "This was many years

262 A *banalinga* is a smooth, naturally occurring ellipsoid stone found in the bed of India's Narmada River and said to embody Lord Shiva.

ago, and yet recently I read a scientific article theorizing that all forms in the universe are holograms, which collapse into two dimensions when absorbed into black holes!" Sundhara said. "My inference was that Saraswati showed him these intricacies well before mainstream science discovered and shared them."

A more mundane possibility is that Guruji, who regularly perused scientific journals, came across an early article on holographic theory and simply explored it more deeply through the prism of his own meditation.

Guruji was also becoming increasingly preoccupied with seeking practical solutions to everyday problems in the world around him. Like his father before him, he found inspiration in the words of Mahatma Gandhi: "If we could change ourselves, the tendencies in the world would also change. As a man changes his own nature, so does the attitude of the world change towards him. We need not wait to see what others do."[263]

As Guruji himself expressed it, "There is more for us in giving than there is in taking. There is more for us in being a little unselfish than there is in being selfish. We can fly better and higher together than alone. Alone we sometimes feel overpowered, helpless and angry. Together, we can commit to improving our own lot through improving the environment around us. In helping others, we *become*. If you are *giving*, it is proof that you *have*."

Accordingly, Guruji was determined to use Devipuram as a platform for creating social improvements while inspiring others to follow suit. "Temples are merely training grounds in which we can expand ourselves," he explained. "What we learn via prayer rituals is to be practiced everywhere, not just in the temple. If we can accept worshiping idols and ideas, why can't we accept worshiping living beings? Devi asked me to build this temple. But as I started living here, the villagers around this place also became a part of my family. Their health and hygiene, housing, food, money issues— they became *my* issues too. Meditation, temple *pujas* and social welfare are not distinct or separate. They are all the same."

When visitors complained to him about the difficulties of focusing on spiritual practice while overwhelmed with the demands of marriage, children and professional

263 A popular bumper-sticker version of Gandhi's quote has been simplified to "Be the change you wish to see in the world"–words that Gandhi never actually spoke. This truncated version of the quote, moreover, comes across as "apolitical, and a little smug," noted Brian Morton, director of the graduate program in fiction at Sarah Lawrence College, in Bronxville, NY. "In fact, for Gandhi, the struggle to bring about a better world involved a steady awareness that one person, alone, can't change anything; an awareness that unjust authority can be overturned only by great numbers of people working together with discipline and persistence." That is also a perfect summary of Guruji's philosophy regarding social improvement.

life, Guruji would often comment that there was no need to consider mundane life and spiritual exploration as two distinct categories.

"We don't have to compartmentalize our lives into different parts," he said. "To worship God only in temples and *tirthas* reinforces, in a way, the belief that God exists only there and not in other places. The reality is that God exists everywhere. As Kabir once said, 'Everybody knows that the drop merges into the ocean, but few know that the ocean merges into the drop.' Spiritual practice can continue at all times, regardless of what you are doing. In fact, it should be the underlying theme upon which everything else continues to be done. That is when it becomes most effective."

Soon after moving to Vizag in 1980, Guruji founded the Sri Vidya Trust with the stated goal of "promoting self-reliance, income-generating opportunities and wealth among the rural poor in India through empowerment programs." In 2000, a group of North American supporters registered the Indo-American Institute for Rural Empowerment as a U.S.-based nonprofit, urging Guruji's followers abroad to "scan for trends and suitable opportunities; dare to dream big and think differently." An earlier group called Gurukul ("The Teacher's Family"), based in Buffalo, NY, had also united Indian students studying in North America for similar purposes.[264]

"We had a lot of fun," said Alok, one of Gurukul's co-founders. "A lot of lasting friendships happened because of this group. We would work ourselves to utter exhaustion but be happy at the same time. There was clearly divine energy in the Gurukul experience."

Within a few years, Guruji's Sri Vidya Trust transformed the educational landscape around Devipuram, founding some 50 village schools, which provided more than 1,500 underprivileged children ages six to 14 with a free education focused both on "skill development and developing positive attitudes towards life and culture."

The trust also helped 2,500 village women organize a rural "cooperative thrift society" called the Jagruti ("Awareness") Bank, which extended microloans amounting to ₹5 million (around US$100,000—a vast sum in India's rural village milieu) that brought them "self-reliance and freedom from the grip of local moneylenders." The trust also coordinated a variety of smaller rural empowerment programs in the

264 Sriganesh Madhvanath described Gurukul membership as "largely drawn from the Indian graduate student population in such places as Buffalo and Pittsburgh," adding that the group "also carried out a lot of fund-raising for the Sri Vidya Trust social programs."

surrounding countryside, relating to everything from health and hygiene to family planning and literacy, to energy generation and conservation.

One such project—involving the conversion of solar heat collected by geodesic dome houses into electric energy—earned Guruji a grant from National Bank for Agriculture and Rural Development in Mumbai. But though he expended a huge amount of time and effort on the project, he lacked the resources to complete it to his own satisfaction—and therefore decided to return the grant money, though he was not required to do so. "This is unheard of in an Indian context," Alok noted. "It sends a very strong message about who Guruji was."

A surviving "to-do" list of projects preserved from his 1999 visit to the United States gives an idea of the sheer amount of intellectual energy Guruji poured into the trust's social-improvement potential during this time:

- Reduce villagers' "dependency on the government to solve their problems; increase their self-reliance."
- Commission and maintain "a competently staffed mobile clinic that can make weekly rounds of 100 villages surrounding Devipuram," with a "focus on prevention, effective alternative medicine, life-saving referrals and social services."
- Develop cottage industries for "products that could easily be made by village women with a little training, for earning an income." (He notes parenthetically, "Are we prepared to give them some training on products, processes, services?")
- Develop telemedicine technology to empower "doctors who want to deliver low-cost services to indigent uninsured people."
- Develop a medical transcription service "to generate employment for fresh college graduates in India."
- Develop digital technology to enrich and broaden the array of resources available for children's education in rural India.
- Develop digital technology to disseminate knowledge of alternative medicine. (As examples, he mentions Ayurveda, homeopathy, Reiki and "stress-reduction meditations.")

- Develop digital technology to "package songs, dances, rituals and algorithms which work to generate transcendental experiences."

"A transformation occurred in Guruji during this period," Alok said. "He became more of a social worker than a spiritual guru! Of course he continued to be a guru and do *pujas* and give spiritual instruction, but what really absorbed him in the 1990s was the social side of things. He told me these social projects were the result of a 'maturation process' within himself, that these were 'the *real* Goddess rituals' he needed to be involved in at that time."

ॐ
ह्रीं

One project that particularly captures the breadth of Guruji's intellectual curiosity—as well as his willingness to experiment with real-world techniques *and* get his hands dirty applying them—was his design and construction of "low-cost, fire-retardant geodesic dome houses for pilgrims and other visitors at Devipuram," with the underlying goal of "demonstrating the viability of such designs in rural India." The domes, which could easily "be built and maintained by rural folk," were also extremely practical for the region's hot, humid climate. They remained "cooler than slab houses and blended much better with nature," Guruji noted. News reports described a prototype constructed (and self-funded) in upstate New York by a group of Gurukul members:

265 The dome was built at the home of Guruji disciple Venu Govindaraju, Ph.D., a research scientist at the university.

University of Buffalo students have constructed a steel, geodesic dome house in a Williamsville backyard,[265] as a cheap, practical form of housing for residents of poor villages in India. To make construction economically feasible in a region where families typically make about [US]$300 a year ... a cement mortar is mixed with locally available gravel materials, then pasted onto steel mesh attached to a temporary framework of geodesic triangles. Once the mortar sets, the triangle framework is removed, leaving a shell of concrete and steel.

With construction costs of about [US]$150, the new homes are providing villagers more than just affordable, sturdy shelter. The dome shape and cement construction also will provide protection from sun and rain, as well as give residents a new sense of permanence. ... Since village homes typically consist of stones, mud and dried palm fronds, they often do not last through the monsoon season, and villagers must rebuild, sometimes every year. ... The geodesic dome in Williamsville measures 24 feet in diameter and has a maximum height of 16 feet. ... So far, five new homes based on this design have been constructed in villages surrounding Vishakhapatnam, a city in southeastern India, midway between Madras and Calcutta.

"The challenge was to build these domes in a way such that unskilled labor could assemble it," Alok said. "Guruji was a great proponent of them because they were low cost, functional and had excellent spiritual vibrations that emanated peace and serenity."

In the early years of Devipuram, Guruji designed and built 12 such domes around the temple grounds and in the nearby village of Gangavaram. The project received considerable publicity in India at the time, generating interest among banks, private entrepreneurs, rural development groups and the Andhra Pradesh Housing Department. With government and private backing, a Sri Vidya Trust-led pilot project saw the construction of one dome house in each of 15 Devipuram-area villages to be used, at Guruji's request, as commonly owned community halls. The Vizag-based Bhagavatula Charitable Trust, a nonprofit rural improvement organization, favorably detailed his building techniques in a 1996 report:

> At Devipuram, half an hour by road from Visakhapatnam city, Dr. Prahlada Shastry [sic] has been experimenting with alternative technologies for better housing. Dr. Shastry ... had built a few residential units using the geodesic dome. We enquired about coconut fibre as a building material and learnt from Dr. Shastry about its use in corrugated cement sheets. He said that coconut fibre is added (2% by weight) to the cement after being dipped in turpentine. A square mould ½-cm thick is used to make sheets from this mix. The mould is placed over a plastic sheet laid out on leveled ground. After pouring the mix and before it sets, the ½-cm thick layer is slipped onto a previously cast coconut fibre/asbestos sheet so that it may acquired the curvature desired. If cracks appear during this stage they are covered immediately with the same mix in liquid form. The size of the mould currently being used by them is approximately 1.2

m × 1.2 m. The sheets have iron hooks embedded during casting so that they can be anchored to the RCC joists used for the houses. A metal wire held the sheet from the hook to the joist. The coconut fibre adds tensile strength to this roofing sheet. At Devipuram, bales of coconut fibre are bought and the fibres cut to 3 cm lengths for use in the mix.

Mrs. SriG Amma recalled visiting Devipuram around this time. "Guruji showed us the domes, the brick-making, the canteen, the solar-energy generation, his early attempts at generating energy from wind," she said, noting with wonder both his in-depth expertise on and infectious enthusiasm for each project. She added, "While technical descriptions of Dr. Sastry's low-cost dome designs may seem dry, the designs themselves are very interesting and to see the actual domes in Devipuram was a thrill."

Shortly before SriG Amma's visit, a terrible fire (caused by a defective kitchen stove) had swept through Gangavaram, damaging or destroying about 80 percent of the homes there—but not the community dome built by Guruji. He drove her to the village and showed her "the 500-square-foot dome house they had put up there some time ago, which had not only withstood the fire, but stopped it from spreading to the houses behind it. Upon our return, we discussed issues relating to [providing villagers with] smokeless *chulhas*."[266]

Amma noted that fire prevention was, in fact, one of Guruji's primary goals in promoting the domes to villagers. "The domes were not only fire retardant; because they were round, there would be no *vastu dosham*," she said, meaning their energy flow was optimal according to *vastu shastra*, the Indian predecessor to Chinese *feng shui*.

SriG Amma left Devipuram as awed by Guruji's social-improvement efforts as she was by his spiritual endeavors. "It is one thing to hear from others about Devipuram—about how the schools are set up and the domes and such," she said. "But it is quite another thing to actually be there in the middle of everything. When you're with Guruji in Devipuram, his boundless enthusiasm for all his little projects rubs off on you, and you feel so *alive* and focused. I would strongly encourage anyone to visit Guruji in Devipuram for at least a couple of days."

ॐ
ह्रीं

By his very nature Guruji was an "early adopter" of new technology. From cameras to camcorders, from VCRs to Blu-ray players, from Walkmans to iPods, from desktops to laptops to tablets—he was always fascinated by the latest technological developments.

Alok recalled the time that Guruji handed him a list of tasks to complete on a desktop PC while he took an afternoon nap. The desktop, however, was located right next to Guruji's bed. "As he lay down, I was clattering away on the keyboard," Alok recalled. "So I stopped and said, 'Why don't I work after you wake up, Guruji?' so as not to disturb him. But he replied, 'No, no, Alok, please keep working. The sound of a keyboard and computer is music to my ears.'"

When I visited Devipuram a few years ago, two gadgets I brought with me were a Tascam DR-07 portable digital recorder, which I used to record many of the conversations referenced in this book, and an Aaxa M2 micro projector. Upon my producing these items, Guruji immediately asked to borrow the instruction booklets for his "afternoon reading."

I had purchased the projector, incidentally, as a last-minute gift for Guruji after Devipuram's projector—an essential teaching tool in his Sri Vidya classes—suddenly ceased functioning. Guruji had, of course, researched the matter thoroughly and knew exactly what make and model he wanted. But my flight was only a few days away and the micro projector proved very difficult to source on short notice; most shops could supply it only on a backorder of several weeks. Then I called an electronics shop in Brooklyn, NY, which happened to have one in stock.

There was a problem, however: the business was run by a family of Hasidic Jews; it was late in the afternoon when I reached them and they were just about to close early for the start of the Jewish High Holidays. By the time they reopened, I would already be in India. I told the man on the phone about my dilemma, and about Guruji—and his bored, detached tone abruptly changed. "Okay," he said, "this Guruji is a man of God; let's try to help him out." We completed the sale immediately and the clerk promised to drop off the parcel for shipment that same afternoon on his walk to temple—throwing in overnight delivery service free of charge.

In the mid-1990s, when the Internet first began to emerge into the popular consciousness, Guruji saw it as a timely gift from the Goddess herself. It seemed the ideal medium for spreading his message, his talks and writings, mantras, ritual instruction—all free of charge—to the widest possible public.

He promptly became an early citizen of the World Wide Web, publishing Devipuram's first website on the then-revolutionary Tripod.com service, part of the Internet's first wave of user-generated content. Guruji titled his site, straightforwardly enough, Guruji: Sri Amritananda Natha Saraswati. It contained a brief biographical sketch, a selection of writings, some downloadable MP3 and PDF files of mantras and ritual instruction, photographs of the Sri Meru Nilayam temple, and his plans for the future development of Devipuram.

"Guruji felt that the best way to teach was to utilize technology so that he could reach out to a lot more people while preserving the guru-disciple connection through voice," said Alok, who was instrumental in helping Guruji develop his online presence. "I was posting *pujas* and *mantra japam* audios in his voice on website, and I asked Guruji if it was okay to do that. He said, 'The *shastras* say that initiation has to be given by the guru's *shruti* (voice), and my *shruti* is there in the audio, so it is equivalent to an initiation.' So you can see that Guruji was both respectful of the *shastras* and innovative in adapting their interpretation to modern times."

A parallel website, established by U.S.-based Gurukul members a few years earlier, focused more on Guruji's social initiatives. That site was called VI-1, a title intended to convey Guruji's idealistic philosophical formula, $V+I=1$: V ("we" as a collective) and I ("we" as individuals) are One.[267]

"VI-1 is an idea, an experiment in synergy," Guruji elaborated. "It asks the question, 'What can people living in high-tech societies do to empower the rural poor of the world?'" The site contained links explaining Devipuram's various projects, along with instructions for joining specific action groups or making donations to projects of interest. These initiatives, he stressed, were not merely his own pet interests, but living laboratories intended to illustrate for India and the world the possibilities of putting one's spiritual values into real-world action.

"Whatever our level of commitment, every one of us has a social responsibility and a role to play in empowering others," he said. "I don't want people to consider these

267 Initially crafted by SriG and later taken over by other U.S.-based disciples, vi1.org was "the main site through which Guruji kept in touch with devotees for over a decade," Alok said. "It was phased out when devipuram.com was formed and became completely functional. Most of the materials on vi1.org were converted from cassette tapes to digital format." Regarding the domain name, Alok notes, "Guruji first suggested using wer1, vr1, ui1 and vu1, but none of those were available. We even tried to bid on them, but finally settled for vi1, which was still available."

as *my* activities, but rather as something that they themselves would like to do, with their own motivation. The only way these projects can be sustained and have a life is through feelings and interests that come from your heart."

As for himself, he said, "I don't have any preset agenda; my role is only as a catalyst in empowering others to help themselves and, in that process, to help both their immediate environment and faraway environments," he said. "All are free to accept or reject my suggestions. I don't want anyone to feel pressured—only motivated. My commitment is only to see you happy, contented and growing. Your choice is mine too, for *we are One*!"[268]

268 Here Guruji echoes Hladini's parting words to him following the *Maha Kumbha Abhishekam*: "I will come as a thought...for we are one."

ꣳ A *homa kunda* (ritual fire pit) inside the *Yagna Shala* dome at Devipuram.
(Giri Ratna Singh)

24 The Powerhouse of Devipuram

But even as Guruji immersed himself in transformative community development projects, working tirelessly to improve the lives of the villagers around Devipuram, a number of self-appointed guardians of social and religious propriety stepped forward to accuse him of undermining India's public morality and cultural dignity by constructing a "pornographic temple." Predictably, the attacks were driven mainly by outrage against the explicit sexual imagery at Sri Meru Nilayam and Kamakhya Peetam.

The central granite image of Sahasrakshi and the *panchaloha* idols within the Sri Meru temple were all more or less in keeping with typical South Indian temple practice, and therefore elicited no particular comment. But the brightly colored, life-size, flesh-toned deities of the lower *avarana*s—many of them displaying bare breasts and exposed (though not anatomically detailed) *yoni*s—were another matter altogether.

"The initial reaction was almost totally negative," Guruji said. Of course, none of the critics were interested in parsing matters of theology, semiotics or history. They went straight for the lurid sound-bite, portraying Guruji as a purveyor of dangerous Tantric immorality. "Very few people said, 'Here is a man brave enough to show himself for what he is and stand up for what he believes in,'" he recalled. "Instead it was, 'This guy's stark raving mad! He's trying to spoil our culture! He should be put behind bars!' Television people used to come to interview me and they would ask things like,

'How can you prove that you're not ruining the country and corrupting our younger generation?' I would answer them to the best of my ability."

He began by explaining that, while the nudity of the *devis* could have an initially shocking effect on some visitors, this tended to fade very quickly. "When you're used to everything being clothed and then you suddenly see something new, that reaction is to be expected," he said. "But still, a woman who is usually dressed and now suddenly removes her clothing is far more exciting to see than a woman who is nude all the time. So maybe when some visitors looked at these devis for the first time, they felt a stirring of passion. But by the time they reached Sahasrakshi at the *bindu sthanam* and did *namaskaram*[269]—that one, single *namaskaram* would be the starting point of a change. The next time they went around, they might want to do some meditation. They might want to close their eyes and just sit in the temple. And the time after that, maybe they'd bring their partners and ask them to go around as well. What has happened to the passion? It has been transformed into a flowing of self-love. And that is the intended transformation. That is what happens at Devipuram."

269 That is, by the time they reached the top of the temple and paid obeisance to Sahasrakshi.

During Devipuram's formative period, however, such lofty goals seemed naively idealistic at best.

Indeed, it was not uncommon in those days to find groups of smirking young men arriving at Devipuram, having heard rumors of this "sexy" jungle temple and seeking prurient thrills. "They would go around looking for pornographic things—running from one idol to another, hoping to find something more," Guruji said. "But all they found was beauty and aesthetics. Finally they'd look at each other and say, 'Just to see these things we came all this way?' Then they'd go home and tell their parents, 'You know, there's a temple you should go and visit.'"

Suryalakshmi said she actually enjoyed confronting these young men. "I used to say, 'My dears, every man knows what a woman has, and every woman knows what a man has—so where's the big joke? Why behave like this? She could be your mother, sister, aunt—she's here in all of those forms.' And they would very nicely reply, 'It's true, grandmother, you're right.' They came to leer, but they left wanting to learn *Sri Chakra Puja*."

More serious-minded critics occasionally turned up as well, shaking their heads in disgust and loudly questioning what the world was coming to when such a temple was allowed to even exist. Most of these attitudes, according to Guruji, merely reflected modern Indian social indoctrination—as well as a fundamental (and largely imported) hostility toward the idea of worshiping God in female form.

"In India, of course, we have had so many Muslim rulers, not to mention the Christians who came to do business with India and then made it their own," he explained.[270] Many of these individuals, he said, "did not have the depth of the religions that they brought with them"; rather, they were the sorts of missionaries and zealots who "have always dwelled in duality—who worship only the Father God and could never accept the idea of a Mother Goddess." And over time, some of these prejudicial attitudes inevitably trickled into Hindu self-understanding as well, he said.

It was, in fact, precisely this circumstance that gave his message such urgency, Guruji said. Patriarchal religion untempered by matriarchal wisdom, he asserted, is the root cause of the world's strife and misery today, and balance must be restored.

"We have had enough of aggression and fighting for now," he said. "I think we can hold back until the feminine qualities show up again. Motherly qualities are really what are needed for this generation—the feminine qualities of creativity, procreativity, nourishment, protection, grace, abundance, love, teaching and compassion. It's a transformation that has already begun to happen, and not just in Devipuram—we are just one nucleus for this evolution; there are so many other nuclei emerging. Everywhere in the world people are beginning to realize and accept the idea that God could be a woman."

And though critics and detractors still exist in abundance, the controversies that surrounded Devipuram in its early years have largely subsided. "Over time, as people started understanding us, the criticism became less and less, and acceptance more and more," Guruji said in 2015. "Nowadays about 99 percent of the people who come to Devipuram come in a spirit of prayer and acceptance, with the understanding that it is a truly spiritual place."

270 Muslim conquests on the Indian subcontinent peaked during the 12th to 16th centuries, and culminated in the Mughal Empire (1526–1857). In addition to the British Raj (1858–1947), various parts of India were colonized for long periods by other European Christian powers, most prominently Portuguese India (1434–1833), Dutch India (1605–1869), Danish India (1620–1869) and French India (1769–1954).

But the struggle to gain such acceptance was not an easy one. Just a few years after the Sri Meru temple opened, Guruji posted a notice outside the entrance in an attempt to inform visitors about Devipuram's unique approach, while also addressing some of the most common objections and misunderstandings. It read:

Welcome to Sri Meru Nilayam temple,

the largest, most unique Maha Meru in the world.

Here one can literally walk into and circumambulate a true Sri Chakra,

meeting life-sized *murtis* of all the yoginis within.

This unique temple is built to tell you that you are goddesses and gods.

If you like, you can be like them too. You are free here. Nobody stops you.

All the powers shown here are dormant in you subconsciously.

Your *sadhana* consists in bringing these powers out to use them

for loving yourself, improving yourself and all those around you.

You gain nothing by leering or laughing at the goddesses here.

You gain everything by understanding your own nature as reflected in them.

You are beautiful and lovable, just as you are.

You are erotic. Nothing wrong with that!

You can create your identity and destiny. You are not powerless.

You don't have to be what others tell you to be.

We are with you in empowering you to be yourself.

Sit in front of the icons. Talk to them. Listen to the answers in your mind.

The highest offering you can make to anyone is yourself.

This is exactly what the Goddesses are doing. They have nothing to hide.

They are parts of you. They love you. That is why they have no shame.

They are not afraid of what others say about them. You can be like them.

You have made a special attempt to come here. We love you.

Thank you for your visit.

We hope you have enjoyed the graceful offering of themselves

that the Goddesses have given you.

~ *Amrita*

In fact, some of the most charming stories about Devipuram in this period come from devotees who, while strolling through the Meru temple, came upon Guruji himself doing *puja* to one or another of the Khadgamala deities. One such visitor found him deep in meditation before the goddess Budhyakarshini, whose name means, "She who attracts the power of discrimination," or "wise decision." Curious, the visitor later asked Guruji why he had chosen to worship that particular *devi*. He replied, "I was asking her to grant me the intelligence to get through life."

Another watched as he was making a milk offering to a deity when a large insect suddenly came crawling by between him and the *murti*. "Guruji interrupted his *puja* and started feeding drops of milk to the insect!" the disciple said. "He later explained that the Devi exists in all living things, including insects, plants and flowers. He added that if you ever pick a flower, you should first get permission from the plant by intoning the Gayatri mantra, because the flower is the *yoni* of the plant."

No sooner had the sensationalism and accusations surrounding the "pornographic" nature of Sri Meru Nilayam subsided when the controversy over the shrine at Kamakhya Peetam rose to a new pitch of fury. At its center was renewed debate over Kamakhya's anatomically explicit *yoni-lingam*.

To be sure, the Kamakhya Peetam—especially during this period—presented some seriously challenging imagery. As always, visitors to the shrine were confronted with two massive, rounded boulders, clearly comprising the Goddess's inner thighs. These sloped into a long, wet cleft explicitly representing her vagina, complete with a stylized clitoris dripping with spring water that spurted up from below. But if that were not graphic enough, her consort Lord Shiva was now represented by an erect, anatomically realistic phallus rising out of the vagina. Even lifelong Hindu devotees—fully accustomed to seeing the Shiva-Shakti pairing rendered as a *yoni-lingam*—could not ignore Kamakhya Peetam's powerful and explicitly sexual imagery.

And it made some of them very uncomfortable.

The historical trend in Hinduism has been toward increasingly abstract, aniconic *yoni-lingams*, to the extent that most modern Hindus do not even vaguely associate them with sexuality. "Early *lingams* were explicitly phallic-shaped, but in the last millennium and a half their shape has tended toward abstraction," observed Davidson and Gitlitz. "In many Shiva temples most *lingams* are now little more than domed cylinders, often rising from a stone base in the form of an equally abstract vagina, called a *yoni*."

While Western commentators often note the "phallic" suggestiveness of the *lingam*, Harvard scholar Diana Eck stresses that such "sexualized" interpretations do "not in the least convey what Hindus have seen and understood in this symbol." For most modern Hindus, she explained, the "*lingam* is the emblem of Shiva's unfathomable presence...[while the] *peetam* or *yoni*, the 'seat' in which it is established, is Shakti. Shiva is timeless transcendence; Shakti, the active energy of time and creation. Together, they form the whole of what is worshiped as the *lingam*—both Shiva and Shakti, male and female."

In other words, the subtle and historical sexual undertones of the icon have become essentially invisible to most present-day Hindu worshipers, who see the *yoni-lingam* essentially as an alternative rendering of yin and yang. And indeed, even at Devipuram, it is exceedingly common to find large rural Indian family groups—fathers, mothers, children, aunts and uncles, grandparents, teenagers of both genders—unselfconsciously moving among the nude deities and worshiping the *yonis* and *lingas* without a trace of shame or scandal.

The iconography at Devipuram—per the instructions of Kamakhya as interpreted and executed by Guruji—represented an overt attempt to reconnect with that deeper, lost history; to re-shift human consciousness to a time *before* sexuality was associated with impropriety, immorality and shame.

Yet Guruji's family was fully aware of the prevailing moral and social sensitivities of most educated Indians—and they were worried.

Even in the early days of Devipuram, "Prasad Rao and I tried to dissuade Guruji from presenting the *yoni* and *lingams* in such an explicit form at Kamakhya," Amma confided. "My feeling was, 'Why this form, which people might not find socially acceptable? Why open ourselves unnecessarily to misunderstanding and criticism from the public?' Guruji would always hear us out, but in the end he made it very clear that this was the way the Goddess wanted it. '*Ida na peetam, guru peetam*,'[271] she used to tell him."

The Goddess Kamakhya, Guruji stated, had explicitly instructed him not to be swayed from her wishes. "Some will ask you, 'What will other people think? How will you be judged? How will it reflect on society?'" she told him. "Don't ever worry about that. Make information available. Tell people, but don't compel them. Let people take it or leave it, think it is true or false, judge you as they see fit. All that matters is that *you* are convinced. People will bring bouquets and brickbats. You don't have to change. Be firm in your belief. I will bring the right people to you."[272]

She concluded: "Initially some will listen, but shake their heads in disbelief. They will leer; they will say it is nonsense; they will say you are destroying culture and civilized behavior. That is normal, because that is how they have been programmed by society. It is not your job to convince them [otherwise]."

It has been said that modern, Westernized versions of Tantra essentially revolve around "spiritualized sex," whereas authentic Eastern Tantra is better described as "sexualized spirituality." In other words, while the ritual imagery of authentic Indian Tantra may sometimes appear to be overtly "sexual," that surface-level, "in-your-face" interpretation is only one very thin layer of the onion.

A strong clue to the deeper meanings within can be found in the iconography itself. Note once again that the *lingam* at Kamakhya rose *out of* the *yoni*, rather than penetrating *into* it. On an early visit to Kamakhya, Sundhara commented to Guruji that it seemed to "depict union in the opposite direction, as if it were actually mirror-image of union."

Guruji explained that it was not a mirror view but rather an "interior view" of sexual union. He said, "This temple, and the inner sanctum of any Devi temple, is the *garbhagraha*, in which procreation is initiated. If one were to be inside the womb when union occurred, this is the perspective one would see."

He continued, "The womb is the place where the universe is born, relatively speaking. Because unless you are born, the universe does not exist—because you are not

271 "This is my seat, your Guru's seat," in Telugu.

272 Kamakshya's full instructions to Guruji are recounted in his essay, "What Kamakhya Told Amrita," in *The Goddess and the Guru, Volume II*.

there to identify it! The whole thing is based on relativity, you see? Tantra does not mean merely the exchange of energies between the male and female forms. The whole *universe* is pervaded by the Goddess; all of its dynamics are Tantra. When a tree's leaves sway in the breeze, they penetrate the space around them—and thus the leaves become the *lingam* and the space the *yoni*. When one person talks to another, the sound of the speaker's voice enters the listener's ear and they interact: the sound wave becomes the *lingam* and the ear drum the *yoni*. When clouds embrace a mountain top, the mountain is the *lingam* and the clouds the *yoni*, and so on.

"So anything dynamic is the divine Tantra," Guruji concluded. "For the universe to exist, there must be constant interaction. Tantra is the technique by which we harness the power of procreation in order to transcend it. Tantric *puja* between human beings is the speediest route to self-realization, but at the same time it is like walking on a knife's edge at the speed of light—there is no room for error. Any emotion could impede the process. Mutual respect is the mandatory ingredient. We must recognize the Goddess in the other person and worship them regardless of who they are or what they do. Whenever you see a woman who is pregnant, or an animal giving birth, or a bird laying eggs, you must realize and recognize that you are seeing the Goddess's dynamics at play."

Though the vast majority of rituals taking place at Devipuram were of a decidedly conventional nature, many remained curious about these "Tantric *pujas* between human beings." In a 2002 conversation with Guruji, Gupta asked him about them specifically.

He replied by recounting his 1983 encounter with the goddess Kamakhya. Guruji explained that "the Goddess instructed him to build a temple on the site and worship her in the explicit *lingam-yoni* form which is now Kamakhya's central image and focal point. The Goddess also told him to worship her in the form of living women. Since establishing Kamakhya," Gupta added, "he has regularly conducted *pujas* in which the women are seated (sometimes naked) in the position of the Goddess."

Observing that the worship of the Goddess in a woman's body, naked or clothed, is not unusual within the esoteric Sri Vidya tradition, Gupta pointed out that what truly distinguished Guruji's approach was not so much the Tantric practices themselves as his straightforward openness about them.

> What is most unusual is the lack of secrecy, the extent to which he has allowed the news of these rituals to travel. The relatively "open" manner in which Amritananda conducts these *pujas* is unique to Devipuram and central to de-esotericization and the transformation of meaning: While sexual rituals have in the past been employed by the tradition as a path of transcendence, such rituals have always retained a "transgressive" quality and hence have been kept secret.

A key to understanding Guruji's powerful break from tradition, Gupta added, was also to be found in the enormous agency afforded to female Sri Vidya practitioners at the temple.

> In the *puja* I witnessed, three women performed the *kumbhabhisekham* (ritual bath) on a young woman who sat naked on the three-foot *lingam* while [Guruji] chanted the mantras outside the closed door. The idea of women worshiping each other's naked bodies is an extremely radical move on Amritananda's part, and not only because of the strong taboos against nudity among upper-caste Hindus. It is rather the role of a woman as the performer of the ritual that marks a major departure from tradition, for in the past only under highly controlled circumstances have women been allowed to perform the more esoteric rituals within this upper-caste, male-dominated tradition.

Typical of Hindu Goddess temples, Devipuram draws particularly large numbers of women seeking help with personal and familial problems. According to Guruji, the most common problem presented is infertility, with marital discord running a close second. Devipuram's reputation for treating both problems effectively—success rates

273 The 90 percent figure comes from anecdotal estimates collected by the author, not from Gupta's research.

274 Gupta notes: "An equally pertinent question is why Amrita-nanda does not encounter *more* opposition than he does given the ostensible sexually conservative character of Indian society. If such rituals were taking place as openly in middle class American society, I am sure that the Guru would be either arrested or deported. Witness the treatment accorded to the tantric guru Bhagwan Rajneesh [Osho] in both this country and in India for openly advocating free love. While his agenda was similarly 'therapeutic,' he catered primarily to Westerners and I suspect he was rejected as 'inauthentic' not on moral grounds *per se*, but primarily on the grounds that he was misrepresenting Hinduism to the West."

275 The *Triveni Kalpam* was published during the *Navratri* season of 2008.

hover anecdotally around 90 percent[273]—has fed into its fame as a *siddhapeetam*, a "place where one gets results."[274]

Devi Parvati, who spent 18 years as a swami—a celibate nun—in the Shankara-charya Order, participated in a number of nude but nonsexual ceremonies in the early days of Devipuram, and said she found them both beautiful and transformative. "It was very powerful," she said. "Just to sit there and be part of the *puja* was a wonderful experience. It was an amazing Tantric temple, though many people just didn't know what to make of it."

Sunita, the disciple whom Guruji had considered as his possible successor at Devipuram, said Kamakhya told her that sexual rituals were "very sacred and auspicious in the olden days." Back then, the *pujas* were performed at "particular days and times" as a cure for "infertility or impotence," Sunita continued. "They were done with lot of mantras; the idea was to awaken the reproductive cells in the woman's womb by doing *puja* to her *yoni* and her breasts simultaneously. If the woman was having her period, the blood flowing from her *yoni* would be offered to the Devi as *prasadam*. Similarly, if the woman was fertile but the man impotent, *puja* would be done to the man's *lingam*. And ultimately, the couple would have children."

One secret to the ritual's efficacy, the Goddess told her, was that "*kama*, the desire for sex, had to be experienced as holy and sacred, without any lust." If either the performer or the recipient harbored any lustful feelings, all bets were off—and the *puja*'s outcome "could be very dangerous."

ॐ

Years later, Guruji would introduce yet another *puja*, this one intended for either individuals or couples, in which nudity was not required; the ritual could be done clothed and in public if desired, and it was called the *Triveni Kalpam*.[275] "Invite the Goddess into you," he wrote in his introduction to the *padhatti* describing the ritual. "Ask her to bless the people around you and to be with you always, answering your questions and giving you directions at every step. Experience the power of Tripura flowing in your body. Do it every day. It only takes half an hour. It is a short form of the *Sri Chakra Puja*, and people seeking *nirvana* will find it easy, authentic, tested and quick."

"Without any reservation, he wrote and published this completely new *puja* methodology as a teacher, guardian, father and evolved sage, as an authority in *Sri Chakra Puja vidhana*,"[276] Sundhara noted. And for the record, none of it came naturally at first—even to Guruji himself.

"One day, Guruji laughingly told me that when he first started doing *japa* and had to concentrate on the different chakras of the Devi, he felt shy because some of them involved the female private parts," Sundhara said.[277] "Immediately, Guruji said, the Devi appeared to him and told him not to be shy. She said, 'There is no difference between me and you or anyone else. I am you, I am your mother, your sister, your wife, etc.' Guruji said that this statement cleared his path of shyness about nudity—indeed, that once he had accepted all of this as Devi's will, no amount of shyness or embarrassment would stop him from performing the *pujas* he understood to be her desire."

Guruji was, of course, fully aware that many Hindus would never accept his interpretations. But their judgments, he said, were not his concern. An orthodox-oriented temple visitor once told him that while he enjoyed Devipuram and found the temples beautiful, he would never, under any circumstance, worship a *yoni*. As the man walked haughtily away toward the sanctum of Sahasrakshi at the peak of the Meru, Guruji leaned over and observed, "The poor fellow will end up worshiping a *yoni* anyway, you know. Lalita sits with her feet up in a lotus posture—so when he places flowers at her feet, he will by default also be placing them at her *yoni*!"

Guruji's total openness about such matters was thoroughly consistent with his interest in opening the benefits of Sri Vidya to a wider audience and revealing the secrets of authentic Tantric practice for the benefit of all who wished to learn it.

But despite his continuing efforts to educate visitors about Kamakhya's symbolism—including routine explanations by staff members and even detailed printed pamphlets—the explicit imagery simply proved too much for many people to take. "When it became clear that the public was not prepared for this form of *lingam*," Gupta noted, Guruji "finally agreed to encase the explicit *lingam* and *yoni* in concrete, in a less explicit form."

276 *Vidhana* means a process or methodology.

277 Guruji is here referring to a visualized or *murti* version of the Devi.

Yet while this solution may have appeased some of his critics, it left Guruji miserable. His attempts to obscure the imagery, Gupta wrote, "led to tremendous feelings of inner conflict and nightly visions of the Goddess, who would not let Amritananda sleep. She demanded that he restore her to her original form, and in addition (as a kind of penance) that he establish two more Ananda Bhairava *lingams* on the property.

"Following her directions, after only a few months, he uncovered the *yoni/lingam* once more, and the temple was thereafter kept locked (except for ritual use) with only a small window for viewing." (Guruji later confided that this small window had a second function: it allowed him to enter Kamakhya and then, reaching out from the inside through the window, to put a lock on the door. Thus it would appear that the temple was closed and locked, so nobody would guess that he was there or disturb him while he meditated.)

Around this time Guruji once again augmented his educational efforts by posting a lengthy, hand-painted sign—this one on the outside wall of the Kamakhya temple—that attempted to further elucidate its symbolism, in what Gupta called "an example of de-esotericization *par excellence*." Guruji's notice read:

KAMAKHYA TEMPLE

A Sri Chakra Meru was discovered here by Amritananda. The Meru was dug out from the middle of a rock formation resembling the private parts of a woman. He also saw Kamakhya Devi in person and received initiation into Shakti *puja* from Her.

The *Sivalinga* represents four levels of understanding: (1) In Creation, Siva is the phallus and Shakti is the birth channel. (2) In Preservation, Siva is the power in the Sun and Shakti is the love of the created world, coming from the breasts. (3) In Annihilation, Siva takes us into space and Shakti is the time which flows through it everywhere. (4) At the Fourth Level, there is no time, no space, no world; only the seed of a world yet to be manifested. Thus the symbol of God is the *lingam*, *yoni* and the Seed coming out of their Union as time, love and semen.[278]

The form here contains all of these ideas. The phallus does not penetrate from outside as in normal intercourse, but is projecting out from the *yoni*. This

278 Guruji is referring to the (1) *sristi*, (2) *sthiti*, (3) *laya* and (4) *turiya* phases of consciousness, respectively.

shows that pleasure need not be sought from anywhere outside, really. We are self-fulfilled; half-male, half-female. The seer and the seen are one. This is the concept of being *Svayambhu*, self-born.

The Shakti *puja* is to be performed according to the rite of Five Ms. These are *Madya, Matsya, Mamsa, Mudra* and *Maithuna. Madya* intoxicates. The intoxication of constantly experiencing the release of all tensions as they arise is meant. *Matsya*, the fish, roams freely in all directions in waters. Water is the symbol of life. Life is to be lived freely, without limits of I and Mine. *Mamsa* means meat. The tongue touching the palate is called meat. *Mudra* means a gesture; Shakti *chalana* and *sambhavi* mudras are well-known. *Maithuna* means intercourse. We are continuously interacting with the world through hearing, touching, seeing, tasting and smelling. All this is called intercourse with the world at large. Shakti *puja* is done to a living woman who agrees to be worshipped as Devi (*Suvasini* if married, *Kumari* if single).

The Agama *shastras* prescribe the actual ingredients. These ancient traditions are not to be looked down upon as Tantra is the art of getting rid of all attachments and inhibitions, gaining freedom from the limiting concepts of uniformity, [expectations] of one's culture, etc. We follow the *Datta[treya]* tradition which insists that *moksha* is for everyone, not only for the elite. All that is required is to follow the tradition told to us by the Guru.

It was a valiant effort (not to mention one that could keep religious scholars busily debating for years). But outrage against the Kamakhya imagery was largely a foregone conclusion. No rational or intellectual explanation—however detailed, spiritually sound or thoughtfully expressed; however historically and semiotically accurate—would suffice to placate those who viscerally objected to Kamakhya's "pornographic" imagery.

Thus in early October 2001, the sign was removed and Kamakhya Peetam was once again remodeled. Gupta bluntly described the resulting state of the temple: "Where the *lingam* once stood in all its explicit glory, now there was only a *yoni*, a small wet hole. The rounded boulders smoothed over with concrete still conjured the appearance of two spread legs. [But] the *yoni-lingam* had been transformed from an anatomically correct penis/vagina into an anatomically correct vagina [by itself]—even the opening itself had shrunken, as if the vagina had returned to its 'normal' size once the protruding penis was removed. The opening held a small pool of water at its center."

In the summer of 2002, Gupta interviewed Guruji at length about this change, and was surprised to hear practical as well as esoteric reasons for his decision.

Guruji explained that for the previous year, he had been "looking for someone to run the temple." The latest full-time priest at Devipuram had (following in his many predecessors' footsteps) moved away some months earlier, once again leaving Guruji with the responsibility of conducting most rituals himself. Soon afterward, daughter Rama and her husband Prabhakar—who had been managing most of Devipuram's and the Sri Vidya Trust's practical, day-to-day functions—had to move away as well.

So in addition to daily *pujas*, Guruji found himself having "to handle the adminis-tration of the temple, as well as the bookkeeping, and meeting with the steady stream of devotees who frequented the temple," Gupta noted. This, in turn, left him "very lit-tle time to concentrate on his more creative work—designing and implementing new interactive computer programs on the teachings and rituals of Sri Vidya."

When a suitable candidate finally appeared to administer Devipuram's affairs, however, he conditioned his acceptance of the position upon Guruji "covering up" the explicit *yoni-lingam*. After initially refusing to make such a change, Guruji "finally agreed to 'consult the Goddess' after a disciple asked him 'Why are you so attached to that form?'"

"That night in meditation, her answer came to him," Gupta recounted. "In a clear vision Devi said, 'Restore me to my original form, but make sure the Sri Chakra [i.e., the original Meru that Guruji had unearthed at the site] is kept inside.' Following her instructions, Amritananda broke the *lingam* and buried the Sri Chakra inside. He also salvaged the *sankastapana*—an abstract, three-dimensional *lingam* shape which was embedded at the core of the *lingam*—and placed it in front of a picture of Shiva, which [he had placed] behind the *yoni*."

For Guruji, the entire experience was traumatic in the extreme.

"I felt castrated," he said. "I was feeling the loss very intensely, perhaps because I had identified so completely with that form. I used to tell my disciples that I would live in that form even after I died."

Guruji's distress, however, passed after a few days and he began to see the situation in a different way: "When the *lingam* was removed, I felt like I had become a woman," he told Gupta, "which in this tradition is not bad—I have many times felt that I would like to be a woman in order to be closer to Devi. So now I identify with the *yoni*. Besides, astrally, [the *lingam* is also] still there. It has just become an *akasha lingam.*"[279]

Having unwittingly caused this massive spiritual, emotional and physical effort, the candidate who requested the *lingam*'s removal decided not to accept the position of administering Devipuram after all. Guruji, in typical fashion, interpreted this maddening outcome as still further evidence of divine will, a mere catalyst toward achieving the Goddess's desired result. "I now understand that what had to happen, happened," he said.

When asked if the nude *pujas* at Kamakhya had stopped or if the removal of the *lingam* had detracted from the *pujas* in any way, Guruji replied, "On the contrary, people are responding even more favorably to the atmosphere in Kamakhya now that the image may be perceived as being somewhat less harsh or threatening. All the aggressiveness has been removed."

Still, many longtime disciples were taken aback. "I was shocked when I heard that Guruji had come in and destroyed the *lingam* and then remodeled the temple in this more user-friendly or politically correct form," said Devi Parvati. "I understand Guruji's position, and how aggravating it must have been to deal with some of those more conservative devotees. But still, I thought it was such a sad thing."

Unfortunately, the situation had simply become too much of a distraction, and decisive action was required to ensure Devipuram's continued existence. At one point, there were even legal threats. "Some mischief monger complained to the District Collector—who also has magisterial powers over the Kamakhya area—saying that foreign visitors were making blue films and so on at Devipuram," Guruji recalled. "The Collector sent a subordinate to investigate; he was a Christian fellow. He sat with me for about three hours at the Meru temple, questioning me very deeply. But in the end,

279 *Akasha* is ether, therefore imperceptible.

he was satisfied and put an end to the inquiry, saying, 'Good. This case is now closed eternally. Hereafter, nobody will disturb you.'"

In accordance with the Goddess's wishes, soon after the *lingam* was removed and the *yoni* reshaped into its present form, the ancient Meru that Guruji had dug up following his vision was reinterred under the temple. "That old Meru had been worshiped in Sivalaya for some years," Guruji said. "Later on it was shifted back to Kamakhya, where it was successively worshiped on top of the *lingam*, then at its base, where the clitoris is—and then finally I reburied it at the place where I first found it."

But despite all the controversy and oft-changing forms surrounding Kamakhya's imagery, the original force that drew Guruji to build a temple there—indeed, the very force that had, he said, manifested Devipuram in its entirely—continued to flow unchanged.

As Haran Aiya recently observed, "Kamakhya Peetam remains, even to this day, the powerhouse of the Devipuram complex."

25   I'm Not the Chosen One

Hardly had the situation at Kamakhya been resolved when yet another traumatic loss was visited upon Devipuram: Swami Swaprakasananda—Guruji's beloved Anakapalle Gurugaru—passed away at 6 p.m. on *Guru Purnima* Day, Tuesday, July 23, 2002.[280] He was just a week shy of 87 years old.

That same morning, Amma—sensing the coming transition—had insisted that they visit Gurugaru, who was hospitalized in Vizag. "Somehow I had been feeling this urge inside to see him since the day before," she said. "I had never felt like that before. In fact, I had rarely gone to see him even on *Guru Purnima* days. But this time I kept telling Guruji, 'I want to go see Anakapalle Gurugaru!' I wanted to go that very moment."

Of course, breaking away from Devipuram wasn't so easy—Guruji was tied up with the steady stream of disciples and visitors who had traveled to pay their *Guru Purnima* respects to *him*. So finally Amma said, "Look, if you can't go I will just take the car and driver and go to see him myself." Her show of determination sufficed to convince Guruji and the pair headed into the city together. They found Gurugaru in his hospital bed, surrounded by family and a few close disciples.

"A lot of his dear ones were with him due to it being *Guru Purnima*," Guruji said. "He had been refusing to eat, but when we arrived he took some food and had some coffee. He was giving me a lot of love and seemed very happy to see me." But he was

280   By the standard calendar, *Guru Purnima* fell on Wednesday, July 24, 2002. But Guruji noted that by the Hindu lunar calendar, "*Guru Purnima* actually started at 1 p.m. [on Tuesday]. So 6 p.m. [Tuesday] was already *Guru Purnima*." Moreover, he added, "6 p.m. is *sandhya* time [a transitional hour of the day; i.e., dusk], which is auspicious in the spiritual context and especially for Tantric tradition."

clearly unwell. "He was quite weak, but he was still able to recognize us, no problem," Amma noted.

Guruji instinctively understood that the end was near. "Even as I sat there chatting with him, I already had the feeling this would be the last time I was going to meet him," he said. Gurugaru did nothing to discourage the perception. In fact, "he told his son to give all his pictures to me." A priceless collection of sepia-toned photographs—some showing a younger Gurugaru performing *Sri Chakra Puja*—was placed in Guruji's hands.

Gurugaru then made an unusual gesture toward Amma as well. "He asked me to touch his feet," she said. "In my life, this was only the second time I touched Gurugaru's feet."[281]

After a few hours, Guruji and Amma bid their final farewells to Gurugaru and returned to Devipuram. Gurugaru died later that same evening, but news of his passing did not reach Devipuram until late the next morning. When they heard, Guruji and Amma hurried off to Anakapalle for the burial.[282] "His body was taken to the *smashana* in a sitting position and then buried amidst the sounds of music and celebration," Guruji said. "Gurugaru's son broke a coconut over his father's head before the burial was performed. This is normal practice for *sannyasis* who don't die through *kapala bhedanam*, voluntary death ensuing from *samadhi*."

Amma was struck by Gurugaru's ecstatic, almost childlike expression of joy. "His eyes were wide open," she said. "There was still so much power in his facial expression." There would be no further births for him, she concluded. "He is gone," Amma said, categorically. "You should have seen his eyes."

In years past, Guruji and Gurugaru had occasionally discussed the possibility of Gurugaru's body being interred at Devipuram, but it was apparently not to be. "His family had already decided on a spot for the burial before I got there, and I did not wish to create any inconvenience by suggesting anything different," Guruji said. "I was perfectly fine with their arrangements."

And while the loss of his longtime friend and mentor must surely have come as a psychological blow—especially during such tumultuous times at Devipuram—Guruji was quite far beyond conventional rituals of mourning and grief: he had learned Gurugaru's lessons all too well.

281 Rama explained, "Because Gurugaru was a *sannyasin*, women were never allowed to touch him. Any *namaskaram* was always done at a distance, touching the ground at least a half-foot away from him."

282 *Avadhutas* are not generally cremated in the typical Hindu practice. Guruji noted, "Burial is the way in which the bodies of *sannyasins* and other realized people are finally put to rest, in a cross-legged sitting posture."

"When I woke up Wednesday morning, I did not yet know of his passing away the night before," Guruji said. "As I walked up the steps of the Sri Meru, it was a lovely day. The sun was peeking out from between the white clouds and shining beautifully on the temple. All the nearby hills and peaks were visible so clearly. The atmosphere was really heavenly; the birds were singing. I thought to myself, 'What a perfect day to celebrate *Guru Purnima*.' Then, just a few hours later, I learned of Gurugaru's passing."

It was late that night before Guruji had a chance to remember the contentment he had felt in his morning reflections. "I realized that my Guru had given me a beautiful *darshan* that morning," he said. "It was the perfect end to a perfect life.

"He merged with nature, didn't he?"

As Devipuram's popularity and reputation spread, Guruji continued to travel widely, both in India and abroad, giving lectures, writing essays, teaching classes in Sri Vidya, and of course presiding over numberless *homas*, *pujas*, marriages and other events; meeting with and advising the troubled, sick and dying; initiating thousands.

At the same time, he never stopped refining, adjusting and simplifying the *pujas* that he was continually performing and teaching. As daughter Rama noted, "Rituals were always being simplified by Guruji. Apart from *Shodasi Upachara Puja* and *Navavarana Puja*, he also simplified various *purascharanas*, *homas*, *abhishekams*, *yantra pujas*, *tarpanams* and *japams*."

In addition, he spent considerable time developing new rituals. "It is often possible to identify when someone took *diksha* from Guruji by the mantras they use, the *pujas* they favor and the attitude they take toward their *sadhana*," said Lalitha Sarma, a Mumbai-based disciple who received *diksha* from Guruji in the early 1980s. "Depending on the period when they met him, they all know a slightly different 'phase' of Guruji." Sarma said watching disciples from various places and decades meet at Devipuram and compare notes is akin to the old Hindu folktale of the blind men and the elephant: each starts with his or her own limited, subjective view of who Guruji is and what his teachings are, but leaves with a much fuller picture.

Guruji also put increasing amounts of time and effort into creating online teaching tools for those who could not reach Devipuram personally, and providing information and resources for faraway disciples who wished to develop their spiritual practices in his absence. Some older disciples were disappointed by this development, seeing it as the end of an era—a break with those early days of one-on-one instruction and intimate, personal conversations with their guru.

"By this time, Guruji no longer had the luxury of giving his disciples individualized attention," Jana said. "There were just so many people coming from so many places around the world to meet with him—and accordingly, his focus changed."

In truth, though, no one could accuse Guruji of not trying to stay in touch. He remained surprisingly accessible to visitors at Devipuram, and when attending events in India and abroad. To the end of his life, visitors and disciples would marvel at their ability to meet and speak with Guruji directly, one-on-one. He took phone calls at all hours from disciples and strangers alike from around the world. To the end, he administered his own email and sent countless brief (and sometimes lengthy) personal replies. His sheer level of personal availability—to so many, so constantly, with no expectations in return—was in many ways his greatest gift to those who admired him.

Unfortunately, however, human nature tends to devalue that which costs nothing. "We do not realize the value of some things, especially if they are given for free," Sundari Amma noted. "But attach a price tag of a *lakh* of rupees for *shaktipat*, and people throng to such gurus."[283]

Guruji didn't seem to particularly care whether people revered him and took his advice to heart or not. He simply enjoyed meeting them and exchanging ideas. What it all led to, if anything, was entirely up to the Goddess.

ॐ

Jana for years told his closest acquaintances about the extraordinary Sri Vidya guru he had encountered in his youth and frequently encouraged them to visit Devipuram and experience this amazing man for themselves. But as the years passed, he noticed their reactions grew increasingly underwhelmed. They often expressed surprise or disappointment at encountering not a detached, mystical, otherworldly saint—but an energetic, dynamic, decidedly of-this-world project manager and social activist.

By the early 2000s, when Jana would describe Guruji as a powerful Tantric adept, "people would no longer understand what I was talking about," he said. "A lot of them

283 That is, commercial gurus who charge large sums for their teachings are often perceived as giving something of greater value.

found him to be mostly involved with his website and various computer issues—one of them told me that he seemed more like an IT guy than a spiritual teacher!"

Guruji was singularly unconcerned about any social impressions he might be making; he preferred to remain totally immersed in his work. His talks, writings and animations were regularly posted online for free, consistently offering some of the most accurate, detailed and authentic explanations of Sri Vidya available anywhere. Those "who were meant to see" these documents (as Guruji liked to express it) would download, copy and share them—some of these individuals, Guruji would add with a chuckle, "might even read them." His job was simply to make the information available—the rest, he insisted, was up to the Goddess.

"Guruji's attention was always focused on whatever engaged him," Alok said. "And at that point in time, what engaged him was multimedia, technology, Internet learning and so on. So many disciples who were interested in sitting with him to do *pujas* and *homas* often would not find that satisfaction in those days, because Guruji would much rather spend his time explaining via a PowerPoint or sitting in front of a computer."

Another reason Guruji spent so much time on non-spiritual affairs at Devipuram was even more straightforward: there was no one else to do it. And unfortunately, there always seemed to be more and more to do. As he became better known as a guru, he had begun attracting a greater number of hangers-on, sycophants and yes-men—people who would appear on the scene, set ideas and projects into motion, make lots of big promises, and then disappear, leaving Guruji to clean up the mess.

"People like that began coming and going," Jana said. "He would entrust them with various tasks; they would say, 'Yes, yes, yes!'—and then nothing would ever materialize. So a lot of responsibilities ended up falling on Guruji's shoulders, and eventually—out of necessity, really—he just adopted the attitude that if you need to get a job done, you'd better do it yourself."

Guruji readily conceded the difficulty of finding a suitable "replacement" for himself. "It requires a lot of effort, patience, energy and competence in different areas of science, Sanskrit, Vedic, Tantric and information technology to do all these things," he said. "Slowly the Mother is sending me help in the form of people who are willing to work on these projects selflessly. But it has often been an uphill task to do them singlehandedly."

And the more mundane jobs he had to handle by himself, the less time was left for more traditionally "spiritual" endeavors. "He was desperately in need of foot presence and help," Alok said. "That, coupled with his general trust in people, and the fact that many feel it's inappropriate to express any disagreement with one's guru, caused some big problems. Because, you see, Guruji is not at all a manager. He is a very hard worker. But he is a visionary and an idea man. He cannot sit and tell people what to do. He cannot manage them."

The last and perhaps the most fundamental reason for Guruji's increasingly "un-guru-like" interactions with disciples and visitors was a profound evolution in the way he saw other people. Increasingly, he was experiencing everyone he met as embodiments of the Goddess, each one expressing some beautifully unique facet of her totality. As such it had become much less interesting to simply teach them what he knew—instead, he wanted to learn from them as well, to see the world as they saw it. "He began to see himself more as the student," Jana said. "He began to balance teaching with learning."

This dynamic was strikingly apparent whenever Guruji met visitors at Devipuram: his intent focus on their words; his thoughtful and pertinent questions about their lives, projects, interests, talents and expertise; his habit of introducing them to others who might share complementary interests. In short, though he clearly remained the man whom everyone had come to see, he seemed genuinely unable (or unwilling) to consider himself "the most fascinating guy in the room"—quite the contrary, it was everyone else who fascinated him.

In a sense, he was always seeking connections, searching for people who shared an interest in the questions that consumed him.

"Guruji sometimes spoke of being a 'lonely traveler,'" Ahalya said. "He would say he still had so many questions yet to be answered; for example, what happens in the absence of time? How can one look at the world in four dimensions? How and to exactly what extent are we limited by our senses? Can we train our consciousness to travel backward in time—or is that attempting to separate time from space, subject from object, or Shakti from Shiva, in a way that is fundamentally impossible?"

More worldly matters engaged him just as thoroughly.

"Guruji was always wanting and willing to learn from all," said Sundhara. "For example, during the period from 1999 to 2006, I remember Guruji putting a lot of effort into studying the fundamentals of Reiki." To the end, whenever someone with knowledge of Reiki arrived at Devipuram, Guruji would frequently spend hours with them, comparing notes, asking questions and further refining his own understanding and practical skills. He also invested a great deal of time mapping the correspondences between Reiki's understanding of energy flow and the chakra system of Kundalini Yoga.

In all cases, Sri Vidya remained his baseline—the filter through which he tried to assimilate wisdom and teachings from other sources, whether they were major religions or self-help advice books. Every person, every piece of knowledge presented an opportunity to peer more deeply into the Goddess's infinite kaleidoscope of manifestation.

"Guruji does not operate from the principle, 'I am up here, you are down there,'" Alok explained. "When you talked to him, he would often ask you as many questions as you asked him. He might request your guidance on as many things as you wanted his guidance for. Why? Because he always believed that there was something precious you had to offer. He had an intrinsic faith that everyone had something to contribute. He always searched for their strengths and then worked with them."

Alok continued: "For example, Aiya's focus and strength is in ritual, so that is what Guruji brought forth in Lusaka. By contrast, when Sudhir Mylavarapu, a former British Council administrator, came to Devipuram, he was not much interested in ritual but fascinated by dome technology—and Guruji engaged his interest and competence accordingly. When he observed that the local women workers from the villages had natural *bhakti* and an interest in learning, he focused on that. When Guruji got involved in developing village schools, it was because those were the needs in the area where he was physically located. Guru never had his own agenda. He was a medium, a catalyst who brought forth what was needed in any particular situation."

Sometimes that could lead to concentrated activity, sometimes to intense intellectual engagements—and sometimes to silence.

"When I sat with Guruji, it was often in silence," said Megha, the Toronto writer. "His gaze and presence alone engaged me—you'd look at him, he'd look at you and you'd know that some exchange had happened. Maybe you didn't really understand what it was, but you were very comfortable with it. You never felt threatened; you knew it was nothing wrong."

Haran Aiya confirmed it was often at such moments that Guruji's efforts were at their most powerful. "That's when things really got done," he said. "He was like Dakshinamurthi: even if he was silent when you were sitting next to him, volumes were being revealed to you."

Asked how he managed to deal with so many different sorts of visitors and disciples—the ritualists, the intellectuals, the devotionalists, the skeptics—at so many different levels of spiritual development and understanding, Guruji replied that he made no real distinction at all. "They're all equally valuable," he said. "All that I experience is me. They are all the Goddess. There are no levels. I find it very hard to believe that any one is better than any other."

When Saru was younger, Guruji sometimes used to tell her she was "like a fourth daughter to him." This, she emphasized, denoted no special status—it was, rather, a typical expression of affection that Guruji shared with many disciples over the years. "That was the whole point," Saru said. "We were *all* his fourth daughter."

As he approached 70, however, the sheer weight of "being Guruji" was taking a greater and greater physical toll. He struggled with worrisome symptoms of ongoing cardiac and other health issues. His legs, along with the "lotus feet" so many disciples longed to touch, were increasingly swollen, discolored and painful. Amma and a handful of early disciples pleaded with him not to overextend himself with so many new plans and projects. But while they succeeded to some extent, Guruji's force-of-nature personality—happily for thousands of spiritual seekers, if somewhat frustrating for those closest to him—remained more or less unstoppable.

He kept intense hours, employing a polyphasic sleep schedule—also known as "the sleep of genius" (since it was practiced by the likes of Leonardo da Vinci, Thomas Jefferson, Napoleon, Thomas Edison and Nikola Tesla, among many other illustrious exponents). Advocates of polyphasic sleep say it generates much additional free time in one's day, while enabling clearer, more creative thinking, more access to the subconscious and dream states, and stricter control over the body itself.

Guruji's approach involved seven hours of sleep spread over three segments of time throughout the day: at Devipuram, he would generally sleep from 10 p.m. to 2 a.m., then awaken. The quiet hours from 2 a.m. to 5:30 a.m. were his personal time—for meditating, writing, working on the computer and so on.[284] He would return to bed from 5:30 a.m. to 7 a.m., and then rise for morning prayers, temple business and meeting visitors. After lunch, he would again take a short nap from 2 p.m. to 4 p.m. (which he jovially referred to as his "beauty sleep"), and then remain awake and active until 10 p.m., when the cycle began once more.

"Guruji recommended this distributed-sleep habit and said that, when using it, the brain can work at 100-percent efficiency throughout the day," his former assistant said. Daughter Anantalakshmi added that sleep has never been a particular problem for Guruji. "He was always able to take a nap and, fortunately for him, he never needed absolute quiet to do so," she said. "He was always quite capable of getting 'into his zone'—be it in meditation, sleep or whatever—quite independently of his surroundings."

Aiya, for example, recalled the time the two of them attended a spiritual conference together. When Guruji's presentation ended, he left the stage but never reappeared. After almost an hour had passed, Aiya became concerned and began searching the conference environs to no avail—until he finally located Guru in the backstage area, contentedly curled up on the floor under a folding table, sound asleep.

In his personal *sadhana*, Guruji continued to have immensely interesting meditational experiences—but with very few exceptions the Goddess remained true to her word and rarely appeared to him in human form anymore. Guruji continued to watch for her, however—and he occasionally found her.

After participating in the *Kumbha Abhishekam* of the Rajarajeshwari Temple in Tiruvannamalai, Tamil Nadu, in 2003, he excitedly reported, "I had experiences of the Goddess there on two different occasions. The first was when a sculpture of Durga was

284 Interestingly, these "wee hours" correspond to the time of the day known as the *Brahma muhurta*: "Yogis, Paramahamsas, Sannyasins, aspirants and Rishis start their meditation during the *Brahma muhurta*; sending their vibrations throughout the world, benefiting all. Meditation will come by itself without any effort."

being videotaped—my God, she was ravishingly beautiful, looking all over the assembly of devotees there. I was reminded of my *darshan* of her at Kamakhya 20 years ago! She was *that* resplendent, though fully clothed and fully covered in jewelry."

The second sighting took place "when the four priests started [the procession] for the *Kumbha Abhishekam*. Drums were playing loudly, and when the priests passed by me, I saw a very pretty girl following behind. I had noticed her earlier, thinking, 'Hmm, possibly. Maybe.' People were tossing flowers at the procession and one yellow flower bulb landed on her left breast. She turned to me, looked at me squarely in the face and gave me a smile—and what an out-of-this-world smile it was. I almost fainted. Nobody noticed her, but I knew she wasn't any ordinary girl. She was the Devi."

In 2003, Guruji made a final triumphant tour of the United States and Canada. It was an extraordinary few months, drawing crowds that surpassed those on any previous visit, as he crisscrossed the United States and Canada from Boston to New York to Toronto to Los Angeles. Near the beginning of the visit, he presided over two unusual events in the rural New England state of New Hampshire. One was a massive *Sri Chakra Homa* attended by more than 600 people and performed on (of all places) a football field at Oyster River High School in Durham. The second involved a group recitation of the *Lalita Sahasranama* atop 6,288-foot (1,917-meter) Mount Washington, the tallest peak in the eastern United States.

Later, on a visit to Toronto's CTV broadcast center, Sundhara was astonished to see Guruji "radiating so much effulgence and compassion that ordinary Canadians, who had never seen or heard of him before, were instinctively clasping their hands together and greeting him with *namaskarams* as he walked along the streets." During a subsequent stop at Future Shop in suburban Scarborough, Ontario, the unexpectedly reverent public reaction was repeated in a consumer electronics setting.

Guruji remained in North America for three months, leaving shortly after a massive *Guru Purnima* celebration at Aiya's Sri Rajarajeswari Peetam—by then no longer confined to Aiya's suburban Rochester garage, but spread over a spacious former dairy farm in nearby Rush, NY.

ॐ
ह्रीं

His tour clearly affirmed that Guruji's reputation had spread far and wide; his message was being heard by an ever-broadening audience. Back at Devipuram, however, he still sometimes wondered aloud why his efforts never really seemed to, in his own words, "catch fire" with anything even remotely approaching the colossal popularity of India's mass gurus such as Sri Ravi Shankar or Mata Amritanandamayi. It was not that he sought fame or adulation; if anything, he instinctively avoided both at every turn.

But what he wanted very much was for his message to rise sufficiently high above the cacophony to be heard by all who were ready to receive it.

Yet it remained fundamentally impossible to picture Guruji at the helm of any sort of mass spiritual juggernaut. He was too down-to-earth; too straightforward and unpretentious. As scholar Hugh Urban wrote (of another pair of spiritual leaders in a different scholarly context), Guruji and Amma were most likely *too* genuine, *too* authentic to find success on such a vast domestic and international scale.

> Unlike the neo-Tantric sex-gurus and gurus of the rich like Bhagwan Shree Rajneesh [Osho], [they] are remarkably low-key and seem relatively uninterested in the mega-guru, mass-profit business. Indeed, despite their odd hybridity of religious styles, they appear quite resistant to the commodification and consumerism that is so rampant in American-style Tantra.[285]

Guruji was also profoundly uninterested in gaining or exercising any charismatic power over others. "If you are given some power and you exercise that power to control people, then you get stuck at that level and will likely be unable to help others," he explained. "But if you use your power to *empower* others, then you elevate both yourself *and* others."

Moreover, Guruji offered no miracles or instant solutions, no quick-fixes or easy answers. Even the streamlined and simplified Sri Vidya rituals and meditations he developed and taught could take years to fully understand and master. "Sure, we may question why one should go through all this trouble if shorter methods are available,"

285 Urban's comment referred to Swami Satyananda and Sree Maa, whose Devi Mandir Ashram near Napa, CA, thrives on a small scale, in sharp contrast to the surrounding "spiritual businesses and get-rich gurus of California-style Tantra."

Guruji agreed. "And I do think the shorter methods work, too, but each method has its own reward in proportion to the effort invested."

In addition, his philosophical writings dug uncommonly deep, challenging and surprising readers rather than providing straightforward inspiration and comfortable platitudes. And when Guruji spoke of the connections between science and spirituality, he did so with the complexity and authority of an experienced nuclear physicist— his learned scientific references were never the lightweight "quantum-everything" that has become the bland stock-in-trade of so much New Age spiritual literature. It took a lot of time and effort to digest and follow.

Finally, of course, his liberal teachings on nudity and sexuality in Tantric tradition—despite their historic authenticity—landed him in a rather sparsely inhabited spiritual middle ground: he was sufficiently frank to scare off many socially conservative Indian worshipers, yet too resolutely authentic, practical and non-sensational to excite the imaginations of many Western neo-Tantrics seeking X-rated "sacred sexuality" in the Mystic East.

Yet while Guruji's teachings spread comparatively slowly, their influence steadily deepened and entrenched itself over the decades, carried by the countless devotees with whom he has shared. "While Amritananda is nowhere near as famous as Rajneesh [Osho]," Gupta observed, "he is the Guru of Chaitanyananda [Haran Aiya], founder of the Rajarajeshwari Peetam in Rochester, NY, America's fastest growing Sri Vidya community, [and his] other disciples have founded Sri Vidya Peetams in other countries as well."[286]

Matters of influence and legacy aside, however, the temples at Devipuram required maintenance, bills had to be paid, and—most of all—Guruji wanted people to learn about, see, share and experience the extraordinary complex that the Goddess had inspired him to build in this remote wilderness. A note penned close to the Diwali holiday in 2003 poignantly captured Guruji's potent joy and confidence in his vision, tempered by the persistent sense that he was somehow not doing enough to communicate it.

286 Guruji's disciples have established *peetams* in Australia, Canada, Germany, India, Japan, New Zealand, Singapore, Sri Lanka and many other countries.

"I feel throttled," he wrote. "I don't have the vocabulary to express my thoughts independently of time. Words like 'change,' 'flow,' verbs, predicates—they force me into speaking in the language of linear time, whereas reality seems to have no such limitations. What am I to do? How am I to communicate, if that vocabulary is denied to me? I feel like an inarticulate speck of sand on the shore of a vast ocean, trying to describe this ocean I see to the world. My throat is gripped by pitiful inadequacy. It brings to mind a Sanskrit saying, *Yato vaacha nivartante apraapya manasa saha*—'Whence words return vanquished, unable to express the immensity of what they have beheld.'"

He implored the Goddess's grace one more time: "Oh Mother, when will you lift me out of pettiness?" he asked her.

And against all hope and expectation, she appeared to him—though still not quite in human guise. Guruji struggled, in fact, to describe the vision she presented.

"What beauty, what perfection, what harmony, what richness!" he recalled. "I saw her bright form; I saw her dark form. Pastel shades and dark hues. Infinite variety; a tapestry of beauty woven upon beauty and expressed in pure excellence, pure perfection. Vector-graphic[287] faces in the most beautiful colors, from every culture, from every era. Perfection personified. Crystal facets, jewels, rainbow colors, all vying with each other to display their wonders, then vanishing—fleeting moments of glory. The vision lasted about 20 minutes."

As she faded he asked her, as he always did, "When will I see you next?"

And she replied once again, "My sweet child, look into the eyes of every devotee and you will see me there."

ॐ
ह्रीं

Meanwhile online, the Yahoo Group Shakti Sadhana[288]—for a time, during Yahoo's early-2000s heyday, the largest group in the network's "Hinduism" category, with thousands of subscribers and dozens of messages posted per day—undertook a nearly two-year discussion of the goddesses populating the *Sri Yantra*, using photos of Devipuram's *Khadgamala Devis* as header illustrations for each. The group also published a detailed guide to performing the *Khadgamala Stotram*, which incorporated Guruji's commentary.

287 Vector graphics is the use of geometrical primitives such as points, lines, curves, and shapes or polygons to represent images in computer graphics.

288 The Shakti Sadhana group peaked in user activity in the late 1990s and early 2000s.

This wider exposure, in turn, prompted renewed discussion—via the Web this time, and among spiritual practitioners from across India and around the world, most of them hearing of Guruji and Devipuram for the first time—about the propriety of sharing Sri Vidya's long-secret wisdom by electronic means, thereby reaching an audience orders of magnitude larger than earlier generations could ever have imagined. The discussion eventually reached a fever pitch, with several traditionalists attacking Guruji's practice fiercely, some murmuring that the Goddess would extract a heavy price for his transgressions. At last, Guruji responded with an exceedingly rare online defense of his approach.

"Yes, I have published mantras on the Web," he replied frankly, referring to his Tripod and vii sites. "I am trying to do everything possible to make information available to people through interactive teaching media. So you have my take on this. It is true that I am taking on the karmas of all those who misuse it. Let me suffer gladly for that. If I am connected to Goddess, she is taking on the karmas made by her own self. Let her enjoy it."

Guruji then reiterated his oft-stated belief that the Goddess would ensure that only those who were ready to receive this wisdom would ever stumble upon it—*and* recognize its authenticity and value—amid the plethora of competing materials online. "My feeling is that the information should be made available," he said. "Just because it is available, it does not imply that everyone looks at it."

Next, Guruji cited the long historic precedent for public sharing of religious "secrets."

"Ramanuja went to the top of the roof and shouted the mantra given to him by his guru, who had extracted a promise that he would not reveal it to anyone," he said.[289] Later, with the advent of books, such secrets reached an even wider audience—which is, after all, the whole point of publication. "It is in this spirit that books, for example, on the *Parashurama Kalpasutra*[290] are published. Do they not contain the decoded mantras? What is the essential difference between publishing it in a book or publishing it on the Web?"

In fact, Guruji argued, the Internet had solved one of the largest, most substantial objections raised by opponents to the publication of mantras and other holy scripture

289 Ramanuja (c. 1017-1137 CE) was a Hindu theologian, philosopher and scriptural exegete, born to a Brahmin family in Tamil Nadu, India. He is revered as a great teacher who–not unlike Guruji– often challenged prevailing views on religious matters, for example championing the role of personal devotion over formal ritual and insisting that caste and gender are not bars to spiritual advancement.

290 A medieval ritual source book still used in some lineages of Sri Vidya, including Guruji's.

in books. "The main problem with books was that the soundtracks were not there," he said. "Interactivity was not there. Now they *are* there, courtesy of the Web."

Then he restated another of his boldest assertions: that an online audio file, properly pronounced and explained in the voice of a qualified guru, could in fact serve as "*a proper auditory transmission from a guru to shishya.*" In other words, technology *could* legitimately be used to reach larger numbers of people than ever before while still preserving the essential, traditional guru-disciple connection through voice.

After all, he argued, "How many so-called gurus are actually giving the information in such detail to *shishyas* now? The gurus themselves are just throwing the mantras out there without knowing any of their intricacies." Here Guruji pointed to the avalanche of blatantly inaccurate information about Tantra that was proliferating on the Internet even then.

"Just look at all the play with Tantra in the form of sexual license," he said. "When our learned gurus don't publicly share the *real* secrets, then all kinds of wrong interpretations will go 'round. Given that what we [i.e., qualified gurus properly initiated and trained in authentic Indian Tantric lineages] are saying is probably less than .01 percent of what is out there on the Web, should we not break the silence? For example, who [among uninitiated persons exploring Tantric philosophies] does not know about the use of *panchamakaras*?[291] Is that really any secret now? Instead of pretending to guard such 'secrets,' we need to instead direct people toward the proper ways of using them—by channeling the correct information rather than hiding it. The times of puritanical rejection of disseminating information have to change in order to prevent further damage. The wise must choose to speak; otherwise, the unwise shall have their way."

ॐ

Guruji's 70th birthday was elaborately celebrated at Devipuram on September 26, 2004, and marked by the publication of *Chidagni* ("Fire of Consciousness"), a hagiographic account of his life up to the opening of the Sri Meru temple. Penned by Mrs. Neti Sitadevi, it has achieved considerable popularity among Telugu-speaking disciples over the past decade and remains available in Devipuram's bookshop.

291 The Five Ms of Tantra, discussed earlier.

But even as he continued to take on new disciples, preside over innumerable *pujas* and expand and improve upon Devipuram's material and spiritual offerings, Guruji remained unable to shake the suspicion that his personal spiritual abilities had begun to fail him—or at least that they had reached their outer limits. Of his meditations around this time he said, "I used to see hieroglyphic scrolls—sometimes written in Egyptian or Atlantian, sometimes more like mathematical symbols, describing some sorts of advanced theories." He tried desperately to hold onto these messages in his memory, feeling compelled to deliver them safely to the world—but found he could not.[292]

"How I wished for an instrument that could video-record the experiences happening in a person's mind without loss!" he said regretfully. "I was not mathematically trained enough to understand the gift that was being given to me; I didn't even know how to transcribe it. And so that gift, which came unasked for, went unutilized. How sad! At 70 years of age, my memory was failing me. I rued the day that I lost my photographic memory. That might have saved the day."

"But," he added, with a generous dollop of wry humor, "that is how I learned that I was not the Chosen One. Not like that guy in *The Matrix*..."

292   Toward the end of his life, Guruji again referenced this phenomenon, stating that all the transmutations of matter in the history of the cosmos had been "preserved in scrolls, most of them written in Sanskrit. You can retrieve this information by accessing [via meditation] a particular region of gravity, space and time [and] see yourself at different ages, or in previous births, far into the past. I can read the Sanskrit; that is not the problem. But these scrolls are being written so rapidly, and their content is so voluminous, that I just can't remember any of it except for a few headings here and there. Some of them were changing before my eyes even as I tried to read them!"

26   Precisely What I Wanted

Despite his occasional frustrations, Guruji forged onward, accepting all of the ups and downs as Devi's will—"all part of the game," as he liked to phrase it. The universe, he remained confident, was unfolding precisely according to her divine intention. So he played his part as best he knew how, and Amma helped him along by exerting "a sublime influence on Guruji when he struggled with these things," Alok noted.

All the while, Devipuram continued evolving into an ever more beautiful rural retreat, with a life and rhythm all its own. A typical March day in the mid-2000s was evocatively captured by a staff member, revealing a morning routine that still pretty accurately reflects life at the temple complex:[293]

> Around 5:45 a.m., the kitchen's huge, wood-fueled country stove is fired to boil hot water for tea. Shafts of sunlight stream through the tall coconut trees, illuminating clouds of swirling wood smoke as Ammatalli, a farmer from a nearby village, arrives at 6:00 to feed and milk the cows. He's also in charge of the vegetable gardens, which are now producing tons of the tomatoes, *brinjals* [mini-eggplants], ladies' fingers [okra], black gram [lentils], coriander and green chilies used every day in the canteen's menu.

293   Due to Cyclone Hudhud's destruction, much of Devipuram's more mature greenery disappeared in 2014, but systematic replanting initiatives have largely restored the area's natural beauty.

Meanwhile, Somayya [another farmer] ventures through Devipuram's gardens, collecting flowers for the day's *pujas*. He returns with four baskets brimming with roses, *champa, kanakambara, parijata, bilwa* leaves, *tulsi* and hibiscus, to name just a few. The fresh-plucked flowers are placed on a huge plate, and Amma begins dividing them for Devipuram's shrines. March is also the season for mangoes, gooseberries, guavas and cashews. The mango trees at Devipuram start blooming in January. By March, you can pick and enjoy "tender mangoes"—*maavidi kaaya pinja* in Telugu. Half of Devipuram is covered in cashew trees; the whole place is suffused with the fragrance of cashews and jackfruits through April.

The staffer went on to describe an ordinary evening there:

When the sun sets at around 6:15 p.m., the birds settle into their nests and darkness falls with pin-drop silence. If you linger atop Sivalaya, you can watch the sky fill with stars; there is no light pollution to disturb your view. Guruji normally spends this time outside the Ashram enjoying the gentle breeze and perhaps listening to meditative music. Often you'll find him speaking to visitors about physics or answering questions about spiritual practice. When he's speaking with an advanced *upasaka*, the language can become highly philosophical—one would need enormous knowledge and experience to even follow the conversation! At 8 p.m. the canteen bell rings, calling everyone for dinner, and it's another sumptuous meal: various curries, fruits, chutneys and thick buttermilk with the fragrance of fresh butter are served, making it a most enjoyable pastime.

Yet the very remoteness that made Devipuram so idyllic continued to make it difficult for Guruji to find qualified people willing to come there and settle. He tried to keep his options open as he continually sought divine guidance on what should happen next. He felt that he either had to "hire an administrator to oversee the entire complex," or, failing that (and if the Goddess allowed it), transfer ownership to an organization with the resources to properly operate the place.

However, several serious inquiries in the latter direction failed to bear fruit.

"Devipuram's location is anathema to most Indians, who prefer to live in cities rather than rural locations," noted Gupta. "Cinema, shopping and good schools are all located in the city. Priests and *pujaris* do not like to live in the country because there is much more money to be made performing rituals in the cities. It is mainly retirees who are drawn to a quiet place like Devipuram," which is, she concluded, "a nice place to visit, but for various reasons, a place where very few people want to live."

At one point, Guruji explored the possibility of transferring the property to the Sankaracharya of Kanchi Kamakoti Peetham, the South Indian seat of the monastic order most closely and openly associated with Sri Vidya. A delegation from the order once visited Devipuram and toured the property, but Guruji never heard back from them. "He attributed their lack of response in this case to the explicit nature of the images in [the] temples," Gupta noted, "as well as the fact that Devipuram [follows] the Dattatreya lineage, initiating devotees into the worship of Sri Vidya without regard to caste or gender."[294]

Later, a pair of disciples suggested that Guruji contact Ganapathi Sachchidananda Swamiji, a prominent Sri Vidya guru from the Avadhoota Datta Peetham in Mysore, who identified himself as a member of the Dattatreya lineage but still called himself a *samayacharin*.[295] Guruji recalled, "They used to tell me, 'Devipuram will benefit a lot if we give it away to him. He has the resources to develop it. If you don't give it, there is a chance endowments will take it over.'"[296]

Guruji visited the Swami in Mysore; the Swami in turn came to visit Vizag, but negotiations never really gained much traction. The Swami was impressed with Devipuram in general, exclaiming, "Guruji, Kamakhya Peetam is a treasure! Tantric *pujas* must continue there; that is very important! Normal [Vedic] *pujas* can go on in the Meru temple." Yet he expressed reluctance to take on the administrative burden of the property, and Guruji did not feel inclined to talk him into it.

"I just listened politely and kept quiet," he said. As they walked the property, the disciple who brokered the meeting "kept nudging and prompting me to offer Devipuram to him, but I made no such move. My friend was frustrated, and afterward he told

294 Gupta added, "It is not irrelevant to note that the Kanchi Kamakoti Peetham occupies a somewhat controversial position as a 'fifth' headquarters of the Shankaracharya Order. Some of the more orthodox Shankaracharya branches recognize only four Peetams and exclude Kamakoti and the tradition that claims Shankara established the *Sri Chakra* there. In light of this, the need to distance themselves from any association with *Kaula* Sri Vidya probably played a major role in their hesitation to acquire the property."

295 The most socially conservative of Sri Vidya schools.

296 That is, the government would take over management of the temple.

me, 'You lost a golden chance! Both of you acted like politicians! You did not make an offer to him, and he did not offer to take Devipuram!' And thus ended that episode."

Yet Guruji continued to nurture a deep passion and urgency toward the mission that Kamakhya had charged him with a quarter-century earlier. He tirelessly generated new ideas and projects in an attempt to broaden Devipuram's international appeal and increase the effectiveness of its social outreach. His old Bombay University marketing certificate came in handy as he worked to "rebrand" Devipuram as "A Global Resource for Goddess Worship."

In the summer of 2005, he secured coverage in the national newspaper *The Hindu* of his ambitious plans to develop Devipuram into a spiritual retreat called *Manidweepam*—Sanskrit for "Isle of Jewels," the Supreme Goddess's heavenly abode as described in the *Puranas*:

DEVIPURAM TO GET A SPIRITUAL RESORT

VISAKHAPATNAM, JULY 13: A spiritual resort will be set up at Devipuram near Sabbavaram by the Sri Vidya Trust, the trust founder, Amritananda Natha Saraswati (N. Prahalada Sastry) announced here on Tuesday. ...

"Devipuram, which has the Sri Chakra temple of Goddess Rajarajeswari, will be known as *Manidweepam*—a *Maha Shakti Peetam* containing all the 51 Shakthi Peetams in the world in the form of Devi's body in an area of 2.5 *lakh* square feet," Prof. Sastry, who quit as a scientist in the Tata Institute of Fundamental Research (TIFR) to build the temple at Devipuram in 1983, said.

Claiming that he had the vision of the Devi several times, Prof. Sastry said that he was directed by the goddess to consecrate a temple at Devipuram before quitting a lucrative career in TIFR. "With Her constant guidance, the temple work was completed in 1994," he said. With devotees all over the world, raising funds for the spiritual project would not be a problem. The resort would be completed by 2010 ... transform[ing] Devipuram into an island of jewels called Manidweepa. "Once completed, the landscape becomes the physical body of

Devi. Its life is Sri Chakra and its power manifests in the people who visit it," he said.

The idea of reshaping the temple complex into "the body of Devi" was quite literal—as Guruji pointed out, the natural lay of the land already contained all the basics. "From the Shiva Hill to the Sri Meru temple, it's all one body," he said. "The face, the breasts, the navel; it's all there."

This striking physical vision was complemented by Guruji's emerging conception of Devipuram as "a laboratory of consciousness," with the Sri Chakra temple at its center "like a jewel set in a lotus." In keeping with that vision, the *Manidweepam* proposal also included classrooms, lecture halls, performance venues and lodging facilities, "all set in an enchanting array of gardens and groves" (including a sculpture garden with large sculptural renderings of human hands performing the 10 *mudras*).

The first phase of *Manidweepam*'s construction began in 2005 in the form of "Srivilla," a residential complex projected for completion in 2009. As Devipuram grew in popularity, guests had begun to complain about the lack of proper accommodations. Those wanting to organize seminars or workshops at Devipuram, or groups coming on pilgrimage, had no convenient place to stay or meet on site. Thus Srivilla's construction was viewed with some urgency, prioritized and partially financed by marketing some of the larger rooms as timeshares.

But while Srivilla would see completion on schedule, most of the *Manidweepam* plan was eventually set aside as impractical. "There would have been no room left for people!" Guruji later joked, dismissing months of planning, discussion and design with typically good-natured detachment. Nonetheless, a wall poster displaying an artist's rendering of Devipuram's landscape reimagined in the form of the Goddess's body remains a popular and widely distributed artifact among disciples and other visitors.[297]

Though Devipuram remained central to his life and mission, Guruji still traveled frequently during this period—though largely within India for health reasons. His large enclaves of disciples in Bangalore, Hyderabad, Mumbai and other Indian cities often

297 In November 2014, the *Manidweepam* plan was revived, albeit on a more modest scale. Construction and plantings began in early 2015, as discussed in the epilogue.

invited him to speak, perform *pujas*, conduct weddings and so on, and Guruji was generally happy to oblige.

On visits to Bangalore, he and Amma often lodged at the home of longtime disciple Sriganesh Madhvanath (known to most simply as SriG). "Guruji enjoyed staying with us because we did not put him on a pedestal; we used to treat him like a favorite uncle," SriG said. "He would spend his time here working on his computer, watching movies he wanted to see and meeting with anyone who dropped by to see him."

His preference was for films displaying "scientific logic, art and creativity," according to Sundhara, who said Guruji enjoyed—in addition to a robust diet of Bollywood classics, regional Telugu cinema and Hindu "theologicals"—such Western titles as *Atlantis: The Lost Empire*; *Contact*; *The Matrix* trilogy; and *Monsters, Inc.* SriG added that he was impressed by *The Abyss*, *The Last Mimzy*, *Titanic* and *What the Bleep Do We Know!?* More recently, Guruji's English-language favorites included two scientific television series—physicist Brian Greene's *The Fabric of the Cosmos* in 2012 and *Cosmos: A Spacetime Odyssey*, Neil deGrasse Tyson's 2014 update on Carl Sagan's groundbreaking 1980 public-television series.

Aside from such entertainments, one of Guruji's relatively few "vices"—to Amma's eternal exasperation—was snacking. "He was a major foodie," SriG laughed. "He savored all the different regional cuisines of India—Punjabi, Maharashtrian, Gujarati. He greatly enjoyed the spicy chutneys that my wife Radhika and my mother came up with. He also had a really soft corner for fried snack foods like potato chips, French fries, *batata wadas*[298] and *samosas*—all unhealthy, unfortunately! But he would indulge on those rare occasions when Amma and we allowed it!" Ice cream and pizza were among his other favorite snacks, with a new villain added to the list in 2012, when Cadbury introduced non-melting chocolate bars to the Indian market.[299]

Guruji's signature culinary weakness was his love for *pakodas*, the universally popular Indian snack made of chopped vegetables deep-fried in chickpea flour. "That obsession has always been there," daughter Radha said. "When I spoke to him on the phone a few years ago, he told me he was researching and experimenting with the art of baking *pakodas*," rather than frying them. When the family lived in the old Vizag house back in the '80s, "Guruji used to joke that he wanted to be reborn as a street

298 Potato-stuffed fried dumplings.

299 In 2012, Cadbury patented "new Dairy Milk bars [that] remain solid even when left in 104°F (40°C) heat for three hours. But the company … will only sell the product in warmer countries like India and Brazil." Guruji, ever in the first wave of new technology adopters, quickly developed a taste for them—especially the kind with almonds.

vendor of *pakodas*," she added. "Horrified, his aunt Tatamma would forbid him from even uttering such fantasies!"

Snacking and spirituality came together in a particularly productive manner when Guruji inherited a sizable group of followers by giving Sri Vidya *diksha* to Professor P.A. Seshan, a senior yoga and Zen master who already had a group of disciples in Bangalore. Before long Seshan's students were holding frequent *satsangs*, workshops and events, and Guruji would sometimes use them to "test-drive" *pujas* he was still in the process of developing.

"This was a really dedicated group, very serious about *sadhana*, but a lot of fun as well," SriG said. "But since they were more inclined towards meditation than *pujas*, Guruji also took to giving discourses and talking about visualizations and so on. They were also forever ready to indulge Guruji's eclectic taste in food—they'd have Chinese noodles catered one day, and *udipi vada sambhar* the next."[300]

Enjoyable though such gastronomical explorations could be, they were of dubious value for a man with heart problems, and Amma fought to "always keep healthy snacks within Guruji's easy reach, while putting unhealthy ones out of the way," Ahalya said.

Nonetheless, in October 2005—more than 14 years after his hospitalization in New York—Guruji suffered a second heart attack in Vizag. He was transported to Bangalore for treatment. "The situation was pretty grave, with about three major blocks and a couple of minor ones," Radha said. "The doctors were advising bypass surgery, but Guruji was not in favor of it."

Eventually, doctors settled upon a less invasive angioplasty option, with tiny balloons inserted through catheters and inflated to reopen the arteries, after which stents—small, expandable tubes—were permanently inserted to maintain a healthy blood flow. As Guruji recovered following successful completion of the intervention, strict dietary and exercise regimens were advised (and, under Amma's constant vigilance, strictly enforced)—and soon Guruji's attention turned back to Devipuram.

"It was during this time in Bangalore that his vision of creating a new Maha Meru, modeled after the one he had originally excavated at Devipuram, truly took shape," said SriG Amma. "In the 18 months following that visit, the Meru went from an idea

300   *Udipi vada sambhar* is a regional, Karnataka-based variation on *sambar*, the spicy vegetable-and-lentil stew that is a staple of South Indian cuisine.

301 Computer-aided design (CAD) is the use of computer systems to assist in the creation, modification, analysis or optimization of a design. CAD output is often in the form of electronic files for print, machining, or other manufacturing operations.

to a CAD design[301] to a prototype, and finally to production in two different sizes and many different finishes. That all happened right here in Bangalore."

For Guruji, it was nothing less than the consummation of a long-cherished dream.

The Meru project began when Guruji's new disciple, the eminently well-connected Professor Seshan, introduced him to a recently retired corporate executive, Mr. Shrikant Welling. As director of corporate planning for the massive Indian conglomerate HMT Limited, Welling had overseen the production of goods ranging from machine tools to fine watches, and from printing machines to tractors.

He was, in many ways, however, the very antithesis of a stereotypical corporate high roller. His notably compassionate and altruistic approach to his work, in fact, landed him a profile in the international business textbook, *Leading with Wisdom: Spiritual-Based Leadership in Business*. "I think the ultimate game of business is that we should have happiness for all stakeholders of the business: employees, customers, suppliers and shareholders," Welling observed in its pages. "The happiness I am talking about is the faith and commitment you must have to achieve something together. The totality of all this happiness is what business is."

He was, in other words, exactly the sort of businessman with whom Guruji could readily "do business." Perhaps Professor Seshan had already guessed as much the day he invited Welling to meet Guruji during one of his group's *pujas* at SriG's Bangalore home.

"I'd never heard anything about Guruji or Sri Chakras, nor did I know anything about Sri Vidya," Welling recalled of that first encounter. But the moment he entered the house, Guruji greeted him like an old friend.

"I stepped into the living room and I saw Guruji sitting on a sofa alone," Welling said. "He called to me, 'Sir, please come and sit next to me. I have a job for you.'"

After a few minutes of polite small talk, Guruji led him to a computer he had set up in an adjoining room. On the screen was the image of a Sri Meru based on the one he had unearthed at Kamakhya, but reconfigured to an extraordinary degree of geometric precision. "This is called a Maha Meru," Guruji told Welling. "I discovered it at a site shown to me by *Adi Parashakti* herself.[302] It is unique—exactly in the form you

302 The appellation *Adi Parashakti* refers to the Goddess as the ultimate and highest divinity. Here Guruji is describing Kamakhya as such.

see, with extra plates between the star shapes.[303] Several people from around the world have tried to help me create one, but we have not managed it so far."

Guruji then took a piece of paper, wrote a list of nine dimensions in inches (to the fourth decimal place!), and handed it to Welling. "I have done a lot of research on this," he said. "Can you please go ahead and design a Meru for me based on these figures?'"

Welling nodded, put the paper in his pocket and promised to try.

For starters, he contacted an old friend who ran a design shop. That gentleman agreed to have two of his younger engineers work up a three-dimensional CAD design in their spare time. But almost immediately, the project displayed an unusually attractive energy—the two young men working on the Meru design began acting as if they were thoroughly obsessed.

"What *shakti* entered into those boys, I do not know!" Welling recalled. "But they didn't go home for three or four days. They worked on that design around the clock." Within a week, they had a "wonderful" schematic ready, which Welling brought to Guruji for review. After intently studying the design from every angle for nearly 45 minutes, Guruji looked up and told Welling, "It is precisely what I wanted. You have done it." His only substantive change was to add directional deity emblems at each of the Meru's four corners.[304]

And with that, it was time to convert the CAD design into a three-dimensional model.

"I got in touch with an acquaintance who had a CNC rapid prototyping machine,"[305] Welling said. Having initially complained that he had no time for new projects, the man impatiently agreed to look at the design—and immediately changed his tune. "When he saw it, he said, 'Wow, Mr. Welling! This is a divine object! It's giving me a lot of good vibrations. I will do this for you. Can you come back in four hours?'"

When Welling returned, he was handed a three-inch-square, one-and-three-quarter-inch-high model, which he carried back to Guruji—who was once again overjoyed. "For years I have been waiting, and now it has finally happened," he told Welling as he examined the model in his hand. "I want this Meru to go all the world over, into everybody's home. How can we get it into production?"

But that task was easier said than done.

303 See Guruji's detailed description of the Meru he found at Kamakhya Peetam in chapter 14.

304 See n. 206, *infra*.

305 Rapid prototyping is a set of techniques used to quickly fabricate a scale model of a physical part or assembly using three-dimensional computer aided design (CAD) data. Construction of the part or assembly is usually done using three-dimensional printing or "additive layer manufacturing" technology. CNC indicates a "computer numerically controlled machine"; that is, one that calibrates models based on digital input.

The main problem was the design's complexity. "I ran helter-skelter everywhere, from Chennai to Coimbatore to Bangalore, to all the production managers I knew," Welling said. "Everybody flatly refused, saying, 'There's no way we can machine so many sharp angles and edges; it has to be done by casting instead.'"[306]

Which presented yet another problem. Because while a machined object can be cut and produced within hours, casting requires an expertly crafted mold. And preparing a mold for an object of the Meru's geometric complexity could take months—surely no skilled caster or mold maker would be able to invest that kind of time, and even if they could the cost would be prohibitive. "I just didn't know what to do," Welling said.

Professor Seshan again came to the rescue, introducing Welling to one Mr. Sudhakaran, an experienced mold-maker who had fallen on hard times since developing severe arthritis in his hands and legs. Welling showed him the Meru prototype and the man nodded. "Yes, I can make a mold for this. But it will take about a year to complete."

"A *year?*" Welling asked in surprise. "Why so long?"

"Well, it will have to be made partly by machine and partly by hand, which will take time," Sudhakaran explained. "Also, with my arthritis I can't work as quickly as I used to."

"So I told him, 'Okay, that's fine. Go ahead. Let's do it,'" Welling recalled. "Because really, there was no other solution in sight."

The first mold created by Sudhakaran was for a large (10-inch-square by five-inch-high) Meru. Working with aircraft-grade aluminum, he immediately got down to business. "I used to visit his shop almost every week," Welling said. "He was working eight or 10 hours every day. No breaks, no Saturdays or Sundays off. Plus he was telling me, 'I have no leg pain, no hand pain anymore, nothing! I am working without any problems. Absolutely all of my ailments have gone away!'"

ॐ
ह्रीं

Thanks to Sudhakaran's improved health, the mold was complete nearly four months ahead of schedule. Welling took it to a "sand expert" to determine the proper mix of sand and resin for optimal, defect-free casting,[307] and then went about choosing a foundryman who could produce the Merus with appropriate quality and care.

306 Welling is referring to two principal methods for fabricating metal objects. Machining refers to production using modern milling machines and other CNC machine tools that literally carve complex parts from solid chunks of metal (billets). Casting refers to the forming of metal parts by pouring molten metal into a mold. There are many complex technical and cost factors that dictate the choice of one method or the other.

307 Sand casting is a metal-casting process using sand as the mold material. The aluminum mold is used to create a sand mold, which is baked. Molten metal is then poured into the sand mold to create the object. The proper resin ratio enables the sand to hold the mold's shape. Sand castings are produced in specialized factories called foundries. More than 70 percent of all metal castings are produced via sand casting.

He finally settled on a Mr. Chandru, proprietor of a "very small roadside foundry" near Bangalore.

The result of Chandru's test casting was nothing short of stunning.

"That first Meru was very, very beautiful," Welling said. "A lot of foundry engineers came to look at it and said, 'This is impossible! You can't get this type of finish with a casting. It's too nice.' And you know, it really did look like we made it with a machine. But it was just a raw casting!"

After having the Meru polished and gold-plated, Welling drove it to Chennai, whence Guruji was preparing to embark on a tour of India's Deep South. "I personally carried it straight to the hotel where he was staying," Welling said. When he walked into the room Guruji said, "I have been waiting for you."

Welling handed him the Meru, and—even though it weighed about 6.5 kilograms (over 14 pounds)—Guruji held it on his lap for the entire visit. When Welling rose to leave, Guruji smiled and said, "I am not going to give this back to you. I am going to carry it wherever I go."

Welling smiled back and replied, "I don't need it, Guruji. It's yours."

Guruji was, of course, as good as his word. "Within one week of its making," he recounted, "the Meru had been to Sringeri Peetham;[308] it had been worshiped as the presiding deity at a *Satachandi Homa* in Tamilnadu Kalaiyar Kovil;[309] it was placed at the feet of Meenakshi Amman Sannidhi, where it received special honors and a sari worn by Raja Matangi Amma there;[310] it entered Kanya Kumari temple;[311] and it visited Anantha Padmanabha Swamy Temple,[312] in whose vaults the jewelry of Manidveepa is kept."

Following this grand tour, production began on a series of smaller (five-inch-square by two-and-a-half-inch-high) Merus, sized to be more portable and convenient for home use. A first run of 108 five-inch Merus and a smaller number of 10-inch models—all of them spoken for in advance by disciples around the world—were prepared for consecration by Guruji himself at the upcoming *Kumbha Abhishekam*. Later, a premium two-inch-square by one-inch-high sterling silver Meru would be added to the line.

308 A renowned eighth-century temple in Chennai.

309 A large Shiva temple in Sivaganga District, Tamil Nadu.

310 Meenakshi Amman Temple, a very famous Shakta- and Sri Vidya-oriented Shiva temple in Madurai, Tamil Nadu.

311 Kanya Kumari Devi Temple at Kanyakumari, Tamil Nadu, at the southernmost tip of India.

312 Sree Padmanabha Swamy temple in Thiruvananthapuram, the capital of Kerala. Believed to be one of the richest temples in the world, the jewels of *Manidweepa*– the celestial palace of the Goddess in *Puranic* lore–are just one of the treasures rumored to lie in its storied vaults.

By mid-2016, Welling said he had personally processed around 5,000 orders for Merus. "I don't keep an exact count, because the orders keep coming!" he added. To date, they have shipped to more than 27 countries,[313] and have doubtless been carried by Devipuram visitors to many more.

And surprisingly enough, the original two molds remain still in active use. "Normally after about 1,000 pieces a mold has to be redone," Welling said. "But amazingly, these molds are as good as new. Chandru told me they're good for another 5,000! And as I told Guruji, that beats any engineering theory, because there are just so many things going on here—from the Meru's extraordinary finish and sharpness to the life of the molds. I really consider them miracles."

When Welling expressed his apprehensions about whether the molds could ever be recreated, Guruji replied, "Don't worry. It is all Devi's play. It will all be according to her wish."

In the meantime, Chandru (the foundryman) and Sudhakaran (the mold-maker) have both prospered. Chandru's roadside workshop has expanded into a state-of-the-art plant in Bangalore—and he remains the sole manufacturer of Devipuram Merus. "For Chandru, casting the Meru is a divine job," Welling said. "Whenever a little time passes without my calling him, he'll contact me and say, 'What is happening, Sir? Why am I not getting any Meru orders?'"

As for Sudhakaran? He's out of the casting business entirely, having made a fortune in real estate investments. His arthritis never returned.

Since production of the Merus began in 2007, they have come to play an integral role in Guruji's efforts to demystify Sri Vidya.

"It is in this spirit that he conceived of the Devipuram Meru," SriG Amma explained. "It is a *yantra* suitable for keeping in homes and offices, bringing peace and prosperity and supporting the various spiritual and social programs of Guruji's Sri Vidya Trust in Devipuram."

Traditionally, a Meru's hollow interior is filled with various sacred substances, placed therein and blessed by the guru. Guruji at first planned to do the same, noting in his original proposal that "the powders of 150 roots will be kept inside and sealed.

313 According to Welling, Devipuram Merus have shipped to Australia, Bahrain, Brazil, Canada, France, India, Ireland, Italy, Luxemburg, Malaysia, Mexico, the Netherlands, New Zealand, Nigeria, Russia, Saudi Arabia, Singapore, South Africa, Sri Lanka, Switzerland, Thailand, Ukraine, the United Arab Emirates, the United Kingdom and the United States.

I will personally do the consecration." But he later reconsidered, asserting that the practice was an unnecessary complication—once again, a social custom disguised as a spiritual requirement.

"Even an atom is hollow," he reflected. "Even the atom's *nucleus* is hollow. Even the quarks that *comprise* the nucleus are hollow. There is no matter anywhere; it is all only probability in your consciousness. Thus, even if the Merus were full of material stuff, they would still always be hollow, because there is no material within them." (When a visitor asked the scriptural basis for his position, Guruji replied, "I don't go by *shastras*. I make *shastras*.")

In a later conversation with another disciple, he remarked that the "cupped" space within the Meru additionally evokes "the Mother's womb, which creates, nourishes and heals."

For years, people closely associated with Guruji knew he was on the lookout for someone to replace him as head of Devipuram, so that he could devote more time to what he now perceived as his true calling—the development of Sri Vidya teaching materials, both written and digital.

A dozen years after its opening Devipuram still lacked the Internet and telecommunication connectivity he needed to accomplish this; he had to be in Vizag. Moreover, at Devipuram he increasingly found himself entangled in routine administrative issues that appealed neither to his nature nor his skill set.

So it was no real surprise when Guruji announced that he was handing Devipuram's leadership over to a new *peetadhipathi*. His choice of successor seemed a logical one as well: Mr. Subbarao Kompella, also known by his initiatory name, Sri Karunamaya Baba, and later as Chinna Guruji ("Little Guruji"), was a distant relative and early disciple, having taken initiation in 1978 when Guruji was still living in Bombay and working at TIFR. A knowledgeable ritualist, Subbarao's particular strength lay in organizing and presiding over large-scale, participatory ritual events—which also seemed to fit Guruji's paradigm of empowering as many people as possible to learn Sri Vidya *pujas* and other teachings.

Born in Chennai in 1953, Subbarao graduated from the University of Madras with a B.E. in civil engineering. Like Guruji and Haran Aiya before him, he first found his calling in the course of providing religious rituals for ethnic South Asians living abroad. While working in New Zealand in the mid-'90s, Subbarao began, according to his biography, "performing and teaching *pujas* for the Indian community there in order to spread cultural and religious awareness."

One night before sleeping, during a particularly difficult eight-month contract assignment in the United States, Subbarao—depressed, lonely and missing his family—asked his small icon of the Goddess "whether she was with him or not during these dreary times." His official biography continues:

> [The next morning] he awoke to find that the icon of the goddess and the area surrounding it were a little sticky; but in his inattentive state of mind he did not give it much thought. On returning from work that evening, however, he returned to the goddess only to find her drenched in honey. This honey flowed from the icon steadily for two full days. Seeing this extraordinary sight, Sri Subbarao was ecstatic—and his faith in the Divine Mother has been unerring ever since.

314 "Waves of Beauty," after a famous hymn to the Goddess revered in Sri Vidya circles.

From 1999 until 2006, Subbarao; his wife, Usha Ratna; and their two daughters, Yashoda Sri Lakshmi and Purnima Sri Vidya, lived in the Boston suburbs, where he founded a nonprofit organization called Soundarya Lahari.[314] From its origins as a small group of expatriate South Indians gathering to chant the *Lalita Sahasranama* and other prayers on weekends, the organization soon grew into a powerhouse boasting more than 600 active participants on a mission "to promote spirituality and render community service." In the process, Subbarao displayed a knack for organizing large, complex and unusual ritual gatherings. His biography elaborates:

> Sri Subbarao conducted many landmark events in the Boston area, all covered by the local media, such as the first *Lalita Sahasranama Parayana* outside India, [in which] 800 devotees sat through 24 hours to complete the 10,000 recitals of *Lalita Sahasranama*. ... He is credited for awakening an extreme sense of Hindu

community and for spreading the name of Goddess Lalita in a land where the majority cannot pronounce the word properly. His determination—from the moment the thought of a *puja* enters his head until the final second of executing the event—is appreciated and revered by one and all.

Subbarao's installation as *peetadhipathi* was formalized under the full *Guru Purnima* moon of Tuesday, July 11, 2006. In giving this able and energetic man charge of Devipuram's everyday affairs, Guruji's aim, again, was to recover more time for his personal projects and spiritual practice. "Hopefully," he wrote to me at the time, "by August, much of what has been tying me down will have cleared."

The plan was that Guruji would shift to more of a figurehead role, making appearances at major functions as Devipuram's founder and spiritual lodestone. For his part, Subbarao said he was pleased that his own spiritual journey had "taken yet another beautiful turn with his Guru consecrating him as the new pontiff of Devipuram." As someone who understood "the workings of both a temple and a nonprofit organization," he felt certain that his services would be "monumental for the growth of Devipuram as a peaceful and sacred retreat, and of Sri Vidya Trust as a valuable organization for the betterment of the community."

🔆 Guruji and Amma standing before the pyramidal altar of the Dakshavati temple at Devipuram, 2012.
(Giri Ratna Singh)

27 Coming of Age

High-profile public debuts for both Subbarao and the new Devipuram Merus took place as part of a massive reconsecration ceremony in early 2007. Marking 12 years since the temple's original consecration in 1994, this event—formally called the *Punaruddharana Maha Kumbha Abhishekam* (literally, the "Grand Restoration and Reconsecration," or more colloquially, the "Coming of Age" festival)—offered disciples and others an opportunity to celebrate Guruji and his vision while also showcasing Devipuram's continuing evolution.

Once again, the motivating principle behind a *Maha Kumbha Abhishekam* is the belief that "it is not enough to just build a temple; it must be maintained both physically and spiritually." So in the months and weeks leading up to the big event, Devipuram was given an impressive facelift, with the grounds being further groomed and improved, and the temples and deities enjoying needed maintenance, repairs and aesthetic touch-ups. The formal event spanned four days—from Tuesday, January 30, until the particularly auspicious full moon known as *Magha Purnima*, on Friday, February 2, 2007—with the first three days dedicated to the elemental triad of Lalita's manifestations: first Shyamala (also called Matangi or Meenakshi), known in Sri Vidya as the Prime Minister to the Goddess; then Varahi, the fierce, boar-headed

Commander-in-Chief to the Goddess; and finally Rajarajeshwari, the Empress of Emperors herself—the "royal" manifestation of Lalita or Sahasrakshi.

By the time the festival started, "the whole place looked colorfully decked and freshly painted," recalled Prakash Krishna, a disciple who flew from the United States to attend the event. "All the deities in the temple complex, including the *Khadgamala Devis*, were freshly garlanded and looked enchantingly beautiful. Devotees gathered from many countries and across India. Getting to know them, living with them, sharing our experiences, recounting our stories, was a memorable experience. Even while I was still there, I remember thinking, 'These are some of my best days.'"

Aiya's longtime disciple Kathy Allen, who had also traveled from the United States, also noted the electric excitement and camaraderie among the gathering crowds. "Arriving in Devipuram on the eve of the *Maha Kumbha Abhishekam* felt like a huge family reunion," she said. "Each day was a full feast of offerings—divine *pujas*, chanting, music, friendships new and old, chatting, sharing food and relaxing in the cashew groves—all amid the divine company of true *Mahatmas*."

Among those spiritual luminaries was Sri Yanamandra Venugopala Sastry from Vizianagaram, about an hour north of Vizag, who presided as *Acharya*, or Vedic high priest. In the absence of Krishnayaji, who was unable to attend, he would return for a fond reunion with Guruji during the latter's 80th birthday celebrations in 2014.

Guruji, Subbarao and Haran Aiya (who had come with around 20 of his disciples from the Rochester temple) also played leading roles in the event. Notable Sri Vidya *upasakas* from all over South India were in attendance as well, including 40 from the renowned Sri Bala Tripurasundari Peetam some 600 miles to the south in Nemili, Tamil Nadu.

"Devipuram was pulsating with a unique energy throughout the *Abhishekam*," recalled Ahalya, who traveled from Canada for the event. "In the early morning, Guruji's chants in a soft, tender voice exuded life in every particle and granule, while the *homas* conducted by Haran Aiya"—whose vocal tone is deep and booming—"resonated in the air with an invigorating energy. The effect was enchanting and electrifying."

Ceremonial details reflected the tremendous growth in Devipuram's reputation—and in the sheer ranks of Guruji's base of devotees and admirers. For example, rather than the nine brass *kalasam* pots used in the 1994 *abhishekam*, the *re*-consecration involved no fewer than a thousand clay *kalasa*, each sponsored by a devotee or family that was, in turn, invited to carry "their" *kalasa* to be poured over the temple at the conclusion of the event. In addition to the thousands who attended in person, countless more participated from temples and home altars scattered all around the world, each with a *sankalpa*[315] dedicating the vibrations of their chants to the *kalasa* at Devipuram.

315 Formal, stated intention.

Inside the Sri Meru temple, dozens of the new Devipuram Merus were arranged on an eight-foot-square, gold-painted wooden Meru—specially constructed on the second floor, there to be infused with the energy of the *Kumbha Abhishekam*—before being carried or shipped off to homes around the world. Guruji personally performed a daily *Sri Chakra Puja* to these Merus—an event that was, in Haran Aiya's memory, "always the highlight of the day."

As the festival began in earnest, Sri Yanamandra and his *ritwiks*[316] led Vedic chants and rituals in front of the *Yagna Shala*. "*Surya Namaskaram, Sahasralinga, Mahaling-archana* and *Mahanyasa Purvaka Rudrabhishekam* were all performed by these men daily," Aiya said. These harmonized with the Tantric goddess *pujas* simultaneously occurring in the Sri Meru temple, Kamakhya Peetam and Sivalaya—to hypnotic and transcendent effect. A large group of women from Hyderabad added to the intense spiritual energy of the event by leading chants of the *Saundarya Lahari* and *Sri Lalita Sahasranama*; others performed additional *pujas* and *homas* all over the temple complex.

316 Assistant priestess.

Ritual and spiritual activities took place each morning, leaving the afternoons and evenings free for relaxation, entertainment and socializing within the temple complex. Each night featured cultural performances by classical Indian musicians and dancers; some famous, others little known. And despite the huge crowds, hunger was never a problem. "There were excellent arrangements made for the food," Haran Aiya recalled. "A team of expert cooks were there preparing tasty, nutritious and timely meals for all the people attending."

On the *abhishekam*'s final day, Guruji, Amma and their three daughters; Haran Aiya and his wife Sakuntala; Sri Subbarao and his wife Usha; and Sri Yanamandra with his *ritwiks* all assembled in the *Yagna Shala* for a final *homa* ceremony before ascending the spiral stairs and scaffolding to the top of the Sri Meru, where the *Kumbha Abhishekam* itself would be carried out. At the age of 72, Guruji's progress was notably slower than it had been 12 years earlier—but no less determined.

"I was moved to tears when I saw Guruji at the top of the temple dome after he had climbed up those makeshift stairs with considerable difficulty," said Prakash Krishna. "It was a magical and powerful moment as he poured the first *kalasam* of water over the Sri Meru temple spire. That tiny moment in time will stay forever frozen in my memory. For me, it symbolizes the culmination of a festival in a small slice of time— yet it simultaneously reminds me of the timeless, eternal relevance of Devipuram and Guruji's vision."

Another attendee, Dr. Devi Padmanabai, was sitting inside the *bindu sthanam*, finishing the adornment of Sahasrakshi with a few others as the ceremony began. "Suddenly, water was dripping from the sanctum roof outside," she said. "We realized that it was the *kalasam* water being poured on top of the *kumbha*! We all paused to acknowledge the fact that the Mother was showering her Grace to us in this form."

For the next few hours, those who sponsored *kalasa* ascended the Sri Meru in a long queue, handing their clay pots up to the priests in a line that snaked around the temple several times. Those who hadn't sponsored a *kalasam* partook of the blessings in their own way. "As the water flowed off the temple, some devotees held up empty bottles to collect it," Kathy recalled. "Others simply stood under the downpour and let it drench their souls."

After the ceremony, Guruji and Amma descended from the temple and sat to meet and offer blessings to their thousands of visitors. As a huge crowd closed in around the couple, volunteers formed a human chain to protect them and keep the line moving. This became an increasingly difficult task as many who had already received *darshan* lingered to watch others receive it, and nearly everyone paused to personally offer Guruji and Amma their congratulations and respects. As the traffic jam thickened, some members of the human chain became nervous and started shouting at visitors to back away.

"The prime screamer was me," said Dr. Sunandini Lakshminath. "I was saying, 'Please don't overcrowd them! Please make it faster! Please don't talk now!'" Guruji, however, was relaxed and content, as always more concerned about the discomfort of others than his own. Lakshminath recalled, "He pulled me close and said, with his usual smile, 'It's okay, why hasten them?' He pointed to a portion of the waiting line some distance away and said, 'See how the people in that queue over there are all standing in the sun? Why don't you go over and help them find a place in the shade?'"

Though no mysterious light phenomena were reported at this festival, as had happened in 1994, many in the crowd pointed excitedly to three eagles that continually swooped through the air over Devipuram as the ritual played out. "In South Indian temple tradition, such presence of *garudas* or eagles during a *Kumbha Abhishekam* ceremony is considered highly auspicious," Prakash Krishna explained. They were seen as "a reassuring, visible symbol of the sacred presence of the gods, rishis, sages, *siddhas* and *yoginis* assembled to witness and to bless such a highly powerful ritual, offering their wholehearted well-wishes to the temple."

"When Guruji did the *abhishekam*," he added, "I had this refrain on my lips—'*pallaandu, pallaandu, pallaayirathaandu, pala koti nooraayiram.*' This is a Tamil devotional song sung during blessings, which translates roughly as, 'May blessings shower for years, thousands of years, millions of years...' And that is what a *Maha Kumbha Abhishekam* is in essence—a collective prayer, a wholehearted blessing, a spiritual re-affirmation and a timely reassurance that the symbol and legacy of this *Shakti Peetam*, Devipuram, will live on forever."

Autumn 2007 was marked by a whirlwind two-week tour during which Guruji and Amma traveled to Sydney to greet their devotees in Australia—celebrating Guruji's 73rd birthday along the way.

Soon after returning to India, he attended a *Devi Yagna* in Hyderabad conducted by a swami named Maitreya,[317] a close friend of one of Guruji's senior disciples. "He was a very advanced Kaula guru," Guruji said. "So we invited him to repeat the *yagna*

317 Maitreya was an exponent of "Nikhil Tantra," a breed of commercial *ashrams* in India that have made a business of selling various "Tantric *sadhanas*" through magazine ads, websites and other channels. The firms are often led by "gurus" with genuine knowledge of Tantra, and the *sadhanas* they sell are generally harmless and noncontroversial. But initiated practitioners in authentic Tantric lineages tend to regard them with a degree of distaste and disdain.

in Devipuram, and he did—though he used heavy doses of alcohol in the ritual, which I did not like."

During his visit, Maitreya also claimed to sense a spiritual "imbalance" stunting the development of Devipuram. "He commented that Devipuram was totally Shakti-centric, and that therefore a lot of *pishachas*,[318] *vetalas*[319] and other evil spirits were hanging around and preventing the growth of the place," Guruji recounted. "He said, 'They just won't go away unless Shiva is appeased.'" The disciple who arranged Maitreya's visit chimed in, saying, "If only you will give me your permission, Guruji, I will build a thousand-*lingam* temple, every bit as grand as the Sri Chakra Meru! I will cover all of the expenses and I will personally manage the place."

"Innocently," Guruji said, "I acceded to the request."

The disciple undertook the job in grand style, overseeing the clearing and grading of the building site and ordering massive quantities of concrete and other materials. But soon after having done so, he abruptly vanished from the scene, leaving Guruji with a large, disorganized construction site. "I had to complete the whole work by myself, using whatever contacts and resources I could muster," he recalled, with a resigned sigh. "I had to design it, build it, perform the *Kumbha Abhishekam* and construct a roof for this 120-foot-by-120-foot structure—and I had to bear the costs."

At this point yet another disciple stepped forward and told him, "Don't worry Guruji, I will take care of it from here." Still more materials were ordered. "At one point they even suggested installing a massive Nandi sculpture that would have cost a couple of *crore* rupees," said Guruji, who quickly put a halt to that idea. "I told them, 'Even if you drag me down the street, that much money won't fall out!'" he laughed. Of course, "none of the promises worked out well," and the second disciple abandoned the job too. Once again, Guruji was on his own.

"At that point he needed help in drafting a workable design," recalled Ahalya, who happened to visit during this bleak interlude. Guruji narrated the whole sordid tale to her, and she asked what he was going to do now. Guruji replied that he was going to do nothing—he had completely surrendered the project to the Goddess in hopes that it would at last begin to move productively forward. And sure enough, it soon did.

"Devi was playing her usual games," Ahalya said. "All of a sudden, some disciples from Russia arrived at Devipuram, visiting for the first time, and—you guessed

318 *Pishachas* are minor demons in Hindu mythology. They are said to prefer darkness and feed on human energies. They are traditionally given an offering at the outset of Hindu religious rituals to prevent them from interfering.

319 *Vetalas* are ghost-like beings in Hindu mythology, said to haunt cremation grounds and inhabit corpses.

it—one of the young ladies happened to be a structural engineer! So she began work-ing with Guruji and they very quickly came up with an optimal structural design for the project."

With the help of this and a few other serendipitous connections, Guruji eventu-ally completed the project, taking the entire ordeal as a vivid object lesson. After all, he said, he had doubted his own instinct and followed human advice rather than the Goddess's direct instruction. He hadn't "done as he willed"; he had trusted in human promises rather than divine protection and guidance.

"And so now, there it sits," he said, motioning in the direction of the temple. "A product of pride, and my burden to support it."

Still, the finished temple was a beauty. Covering 22,500 square feet and funded mainly via disciple sponsorships of the individual *lingams*, it was finally completed in 2008 and named Dakshavati. "Sati Devi left her body during the *Daksha Yagna*, which re-sulted in all the *Shakti Peetams*," Guruji explained. "So the name serves to connect it with the nearby Kamakhya Peetam."[320]

Indeed, if the Sri Meru temple could be considered in some ways an elaboration upon the smaller Kamakhya shrine, then Dakshavati might be understood as an analo-gous expansion upon the hilltop Sivalaya temple. At its center, a large altar rises under the gaze of a formidable black granite Nandi, Shiva's iconic bull *vahana*[321] and com-panion. It is surrounded on all four sides by eight enclosures containing a total of a thousand additional Shiva-*lingams* intended for individual worshipers.

Its altar is dominated by the so-called Kailasa Peetam—a large, polished black-marble pyramid, inset with 365 *lingams* representing Shiva's home at the peak of Tibet's Mount Kailash—but that was not the initial conception. "Originally, the centerpiece was a thousand-*lingam prastara*,"[322] Guruji explained. "It was on a flat marble slab, and small, colored marble *lingams* were inset with what we thought was a good adhesive. Unfortunately they started coming out, and then some visitors started removing them and taking them as souvenirs. When their number had dwindled to about 800, we finally had to do something about it."

320 This *Daksha Yagna* lies at the center of a pivotal story in both Shakta and Shaiva schools of Hinduism. Daksha Prajapati was a powerful king and the father of Sati, an incarnation of the Great Goddess. Sati married Lord Shiva against Daksha's wishes. So when Daksha held a great *yagna*, inviting all the gods and goddesses to attend, he intentionally snubbed Shiva. Unable to bear this insult, Sati appeared at her father's event and immolated herself in the sacrificial fire. Crazed with grief, Shiva scooped up Sati's body and carried it with him on a dance of destruction that threatened the entire universe. Lord Vishnu stopped the rampage by throwing his discus at Sati's corpse, which thereupon fell in pieces all across the Indian subcontinent, each piece becoming the site of a Great Goddess temple–now collectively known as the *Shakti Peetams*. The Kamakhya shrine at Devipuram is a *yoni peetam*.

321 A mount, or associated animal.

322 Staircase.

So Guruji constructed the pyramidal altar that stands there today, using four triangular slabs, each containing 91 smaller marble *lingams* (now drilled into place rather than glued). "That added up to 364 small *lingams*, and in the center we placed big granite *banalinga* from the Narmada River for a total of 365," Guruji said. "Then we consecrated it yet again."

As 2008 wound to a close, Guruji announced that a *Satachandi Homa*—a giant fire sacrifice to the Goddess involving 120 fire pits simultaneously receiving offerings in conjunction with recitation of the *Devi Mahatmyam*—would be held on the beach in Visakhapatnam on Friday, December 28. Its goal was "to promote protection, peace and prosperity for all," a promotional flyer read, "in front of Kali Ma, at the junction of Land and Sea, with the Guru of Devipuram, on a New Year's Eve—what better way to enjoy your time spiritually at the beach?"

Just a few days before the huge event, however, Guruji suffered his third heart attack. It had been 17 years since his first in the United States, and just over two years since his second. He was immediately hospitalized and underwent another angioplasty. When the event organizers took steps to cancel the event, however, Amma insisted that everything proceed according to schedule. "She took charge and said the event would go on as planned, because this was a long-cherished dream of Guruji," Radha recalled.

So the necessary municipal permissions were obtained, the fire pits were dug, and industrial quantities of *puja* materials—*ghee*, parched rice and other items—were delivered to the beach. By the appointed day, as the sun set over Vizag's Rama Krishna Beach, its expanse was aglow with flames and echoing with more than 1,200 voices chanting the Goddess's ancient hymn of praise and praying for Guruji's swift and full recovery. "The sight of a hundred *homa kundas* blazing on the sand, covered by a canopy of lights, was simply majestic," Radha said. "As we watched it together from the main pavilion, Amma told us she'd had a vision of precisely this scene just a few years earlier."

From the hospital's intensive care ward, Guruji called in to wish his blessings to all. He was overwhelmed and gratified when apprised of the spectacular result—not only the *puja* itself, but Amma's strong and effective management of the event. "I was grateful to Goddess for using this opportunity to throw up an unquestioned leader," he said. "It was an occasion that demonstrated Amma's courage in planning and conducting a *yagna*. My son-in-law Balkumar came up to me soon afterward and said, 'Why did you ever think of any other *peetadhipathi*? Why not Amma? A natural choice!'"

श्री A mantra devised by Guruji in about 2007, combining the Panchadasi mantra of Sri Vidya with his own *dikshanama*. At the time he described it as "the only mantra you will ever need." Shown here in his own handwriting, in both Roman and Telugu script.
(Sri Vidya Trust)

28   It's Her Worry Now

Though Guruji recovered from his third heart attack as he had the other two, he felt distinctly weakened in both body and mind. Approaching *Guru Purnima* observances in July 2009, he wrote to me, "With failing health, at 75, my memory is fading and I don't know how much longer I can be productive and understanding. It is getting more and more difficult to organize my thoughts and communicate them coherently."

Concluding that death was probably not far off, he began preparing for his own passing as he would for any other journey: "I am trying to tie up loose ends and waiting for my visa," he wrote. It was neither depressive self-pity nor an admission of defeat; from Guruji's viewpoint, it was simply a realistic attempt to assess the situation as it stood and respond accordingly. Having done so, he gamely threw himself back into the needs of visitors, disciples and Devipuram itself with typical gusto.

In October 2009, a *grihapravesam*[323] was thrown to celebrate the grand opening of the Srivilla guest house—the most tangible outcome of the otherwise abandoned *Manidweepam* project. The finished structure was lovely indeed: three stories high, it was clean, spacious, breezy and bright, with a function hall and institutional kitchen facility large enough to accommodate 200 guests for rituals, weddings, concerts or conferences. Three smaller conference halls were available for workshops and classes, plus dormitory-like accommodations for around 75 individuals, and 30 larger rooms

323 Housewarming party.

for couples and families. To formally solemnize the grand opening, Guruji personally led a *Satyanarayana Puja*—traditionally performed to Lord Vishnu upon the successful completion of any particularly difficult task.

Soon afterward, he installed an industrial-grade water filtration system to free Devipuram's guests from the tyranny of continually purchasing, transporting and restocking bottled water during their visits. Water coolers, replenished daily with safe, potable H_2O, began springing up throughout the corridors of Srivilla and across Devipuram.

Guruji then turned his attention to the state of the Sri Meru itself. In 2014, the temple would be 20 years old and its future had to be considered. The black granite *vigraha* of Sahasrakshi at the peak of the Meru was fine; she would survive indefinitely. Likewise, the *Khadgamala* goddesses of the inner *avaranas*, which were cast of durable metal alloys and designed to last centuries—they all still shone like new, aglow with constant worship.

The main problem was presented by the 90 cement-mortar *Khadgamala Devis*. Those residing inside the temple, protected from the elements, were still in relatively good condition. Though subject to wear and tear from frequent touching and worship by devotees, their details remained sharp, their enamel colors bright and lifelike. But the *murtis* in the outer, *bhupura* section of the temple were visibly deteriorating—despite a frequent regimen of worship, washing, repair and repainting, they were worn, faded and in some cases actually crumbling in the heat, humidity and heavy rainfall that characterized the local environment.

Several years earlier in 2010, Guruji had announced that the *Khadgamala Devis* would gradually be replaced by red sandstone *vigrahas* "similar to the ones used in temples such as Konark, Bhubaneswar and Lingaraja"—famous medieval temples in the nearby state of Odisha—and having "a minimum life of 300 years." As with the Dakshavati temple, the project would be primarily financed by devotee sponsorships; in this case of ₹16,000 (about US$300 at the time) per goddess. "These sculptures are poised to be as beautiful, graceful and powerful as the original cement sculptures," Guruji said, as the work began, "but they will require much less maintenance in terms of painting and upkeep."

The sculptor commissioned to create the new images was Sri Raghunath Mohapatra (b. 1943), an architect and stone carver from Odisha. Known for his mastery of Hindu temple design, ornamentation and aesthetics, Mohapatra's work graces India's Central Hall of Parliament, and his 1968 masterpiece "Konark Horse" is a landmark in Odisha's capital city of Bhubaneswar. He has received three of India's four highest civilian honors—the *Padma Shri* in 1975, the *Padma Bhushan* in 2001 and the *Padma Vibhushan* in 2013. His ancestors were reputedly the same masters who "created the world-famous Konark Temple, and the 12th century Shri Jagannath Temple at Puri." Even today, Mohapatra "wields [his] hammer with incredible precision and his chisel carves life on hardy stones with utmost ease," a newspaper profile noted. "During the past five decades, his countless strokes on chisels have created scores of monumental sculptures that many in his profession can only aspire to achieve."

In late 2011, Mohapatra's first *Khadgamala Devis* began arriving at Devipuram—each following the same specifications visualized by Guruji in his original meditations a quarter-century earlier. Over the next three years, additional shipments regularly arrived. In mid-2014, Guruji wrote, "there are still some gaps, but the sculptor is busy and I can't force his pace." By 2015, however, the work was complete and the statues given their final finish according to their location in the Sri Meru. "They are not all painted alike," Guruji explained. "Some are in dark stone hues, those in the 16-petalled lotus are light stone hues, the eight-petal deities look like bronze, the 14 triangle *devis* are painted in golden hues and the rest are multicolored just like the old ones."

As the new sandstone *vigrahas* gradually took their places in the Sri Meru temple, the original cement sculptures were deconsecrated and removed—a bittersweet development for at least some longtime disciples. For all the elegance of the new sculptures, the original *Khadgamala Devis* vividly conveyed the brash, youthful immediacy and impact of Devipuram's early days as an upstart challenger to the status quo. By contrast, the new *vigrahas* are mellower and more classical in look and feel—perhaps signaling the maturity and confidence of the more established institution it has become.

For a time during the transition, many of the deconsecrated *Khadgamala* statues were placed along the walkways of Devipuram, and it was not uncommon to see passersby—visitors and staff alike—pause or even sit before one or another image to contemplate, offer *namaskaram*, pray or meditate. Fading and crumbling though they had become, the images still held a cherished and honored place in the hearts of admirers of both Guruji and Devipuram, as reminders of how it all began.

At the same time, this same sense of habitual, somewhat nostalgic attachment was undermining Guruji's attempts to withdraw from the daily life of Devipuram.

In the several years since Subbarao's appointment, the new *peetadhipathi* had undoubtedly left his mark on the place. He was an active and ubiquitous presence around Devipuram; large numbers of devotees had accepted him as their guru. Yet nearly every visitor still wanted to meet and interact with—and, not infrequently, receive *diksha* from or perform *puja* to—Guruji himself.

While initially content with this arrangement, Guruji eventually decided that a more dramatic and emphatic break from Devipuram was required. His plan was to spend his time at home in Visakhapatnam rather than at the Ashram, and to entirely cease taking on new disciples. In publicly announcing this decision on *Guru Purnima* day, Sunday, July 25, 2010, Guruji offered one of the most eloquent, candid and definitive public statements he had ever shared with his growing family of followers.

"I have always done what I felt was the right thing to do in my life," he began, "whether resigning from a plush job in Bombay without consulting anyone, or building a temple in the middle of nowhere, or sharing my experiences of the erotic nature of the Goddess through her lovable nude forms in the *Khadgamala*, or ignoring the public anger this generated, or taking care of thousands of devotees by giving them mantras and taking on their karmas."

With the passage of time, however, the radical freedom and generosity that guided him throughout his life had become compromised. Rather than "doing as he willed"—as his father, Gurugaru and most of his life experiences had taught him—he too often found himself being used as a mere *diksha* resource, "giving mantras to devotees on demand rather than giving only what I felt was good for them."

This particular departure from tradition had, he now felt, been an error. "It is not the tradition that the disciple asks the guru to give this or that mantra," he explained. "The guru decides which he thinks is the best for the disciple. Yet, so many devotees requested me to give Maha Shodashi, *Mahavakyas, purnadiksha*; to make them *pee-tadhipatis* and so on—and I accommodated most such requests."[324]

Guruji's motivation in doing so, he said, was never personal gain. "I went out of my way to do this out of pure compassion," he said, "without expecting any return for *shaktipat* or initiation. If anyone gave me anything for my personal use, I spent it for Devi. God has given me enough to survive on; I have no need to appropriate what is given to God as mine."

Nonetheless, the situation had depleted him physically, and his health was steadily deteriorating. For too long, he said, he had disregarded the growing chorus of warnings from his family and other well-wishers—but now the stark reality of his situation had finally come home to roost. "Having grown old and suffered three heart attacks—and having been operated upon thrice for those—I now feel I have a right to spend the rest of my life peacefully with my family, without taking on any further tensions," he said. "I request all people to show some respect for my age and health, and understand my need to rest and spend time with my family, whom I have too often ignored for all these 30 years."

Guruji hastened to add that he had no intention of abandoning his work; quite the contrary, he wanted to spread it even further, specifically by "producing media for a course on teaching Sri Vidya, so as to make it available for all people instead of a selected few."

His personal availability, however, would be limited.

"Henceforth, it will not be not possible for people to do *puja* to me personally," he said. "If I am unable to accommodate anyone for this, they should not feel that I have disowned them, or get hurt by this decision. I am still their guru, except that personal *pujas* are not possible any more. If anyone is still hurt, I will apologize to them personally if given a chance."

As if to underscore his resolution, he began for a time discouraging use of the name "Guruji," instead introducing himself and signing his correspondence simply as "Amrita," presenting himself as a friend and advisor rather than any kind of leader or authority figure.

324 "I remember many devotees in the late '80s and early '90s, traveling from particular countries to India to ask for *purnadiksha* from Guruji," Alok said. "Guruji was, for the most part, amused by this and his innate sense of humor would become quite evident when he gave them their *dikshanamas*, which would often reflect their worldly occupations or personalities. Some of us back in the U.S. would even try to forecast what name Guruji might give to a particular person, keeping in mind this sense of humor. I also remember a case when a student from Buffalo came to Guruji asking for the Gayatri mantra. Guruji told him, 'Why do you want Gayatri? It is a Vedic mantra and requires you to give up meat, etc. Why not take a Tantric mantra with higher potency and no such restriction?' I could see he was uncomfortable with being put in a position where the disciple was demanding a particular mantra."

It was a valiant attempt at final separation—but, once again, the Goddess had other plans: within less than a year, Devipuram was once again left without a leader.

In 2011, Subbarao suddenly, quietly announced his intention to step down as *peetadhipathi* and establish a new *peetam* in his home city of Rajahmundry, Andhra Pradesh, about 225 kilometers (140 miles) away. There was no public announcement and very little private discussion regarding his departure.

Shortly thereafter, however, in accordance with "instructions I received from Devi," Guruji publicly announced the dedication of Devipuram to the *Sri Guru Padukas*—a pair of his sandals, the right representing Shiva, and the left, Shakti. Referring to the guru mantra of his lineage, Guruji explained, "It is our tradition to say '*Sri Guru Sri Padukam Pujayami Tarpayami Namah*' and not '*Sri Guru Sri Padau Pujayami Tarpayami Namah*'"—in other words, gurus are symbolically represented by their sandals, rather than by their feet as in most other lineages.

Devipuram, he said, now belonged solely to the Goddess; it had been built "under her supervision and the direction of her *padukas*, one of them being *Prakasha* and the other *Vimarsa*.[325] One *paduka* belongs to Sri Devi and the other belongs to Shiva. They are our real Gurus."

Holding their ceremonial sandals upon his head—symbolizing, in the traditional gesture, his place in a lineage reaching back through time immemorial—he added, "These *Sri Guru Padukas* have been blessed by me, by my wearing them while a full *Navavarana Puja* was completed. I have placed one pair at Devipuram, and another pair in my home. Anyone can do the *puja* to the *Sri Guru Padukas*, offering the fruits of the *puja* to my feet personally as long as I am alive. Once I am gone, the *padukas* will keep blessing everyone. This is the tradition followed by every major *peetam*."

A few months later, Guruji further clarified that, in the event of his own departure or passing, "Devi's *padukas* will be in charge of Devipuram, not any human being. There will be no more *peetadhipatis* here, only administrators of the Sri Vidya Trust to look after all matters concerning Devipuram."

In 2013 he added that since "Devi is now the Guru" at Devipuram, *Guru Purnima* would no longer be celebrated there in the usual month of *Ashadh* (June–July), but rather during *Sharad Purnima*, a harvest festival celebrated on the full moon day of *Ashvin* (September–October), dedicated to Lakshmi and marking the end of monsoon

325   *Prakasha* is enlightenment, and *Vimarsa* is analysis.

season. "The force that brought Guruji to Devipuram preceded him and will remain after him," Alok reflected. "That is why Guruji maintained that he was merely the vehicle and that that Goddess herself would be his only successor at Devipuram."

"I am not the decision maker," Guruji affirmed. "It is Devi's worry now—and she is the one who is choosing."

ॐ Doused in energized holy water, Guruji casts a piercing gaze as he leaves the Sri Meru temple.
(Sri Vidya Trust)

29   The Goddess and the Guru

So as he approached his 80th year, Guruji found himself once again at the helm of Devipuram. "For years I kept trying and trying to give it away, and she keeps giving it back to me!" he laughed. "So I am here. Let her have her way."

And it was precisely this attitude of relaxed good humor that best characterized Guruji's final years at the unlikely retreat that the Devi and he—the Goddess and the Guru—had created together. Gone were the dark intimations of illness and mortality that had characterized his talks and writings during his attempts to withdraw from Devipuram. Asked about the shift in attitude, he merely shrugged and said, "I got better," without further explanation.

This re-energized outlook was also apparent in the palpably renewed engagement and energy he brought to his interactions with visitors—whose ever-increasing numbers no longer hailed just from India and other English-fluent enclaves such as the United Kingdom, the United States and Canada, Australia and so on, but more and more frequently from Mexico, Central and South America, and a plethora of Central and Eastern European countries—Russia, Ukraine, Latvia and beyond.

Guruji's similarly reinvigorated focus on teaching became apparent in Devipuram's intensive "Sri Vidya Courses," organized and taught by a variety of disciples, with Guruji delivering occasional keynote lectures throughout. The courses aimed to provide—in high-concentration, one-week sessions—a volume of knowledge and practice that would otherwise take months of concentrated effort to acquire organically during a more extended stay at Devipuram. Participants left with a supply of *yantra*s, instruction booklets and CDs loaded with videos and animations; they filled pages with copious notes and recorded hours of video and audio that would themselves take years to fully process and absorb. The programs have become increasingly popular, packing the Srivilla guesthouse to room-sharing double and triple capacity during the *Navratri* holidays each year.

To accommodate a growing wave of devotees and disciples unfamiliar with Sanskrit language or authentic Hindu tradition, Guruji redoubled his attempts to simplify and streamline the rituals—seeking to preserve the essential energy and focus they offered spiritual seekers, while removing as many cultural and linguistic barriers to participation as possible. Still, he emphasized that students had to meet him at least part of the way. "We can go to America; we can go anywhere," he said. "But how much will be understood depends much on the effort and preparation that has been invested ahead of time. Great efforts are needed to effect great changes. And the most important part of such efforts is self-improvement."

In 2012, he introduced a entirely new ritual called *Siri Jyoti* ("Abundant Lights"). A briefer, more concentrated variation on the demanding *Navavarana Puja* that stands at the center of Sri Vidya tradition, *Siri Jyoti* focuses on harnessing the energy of group participation. "We join together to put our life forces into a light in the center of a power diagram that we draw," he explained, referring of course to the *Sri Yantra*. "It is easy to learn and do. It is catching on."

He also established a new media lab at Devipuram, staffed by local disciples who videotaped, archived and occasionally posted Guruji's various talks and classes online, whether on Devipuram's current website, www.devipuram.com, or its YouTube channel, devipuram1. Thanks to improved technology and telecommunication tools, the volume of teaching material now being produced at Devipuram today exceeds that of past years by several orders of magnitude. Ever the innovator, Guruji also tried offering free, interactive online classes in various media, including Facebook—with decidedly mixed results. In true scientific fashion, he continued to tweak, retool and retry these approaches. Meanwhile, disciples and visitors from around the world augmented Devipuram's internally produced presentations by creating and posting their own videos and teaching tools, using Devipuram materials or interviews filmed during visits there.

Guruji saw this explosion of new data and multipolar participation as the Goddess's own intent—her way of fulfilling the promise of an ever-smaller, more interconnected world.

"I believe in the power of nature as a loving goddess," he said. "I have seen her physically manifest, and she has been my mentor through decades of meditations. She made me build a temple for love, for *Rati*,[326] at Kamakhya, in the form of her creative center, the *yoni*, and another unique temple in the form of her bosom, called Sri Meru, for the protection and the nourishment of humanity. Now she is asking me to build an international temple on the Internet, not confined by walls. She made me create graphic learning modules for connecting to her. She made me use technology as a means of initiation or immersion, and to accelerate the learning curve. Her purpose is to promote a better quality of life for all."

In an age of cell phones, tablets and cloud technology, he added, the Internet has emerged as a powerful teaching tool for even graduate-level coursework—and as the medium of choice for the young. "If we don't adapt our methods of teaching to the current generation's way of thinking and doing things, then it's natural for them not to have any interest," he explained. "We need to find more meaningful ways of involving them, using their ways of doing things."

Online teaching is not only a convenient resource, he said; it is also an eminently effective one for teaching Sri Vidya. "The power of mantras travels through the voice; it *can* be transmitted as an audio file," he said. "That allows the learning to happen at a place and time of your choice—even while driving to work—at whatever speed is comfortable for you. Love can and should transcend boundaries of country, color and creed. I ask you: If organizations can deliver threats to nations through videos, why can't we use them to deliver care and love?"

326 Rati is the Hindu goddess of erotic love. Usually described as a daughter of Prajapati Daksha, she is the consort and constant companion of the god Kama (Desire, Eros), and is noted for her extraordinary beauty and sensuality. She is also considered to be Krishna's *shakti* in the elemental *Puranic* story of the *Rasa Lila*, or "Dance of Divine Love."

From the moment he initiated his brother and sister-in-law into Sri Vidya in 1977, Guruji never seemed to pay much attention to the number of disciples he'd accumulated. But that number rose steadily, with almost every passing day, for nearly 40 years. Pressed to venture an estimate, he shrugged and said mischievously, "Maybe *sahasra*—a thousand—by now? Or maybe even more?" In the process of defining that term, however, he edged closer to a true answer: "*Sahasra* consists of the number one followed by three zeroes. The one is our invariant Self; the three zeroes represent each of our states—*jagrat, swapna* and *sushpti*; waking, dreaming and deep sleep. In effect, then, it covers the gamut of all possible experiences—and therefore corresponds to infinity."

For decades, Guruji had traveled the length and breadth of India and circled the globe, constantly initiating new members into his lineage. But age and fragile health had taken their toll, and for most of his final decade he rarely left India at all. The world had to come to him.

"Recently there was a learned man from Tampa, Florida, in the United States, who came to my home while he was in Vizag conducting *yagnas*," Guruji told me in 2015. "Every year, this man invites realized souls like Sri Paripoornananda Swami, Samavedam Shanmukha Sarma and Sri Siddheswarananda Bharati Swami to visit him in the United States. And he said to me, 'Come, I would love to receive you in my home.' But I told him I could not come." Still, Guruji asked the man, "Why would you want to invite me anyway? I am a small fry compared to these people who command millions of followers."

In response, the gentleman extended his arms as if he were giving away a large gift and said: "Guruji, you tell people, 'Here, you can have this—come and take it. Or if you can't come, you can take it for free from the Internet.' That's what you are like, Guruji. The others give too, but there is a difference: they always hold something back, some small thing close to their hearts. They say, in essence, 'I have this and you don't. If you want it, come to me and you just might get it after I have tested you enough.'[327]

"This, Guruji, is why I want *you* to come, specifically," he concluded. "*So* many people will benefit."

"It touched my heart," Guruji said. "But I was unable to go."

327 In this regard, Guruji has said, "Maintaining a difference in level between guru and disciple shows that the guru is still working within the realm of gravity. The *akasha tattva* [ether element] of complete freedom without difference has not yet been reached."

ॐ
ह्रीं

To all appearances Guruji retained the energy, engagement and demeanor of a man decades younger, but the wear and tear of age were ultimately inescapable. On October 31, 2012, while climbing a stairway to preside over a *Siri Jyoti* event in Vizag, Guruji took a hard fall and broke his right arm.

"He claimed he was fine and refused to go to the doctor until after the event was over," daughter Radha noted. "But it turned out to be a fracture in his lower right arm, which had to be set with the insertion of a rod along the entire length of his arm up to the elbow." Making light of the situation, Guruji wrote to me, "I took it as a sign that Devi wanted me to stop writing B.S." After a few weeks in a cast and several months of rehabilitation exercises, Guruji was back to his usual routine, though his arm remained "a little weak and twisted," he said.

He was also suffering from degenerative joint disease in both knees and chronic pain in his lower back. In early 2014, he and Amma spent two relaxing weeks at an Ayurvedic retreat in Bangalore, which resulted in some marked physical improvements, as well as the institution of a new dietary and medical regimen. Meanwhile, most of Guruji's health-related difficulties remained very much in the background for disciples and visitors, who in fact often commented that he seemed more glowing and lucid than he had in years.

On any given evening on the benches outside the Ashram at Devipuram, he would still hold forth on the political, corporate and environmental scourges of the day. One night in late 2012, for example, he expressed consternation over the Monsanto Company's practice of patenting and aggressively controlling access to genetically modified seeds and organisms (GMOs) as "the first time in history that human beings have displayed the hubris of trying to take ownership of not just life, but the very act of creation."

He noted that the damage inflicted by such extremities of greed had become a threat to human survival itself. "The opposite of love is not hate," he said. "The opposite of love is greed. Love is the infinite capacity for giving; greed is the infinite capacity for taking. But I firmly believe that love is born from the wisdom to overcome greed and manipulation. I dream of *not* destroying the greenery on this Earth. I dream of preserving the oxygen that sustains its life. I dream of a generous world in which the haves support the have-nots instead of exploiting them."

Not surprisingly, gender inequality in India, and globally, incensed him—in particular sexual violence, which he blamed on repressive social norms. "Sexual crime increases by suppression not by expression," he said. "It is extinguished by expression, not enhanced by it." Following the brutal gang-rape and murder of a young woman in New Delhi in December 2012, a case that garnered worldwide media attention, Guruji was shaken. "So this is how we worship the Goddess in India!" he fumed. "And as if to rub salt into the wound, we repeat like a parrot, *Matru Devo Bhava*[328] Oh Goddess, when will you awaken to establish equality and respect between the genders?"

Global climate change presented yet another topic of concern. That threat was brought home in powerfully October 2013, as Guruji watched Cyclone Phailin—a rare Category 5 tropical cyclone, with sustained 260-kilometer-per-hour (160 mile-per-hour) winds—prowl the Bay of Bengal, for a time menacing Visakhapatnam with the threat of a direct hit. "There are two kinds of laws," he said. "Those made by us, and those made by nature. As long as our laws match those of nature, she will give wisdom, bounty and creative purpose to our lives. But when she is abused and raped, she turns violent." (Just a year later—almost to the day—Cyclone Hudhud followed through on Phailin's threat, becoming the first such storm to make landfall in an Indian city in more than a century.[329])

Seeking ways to live in harmony with laws of nature, Guruji hoped, would be part of the legacy of his life and teachings. "However small I am in the vastness of this world, there is yet a purpose and goal for my life," he said. "I have made every effort to discover that purpose and to live by the truths I learned. If you are like me, perhaps you will do the same. Your purpose and dreams may be different from mine, but they all spring from the same fountain of care and love. Everyone preaches love—but it is high time we start walking the talk. We owe it to our future generations."

Guruji's dreams, as always, began literally in his own backyard; in the towns and villages surrounding Devipuram—and a lot of them involved solar power. "Solar is green technology," he explained. "It preserves the ecology for our descendants. It can provide clean water, comfortable homes, and electric power to increase time available for learning, so the poor can have light by which to study after the sun has set. Solar power can shift the capacity to dream—and to execute those dreams—from urban to rural areas, providing a level playing ground for enterprises large and small. Instead of chastising China for dumping cheap but excellent solar panels on the market to compete with the established power grids, we should thank it for making its human resources available to solve the power problems of the world."[330]

But though Guruji remained excited about and hopeful for the possibilities of science (especially when combined with love in the service of humankind and the material world), he was even more passionate about taking that synergy to the next level—by employing science, love and service as springboards from which to achieve liberation of the spirit.

"On a daily basis we are conditioned to believe that the world we see is the only world that exists, that *it* is the only constant," he said. "But in fact we have now moved as a species far beyond that misperception in virtually every scientific endeavor. And as humankind advances in understanding, things that were once impossible become possible. Take flight, for example: once it was an irrational fantasy; now it's a daily part of ordinary life for millions of people. No big deal. Nothing mystical about it. Totally rational. The things that we think are irrational today can become rational tomorrow."

"In this way," he added, "humankind is continuously moving the line between science and spirituality. In fact, this whole divide between spirituality and science began crumbling with the advent of the quantum period in physics, when we first confirmed that the observer has a say in what is being observed. He chooses what to see, and that is what he sees. The very act of observing a phenomenon at the quantum level makes it change; you cannot observe it without changing it. Therefore the observed and the observer are, somehow, one. And that's a very hard pill for any classical physicist to swallow, because ultimately it implies that each of us is capable of creating a universe, that each one of us really is a creator and that—by extrapolation—anything is possible. Which is totally irrational, right? A bunch of mystical nonsense! So says our conditioning—but that is where the science is heading."

It's also where Guruji's own personal spiritual inquiries were heading in his final years. Four decades after Sastry the Scientist became Amritananda the Guru, he

330 "As far as I know, nothing makes Guruji happier than coming up with inexpensive, renewable technologies that can be used in a decentralized way in the remotest parts of the words," Alok said. "I have seen him glow with happiness upon seeing a simple thing like a rotor blade serving as a fan, powered by solar energy. He has spent countless hours thinking about deriving pure water from the air using solar energy. At heart, he is rooting for the rural people who are living in remote areas, to benefit from technology without having to move to urban areas."

remained certain that these two aspects of his mind and experience were ultimately reconcilable, and that both were pointing to the same conclusions.

"I was never a great scientist, but I have always had a very good scientific temperament," he said. "And I am still trying to explore and understand myself in a way that is both spiritual and scientific—because there are just so many connections. I am oscillating, maybe even *vacillating* between those two poles. Even today I try to be rational: why does it have to be the way it is, all of this?" He raises his hands and looks around, gesturing toward the world around him. "I keep questioning myself. I keep questioning everything that I see. And this questioning keeps driving me onward, both at the level of spirit and of science. If I hear some spiritual person say, 'Oh, the sciences are a bunch of bunkum!'—it hurts me still, because I know how much time and care go into those disciplines. Such people know not what they are railing against."

Yet the spiritual side of the equation was ultimately the one he chose to pursue as his life's work—by liberating and freely teaching the spiritual techniques employed by Sri Vidya *upasana* in the service of the Supreme Mother Goddess, and making them accessible to all who wished to learn.

"Over the years, I have come to understand the concept of ritual," he explained. "And one of the finest rituals I know of in the world today is that of the Lalita *upasana*. There is no comparable ritual in existence. It is very broad in scope. It operates at once on the physical, astral and even deeper levels. And, I would add, it is very beautiful. I wanted to teach it to all who wished to learn it. Not to thrust it upon anybody who wasn't interested, but to help all of those who wanted to understand it."

That he did for half of his lifetime with a singular focus and devotion. Thanks almost entirely to Guruji's persistent, often lonely efforts, scores of previously secret, forbidden, inaccessible rituals, prayers and mantras—concealed from most of humanity for at least a millennium—are now a part of daily life and common parlance in countless homes across India and beyond, spreading through *ashrams*, yoga studios and temples in the United States, Canada, Mexico, Central and South America, Western and Eastern Europe, Australia and Asia.

Yet for all the depth of passion and conviction he brought to his "mission," what remained notably absent was any sense of missionary zeal. Not only was he perfectly comfortable with people rejecting his teachings; he seemed entirely at peace with the prospect of their disappearance altogether. "Everything has a life—it is born, it grows, it flourishes and then it dies," he said. "Why should we assume that the Sri Vidya tradition is something special that will defy the laws of nature? If the tradition has to die, it will do so. If it has to live, it will live. Goddess's wisdom far exceeds ours."

Despite his many successes, however—and probably, to a large extent, because of them—one of Guruji's greatest unfulfilled wishes was to simply find himself a little more downtime, a bit more space in which to be alone with his thoughts and meditations.

"When you're in meditation you are yourself; nobody disturbs you," he explained. "But people *do* disturb me. They don't give me the time to sit and meditate. Once you become a guru, it's very tough to get time for yourself. People intrude on you. They make you do things you don't want to do. They put you on a pedestal and start carrying on..." He shrugged. "It's not me."

So why stay around and put up with all the fuss? "I could have stepped away, yes, but I didn't see the point of it," he explained. "It's a challenge, and challenges are necessary for creativity. Problems force the mind to find solutions. Ultimately, it's all a game."

Lalita's game, to be precise. The Playful One's play, unfolding across the cosmos in an infinite multitude of dramas and narratives, experienced via endless segments of space and time. Some of these dramas are vast, violent galactic spectacles, spanning light years of space and eons of time. Others are minute, unimaginably intense exchanges of matter and energy occurring at the atomic and subatomic levels, playing out in fractions of nanoseconds.

But most of the dramas—in the sphere of Guruji's everyday work, at least—were of the mundane, human variety: love, marriage, birth, school, wealth or lack thereof, employment won or lost, ideas born and nurtured, dreams realized or dashed, first meetings and final separations, loyalties and betrayals, youthful enthusiasm, middle-age crises, elderly wisdom, illness, loss and death—billions of individual dramas continually proliferating here on the planet Earth on the timescale of human lives and generations.

The role of the guru, he said, is to teach people how best to play this "game"—what the rules are, both obvious and non-obvious, written and unwritten; what the goals are; which mental and physical attitudes work best in achieving these goals; where the traps lie; how to cope with disappointments and setbacks; how to live joyfully, regardless of one's circumstances at any given moment. How to never forget who and what you really are.

"Spirituality and society are at war, and people get caught in the middle," Guruji explained. "Society demands obedience; it thrives on obedience. But inquisitiveness, curiosity, wonder and creativity—these qualities thrive in freedom. Thus we live in a dichotomy, and I think that this dichotomy consists, in part, of the stress between spirit and science. Between society"—he closed his fist tightly for a long moment—"and freedom." He opened his palm wide.

"As a result, people need guidance, information, someone who's looking out for them—for their true selves, for their spiritual interests," he continued. "The role of the guru is to tell you that you are perfect the way you are. To love you so that you can learn to love yourself. When everyone is in perfect health, no one needs a doctor; when everyone is a saint, no one needs a priest. But there *is* a need. Because everyday reality is always there to pull us downward, to ground us, and yet there is another part of us that is able to soar to whatever heights we desire. Meditation is the place where we can soar."

To the greatest extent possible, Guruji said, he always tried to follow Anakapalle Gurugaru's advice and rely on his own internal guidance, the Goddess's guidance— the wisdom that comes from one's own deepest Self rather than the more mundane external variety.

"You should always trust your own experience," he said. "Many of my meditational experiences led me to break societal norms and defy the way I was taught to think. Yet it was only when I learned to trust these experiences that Devi revealed herself to me more fully. So my advice is to be, whenever possible, self-referred."

All in all, he said, his choices and decisions in life—difficult though they were at times—have made for a spiritually rich and fulfilling existence. "I've been an infant, I've grown, I've loved and I've been loved," he said. "To the best of my ability, I've tried to do something for others. Not because I expected something back from them, but because it was in my nature to do something and because it made me happy to do it. Our happiness is Devi's happiness."

The prospect of his own bodily death—unsurprisingly—elicited barely a shrug.

"Ultimately, if I can go when I decide to go, and not feel much of a pinch, then I've accomplished something great," he said. "That's the kind of transition I'd like to make. I want people to celebrate when I go, not cry. I want people to be happy. When your integration with the body is broken, you become one with nature. You go back to nature, and that is something to be celebrated. Why cry over it? That's my attitude toward life."[331]

In the meantime, Guruji enjoyed toying with the idea that he might one day throw off the burden he had taken on with the building of Devipuram—and simply walk away. He recalled his early days at TIFR, when he used to get bored with the various scientific disciplines he undertook almost as quickly as he had mastered them. Now, he mused—only half-jokingly, it seemed—that a similar dynamic was at work regarding Devipuram and his guruhood.

"Perhaps the same story is repeating itself all over again," he said. "Now that I've built this place and it's time to get the reward, maybe I'll just walk off again! Maybe I'll resign as a guru! I think it's the same pattern continuing: I still want to move away from the applied sciences and go back to pure research—in a way, the same tension applies as much to my current specialty as my previous one!"

But the time for chatter had passed.

Dusk had fallen, and the temple bell was ringing for the evening's final *aarti* at Sri Meru Nilayam. Somewhat laboriously, Guruji stood, took his leave, and began the slow walk toward the temple he built: Her temple. His temple. The Goddess and the Guru. Just one of many proofs in his life that even the most impractical and unlikely dreams of our hearts stand a chance—with time, faith, effort and courage—of eventually manifesting and taking shape before our very eyes.

THE END

331 One early disciple mentioned that back in the mid-1980s, "Guruji told me one day that when he leaves this body he would like his body left in the jungle for the animals and birds to feed on." The disciple added, with a lingering hint of incredulity, "I do not think any of his admirers would ever allow that to happen!" Another said, "Guruji once told me that, upon his physical death, he would merge into the breasts of the Divine Mother, giving *amrita* [divine nectar] from one breast and *ananda* [divine bliss] from the other, for the benefit of all creation."

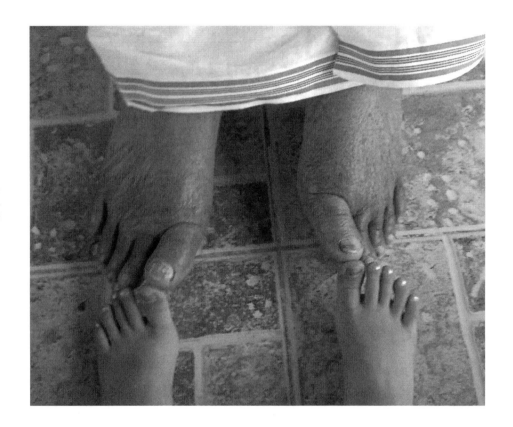

ॐ Passing on the *shakti*:
Guruji with a young
visitor, December 2014.
(Kathy Allen)

Epilogue

Matter Becomes a Wave

TO CONQUER DEATH YOU ONLY HAVE TO DIE.
~ *Tim Rice & Andrew Lloyd Webber,* Jesus Christ Superstar (1970)

In the days and weeks following Cyclone Hudhud's direct hit on Devipuram in October 2014,[332] some critics suggested—albeit mainly from the safe anonymity of social media—that Devipuram had been punished by the Goddess, in a rebuke against Guruji for his decades of revealing her deepest secrets, of teaching her worship to the unqualified and the unworthy.

332 See the introduction.

More impressive, however, was the abundant evidence to the contrary.

"Back when Guruji first proposed constructing the Sri Meru temple, there were eminent engineers and experts who vehemently insisted (A) that the structure would prove impossible to build, and (B) that even if it *was* built, it would be inherently weak and vulnerable," said son-in-law Balkumar Marthi, now a director and microbiologist with a major agricultural corporation in Holland. "Well, not only has the temple stood firm for the last couple of decades, but it has now withstood the sustained force of 200 kilometer-per-hour winds in a cyclone that destroyed everything but the hills around it!"

Nonetheless, detractors jeered that if Guruji were such an accomplished *siddha*, he would surely have deflected the brunt of the storm's destruction away from Devipuram. Apprised of this argument, Haran Aiya scoffed, "Deflected it toward whom? Which of the Mother's children should have suffered the destruction in Devipuram's place?" On the contrary, he asserted, the relatively minor damage to the temples—not to mention the complete absence of human casualties—offered a prime illustration of Guruji's selfless compassion, his willingness to draw harm away from others and his indifference as to whether or not those efforts were recognized.

Yet as donations poured in from around the world and the hard work of cleanup and reconstruction commenced in the autumn of 2014, the Sri Vidya Trust erected a Telugu-language sign at the entrance to the complex:

> Cyclone Hudhud left Devipuram largely shorn of its greenery. But Goddess Sahasrakshi, along with Her 108 attendant deities, protected all living beings in the vicinity of the Sri Meru temple. Battered by wind speeds exceeding 200 kph, the spire and ceramic tiles of the Sri Meru's dome were ripped away. Yet inside the sanctum, whose doors remained open throughout the storm, even the pleats on the Blessed Mother's sari remained undisturbed. An imposing *peepal* tree, weighing a few tons, was uprooted and cast aside by the cyclone. But *murtis* weighing only a few kilos went unharmed. All around, trees and rooftops were blown away—but Hudhud did not budge the ultra-lightweight fiberglass roofs sheltering Sri Meru's 24 outdoor deities. Why? Because Goddess Sahasrakshi had fully enfolded Sri Meru and its environs within Her protective embrace.

Nearly a decade earlier, Guruji had developed ambitious plans to transform Devipuram's landscape in a project known as *Manidweepam* ("Isle of Jewels").[333] Though the concept was ultimately set aside as impractical, the post-cyclone period saw its revival on a somewhat more modest scale.

333 The *Manidweepam* project is detailed in chapter 26.

"Hudhud's damage to the vegetation actually helped us in a way," Guruji explained. "When we first considered the idea some years back, I worried that clearing the tree growth would be too labor intensive, and also that it would be too difficult in the sense of destroying so much life. Yet via Hudhud, the Goddess has removed these obstacles. The energy at Devipuram today is just tremendous. People come here expecting to feel bad about all the damage, but they leave feeling that something new and powerful is just beginning."

That sense was strikingly palpable during the final week of 2014, when disciples from around the world converged on Devipuram to celebrate Guruji's *Sathabhishekam*. Largely the brain child of Haran Aiya, the event was a sort of combined celebration of his 80th birthday, which had happened three months earlier; his one-thousandth full moon, which was upcoming in July; and, in a general sense, Devipuram's continuing rebirth in the wake of Hudhud. Another highlight of the event was the formal unveiling of Gurugaru's new resting place within a small shrine near the entrance to Devipuram, where a marble statue of Dattatreya had been installed some months earlier. In addition to Svaprakasananda's remains, the shrine also housed a jade Shiva linga and a jade Nandi bull.

According to witnesses, the collective impact of these observances was powerful indeed.

"The energy was out of this world!" marveled lifelong disciple Saru Janahan, making her first visit to Devipuram in more than a decade. "I mean, the energy has always been there, but it was almost as if the lack of trees made you more aware of it. Perhaps not having the 'distraction' of trees made it easier to *perceive* the energy."

Evgeniya Bratslavskaya, who traveled from Kiev, Ukraine, to attend the *Sathabhishekam*, experienced a similar sensation. "When we arrived at Devipuram, I couldn't even believe the feeling in the air," she said. "It was as if the cyclone's aftermath had drawn everyone together into a state of complete unity and common purpose—as if the storm had cleared away everything unnecessary in order to make room for the creation of something new."

As to what that "something new" might turn out to be, Guruji shook his head, unwilling to speculate—at least not aloud.

"That depends entirely upon her will," he said. "And her will, will be done."

Six months out from the cyclone, in mid-April, efforts to repair the physical damage to Devipuram's buildings were well underway. The temples sported fresh coats of brightly colored paint and the surrounding greenery was returning with remarkable speed.

Amid all of this outward progress, Guruji finally found some time to return to his inner work, experiencing meditations that seemed to echo and amplify numerous threads drawn from many different phases of his spiritual life.[334]

"I have been living in an ocean of utter creativity," he said. "An ocean of silent visions—totally silent, even if galaxies are colliding or being created. There is no way I can describe these visions; I know they are totally incommunicable."

334   Guruji shared these reflections via several media, on Monday, April 13, 2015. However, he had first mentioned his "silent visions" shortly after the consecration of the Sri Meru Nilayam temple. For the previous decade and a half, his meditations had often been accompanied by intense sound or droning hums. But starting in around 1995, many of his meditative experiences became "silent spectacles." Theorizing that he had possibly passed out of the frequency of audio waves, and into the visual frequency range, Guruji observed that "the unstruck sound ceased to be; my body was totally relaxed, my mind was alert, but only seeing in wonder whatever was happening. Perhaps it was precisely these conditions that enabled such visions to manifest."

He tried nonetheless. These were cosmic-scale revelations, he said, that made his everyday, worldly life seem less and less real—and, in retrospect, plainly indicated that a dramatic process of detachment had begun. "I feel I am dreaming when I am in the waking state," he said. "This waking state is not me. The *real* me is totally mad and totally creative. Yes, I am experiencing some mad state—but I see no violence in it, thank God."

In fact, this so-called "madness" reminded him of the time, decades earlier, when he had watched the Saint of Simhachalam affectionately rub Anakapalle Gurugaru's head and call him "*pichi*," the Telugu word for mad or crazy.[335] "I used to wonder what that gesture meant," Guruji mused. "I would ask myself, 'Was it some kind of a *diksha*, or what?' But now I understand what it was."

What the Saint was conveying, Guruji believed, was that Gurugaru had left the ordinary mortal state of *becoming*, and entered a transcendental state of simply *being*, a state that could easily appear as madness to anyone who hadn't experienced it.[336]

"*Being* is what you *are*," Guruji said. "It is called 'now.' It is a continuous state. *Becoming* is what you are *not*. It is a process of creating time by changing 'me.' The process can be sudden or gradual; it can be anything that is ever-changing: blazing lights, galaxies, stars, earths, oceans, people, animals, worms—from the smallest imaginable thing to the largest."

"*Becoming*," in other words, is our ordinary state of existence—the state of birth, growth, decay; of creation and obliteration on every observable scale. It is *Maya*, the experience of separateness—a constant, sequential play of matter upon matter, taking place on the vast performance stage of space and time.

"In this state of *becoming*," Guruji explained, "you see *yourself* as something other than *you* [i.e., what you really are]. That is the creative part, because whatever you see is [actually] spinning out from your own current being. Part of this process is driven by you—by your giving it an intention, a direction. But another part is spontaneous and *not* created by you. And that is the much bigger part."

In Gurugaru's—and now Guruji's—state of "*being*," by contrast, all of these dramas, large and small, faded to insignificance. This, then, was the "mad state" he was experiencing—and quite unapologetically so.

335 This incident is recounted in chapter 18.

336 In a discussion of this incident a few months before making the above comments, Guruji said to me, "My Guru told me it was an initiation into a type of *Sanyasa Diksha called Ativarnami*."

"I am enjoying my madness," he said. "It is the real me. I am myself. That is the most important fact.[337] With whom else can I share my madness?"[338]

Mental, physical and even spiritual activities lost much of their significance and relevance for Guruji in this new state of *being*. In practical terms, the shift translated to a dramatic stepping back from his physical, embodied role as guru and teacher. He was wrapping up his work. A process of profound detachment was underway and was rapidly unfolding.

In his *pichi* state, "this world, including my role in it—as well as [mundane concepts of] gender, caste, name, fame, money, power, status and goals—means nothing," he declared. As if to cement the absolute nature of this statement, he explicitly included the replanting and repairs going on all around him at Devipuram "That goes for *Manidveepam* as well," he said.

Like many accomplished people in their later years—and very much in keeping with his own intensely skeptical and self-questioning nature—Guruji now looked back on his life critically, questioning the value of his efforts and accomplishments: transmitting mantras, teaching ritual, counseling prayer and *sadhana*. These too were losing their relevance for him.

In his new state of *being* rather than *becoming*, he said, he could no longer muster "the power to make others see what I have seen." Over the years, his visions had grown increasingly abstract and mercurial; now, "by the time I help others see them through my will, the visions have changed infinitely," he said, "and they never repeat. So what is the point?"

Even his beloved Sri Vidya rituals seemed inadequate from his new viewpoint. Could he offer "at least a mantra, a yantra, a Tantra or *any* process by which others can [definitely] gain such experiences?"

"No," he said. Not anymore. "It is her choice."[339]

In Guruji's state of "*pichi*" divine madness, even prayer seemed to have lost its efficacy for him. In a world rapidly losing its substance, it too seemed unreal. "When I pray [now], I am in my dream world, not my real world," he explained. "So prayer is useless, too."

337 Just a year or so earlier, on the other hand, he had stated that his Guru role was "not me," and expressed a desire to reclaim and resume his own spiritual journey: "Now that I've built this place and it's time to get the reward, maybe I'll just walk off! Maybe I'll resign as a guru!" (See chapter 29.)

338 More than a lonely call for the empathy of kindred souls, Guruji's statement recalled the *Mahavakya* ("Great dictum") of Shaktism's most venerable scripture, the *Devi Mahatmyam*: "I alone exist in this Universe. Who else is there besides me?" (10.5).

339 Guruji added, "And by 'her,' I mean that part of me which becomes what I see through my intention. Language is so inadequate."

Though such pronouncements may, at first glance, appear harsh and incongruent with Guruji's life teachings, they are in fact very much in keeping with the evolution of his thought. A decade earlier, in a 2006 Diwali address, Guruji told his disciples he would help them as much as he could, but that "finally, you are the architect of your own realization." Even in the presence of *diksha*, knowledge of the mantras and techniques of Sri Vidya, and regular practice, he explained, "results are not guaranteed—but the conditions have been met for them to occur."

And he continued to acknowledge just how much those "results" were worth striving for. Despite his growing state of detachment, Guruji could simply not discount or dismiss the beauty and profundity of the meditative experiences he had enjoyed with the Goddess over the course of his lifetime.

"They will always be my visions," he said, "whomever I happen to be."[340]

Profound though these inner philosophical shifts may have been, outwardly Guruji's daily routine and attitude toward life did not appear to be significantly impacted by them.

"He spent his final months and weeks in pretty much the same way he had spent his entire life," Ananta said. "Attending to people's problems, whether in person, via telephone or by email; recording talks on the *Saptashati* and Sri Vidya for the upcoming *Navaratri* celebrations; planning for various events at Devipuram; constantly researching solutions to global issues..."

As the year's midpoint arrived, Guruji reached his *Sahasra Purna Chandrodayam*—the one-thousandth full moon to occur during his lifetime. It fell on Friday, July 31, 2015, which also happened to be *Guru Purnima*, an auspicious and unusual convergence.

Combining the statistical likelihood of a person reaching 81 years of age with the chance of one's thousandth full moon falling on *Guru Purnima*, Alok Baveja—donning his expertise as a tenured Rutgers business professor—calculated "an approximately 99.9 percent chance of this *not* happening, due to either a person not living long enough or it falling on a non–*Guru Purnima* full moon day. So, from a 'chance' standpoint, it is indeed a very rare event." He added, "Guruji specifically mentioned this

340 Here Guruji suggests a future incarnation, as Haran Aiya suggested in his foreword: "What is it that makes Guruji so different? I think he arrived here with the whole package, whereas most of us have to strive to get the package. I think he's been coming back with it for, oh, to the best of my knowledge, 800 years at least. He keeps coming back with the same package."

event to me and others as being a significant one, even more important than his 80th birthday itself."[341]

341 Indeed, Haran Aiya made a similar statement to me regarding Guru's *Sahasra Purna Chandrodayam*.

In August, Sundhara Arasaratnam—by now retired in Newmarket, Ontario, and only recently recovered from serious surgery—was surprised to receive a call from Guruji asking him to come visit Devipuram. Sundhara quickly arranged the trip, but was puzzled to discover when he arrived that Guruji seemed to have no particular agenda in mind. Their conversations were relaxed and cordial; as old friends, they often just sat in contented silence. But when Sundhara left for the airport at the end of his stay, Guruji and Amma surprised him by riding along to bid him farewell. Just before they parted, Guruji handed him a pair of his *chappals* (sandals) and a few other precious mementos. While touched and honoured by the gesture, Sundhara said he still suspected nothing unusual.

A few weeks later, on Saturday, September 26, 2015, Guruji celebrated his 81st birthday at Devipuram. While he clearly enjoyed the day of special *pujas* and celebrations with Amma and a large gathering of disciples, he did not look well. His arms, legs and feet were all noticeably swollen, symptomatic of advanced congestive heart failure. His face especially, though often smiling and aglow with good humor, had a distended appearance; his expression was frequently absent and detached. His speech was indistinct. He was not his usual self.

Though he had rarely left the south of India in several years, Guruji did renew his passport around this time and spoke tentatively of traveling again, perhaps to Europe. He told one disciple he might even attempt a trip to North America—but added that if the trip did not occur before the end of 2016, it would probably never happen. Later, when informed that Amma had approved booking them for a flight to attend a wedding in Hyderabad at October's end, he cryptically commented, "Ah, but has the other Amma [implying the Devi] also given us permission?"

Amma curiously noted that, after years of mounting good-natured resistance to her attempts to impose a healthier food regimen, Guruji had begun displaying a singular "lack of interest in midnight feasts and all things crunchy and munchy. That was very strange indeed," she said.

A new Telugu-language religious television channel, Gnana Yogi, arranged to record a series of half-hour conversations with Guruji in the autumn. The second taping (and, as it turned out, the final one) was conducted on Friday, October 9. Guruji was visibly suffering throughout, displaying "signs of deep fatigue and a physical inability to talk clearly," daughter Ananta noted. "It was very difficult to view."

The next morning, Saturday, October 10, Guruji rose early as usual at home in Vizag; Amma was already up and cooking his favorite breakfast of *dosas* served fresh from the pan. Guruji's movements were unusually slow and quiet, and he told Amma he was feeling "a bit out of sorts." Amma urged that they should visit his doctor before making the move to Devipuram for the upcoming *Navratri* festivities,[342] but Guruji replied that he would get a checkup afterward.

At that point, Sunita, a disciple who lived in a neighboring flat,[343] arrived and took over cooking duties so that Amma could begin her daily *puja*. Soon afterward, Guruji finished his breakfast, stood up and walked into the bathroom to take a shower.

Moments later, while sitting in the *puja* room, Amma heard a loud thud. For an instant, she assumed it was "construction noise from the street." Then she heard Guruji call out. Still suspecting nothing unusual and thinking only that "he perhaps had forgotten to take his towel," she and Sunita arrived at the door simultaneously—and found Guruji sitting dazed on the floor.

"I felt dizzy and fell down," he told them.

It would be his final verbal communication.

While Sunita called for an ambulance, Amma recruited a pair of neighbors to help Guruji back into bed. He was breathing with difficulty and felt uncomfortable whether sitting or lying down. Amma brought him a cup of coffee. He took a few sips and then handed the cup back to her with a nod that she should drink the rest. As the ambulance crew arrived and wheeled him away on a stretcher, "He did not convey any messages," Amma said. However, "those around him did receive piercing glances of grace."

By 9 a.m., Guruji had arrived at nearby Manipal Hospital, where Dr. M. Bhaskara Rao—the same surgeon who had operated on him some years earlier, and who had been his heart specialist for more than a decade—confirmed that he had suffered yet

342 In 2015, *Navratri* fell from October 13 to 22.

343 This is the same Sunita who was profiled in chapter 23.

another "severe cardiac incident," his fourth and final heart attack. He was admitted to surgery and a pacemaker was inserted; this seemed to stabilize his condition—but only marginally and, as it turned out, only briefly. Following a day of crisis after crisis in the intensive care ward—through which Guruji never again regained bodily consciousness—his journey reached its end at 6:35 p.m. (IST), Saturday, October 10, 2015.

The same social grapevine of near-instantaneous communication between disciples, which had long spread happy tidings of Guruji's *pujas* and other events, now just as swiftly carried news of his passing. By Saturday evening, Ananta said, the hospital lobby "was thronged with disciples, well-wishers and volunteers, and the hard task of making the announcement, accepting the reality and coping had begun for us all."

The next morning, with early-autumn temperatures hovering around 30°C (in the high 80s °F), Guruji's body was washed and prepared for cremation, then enclosed in a clear, refrigerated, flower-bedecked bier and transported in sad procession to Devipuram. His remains lay in repose all day Sunday, alongside the very benches where he and Amma had for years welcomed visitors. As a nonstop stream of mourners flowed slowly by, bowing, prostrating, weeping and praying, "the chanting of devotional songs and hymns—from the *Chandi Saptashati Path* to the *Lalita Sahasranama*—continued through the day and into the night," Ananta said. "It was uplifting and heartbreaking at the same time. So many visitors were pouring in, looking to Amma for solace and strength. And strong she was, for most part."

Thousands more, meanwhile, followed the wake remotely from around the globe via live webcast, many leaving tributes and condolences that scrolled continually below the video. An impromptu shrine to Guruji sprang up at Haran Aiya's temple in Rochester, NY; similar ones were erected at other temples, *peetams* and home shrines by those within his lineage all over the world.

The family's private grief was largely subsumed in the rush of the relentlessly public event, yet there were quiet, almost unbearably poignant moments, such as when Guruji's elder sister Suryalakshmi bowed her wispy white head over her brother's face to whisper her farewells, and when granddaughter Pallavi—whose wedding Guruji was to have presided over in December—tearfully paid her respects. Such moments offered a striking reminder that Guruji was a husband, a father, a son, a brother, a grandfather, a colleague—in addition to being a guru and a friend.

"Guruji's transition from the physical to the ethereal had to be viewed from so many perspectives," Ananta observed. "He was both a householder and a Sri Vidya *upasaka* of the highest order; thus we had our family's grief on the one hand and the *vasudaiva kutumbakam*[344] on the other. It was hard to find any precedent for such an unusual combination."

Even in those dark hours, however, Guruji managed to send comforting words and guidance to Amma. As she was searching through his papers for some necessary documentation, a scrap of paper fluttered from the pile and landed neatly before her eyes. On it, in Guruji's handwriting, was a small fragment of a poem in progress:

> *From whose womb is created this whole world*
> *From whose vision is manifested this entire world*
> *And the one who causes the dissolution of the world*
> *So too am I: what's in a name, or even a place?*
> *Wherever you seek, there I will be found*
> *Call me by any name, and I shall respond.*

"Do not limit him to the name and form of Amritananda anymore," sister-in-law Sundari Amma commented when Amma showed her the verse. "Now he is omnipresent and dimensionless."

Last rites were publicly administered at Devipuram's Ashram on Monday morning. For a few of the rituals traditionally performed by immediate family alone, the priest—recognizing the extenuating circumstances occasioned by a widely beloved spiritual leader—allowed others to participate as well.

"We asked for that [participation] and encouraged it," Ananta said. Even in those rituals that were performed by family alone, she added, efforts were made "to do it on behalf of others too, because it was so important to them. We tried to put our grief aside and accommodate everyone."

Following these ceremonies, the body was removed to a wilderness clearing at the southwest corner of Devipuram, where a funeral pyre had been prepared for the cremation. Guruji was not to be buried in the tradition of the saints and swamis, such as Anakapalle Gurugaru, because he had technically remained a householder and never become an *avadhuta*. Yet it was clear to all who knew him that Guruji had merged with the Devi, so an ordinary cremation would not do.[345]

"Various senior Sri Vidya practitioners were consulted regarding the correct procedure to follow for a Sri Vidya *upasaka* and evolved soul," daughter Rama explained. It was determined that her husband Prabhakar, as Guruji's son-in-law, would perform the last rites.

First a solemn *Sri Chakra Homa* was performed privately at the cremation site by a select group of senior disciples. As the *homa* reached its end, Prabhakar used the fire from the ritual to ignite the funeral pyre, in another traditional Sri Vidya practice. Perhaps surprisingly, in light of Guruji's lifelong teachings about the feminine gender—and the fact that so many considered him to be the Goddess incarnate—the presiding priest closed the cremation to all women, including Amma and Guruji's daughters.

"We were there until they took him for cremation," one female attendee recounted. "We were chanting in groups. But we were not allowed to the place where they performed the *Sri Chakra Homa* and his body was immersed in flames." Many, however, climbed to the higher levels of the Sri Meru temple, and chanted, prayed and cried as they watched the conflagration from afar.

The body of Guruji—Dr. Nishtala Prahlada Sastry, more widely known as Sri Amritananda Natha Saraswati—was cremated at approximately 2:30 p.m. (IST) on Monday afternoon, October 12, 2015. It was a grim and graphic affair; the body was not hidden within the pyre, but clearly visible atop it throughout. "It was difficult to see Guruji in that state," one witness commented later. "And it was really hard to believe it when he was finally gone, even though we all knew he had merged with the *panchabhutas*[346] and become the Devi."

Guruji's physical exit from the world thus complete, it was time for everyone left behind—family and disciples alike—to take a deep collective breath and begin the

345 This decision too occasioned passionate debate among senior disciples, with some insisting that he *should* be buried as a saint and had stated as much himself, while others just as strongly insisted cremation was the proper course and had always been Guruji's preference and expectation.

346 The five elements: earth (*prithvi*), water (*jala*), fire (*agni*), air (*vayu*) and ether (*akasha*).

long process of trying to absorb and comprehend the spiritual and worldly implications of all that had just happened. "The 'ashes to ashes, dust to dust' portion of the process was upon us all too soon," Ananta said. "Sobering, totally unacceptable and yet the truth. And like millions before us, we had to bow down before it."

The joyous festival of *Navratri* was set to begin the evening following the cremation, and Guruji's three daughters announced that celebrations would proceed as usual at Devipuram, urging disciples around the world to celebrate as well. Guruji—who had said, "I want people to celebrate when I go, not cry"—would no doubt have approved. On October 23, the day after *Navratri* celebrations ended with the Vijaya Dashami holiday, a moving *shraddhanjali*, or remembrance ceremony, was held in Devipuram, affording disciples, colleagues and friends a chance to offer their final tributes. A card distributed to attendees showed Guruji's face together with the Telugu message, *Seemitha vyaktini maatrame kaadu. Nee lo daagina sakshi ni nenu*: "I am not this limited body. I am the witness in you."

Six months after his passing, Guruji's ashes were interred in a new building, designated the Guru Dhyana Mandiram—or Guru Meditation Chapel—and located adjacent to Kamakhya Peetam, close to the place where he experienced his first visions of the Goddess more than three decades before. The shrine officially opened at 6 p.m. on April 15, 2016, at the culmination of the Devi Ratha Supratishta Mahotsavam, an event sanctifying a new ritual chariot for transporting the temple's *utsava murti* [347] of the Goddess Sahasrakshi during outdoor ceremonies. Haran Aiya came to preside in person.

347 Processional image.

The focal point of the Mandiram is a life-size—and remarkably life*like*—statue of Guruji created by the sculptor Ravi Chandra. Constructed of fiber-reinforced plastic, the statue stands about seven feet high, including its lotus base. Several hundred devotees attended a solemn consecration of the shrine led by Amma, Sundari Amma, Guruji's brother Prasad Garu and other family members—as well as Aiya.

"We feel his presence everywhere; he is always guiding us," daughter Rama said on the occasion. "Yet as humans, we sometimes need a figure to focus upon—and that's why this statue was created. It is not meant to be worshiped, but rather to inspire us all. The Dhyana Mandiram is a place where one can come and silently meditate in the presence of the guru. Equally important is the need for us to continue espousing his values, by reaching out to more people and sharing this knowledge in the same way that we received it from him—that is, unconditionally."

When I parted with Guruji for the last time at Devipuram before returning to the United States, where most of this book was written, I expressed my hope that I would return soon and hand him a published copy. He casually replied that perhaps I should also bring a copy for Sahasrakshi at the top of the Meru temple. Through the filter of hindsight, that offhand comment later seemed prophetic.

During a telephone conversation with Alok just a few days after Guruji's passing, I expressed my disappointment that I had failed to finish the work in time. The next morning, he sent me a thoughtful note via email.

"As much as you would have liked to put the published book in Guruji's hands while he was still alive, in a way it is fitting that it will be published after he has gone," he wrote. "As you know, he never liked to be in the limelight, preferring that we focus on his teachings and our own growth rather than on him personally. Often when I would show him something that I'd written about him, he would tell me not to make it public so long as he was still around. Then he would smile and add, 'After I am gone, you can do what you want.'"

Full disclosure: Guruji never said any such thing to me (he probably figured the book's progress was already glacial enough; why offer further reason for delay?). But he did take the time and effort to read, edit, verify, augment and finally approve—twice over—the completed manuscript. He was characteristically open throughout the process, censoring essentially nothing, mainly just correcting names and dates and penning in various explanatory remarks and additional stories. When we were finished, he thanked me for what he termed a "Herculean effort"—and I had a chance to thank him for sharing his astonishing life, wisdom and teachings with me.

"He sowed the very best seeds inside each one of us, one person at a time, with supreme care and with nurturing, personal attention," Alok said on the day of Guruji's physical death. "His presence can still be felt and is perhaps even more readily accessible now."

Commenting at Guruji's *shraddhanjali* two weeks later, sister-in-law Sundari Amma agreed. "We do not realize the value of the precious gems he has placed in our hands," she said. "Actions he was unable to perform while alive he can now accomplish without the limitations of his physical body."

Indeed, as Guruji—scientist and holy man, powerful Tantrika and compassionate friend—used to say with a wink of his eye, death has little real substance, merely marking a physical transition through which "matter becomes a wave that can flow freely."

Considering the source, I have no reason doubt it.

Acknowledgments

Guruji often seemed the most rugged of individualists—sometimes referring to himself as a "lonely traveler"—but there was no greater advocate for the power of collaboration when it came to getting a big job done. The research, reporting, writing and editing of this book involved daunting doses of both: long solitary hours of work, frustrating setbacks, disheartening dead ends—and yet just as many thrilling moments of insight, discovery and connection that ultimately made the entire experience inexpressibly rewarding and worthwhile.

For this I offer my deepest gratitude, first and foremost, to Guruji himself—for his radical openness, good humor, patience and generosity of spirit over the long years we spent developing this work. The value of what he taught and shared with me along the way is in a state of continual unfolding, and since I am as yet unable to fully categorize or quantify it, I will simply say *Sri Gurubhyonamah.*

Guruji's immediate family—from Annapurna Amma, his wife of more than half a century, to his elder sister Suryalakshmi Amma, his younger brother Prasad Rao Garu and sister-in-law Sundari Amma—unfailingly treated this looming, prying American interloper with candor and kindness. No one, however, worked harder to bring the book into fruition than Guruji and Amma's three daughters, Anantalakshmi Pisipati, Radha Marthi and Rama Kandarpa, each of whom provided bottomless reservoirs of assistance, explanation, access and resources over the years.

Also essential to the book's completion was the formidable Wijayaharan Aiya, one of Guruji's earliest and most prominent disciples, who gave generously of his perpetually limited time, offering stories, insight, laughter and more (much more, dare I say?), as well as his daughter Saru and her husband Balasingam Janahan. Nor can I fail to mention the erudite and perceptive Professor Alok Baveja of Rutgers University School of Business. Megha Chatterjee—a talented writer and editor, originally from New Delhi and now residing in Toronto, whom I first encountered a decade ago through the strangest of Guruji-related coincidences—provided countless painstaking hours of interview transcriptions, structural advice, pronunciation coaching, general encouragement, tea and sympathy.

I am grateful to every individual who agreed to share their memories and insights in these pages. And there are so many others who made themselves indispensable at various phases of the project's development: Nora Madasamy, the first bridge; the Honorable N. Sankara Menon, who introduced me to Sri Vidya and then to Guruji; and Mrs. Prasanna Nair, the final goad, who encouraged me to stop messing about and wrap things up already.

Also vital to the book, each in their own indispensable way, were (and alphabetical is the best I can do) Kathy Allen, Ahalya and Sundhara Arasaratnam, Mani and Prasanna Avasarala, Eleathea ("Ekta") Barraclough, Devi Parvati Dombkowski, Jana Dunn, Colin Earl, Ekabhumi Charles Ellik, Felice Espinoza, Roxanne Kamayani Gupta, Rita Karina Salgado Fuerte, Maya Devi Georg, Sinu Joseph, Sweta Kamble, Swethambari Koteshwara Rao, Elaine McArdle, Malcolm McQuirter, Sunita Medepalli, Ksenia Moshykhina, Gopal Narayan, Robert Paré, Megha Patel, Cliff Pollick, Meena Radhakrishnan, Prema Reddy, Daniel Ruth, Lalita Sarma, Sreekavya Siripurapu, Alexey Somov, Karthika Sugumaran, Michael Steinberg, Ray Talamo, Ximena Terrés Casas, William Thomas, Sarah Tomlinson, Christopher (Hareesh) Wallis, Dave Yoss and Maria Antonieta ("Toni") Zavala Uribe. And I would be remiss not to mention Eve Rickert and her wonderfully talented team at Talk Science to Me in Vancouver—with a special shout-out to Amy Haagsma, Darinka Aguirre, Jeff Werner, and Sheilagh and Elspeth Simpson. Most especially, however, my gratitude goes out to Julianne Reynolds, Giri Ratna Singh and Oleg Zinkovetsky, whose beautiful photography so enhanced this volume, as well as the website and videos that support it. To the many others whom I have surely forgotten to name here, thank you too—and I will apologize in person if you give me a chance.

In closing, I wish to thank my entire family, in particular my father Paul—my first and most demanding "guru"—whose penetrating intelligence, remarkable self-discipline and startling artistic grace have always been my high-water marks (and whose presence I still miss every day). Special thanks also to my sister Maria—dedicated educator and literary connoisseur—for her deep reading and insightful commentary on an early draft of this book, and to my brother Steve, whose big-picture vision (and serious design chops) informed this project in ways too numerous and complex to express.

Last but far from least, love and thanks to my very smart, very tough, very beautiful (and very patient) wife Dr. Anna Pavlotsky Bowden, whose unwavering love and support made this project possible in just about every way that matters, and to my sons Alexander and Dylan, for being "book orphans" a little more often than they ever should have been. Finally, love to my daughter Sofia Mikhailovna, tiny ambassador of the Devi, who visited all too briefly but set into motion a mighty sequence of events that, quite possibly, changed everything for the better.

Кто влюблён и всерьёз, свою жизнь для тебя превратит в цветы.

Michael M. Bowden
Pennamaquan Lake, Maine,
and Halifax, Nova Scotia
August 2016

Notes

Foreword

xviii   **"a Tantric path"** Dempsey, Corinne G. *The Goddess Lives in Upstate New York: Breaking Convention and Making Home at a North American Hindu Temple*. Oxford: Oxford UP, 2006, 6.

Introduction

1   **Cyclone Hudhud 1   Biswas, Soutik.** "How Cyclone Hudhud Got Its Name." *BBC News* 10 Oct. 2014. Web.

2   **Najar, Nida, and Sriram Karri.** "300,000 Evacuated as Strong Cyclone Hits Eastern India." *The New York Times* 12 Oct. 2014. Web.

2   **TNN.** "Cyclone Hudhud Tears into Visakhapatnam at 195kmph, Wreaks Havoc in City." *The Times of India 13 Oct. 2014*. 19 Oct. 2014. Web.

2   **Rao, Kamalakara.** "Vizag First Indian City Directly Hit by Cyclone." *The Times of India* 18 Oct. 2014. Web

9   **"To the chagrin of many scientists"** Goldberg, Philip. *American Veda: From Emerson and the Beatles to Yoga and Meditation*. New York: Three Rivers, 2013, 288. Print.

9   **"To ordinary readers"** Goldberg, 234.

13   **"Be glad that you have"** Miller, William. "Death of a Genius: His Fourth Dimension, Time, Overtakes Einstein." *Life* 2 May 1955: 64. Web.

16   **"Washington Post photo essay"** "Visions of Faith: Hindu Temple Ceremony in N.Y." *Washington Post* 17 July 2010. Web.

20   **"I don't feel I need to burnish his image"** Godman, David. "Living the Inspiration of Sri Ramana Maharshi." *David Godman - Home Page*, n.d. Web.

III.   The Yogi, the Nazis and the Cyclotron

48   **"I had no food"** Jnanananda, Swami. *The Saint and the Scientist: Life, Writings, and Teachings of Prof. Swami Jnanananda*. Edited by Keshav Dev Sharma, translated by Raju Umapathi Datla, Washington, DC: University Resources Press, 1992, 19-20. Print.

49   **"Bhumananda used to bring me"** *Ibid,* 79.

49   **"continued walking back"** *Ibid,* 92.

51   **"distasteful and deplorable"** *Ibid,* 118-120.

51   **"I challenged them to put me in jail"** *Ibid,* 124-125.

51   **"Although I did not know"** *Ibid,* 124, 128.

52   **"I followed the events"** *Ibid,* 130-131.

53   **"giving them full freedom"** *Ibid,* 145.

54   **"People used to fall at his feet"** G., B.M. "Swami Jnanananda (1896-1969): A Scientist with a Humane Heart." *The Hindu* (Visakhapatnam Metro Plus) 13 Jan. 2003. Web.

54   **"He used to say"** Jnanananda, 167.

54   **"Yogic practices are intended"** *Ibid,* 169.

IV.   The Cradle of Cutting-Edge Science

58   **"It all began"**   A Special Correspondent. "TIFR in Bhabha Centenary Year:
A Base for Progress." *Frontline 26*(26) (19 Dec. 2009). Web.

V.   An Absentminded Professor?

64   **"to vindicate the importance of"**   Goldberg, 50–51.

VI.   On Turning-Point Hill

74   **"It is well known by Shaktas"**   Gupta, Roxanne Poormon. "Embracing Orientalism and Exposing
the Goddess: Devipuram and the De-Esotericization of the Erotic East." *Annual Meeting, American
Academy of Religion*. Colorado Conference Center, Denver, Colorado. 18 Nov. 2001. TS (unpublished).

VII.   A Dormant Volcano Awakens

79   **"Isavasyam idam sarvam"**   "Sri Isopanishad 1." *Bhaktivedanta VedaBase*.
The Bhaktivedanta Book Trust International, Inc. n.d. Web.

84   **"Runanubandha is an existing"**   Kumar, Sreeram Manoj. "Relationships are
Indebted Credits to be Cleared Now!" *SpeakingTree.in*, Dec. 12, 2011.

VIII.   The Wisest of Madmen

91   **"Even as a child"**   Sastry, A. Ramalinga. "Metro Cultural Round-up." *The
Hindu* (Visakhapatnam Metro Plus) 28 July 2003. Web.

91   **"associated with the apparently crazy modes of behaviour"**   Feuerstein, Georg.
"Holy Madness." *Yoga Journal*, Issue 98 (May/June 1991): 68–70, 103–107. Print.

92   **"As the years rolled by"**   Sastry, A. Ramalinga. "Metro Cultural Round-up."

92   **"By treading an austere life path"**   *Ibid.*

94   **Video footage of Gurugaru Vishudha Avatar Baba.**   Vishudha Avatar Baba. "Swami
Srilasri Swaprakasananda Theertha Avadhootha." *YouTube*. 31 Dec. 2010. Web.

97   **"Some people receive a very intense shaktipat"**   Wallis, Christopher D.
Tantra Illuminated: The Philosophy, History, and Practice of a Timeless Tradition,
2nd ed. Petaluma, California: Mattamayura Press, 2013, 153. Print.

X.   Into the Heart of Africa

111   **Aiya's mastery of specialized and complex ritual ceremonies**   "Sri Chaitanyananda, Our Temple
Founder." *The Official Website of Sri Rajarajeshwari Peetam*. Sri Vidya Temple Society. n.d. Web.

111   **"began performing public pujas"**   *Ibid.*

111   **"Worship of the Devi"**   Haran Aiya. Personal conversation. 4 Dec. 2013.

114   **"a reputation for"**   Dempsey, 91.

114   **"We walked into the living room"**   Haran Aiya. Personal conversation. 4 Dec. 2013.

115   **"the intricacies of performing Sri Chakra Navavarana Puja"**   "Sri Chaitanyananda, Our Temple Founder."
The Official Website of Sri Rajarajeshwari Peetam. Sri Vidya Temple Society. n.d. Web. 22 Jan. 2014.

117   **"In 1979, ten devotees"**   "Hindu Temple in South Africa." *Dinamalar* 29 Jan. 2009. Web.

118   **"Aiya, his wife and their young daughter"**   Dempsey, 92.

XI.   A Path Fraught with Danger

122   **Many who took initiation went on to establish affiliated shrines and temples**   Gupta, "Embracing."

128   **"From a theological perspective"**   Dempsey, 92–93.

130   **"destructive powers"**   Egnor, Margaret. "On the Meaning of Śakti to Women in Tamil Nadu." *The Powers of Tamil Women.* Syracuse, NY: Syracuse University, 1980. 1. Print. South Asian Ser., No. 6.

130   **"goddesses bear a seemly, auspicious demeanor"**   Hawley, John Stratton, et al.
Devī: Goddesses of India. Berkeley: University of California, 1996, 11. Print.

130   **"fraught with danger"**   Gupta, "Embracing," 5.

130   **"that the worship of Śrī-chakra"**   Rao, S.K. Ramachandra. *Śrī Chakra.* Delhi:
Sri Satguru/Indian Books Center, 1989. 1. Print. Sri Garib Oriental Ser.

130   **"Even today"**   Wadley, Susan S., ed. *The Powers of Tamil Women.* Syracuse,
NY: Syracuse University, 1980. xii. Print. South Asian Ser., No. 6.

132   **"one of the prime disciples"**   "Dance: My Life, My Passion and Everything
In Between." *Kuchipudi Vaibhavam* 16 July 2010. Web.

132   **"Balakka has her own creative process"**   Smt. A.B. Bala Kondala Rao. Personal conversation. 23 Feb. 2015.

XII.   It Wasn't Meant for Them

140   **Kakinada Severe Cyclonic Storm of 15-18 October 1982**   Datta, Rattan K., ed. *Advances in Tropical Meteorology: Meteorology and National Development.* New Delhi: Concept, 1996, 431. Print.

140   **Rao, V. Kamalakara.**   "Visakhapatnam Gets Chunk of Year's Northeast Monsoon Quota in 3
Days." *The Times of India* (Visakhapatnam Edition) 25 Oct. 2013. Web. 08 Mar. 2014.

XIII.   The Cinema Goddess

148   **"The 18 Maha Shakti Peetams"**   Sircar, Dineschandra. *The Śākta Pīthas.*
Reprint of 2nd Revised Edition. Delhi: Motilal Banarsidass, 1998.

148   **"The whole city of Visakhapatnam"**   Sitadevi, Neti. *Chidagni.* Hyderabad: Sai Likhita Printers, 2004. Print.

148   **"When a pot is filled with water"**   Padma, Sree. *Vicissitudes of the Goddess: Reconstructions
of the Gramadevata in India's Religious Traditions.* New York: Oxford UP, 2013, 85 ff. Print.

148   **"The entire city turned out"**   "Details of Ganesha Immersion." *Sathya Sai:
Ganesha Vinayaka Chaturthi.* Sai Baba of India Group, 6 Sept. 2008. Web.

XIV.   The Jingling of Anklets

153   **"The garbhagriha is small"**   Shin, Jae-Eun. "*Yoni, Yoginis and Mahavidyas: Feminine Divinities
from Early Medieval Kamarupa to Medieval Koch Behar.*" Studies in History 26(1) (2010): 1-29.

154   **"Worship with the Pancatattva"**   Woodroffe, John George. "The Pancatattva." *Śakti and Śākta: Essays and Addresses*. 9th ed. Madras: Ganesh, 1987, 389–401. Print.

155   **"in her digamber (naked) form"**   Gupta, "Embracing," 14.

157   **"Do you believe in God, Dr. Arroway?"**   *Contact*. Dir. Robert Zemeckis. Warner Bros. Pictures, 1997. Film.

XV.   Temples Raised by Woman Power

165   **"Goddess religion predates"**   Padma, 46–47.

165   **"giving birth, prominently displaying"**   *Ibid*, 265.

165   **"The goddess as sakti"**   *Ibid*, 265.

165   **"[Moreover, the Goddess was] admitted"**   *Ibid*, 94.

166   **"Experiencing competition from each other"**   *Ibid*, 265-266.

166   **"Indian culture underwent a kind of reset"**   Zhuravlev, Ilya. "Tantric Roots of Hatha Yoga: Interview with Hareesh (Christopher Wallis)." *Wild Yogi*. N.p., Apr. 2012. Web.

167   **"portrayal of fertility goddesses in naked form"**   Padma, 132–34.

167   **"Kalidasa wrote about sex, romance and the feminine form"**   Arya, Rohit. *The Sacred India Tarot*. Mumbai: Yogi Impressions, 2011, 179. Print.

168   **Tantra definition**   "Tantra." Defs 1 and 1.1. *English Oxford Living Dictionaries*. Oxford University Press. n.d. Web.

168   **"the term tantra and the tantric traditions of Hinduism"**   "Tantra and the Tantric Traditions of Hinduism and Buddhism." *Religion: Oxford Research Encyclopedias*. Oxford University Press, 04 Apr. 2016. Web.

168   **"clearly, some kind of Tantric stuff is going on here"**   Sree Padma. Personal conversation. 6 May 2014.

XVI.   The Chorus of a Thousand Voices

175   **Filmmaker Julianne Reynolds' profile of a village girl named Leela**   *Leela: Portrait of a Priest in India*. Dir. Julianne Reynolds. Romanski Films, 2013.

175   **"wanted to live a much simpler life"**   Julianne Reynolds. Personal conversation. 7 December 2014.

XVII.   You're Asking for Trouble!

182   **"The fortune of a stone"**   Carr, M.W. *A Supplement to the Collection of Telugu Proverbs*. Madras: Christian Knowledge Society, 1868, 356. Print.

XVIII.   Stringing a Garland of Swords

189   **"They are not even nude"**   Sree Padma. Personal conversation. 6 May 2014.

196   **"Swamiji was born"**   *Sri Rama Viswambharanadh (Jatala Sadhu): A Mysterious Sadhu*. Hyderabad: Sri Rama Viswambharadas Adhyathmika Seva Sangam, 2009. Print (pamphlet). *Text condensed, grammar and spelling corrected.*

197   **"If I tell you his origin"**   Svoboda, Robert. *Aghora: At the Left Hand of God*. Albuquerque, NM: Brotherhood of Life, 1986, 139 ff. Print.

197   **"first glance"**   *Ibid*.

199   **"I met Jatala Sadhu"**   Svoboda, Robert E. "News: January 2015." *www. drsvoboda.com*. Dr. Robert E. Svoboda, Jan. 2015. Web.

XIX.   The Backbone of Devipuram

206   **"I saw an old man"**   Amma. Personal conversation. 24 October 2012.
208   **"the sacred and secular"**   Arya, Rohit, and Jane Adams. *The Sacred India Tarot*. Mumbai: Yogi Impressions, 2011, 177. Print.

XX.   Points of Connectivity

211   **"de-esotericization"**   Gupta, Roxanne Kamayani. "Exposing the Goddess: De-Esotericization and the Erotic at Devipuram." *Tantra: Constructions and Deployments of Power* [conference]. Northern Arizona University, Flagstaff, Arizona. October 12, 2002. TS.
212   **"Some argue that"**   Gupta, "Exposing."
214   **"We've all heard of near-death experiences"**   Johnsen, Linda. "Waves of Beauty and Bliss: Deciphering Imagery from the Saundarya Lahari." *Yoga International*. 17 June 2014. Web. 13 Sept. 2014.
215   **"One of the ways Aiya deflects"**   Dempsey, 67.
215   **"The only time Aiya asked me"**   *Ibid.*
217   **Mother Meera**   "Germany's Meera: Reclusive Young Guru Is an Open Door to Cosmic Mother." *Hinduism Today*. Himalayan Academy, Apr. 1989. Web.

XXI.   A Goddess in Upstate New York

220   **"If the Divine Mother wants to come to your house"**   Dempsey, 154.
227   ***A Jewel from My Mother's Crown***   "New EBook for Sri Vidya Upasakas: 'A Jewel from My Mother's Crown.'" *SriVidya.org*. Sri Vidya Temple Society. 22 Nov. 2015. Web.

XXII.   An Impossible Dream Comes True

233   **"Kumbha abhishekam is a general term for the grand celebration"** "Our Thoughts." *Sri Chakra* 11.2 (2007): 2. Web. 18 Apr. 2014.

XXIII.   Beyond Temple Walls

250   **"This was many years ago"**   Greene, Brian. "Our Universe May Be a Giant Hologram." *Discover Magazine* 4 Aug. 2011. 13 Sept. 2014. Web.
251   **"In fact, for Gandhi"**   Morton, Brian. "Falser Words Were Never Spoken," *New York Times* 29 Aug. 2011. Web.
254   **"University of Buffalo students"**   Goldbaum, Ellen. "Dome-Shaped Homes Offer A Safe, Cheap Remedy to Severe Housing Problem In India." *News Center*, 18 Nov. 1993. Web.
254   **"Goldbaum, Ellen."** "UB Students Build Geodesic Dome In Williamsville Backyard." *News Center* 15 June 1994. Web. 28 Sept. 2014.

255   **"At Devipuram"**   Keswani, Kiran. *A Dwelling: Physical Planning and Design at Haripuram, Visakhapatnam, India*. Bhagavatula Charitable Trust, January 1996. Report.

258   **"Guruji: Sri Amritananda Natha Saraswati"**   *gurujiamrita.tripod.com*

XXIV.   The Powerhouse of Devipuram

266   **"Early lingams were"**   Davidson, Linda Kay, and David M. Gitlitz. *Pilgrimage: From the Ganges to Graceland: An Encyclopedia*. Santa Barbara, CA: ABC-CLIO, 2002, 347. Print.

266   **"what Hindus have seen and understood in this symbol"**   Eck, Diana L. *India: A Sacred Geography*. New York: Harmony, 2012, 208. Print.

266   **"lingam is the emblem"**   *Ibid*, 208–209.

269   **"What is most unusual"**   Gupta, "Exposing."

272   **"an example of de-esotericization"**   Gupta, "Embracing," 19.

275   **"When the lingam was removed"**   Gupta, "Exposing."

275   **"On the contrary"**   Gupta, "Exposing." (All preceding quotes in this section are from this unpublished paper.)

XXV.   I'm Not the Chosen One

284   **"the sleep of genius"**   Sterbenz, Christina. "These Alternative Sleep Schedules Could Save You 20 Years Normally Spent in Bed." *Business Insider* 04 Nov. 2013. Web. *18 Apr. 2014; "What Is the Da Vinci Sleep Schedule?" WiseGEEK n.d. Web.*

285   **The quiet hours**   "Brahmamuhurta: The Best Time for Meditation." *The Times of India* 16 June 2009. Web.

287   **"Unlike the neo-Tantric"**   Urban, 183.

288   **"While Amritananda is nowhere near as famous as Rajneesh"**   Gupta, "Exposing."

289   **"Shakti Sadhana"**   *groups.yahoo.com/neo/groups/Shakti_Sadhana/info facebook.com/groups/shaktisadhana*

291   **Chidagni**   Sitadevi, Neti. *Chidagni*. Hyderabad: Sai Likhita Printers, 2004. Print.

XXVI.   Precisely What I Wanted

295   **"He attributed their lack of response"**   Gupta, "Exposing."

296   **"DEVIPURAM TO GET A SPIRITUAL RESORT"**   "Devipuram to Get a Spiritual Resort." *The Hindu* 13 July 2005. Web.

298   **non-melting chocolate bars**   Collins, Nick. "Non-melting Chocolate Invented by Cadbury's." The Telegraph 23 Nov. 2012. Web.

300   ***Leading with Wisdom: Spiritual-Based Leadership in Business***   Pruzan, Peter, et al. "S.K. Welling: A Leader Must Have Concern for Others." *Leading with Wisdom: Spiritual-Based Leadership in Business*. Sheffield: Greenleaf, 2007, 173 ff. Print.

XXVII.   Coming of Age

309   **"it is not enough to just build a temple"**   "Our Thoughts." *Sri Chakra* 11.2 (2007): 2. Web.

XXVIII. It's Her Worry Now

321   **"the world-famous Konark Temple"**   Barik, Satyasundar. "An Award for My Devotion to Sculpture: Mohapatra." *The Hindu* 27 Jan. 2013. Web.

321   **"wields [his] hammer with incredible precision"**   *Ibid.*

List of Illustrations

Index

About the Author

Michael Bowden is an attorney and former New York Times Company reporter with three decades of publishing experience, having written for newspapers and magazines ranging from the *ABA Journal* to *India Today*. A longtime features editor for Lawyers Weekly Publications in Boston, Bowden is currently director of communications for Roger Williams University School of Law, Rhode Island's only law school. His freelance magazine features have appeared in both national and international publications, and he was awarded the American Bar Association's prestigious Ross Award for his legal journalism.

A *magna cum laude* and Phi Beta Kappa graduate of the University of Rhode Island, Bowden earned his Juris Doctor degree from the University of Maine and actively practiced law for several years before returning to journalism. In 1999, he cofounded the Shakti Sadhana group, which collected, published and hosted discussions of Hindu Shakta scriptures online. He and Amritananda met in 2003 and collaborated on a number of projects together.

Bowden is also an accomplished artist, whose paintings have been featured in both group and solo gallery shows. He lives in Rhode Island with his wife Anna and their two sons.

25595316R00244

Printed in Poland
by Amazon Fulfillment
Poland Sp. z o.o., Wrocław